Exclusive Strategy Guide

Other Titles from GW Press

Civilization II—The Complete Guide to Scenario Design
Daikatana—Official Strategy Guide
Dominion: Storm Over Gift 3—Exclusive Strategy Guide
Duke Nukem 64—Official Strategy Guide
Duke Nukem: Time to Kill—Exclusive Strategy Guide
Duke Nukem Total Meltdown—Exclusive Strategy Guide
Oddworld: Abe's Exoddus—Exclusive Strategy Guide
Oddworld: Abe's Oddysee—Official Strategy Guide
Quake II—Authorized Strategy Guide
Star Trek: Starfleet Academy—Exclusive Strategy Guide
Total Annihilation—Exclusive Strategy Guide
Trans Am Racing—Exclusive Strategy Guide
Unreal—Official Strategy Guide
WarGames—Exclusive Strategy Guide

Interactive Strategy Guides (on CD-ROM) from GameWizards
Blood
Duke Nukem 3D
Duke Nukem Atomic Edition
Lords of the Realm
Phantasmagoria II
Redneck Rampage
Shadow Warrior
Star Fleet Academy
Tomb Raider

Order information: Contact The WizardWorks Group, Inc., 2300 Berkshire Lane North, Plymouth, MN 55441 USA. You can also call toll free 1-800-229-2714.

Visit our web site at www.gwpress.com

Exclusive Strategy Guide

Selby Bateman

GWPress
A Division of GameWizards, Inc.
7085 Shady Oak Road
Minneapolis, MN 55344
www.gwpress.com

Publisher
Shel Mann

Associate Publisher
Scott Grieve

Acquisitions/Development
Michael Koch

Design/Layout
Richard Walker
MK Publication Services

Total Annihilation–Exclusive Strategy Guide
Published by
GW Press
A Division of GameWizards, Inc.
7085 Shady Oak Road
Minneapolis, MN 55344

ISBN: 1-56893-779-2
Library of Congress Catalog Card Number: 97-80240
Printed in the United States of America
98 99 00 10 9 8 7 6 5 4 3 2

Contents at a Glance

Contents

Foreword

A couple of years ago I was walking around the first Electronic Entertainment Expo in Los Angeles, checking out what the rest of the world was doing, when I came across a particular product that I had heard about: *Command and Conquer*. I was thrilled with what I saw and was dying to play it. At the time I had just finished developing *Triple Play Baseball '96* for Electronic Arts. I seemed to have made a career out of sports games, working first on *Hardball II* for Accolade, then on *4D Sports Boxing* for EA. When I finally got my hands on *C&C,* I said to myself, that's it, I am going to build a real-time strategy game; no more sports games, from here on out it's tanks and jet fighters!

So I called Shelley Day, an old friend of mine who had started a company called Humongous Entertainment with Ron Gilbert, a developer well-known in the games industry for his successful adventure titles and his sense of humor. I told Shelley that I wanted to build the ultimate real-time war game, and she introduced me to Ron, who thought it was a great idea. We started out with a few basic goals: 3D terrain, 3D units, and a world that obeyed the laws of physics, a world in which the player could interact with forest fires, wind, and water. We were very happy with the results of our early experiments. It was exciting to see a 3D wire-frame that represented a tank driving over a digital mesh. We had high expectations for the way the unit would move. For example, we wanted the barrel to recoil with a muzzle flash and smoke. The shot would emerge from the barrel and fly with exacting mathematical precision across the terrain in a perfect arc. The entire unit would shake when firing the shell, and it would jolt when it was hit. After we had met all of these goals, we said, OK, we have the setting, now let's build a really great game.

I still remember sitting at my desk, staring at the Word document that I was calling my game design. It lacked something essential, something different. I wanted to take gamers to the battlefield and get them involved at a much more personal level than other real-time strategy games. That's when I thought up the Commander. It would be the ultimate unit, the end-all unit, and it would be you. The Commander would be able to generate power, travel underwater, and repair, cloak, and create units. It would have built-in radar and could capture enemy units and reclaim wreckage and turn it into vital energy. It would have a very tough armor and wield the most powerful weapon in the game—the Disintegrator Gun. However, when the Commander went Kaboom, you did, too!

Above all else, the game had to be fun to play. No matter what all the technology gave us visually, we needed to offer the player as many cool units to play with as possible. The units needed to work in harmony with each other and cover all of the major areas—land, sea, and air. We came up with the KBots because we wanted to provide alternatives for players. We knew that some gamers would like more conventional units, while others would enjoy units that did things never before seen. Units are like toys: no matter how many you have, eventually you get bored with them. From the beginning, we knew we would have to build the engine so that we could add new units at any time. This was the inspiration behind making new units available after the game is released.

As it turned out, we achieved much of what we set out to do. I am very eager to start working on the sequel and take the real-time strategy game experience to the next level. If there's one thing I have learned from the challenges of developing *Total Annihilation*, it's this: if you set your goals high and work hard to achieve them, the rewards are tremendous. We at Cavedog had a lot of fun building *Total Annihilation*, and I hope you have as much fun playing it as we did. Come visit us at **http://www.cavedog.com**, and drop us a line or two or three. We look forward to all of your comments and war stories over the coming year.

Chris Taylor
Cavedog Entertainment

Acknowledgments

First, a very special word of thanks to Hartley and Pattie Lesser for giving me the opportunity to work with the great folks at GW Press to create this official strategy guide. Chief among those at GW Press I wish to thank is Michael Koch, a tremendously talented editor who not only helped make this book come to fruition but also improved it in ways too numerous to count.

My deep appreciation as well to Ron Gilbert, Chris Taylor, and the entire *Total Annihilation* team at Cavedog Entertainment. This guide has benefited tremendously from their "total dedication" to creating a great game and sharing their insights, hints, tips, and strategies.

I also wish to thank Michael Rymaszewski, a fellow writer and excellent war gamer, for bringing his strong gaming talent to bear on many mission and multiplayer games, and for his strategic advice. Thanks also to Vince Matthews, who contributed significantly to mission strategies and to multiplayer games.

As always, my deepest gratitude and love to my wife, Sandie, for her unending support and encouragement—especially during the sleepless nights and long days when I battled for galactic peace among the worlds of Arm and Core.

About the Author

Selby Bateman has been writing about computer and video games for more than 13 years. The former executive editor of *Game Players*, *PC Gamer*, *CD-ROM Today*, *Computer Entertainment News*, Selby has been a columnist for *NEXT Generation* magazine, and a writer and reviewer for CNET's Gamecenter.com. He has coauthored two official computer game strategy guides (*SimIsle* and *Ascendancy*), and is a judge for the Software Publishers Association (SPA) Codie Awards.

Introduction

Welcome to the universe of *Total Annihilation!* You are about to join a fight to the finish, the culmination of a war between two opposing forces that have fought ceaselessly for thousands of years. Your role is to take either of the two sides of mechanized robotic fighters—Arm or Core—and ensure that the other side is reduced to a smoking heap of rubble. Sounds like fun! But there is more.

Total Annihilation is set in a real-time, 3D-rendered universe that looks, feels, and plays like no strategy game you've experienced before. The multiple terrains are truly 3D environments in which every hill, mountain, valley, river, sea, island, desert, and lava pit becomes a part of your strategy. Each of the more than 150 units in the game exists in a real run-time 3D form, interacting with each other and the terrain in very realistic ways. Each tank tilts and rocks with terrain it moves in, and weapons recoil with mathematical precision. Finally, with a total of 50 single-player missions and some 30 multiplayer and skirmish maps, the variety of new game play experiences never stops.

To help you get the most out of this war-torn universe, *Unlock the Secrets of Total Annihilation* comes loaded with undocumented secrets, strategy tips, background information, and multiplayer and mission maps. In *Total Annihilation,* what you don't know can and will hurt you. Now, let's get started.

How to Play the Game

Almost everything in *Total Annihilation* belongs in one of four broad categories: Commander, Construction, Resource Management, and Combat.

Commander

Everything in *Total Annihilation* begins and ends with the Commander. The most powerful (but not invincible) unit in the game, the Commander is central to all construction, resource management, and combat efforts. The only time this is not a factor is in the opening mission for both Arm and Core, in which the Commander is rescued. Most of the time, you will be ordering your Commander to build and repair structures and units with a nanolathe on one arm, and to fire his Disintegrator Gun with the other arm.

Construction

To come out a victor, you have to learn what, when, where, and how to build the 150+ units that come with the game. The construction process is initiated by the Commander, who builds energy and metal generators, KBot Labs, Vehicle Plants, Aircraft Plants, Shipyards, plus Radar and Laser Towers—the basics. The factories built by the Commander produce units that include Construction KBots, Construction Vehicles, Construction Aircraft, and Construction Ships. These construct Advanced KBot Labs, Advanced Vehicle Plants, Advanced Airfields, and Advanced Shipyards, which in turn produce new, more advanced Construction units. Turn to Chapter 3 for the complete Unit Build Hierarchy for both Arm and Core, including the top secret Level-3 units and structures that are absent from the manual.

Resource Management

Unlike other strategy games, *Total Annihilation* does not force you to concentrate on the details of managing resources at the expense of what you're really looking for—intelligent combat. Both Arm and Core depend on energy and metal units to create units and structures. While individual sources of energy and metal are limitless—for example, a metal mine never runs dry—finding enough metal sources to tap is a major concern. In fact, metal is the resource that you'll have the most trouble keeping in good supply. Good thing the Commander can reclaim metal from wrecked units and structures—it helps in a pinch.

Combat

Combat is the heart of *Total Annihilation.* It is the most fun and the trickiest part of the game. At first, some players will be overwhelmed by the variety of units they have to choose from, plus figuring out those that are used by the enemy. So keep the Arm and Core Unit Build Hierarchies handy, and you'll pick up quickly who's who and what's what. To help you keep things straight, *Unlock the Secrets of Total Annihilation* comes with an alphabetized unit guide, detailed unit statistics, and a tear-out card you can use as a quick-reference tool when things get muddy—it provides basic information on every unit.

The best way to get started in combat is to simply sit back and watch. When Arm and Core units get near one another, the lasers and explosions start right away. Study how the game's artificial intelligence (AI) leads units under its command as they attack your troops. Pause the game frequently (by hitting F2), and identify which units mix it up at short range, and which stay in the back firing long-range weapons such as rockets, missiles, and heavy artillery shells.

How to Use this Book

There are several ways in which you can use this book. If you're looking for a good overview of strategy hints and tips, start with Part I, Taking Control. Chapter 1 provides a brief overview of the game's most important configuration options. Chapter 2 presents ten commandments for game play that provide fundamental concepts for winning. Chapter 3 provides an overview of winning TA strategies that cover almost every aspect of game play, from using the Commander and the 3D terrain to your advantage, to the best offensive and defensive strategies.

If you need to find out something about a particular unit, Part II, The Unit Guide, offers alphabetical listings of all major Arm and Core units. We define each unit, offer a strategy tip for its use, and provide the name of a corresponding enemy unit. Chapter 4 covers the units and structures that are common to both sides, while Chapters 5 and 6 feature Arm and Core units, respectively.

If you're stuck on a particular mission, or want to see alternative ways to win a mission, then start with Part III, The Mission Guide, which includes mission briefings, strategies, and maps for all 50 single-player missions.

Multiplayer options and strategies are covered in Part IV, Multiplayer Total Annihilation. At press time, there were already 31 multiplayer maps. You'll find all of them in the book, along with some tips on playing each.

Part V, Inside Total Annihilation, features winning hints and tips from ten members of the team that created TA. There's also an interview with TA producer Ron Gilbert and lead developer Chris Taylor that sheds light on the development of the game, and how to play it even better.

For those of you who can't get enough of *Total Annihilation,* The Appendix offers detailed Arm and Core unit statistics that you can dig through for comparisons. Finally, for the cheaters among you, we've placed cheat codes throughout the book—courtesy of the guys at Cavedog Entertainment who invite you to regularly check their web site at **http://www.cavedog.com** for updates and more cheat codes. However, to keep things more interesting, we're not telling you where—you'll have to find them for yourselves.

Good luck, Commander!

Part I

Taking Control

What began as a conflict over the transfer of consciousness from flesh to machines escalated into a war that has decimated a million worlds. The Core and the Arm have all but exhausted the resources of a galaxy in their struggle for domination.

Crippled beyond repair, the remnants of both armies continue to battle on ravaged planets, their hatred fueled by over four thousand years of total war. This is a fight to the death. For each side, the only acceptable outcome is the complete elimination of the other.

+ATM

(Will give everyone 1,000 metal and energy units)

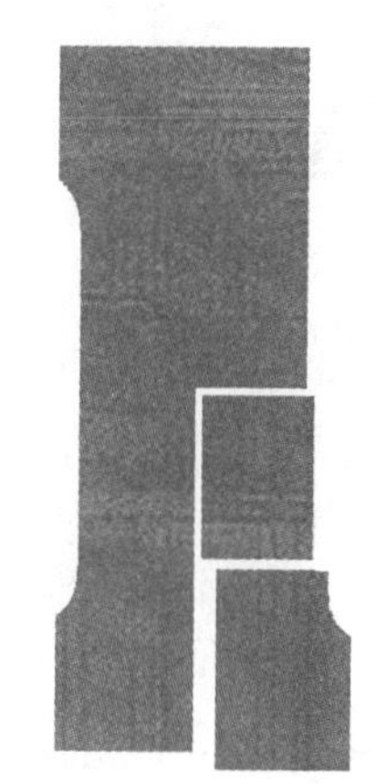

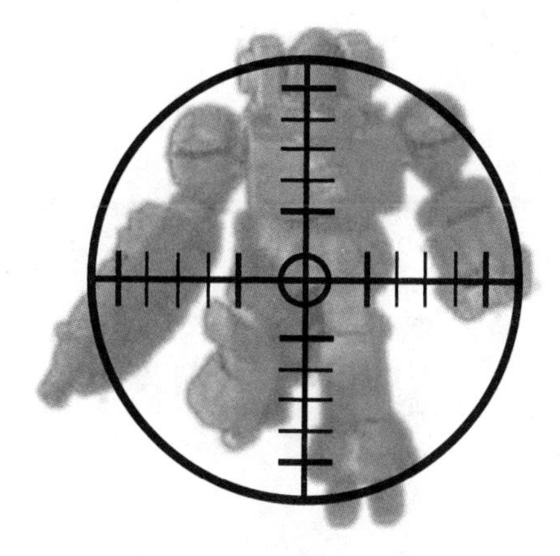

Configuring Your Game

Spend a little time configuring *Total Annihilation* the way you want it to be, and you'll get even more out of the game. You'll be spending a lot of time bringing peace to the universe, so you might as well be as comfortable as possible. It also helps to understand why certain settings are available and under what circumstances to choose them. Here are six configuration and usage tips that I have found to be helpful in making your TA gaming experience trouble free.

A Word on System Requirements

The computer system requirements to play *Total Annihilation* are spelled out in the game manual. However, the following observations on various setting options should help you reduce the risk of potential performance problems.

- **DirectX.** Total Annihilation comes with the newest version of Microsoft's graphics and sound programming interface, DirectX version 5. While your computer may already have a version of DirectX installed, you should install the new version that comes with the game, just to be on the safe side.
- **Ram Available.** Although the minimum requirement to run *Total Annihilation* is a 100 Mhz Pentium with 16MB of RAM, the recommended configuration is a 133 Mhz Pentium with 32MB of RAM. With more than 150 units and structures and some very large battlefield maps, TA pushes a computer's performance very hard. All of the single-player missions in the game are playable if you have 16MB of RAM. However, there are some very large multiplayer and skirmish maps that require 32MB. If your system has 16 or 24MB of RAM, you may still be able to play on some of the 32MB multiplayer maps. Give it try and see if it works. You may also try reducing the number of total units that can be in a game from 200 for each player to 100 or less.
- **Screen Resolution.** TA is optimized for a screen resolution of 640 x 480 pixels. This is the default setting, and I recommend that you stick to it. If you have a fast Pentium system (200 Mhz or faster) and 64MB of RAM, you can try the other possible settings (800 x 600, 1024 x 768, 1152 x 864, or 1280 x 1024). However, be aware that changing the default screen resolution may lead to some video processing glitches that may interrupt the enjoyment of the game. It's best to stick with 640 x 480.
- **Visual Effects.** For computers at the low end of the game's minimum requirements, it helps to turn off some of the graphic detail. This will ease the burden on your computer's memory and processor, and make on-screen action faster and smoother. Try turning off the building and vehicle shadows, the antialiasing that removes the jagged edges on objects, and the shading and object rendering that controls the way an image is drawn and shaded. With Pentium 100s, you should notice your on-screen units pick up speed and performance.

Playing It Medium

There are three difficulty settings in the Options menu—Easy, Medium, and Hard—for the 50 Arm and Core missions. The recommended mission strategies in this book are based on playing the game on the default setting, Medium. The Easy and Hard settings will vary the number of your starting forces and those of your opponents. These same settings also apply to the Skirmish mode that enables you to challenge up to three computer opponents using the game's multiplayer maps. The mission and multiplayer maps do not change when you select a different difficulty setting, nor do the mission goals for Arm and Core.

Chapters 7 and 8 rate each mission independently of the game's difficulty setting. In other words, the difficulty rating for each mission is an estimate of how hard or easy that particular mission is when played on the Medium setting.

If you are having trouble winning a mission on the default Medium setting, try the Easy setting so that you can get further in the mission. By contrast, if you can easily defeat a mission on Medium, crank it up to Hard and find out just how good you really are.

Knowing Your Key Commands

Know your keyboard commands, and you'll be able to speed up your game play significantly. The manual lists all key commands available to you. However, there are a few that deserve special attention, so you can get the most out of them. (See Chapter 10 for information on key commands in multiplayer games.)

- **F2.** This key pauses the game and brings up the Options menu. Note that you can give orders to units even when the game screen is paused. This is helpful when you have units in combat that are headed in the wrong direction or need to be redirected for some reason. With the game paused, click any unit on the main screen and then click the location where you want it to move and attack when the game resumes. You can also use the mini-map in the upper left corner to send the selected unit to a point.

- **Plus (+) and Minus (-).** By pressing the plus key, you can increase the speed of the game up to 10 times faster. The minus key will slow the game down up to 10 times slower. With multiple battles under way on a crowded battlefield, use the minus key to slow things down in order to get a better handle on what your next orders should be. On the other hand, if your units have to traverse a wide-open area on a huge map, increasing the speed will move them along faster.

- **Ctrl plus 1–9; Alt plus 1–9.** One of the most effective strategies to employ is selecting groups of units into squads with the Ctrl plus 1 through 9 key combination. After they are put into squads, you give orders to the squads by first pressing the corresponding Alt plus 1 through 9 keys.

- **Tilde (~).** Make it a habit to press the tilde key at the start of a mission to show the damage level for each unit. This tells you when you need to repair your units and structures. It will also show the number of the squad to which a unit belongs after you have selected a group using the Ctrl plus 1–9 key combinations.

- **Ctrl-Z.** Use this key combination to select all units of a certain type. For example, click on an aircraft unit and then press Ctrl-Z—all of the units of that type are selected. This is a terrific way to control your aircraft, and it also works for other units.

Chatting It Up

There are three levels of Chat that you can select in TA: Off, Medium, and Full. Chat is the selection of the number of messages that scroll across your main screen as units arrive, complete tasks, come under attack, or attack enemies. Some players like to glance at Full Chat. Others prefer to play with the Medium Chat or even Off settings. If you're fairly comfortable with the game or require only minimal assistance, select either Medium Chat or Off. For example, when a unit reports that it is under attack, under Full Chat you can hit the F3 key and the screen will center on the unit that gave you the last Chat information. Once you get used to this pattern, you will find it much easier to check in on building projects and units that may be threatened.

Listening to Music

Total Annihilation has an outstanding soundtrack that complements the action and events in the game. For example, when you are setting up your base or building new structures without being bothered by the enemy, the music is lively but measured; in the midst of combat, however, the music reaches a peak of intensity. Note also that you can play your own music during single-player and *spawned* games by replacing the TA CD-ROM with a music CD of your choice. This is just one of many features that enable you to configure the game to your liking. As Ron Gilbert, the game's producer, said in an interview with the e-zine *Gameslice*, "Hey, it's your game, you bought it! Why should we tell you how to play it?" (For more details on spawning see Chapter 9.)

Mapping Your Field of Vision

TA gives you three options to configure the field or range of vision of your units. Try each of these options to find out which is your favorite.

- **True.** This line-of-sight setting means that the units field of vision depends on variables such as location (i.e. what is their elevation), barriers (i.e. what is in their way), and distance (i.e. how far away things are). For instance, your units will see further from a mountaintop, but their vision will be blocked by a forest or a hill.

- **Permanent.** In this mode, you can see anything that happens on the map wherever your units have traveled on the map—there's no "fog-of-war." It's as if your units dropped tiny cameras behind them when moving, thus letting you keep an area under constant observation.

- **Circular.** Your units will see everything within a radius, and elevation does not affect their field of vision.

Now that you have these configuration options settled, it's time to launch into a description of the most important rules to follow—they will help you blaze a victorious trail across the Arm and Core universe.

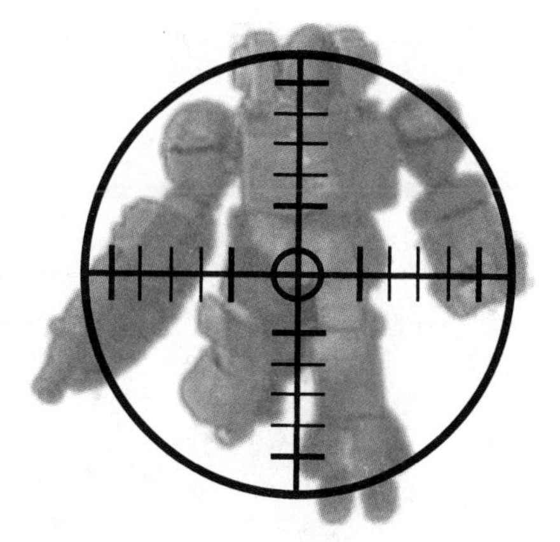

The Ten TA Commandments

The Arm and the Core have battled for thousands of years, and there is much to be learned about their warfare techniques. As a new Commander, you can benefit from the wisdom of those who have gone before you. The following TA Commandments are the bedrock on which you should base your individual strategies—ignore them at your peril.

Don't Lose Your Commander

The Commander is powerful, but not invincible. In the thick of things, it's easy to lose track of where the Commander is located. Press Ctrl-C to immediately center the screen on the Commander at any point in the game. Early on, use the Commander aggressively to set up resource generators. He'll also have to use his Disintegrator Gun more than once when your budding base is seriously threatened by an enemy attack. Be cautious with the Commander once a game is well under way. If the enemy is in command of the skies, try hiding the Commander under water or in a nearby forest for safe keeping. Be careful, however; placing the Commander under water is very dangerous if the enemy has subs, since the Commander cannot fight back when submerged.

Know Yourself, Know Your Enemy

Total Annihilation features more than 150 different units and structures. You should make a point of learning to recognize types of units instantly, and memorizing their special qualities. Otherwise, you'll have a hard time building an army that features the proper mix of units, and organizing them well.

Each side features more than forty mobile units—KBots, land vehicles, ships, and aircraft. The result is a battlefield crowded with diverse units, each of which is ideally used in its own special way. Knowing the difference between a Triton amphibious tank and a Bulldog battle tank is knowing the difference between a surprise-attack sea/land unit and a land-based juggernaut. Each has its own strengths and weaknesses that you should understand.

Although the menus presenting the units and structures are easy to read and work, nothing can take the place of knowing the strengths and weaknesses of each unit. Obviously, you should also know what's required in order to acquire the ability to build any given unit. Many of the better ones become available only after you've done all the building required to reach higher structure and unit levels. See Chapter 2 for the complete Unit Build Hierarchy, including the top-secret Level-3 units and structures that are missing from the manual. Chapters 4 to 6 provide concise descriptions of every Arm and Core unit and structure.

Expand to Conquer

Building a defensive base with tightly clustered structures doesn't lead to victory in *Total Annihilation*. Expand! Expansion means access to more metal and geothermal energy resources, the key to further growth. In the short term, strategy based primarily on creating an unassailable base brings peace of mind. In the long run, however, you'll give up a lot of ground to a hungry and aggressive enemy. The AI is very good at finding resources and putting them to immediate use in its war machine. You cannot compete without making an old-fashioned grab for territory and the resources that go with it.

On large maps with plenty of land, try spreading out the structures in your base so that they are at least a quarter of a screen apart. Later on, when nuclear weapons and long-range cannons are being used, this technique keeps your base from being totally destroyed in one or two missile strikes. In general, think expansion—think aggressively. Use scout vehicles and infantry units to find metal deposits, favorable terrain for your bases and battles, and the enemy.

Choose Terrain Wisely

Total Annihilation brings a new real-time 3D environment to life that affects game play in a variety of ways. Mountains, rivers, lava pits, oceans, and forests offer you opportunities to use the terrain to your advantage when establishing bases, planning ambushes, and attacking enemy bases.

Mountainous terrain, with many trees and forests, creates bottlenecks for tanks. Tanks operate better on open terrain where they can't get bogged down. On the other hand, artillery units can take advantage of rough terrain by firing over hills and forests and shooting from mountaintops.

Real-time game play in *Total Annihilation* is affected by terrain in ways that are different from any game you've previously played.

Scout Early and Often

Locating enemy forces and finding out what they're up to is always a top priority. You should fine-tune your strategy only after you've obtained enough intelligence! Send out scout units quickly to locate and possibly harass your adversary. Set up Radar Towers within the first few minutes of every game—they really help keep tabs on who's where.

Scouting can accomplish two aims. First, it can tell you what you need to know about enemy forces. Second, the appearance of your scouts may panic your opponent into thinking that you're much closer and stronger than you really are.

Don't Let Your Guys Fight Alone

A single unit can't accomplish much in combat. Don't waste troops by sending them out one by one, in a thin trickle; form combat squads. The game interface enables you to control up to nine different squads of troops; you select groups with the Ctrl plus 1–9 keys. For example, small squads that mix infantry, tanks, artillery, and missile launchers are effective raiders in relatively open terrain. Naval task groups are always more effective if they feature a mix of submarines, destroyers, cruisers, and battleships. Launching fighters early to clear way for the bombers is also a good tactic. Base assaults work better when close-combat units (scout vehicles, infantry KBots, rocket launchers) are supported from a distance by artillery and missile launchers that follow behind.

You may succeed by throwing your troops at the enemy in one humungous mass, but in doing so you won't take advantage of what each unit does best. Artillery is ineffective when engaging an enemy face to face; faraway infantry won't be able to engage the enemy at all.

Repair and Recover

The Commander has the ability to repair damaged units and structures, and also to recover usable metal from wrecks, and energy from trees and foliage. These abilities are crucial to your victory in a number of missions. Metal in short supply? Get in the habit of swooping in on the wreckage of units and structures right after a firefight. The

Commander can reclaim multiple wrecks in succession if you click on the Reclaim button while holding the Shift key down, and subsequently clicking on all the wrecks you want reclaimed.

It's easier and cheaper to repair a unit or structure than it is to build one from scratch. The Commander can repair a number of units and structures in quick succession. Once again, you can set up a repair queue by Shift-clicking, as when reclaiming metals.

Beware Friendly Fire

Friendly fire—killing your own troops by accident or through poor management—is a real problem in *Total Annihilation*. In close combat, the Commander's Disintegrator Gun can blow up your own troops that happen to be next to the target. You'll also have friendly fire casualties when your artillery units rain down shells on top of your frontline troops—the long-range Arm Big Bertha cannon and the Core Intimidator cannon are frequent culprits

When using artillery, aim your fire away from your units that are engaging the enemy in close combat. When using the Commander to destroy enemy units, select targets a safe distance away from your own troops.

Focus Your Firepower

En masse or in squads, your troops should always concentrate their fire on selected targets to maximize damage to the enemy. Destroy your targets one after another by ordering an entire group of troops, ships, or aircraft to fire at the same target. This tactic can knock out well-armored laser towers, construction plants, and heavy tanks in record time.

Use Combined Land, Sea, and Air Forces

It takes time and lots of resources to build up combined forces, but the whole entity is worth more than just the sum of its parts. Land forces occupy territory for you, and provide control of resources. Air and sea forces support and extend the ability of land forces to capture territory, and defeat the enemy. *Total Annihilation* was developed so that you cannot build strong, advanced armies, navies, and air forces too easily, and all at the same time. You have to make informed choices about what you develop first.

In general, build up land forces, first. Establish bases, then consider building air and sea forces next, depending on your strategy. Of course, this will also depend on the game you play—whether it's land or sea that dominates the map.

Winning Strategies

Winning IS everything in *Total Annihilation*. There are no awards for second place in a fight to the finish. With that in mind, you have to ask yourself: What is the best formation for an assault against an enemy base? Do I know the secret technique to increase the construction speed of any unit or structure I'm building? How can terrain give me a strategic advantage over my enemy? In short, what do I have to know to kick some serious butt in *Total Annihilation*? Turn this page, and you'll discover the basics on where and how to build your bases, armies, navies, and air forces—including the top secret Level-3 structures and units that are absent from the manual—and how to make the best use of your Commander.

Understanding the Basic Unit Build Hierarchies

There is a definite order to how and what you can build in *Total Annihilation,* and to the ways in which you can use your units and structures. The order in which you can build units and structures in the game is at the heart of your winning strategies. This is what is called the Unit Build Hierarchy. In life, you have to crawl before you walk, and walk before you run. In TA, you have to build the basic units and structures (Technology Level 1) before you can construct the more advanced units and structures (Level 2 and Level 3). In short, you must first aquire certain structures or units before you can build others.

It's not easy to keep things straight with over 150 units and structures, so keep a few points in mind:

- **The Commander builds the basics.** The Commander is capable of building twelve different basic structures, ranging from Solar Collectors and Metal Extractors to the four different Level-1 construction plants for Kbots, vehicles, aircraft, and ships.
- **The construction plants keep things rolling.** The Level-1 construction plants build, among other things, mobile construction units, which, in turn, build advanced construction plants, which, in turn, build advanced mobile construction units.
- **Weapons follow the same build hierarchy.** As the more advanced construction plants and mobile units are built, new weapons become available. You'll find more information on the offensive and defensive weapons hierarchies later in this chapter.
- **Last, but not least—your doomsday units and structures.** The three advanced construction units build the secret Level-3 structures and units that are omitted from the game manual. They include the Advanced Construction Kbot, the Advanced Construction Vehicle, and the Advanced Construction VToL Aircraft.

Figures 3-1 and 3-2 illustrate the Arm and Core Unit Build Hierarchies, respectively. First comes the Commander followed by the various construction units or structures (shaded boxes) and their respective outputs. The secret Level-3 units and structures revealed here include Arm and Core long-range cannons, nuclear missile launchers, nuclear antimissile defense systems, and advanced radar, repair and energy-producing structures.

Since each of the advanced construction units can produce virtually the same Level-3 structures and units, there is flexibility as to whether you pursue the Kbot, Vehicle, or Aircraft technology paths. The only restriction on building any of these Level-3 components is that the nuclear missiles are available only in multiplayer games, not in the single-player missions.

NOTE In multiplayer games, each player can have a maximum of 200 units and structures at any given time.

The ARM Unit Build Hierarchy

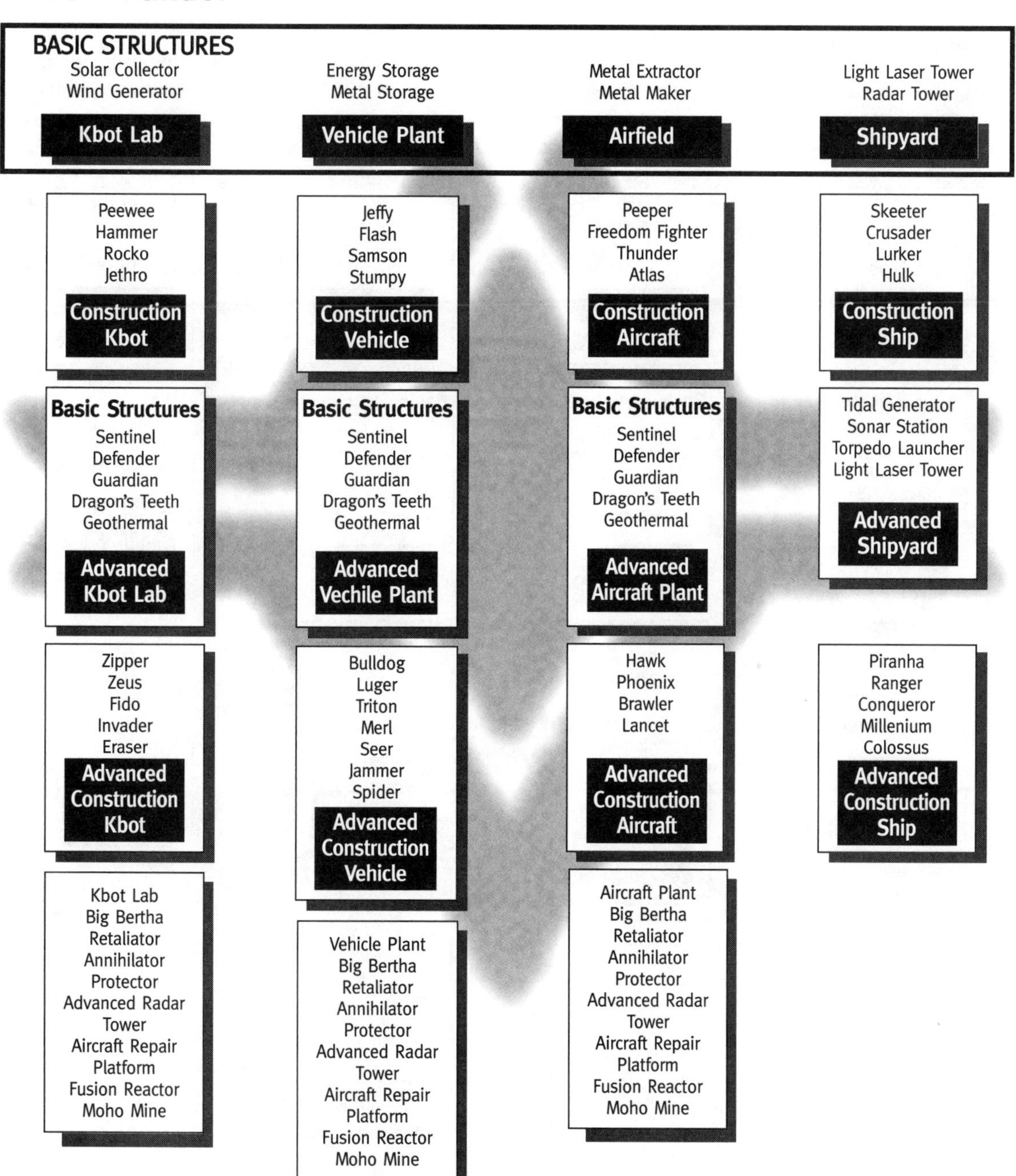

Figure 3-1: The Arm Unit Build Hierarchy

The Core Unit Build Hierarchy

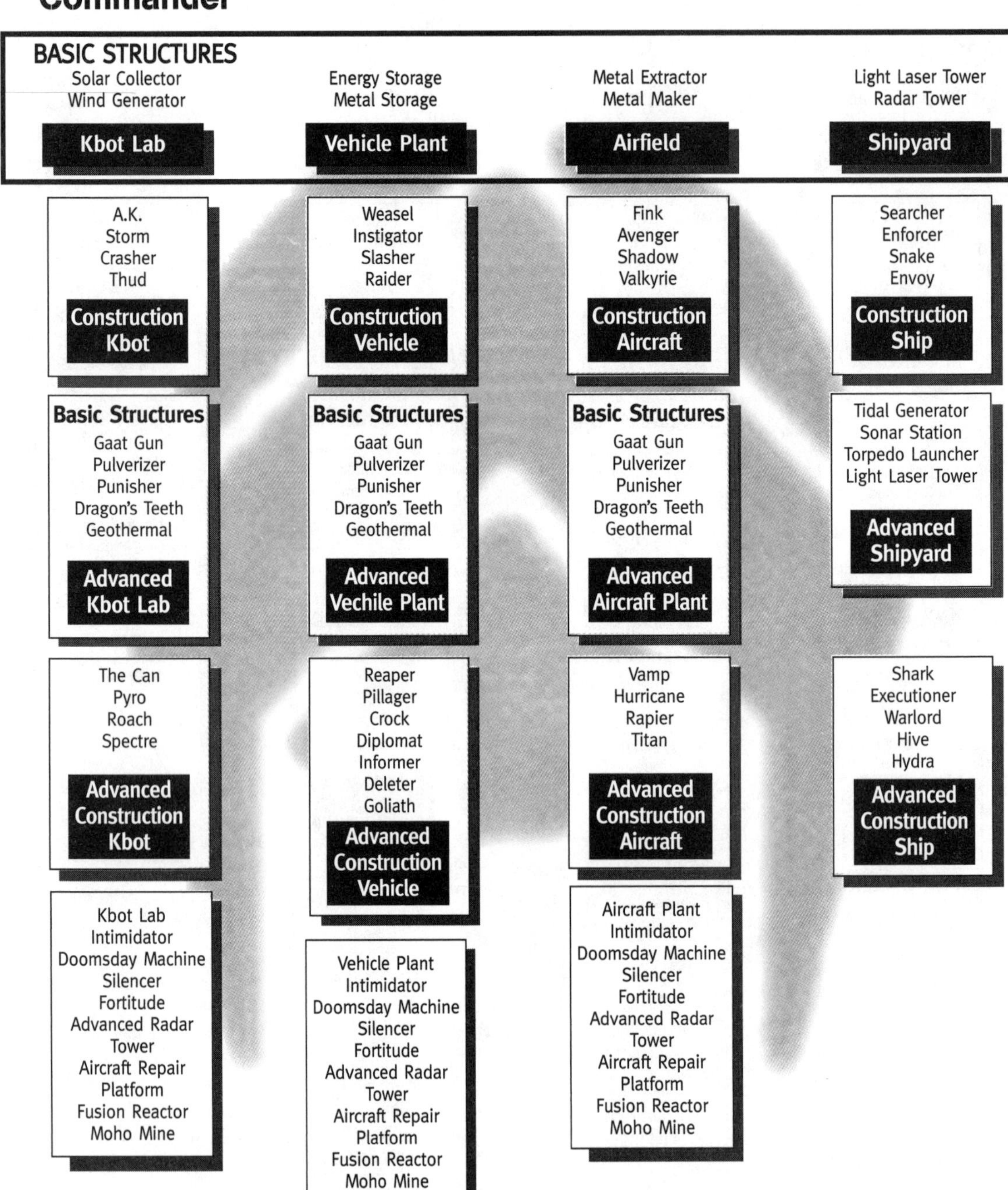

Figure 3-2: The Core Unit Build Hierarchy

Giving Orders

How your units and structures act and react is determined by the settings in the Unit Orders window (see Figure 3-3), which offers you a wide range of behaviors to program. At the top of the Orders window are the Fire options, which control when your units fire their weapons. Underneath you'll find the Movement options, which tell your units how they should move or roam about. The lower part of the Orders window contains additional movement and behavior options.

Fire Options

There are three Fire options, ranging from aggressive to totally passive:

- **Fire at Will.** This setting means that any unit with a weapon will begin firing at an enemy the moment it detects that enemy. You use this setting in combat situations, and whenever the potential for combat is high.
- **Return Fire.** This means that a unit will only fire at an enemy if fired upon first. This is useful in defensive situations when you don't want to open hostilities right away except in self-defense.
- **Hold Fire.** The final Fire option is to not fire at all under any circumstances. This option can be very helpful when your Commander is trying to capture an enemy unit or structure and you don't want any of your troops destroying it in their zeal.

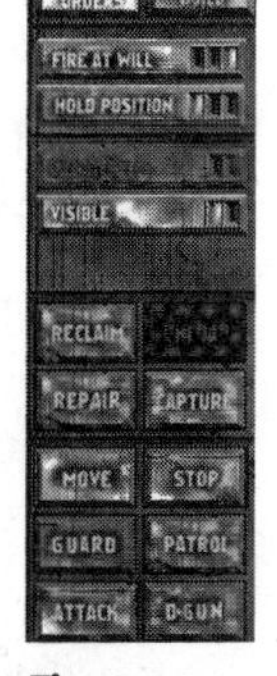

Figure 3-3: The Orders window

Whenever the action on screen gets too busy, use the minus (-) key to reduce the game speed. The plus (+) key increases game speed. You can also press the F2 key to pause the game. You can still issue orders while the game is paused. In Internet games, if the game play is becoming sloppy, try slowing the game down.

Movement Options

How and when your units move about is determined by your choices among the Movement options. At times you may want your units to pursue their attackers; at other times you may want them to stay put and protect your base. There may also be times when you want them to stay nearby, but maneuver to stay out of the line of fire.

- **Hold Position.** In this mode, your mobile unit remains at its post no matter what the circumstances. When coupled with the Return Fire or Fire at Will option, the Hold Position mode effectively turns your unit into the equivalent of a stationary defense structure. When coupled with the Hold Fire option, it turns your unit into the equivalent of a tree trunk.
- **Maneuver.** For a bit more self-preservation, the Maneuver option allows a unit to protect itself by moving around when fired upon—less of a sitting duck, but remains in the general area. Also, a unit will move within a certain area if it allows it to open fire at the enemy.

- **Roam.** The most aggressive movement option is Roam, in which the unit will follow the enemy. If you want to be really aggressive, set your options to Roam and Fire at Will. (A setting of Hold Position and Hold Fire, by contrast, is the ultimate passive mode.)

Mobile construction units have a very powerful ability to automatically repair other units. Set a construction unit on a patrol route and order it to Repair, and it will automatically repair any damaged unit it comes near on its patrol course. When it's set on Roam, the unit will go out of its normal path when it gets near a unit that needs repair.

Additional Orders

The Orders menu has additional specific orders that you give to units to perform certain tasks. These are very helpful when setting your individual unit strategies.

- **Reclaim.** Only construction units and the Commander can reclaim metal from rocks and wreckage as well as energy from sun, wind, steam, and biomass. This is one of the most useful orders in your repertoire since energy and metal are scarce commodities in many situations. In situations where you wish to reclaim material, but the duty is hazardous, always send in your construction units to do the job. Don't risk losing your Commander.

- **Repair.** This is another very powerful command. Construction units and the Commander use this order to keep the troops and structures healthy. However, as with many processes in *TA*, you can set up this option to be automatic by having your construction units patrol back and forth, repairing anything that needs repair as they pass by. Since repairing a unit requires energy but no metal, there's a big advantage to repairing units on metal-poor worlds.

- **Move.** The Move order simply tells a unit to relocate to a new position; but it doesn't cancel out the previous movement order to Hold Position, Maneuver, or Roam once it gets there.

- **Guard.** This is very handy for attaching one unit to another. For example, if you want to create a small squad of troops that should stay together, order each of them to guard one another or, say, the Commander. They will move together as a group, although they will not stay in a formation.

- **Attack.** Like Move, this order does not cancel out the overriding Movement and Fire orders, but does tell the unit to attack the particular target that you click. Once the job is completed, your unit will return to its earlier status.

- **Capture.** Only the Commander can capture other units and structures. It's difficult for the Commander to stop a moving enemy unit long enough to capture it, but if you order a Spider bot to guard the Commander, the Spider can paralyze the unit so that the Commander can capture it.

- **Stop.** This command tells a unit to forget whatever commands it has been given, even if there are several commands lined up.

- **Patrol.** The patrol function is very useful for guarding base perimeters. But, as mentioned earlier, it's also extremely helpful in allowing construction units to automatically repair any damaged units it comes in contact with along the patrol route.

- **Load and Unload.** Air and sea transports make use of this command. Air transports can carry one unit at a time. Sea transports can carry more: Arm's sea transport can carry 20 units, Core's 24 units.

When it comes to the importance of particular units, you must not underestimate the value of Kbot, vehicle, naval, and aircraft construction units. They not only build other units and structures, but also take over a great deal of work from the Commander by repairing other units and structures, and reclaiming metal and biomass for energy. Combine several of them on a building project, and their build speeds are *added* to one another. For most missions and multiplayer games, include several of them in your building plans.

When one of your units destroys five other units, it becomes a "veteran." This status incrementally increases the unit's rate of fire, the power of its weapon, the effectiveness of its armor, and the amount of time it takes for the enemy Commander to capture it. Veteran status will also improve the accuracy of the unit's weapon, including its ability to accurately lead a moving target. Every additional five units that a veteran kills further enhances all of those factors. So, it pays to keep repairing your units and keep your veterans going!

Making the Most of Your Commander

The Commander is versatile, powerful, vulnerable, slow, and over-worked. Like a lot of leaders, he has good points and bad points. It's your job to bring out the best in your Commander as you play TA. Since the death of the Commander can mean the end of a game or a mission, get to know the Commander inside and out.

- **Press Ctrl-C to immediately center the screen on the Commander.** It's easy to lose sight of the Commander when the fighting is heavy and there are many units moving at once. The Ctrl-C option selects the Commander for your immediate orders.

- **Recognize your Commander's "build" speed**. The Commander builds faster than any other construction unit in the game—300 *work units* per second. Appendix A at the end of this book presents many unit and structure statistics, including the *time* (expressed in total number of work units and converted to seconds) it takes to build each unit.

- **There are eight different "build" speeds in the game.** Those speeds are spread among the 16 units and structures that have a construction capability. Although the

Commander builds structures at 300 work units per second, a Level-1 construction plant builds structures and units at approximately 100 work units per second, and a Level-2 construction plant builds them at about 200 work units per second. In short, it takes the Commander approximately 20 seconds to construct a Kbot Lab (6,000 work units) while it would take a Level-1 Construction Kbot a full 60 seconds to do the same job. The Commander builds a Light Laser Tower (1,500 work units) in approximately 5 seconds—provided you have sufficient metal and energy.

- **Assist your construction units**. To increase the speed of construction, the Commander can assist construction plants and mobile construction units in their efforts. You can do so in one of two ways, depending on your mouse interface choice (see *Using the Mouse* in the manual). If you're using the Left Click (default) mouse interface, select the Orders menu option for the Commander, left-click Move, then left-click on the unit under construction. The Commander will move to the unit and begin assisting in the construction process. If you are using the Right Click mouse interface, with the Commander selected, simply right-click on the unit being constructed for the same effect. The Commander's building speed of 300 work units per second is *added* to the current build speed of the construction plant or mobile construction unit that's already building the unit or structure.

- **Experiment with multiple construction orders**—Early in a game, the Commander is the only construction unit. To build Metal Extractors, Solar Collectors, Light Laser Towers, and other structures more quickly, order the Commander to build several of the same structure automatically in succession. Click on the desired structure in the Build menu. Then, hold down the Shift key while clicking on the locations you wish to build in. However, before you give a series of multiple construction orders, calculate your Energy and Metal reserves to make sure you won't unexpectedly run out of resources (see Figure 3-4).

- **Use the Commander's weapons wisely.** The Commander's weapons consist of a laser gun and the Disintegrator Gun. The D-Gun can destroy anything it hits with a single shot. However, each D-Gun blast costs you 400 *energy units,* which can deplete Energy reserves in a hurry. Still, this blasting power means that the Commander can sway the tide of battle upon entering a firefight. The downside to this is that the D-Gun blast can also very easily destroy your own troops, a.k.a. death by friendly fire—something you should avoid at all cost. For example, in battle situations in which troops are tightly bunched against one another, your Commander's blast can kill as many of your own troops as those of the enemy. Try using the D-Gun either with isolated targets, or where the Commander's troops are not engaged in close combat with the enemy.

- **The AI targets the Commander first.** The Artificial Intelligence (AI) used by the computer-controlled armed forces will seek out the most attractive target, which is almost always the Commander. So, don't lead an assault against heavily defended positions with your Commander in the lead—it amounts to suicide. Send in less valuable units just ahead of the Commander. The enemy will target them first, giving you a chance to bring the Commander into action without immediately drawing all the enemy fire. If you are a good player, you can throw a switch and use the Commander as bait; expose him briefly to the enemy, then hide him somewhere safe—behind a big rock, for example. While the AI-controlled units pelt the rock with shots, your units can destroy them without return fire.

- **Capture enemy units.** Your Commander can approach AI-controlled units and structures without immediately drawing fire. This can occur if the unit or structure in question is set to Hold Fire or Return Fire. Select Capture from the Commander's Orders menu, then click on the unit you wish to capture. You can capture multiple enemy units and structures by holding down the Shift key once you have selected Capture. It is possible to capture entire groups of structures this way.

- **Consider using the Cloaked option.** The Commander can become invisible for short periods of time if you select the Cloaked option in the Orders menu. However, cloaking uses Energy at a rate of approximately 200 energy units per second if still (1,000 EU if moving), which is a very steep price. Cloaking should only be used in those circumstances in which you have plenty of Energy resources and the Commander is under extreme enemy pressure.

- **Hide your Commander (if necessary).** Since the death of the Commander can mean the end of a mission or a multiplayer game, one tactic to help save his metal skin is to hide the Commander. You cannot implement this tactic right away, since you need the Commander to build up your base. However, once base development is fairly far along and you have acquired a few construction units, try hiding the

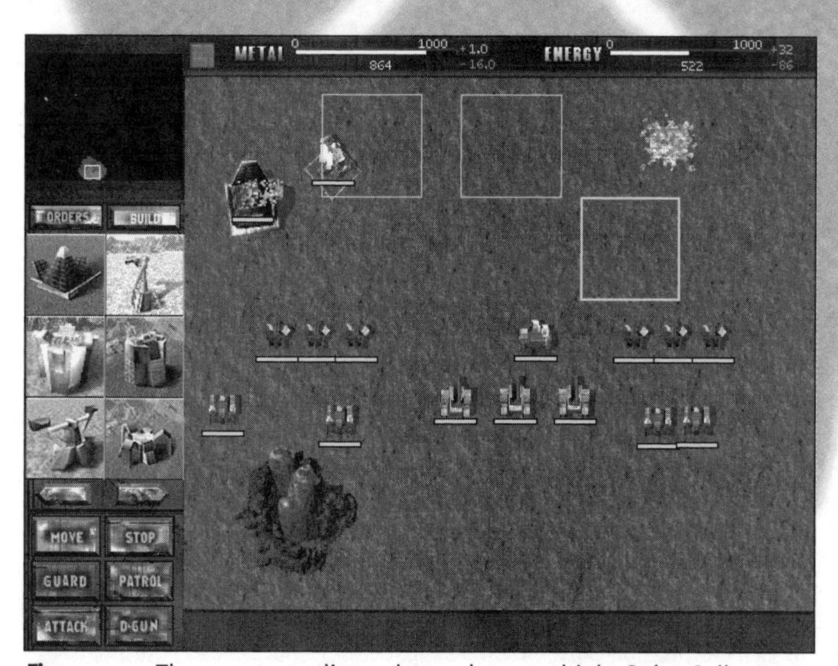

Figure 3-4: The square outlines show where multiple Solar Collectors will be built.

Commander in deep water near your base—making sure that there's sonar and torpedo launcher protection from enemy subs. This is a good way to escape dangerous aerial threats. You can also try hiding the Commander in a thick group of trees—although the computer AI will spot that through its radar, human opponents may overlook it.

Order your Commander to Capture a single Light Laser Tower that is guarding a metal extractor or some other enemy structure. Your Commander will be fired upon, but can withstand the laser. When the conversion occurs, change the LLT's orders to Hold Fire while you Capture the other structures. Then change the LLT back to Fire At Will so that it will shoot on sight any approaching enemy unit.

Building Strategies

Virtually every move you make in TA has something to do with building. How fast and how effectively you can build structures and units has a great deal to do with how long you stay alive. Where is the safest place to build your base? What should you build first, second, and third? Here are some answers to these burning questions.

Designing Your Base

If you want to be the Frank Lloyd Wright of base design, then you have to understand how the location, structure, and purpose of your base fits into your winning strategy. The components of good base layout vary with the terrain, the opponent, and whether you prefer an offensive, expansion-oriented game or a defensive, protection-oriented approach. Still, there are some fundamentals that apply in almost every game.

- **Make good use of the terrain.** Minimize the number of easy geographical approaches to your base. Making good use of terrain while siting the base means limiting enemy access. Dragon's Teeth barriers are great for directing approaching enemy units into choke points. Place laser, missile, and rocket towers so that they have overlapping fields of fire covering these choke points.

- **Always remember to use Dragon's Teeth as a part of your base design.** Dragon's Teeth are very difficult to destroy, and should be a part of almost every base design. They are cheap, and they can funnel your enemies into kill zones. When ordering a construction unit to build Dragon's Teeth barriers, always hold down the Shift key to order the unit to build multiple barriers. By doing so, you can have the construction unit set up rows of Dragon's Teeth while you move on to something else.

- **Place units strategically.** Place anti-aircraft structures and mobile units along the base's perimeter, and at strategic spots within the base proper. Do not cluster multiple AA units, such as Arm Jethros or Core Crashers. Space them out across your base. This offers a number of different firing angles against enemy aircraft. Use Kbots to patrol the perimeter. Kbots, such as the Arm PeeWee and Core A.K. have a longer spotting range than most other units. Site Radar Towers at several points around the base. Don't scrimp here. Build at least three or four, as shown in Figure 3-5.

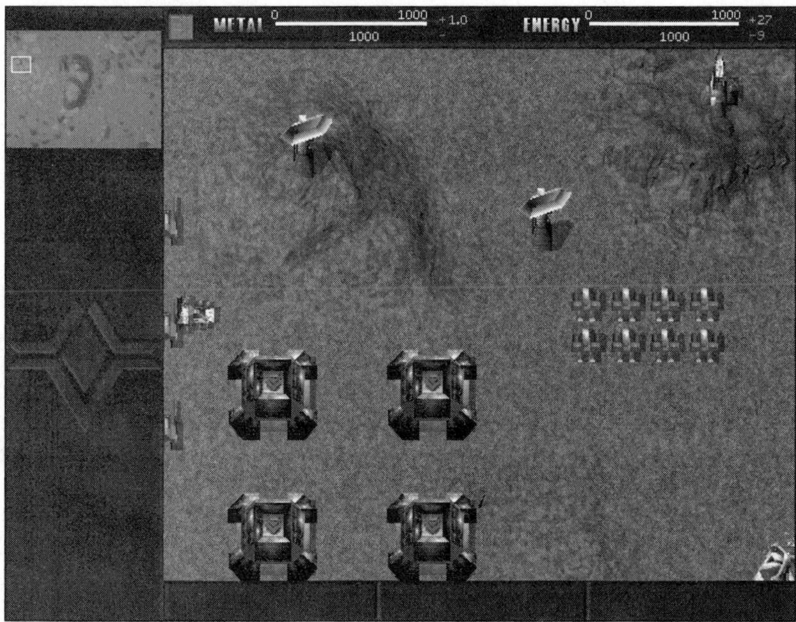

Figure 3-5: Spread out your base and use Radar Towers as soon as possible.

- **Build a strong defense perimeter.** Scout vehicles make good, cheap perimeter patrols. You can also build Light Laser Towers at least a half-screen from the perimeter of your base to give you additional warning and slow down enemy advances. Place construction units and structures close enough to the base perimeter so that the newly produced units can be moved into action without having to travel through the entire base.

If you have an Aircraft Plant, have Level-1 fighter aircraft—such as Arm Freedom Fighters or Core Avengers—fly regular patrols from one end of the base perimeter to the other. They not only spot approaching enemy aircraft and ground units, but can also attack and destroy them.

Building Bases

In TA, you live or die by the kind of base you build. Some players like to construct massive fortresses for protection. Others favor a more open, spread-out look and feel. To a great extent, the kind of base you build in *Total Annihilation,* depends on individual mission objectives, or the specific multiplayer environment. Defensive gamers tend to favor pouring more resources into building formidable but expensive stationary defenses that are difficult to assail. Offensive gamers, by contrast, tend to keep bases spread out, expand quickly into new areas for additional resources, and spend more metal and energy on producing offensive weaponry and scouts. Whatever strategy you use—offensive or defensive—here are a few fundamentals to keep in mind.

- **Assess your potential base site.** In most missions and on many multiplayer maps, your starting location is close enough to resources for you to begin building a base nearby. When possible, try to locate your base in a corner of the map. This provides a measure of protection on two sides. However, when enemy aircraft become operational, the map edge won't hinder them during strafing and bombing raids

- **Find nearby metal deposits.** Scout out at least two or three metal deposits in the area you wish to place your base. Build your base around these deposits, if possible, in order to have a long-term supply within the perimeter of your base. *Total Annihilation*'s AI places a high priority on destroying enemy resource-generating structures, so protect your metal extractors with Light Laser Towers, Kbots, and missile launchers.

- **Analyze the proximity of natural barriers.** Rivers, steep mountain ridges, tall mesas, and buttes restrict or impede enemy access to your base, block the enemy units' line of sight, and possibly provide good sites for defensive structures. River crossing points can be good choke points at which you can station Light Laser Towers, Kbots, and tanks to block access to your base. Mobile units slow down to half-speed when fording these river crossing, making them easy targets. High ridges and buttes are great for Radar Towers and artillery units.

- **Consider building a decoy base.** When starting a mission or a multiplayer game, consider building a false base to confuse the enemy. This might mean placing a few Solar Collectors and Metal Extractors in an area protected by a Light Laser Tower, and then moving your main force away from there to an area with better natural defenses or more Metal resources.

- **Accumulate resources.** In almost any scenario, the first step is to secure a supply of resources: the energy and metal that keep you growing. Metal is the resource that is usually in short supply, since energy is supplied by the limitless sunlight (Solar Collectors) and wind (Wind Generators). Start by building at least one Metal Extractor on a metal deposit, then build two or three Solar Collectors. Ideally, early in a game you should have at least three Metal Extractors built to provide enough metal for construction of a Kbot Lab or a Vehicle Plant, and the units these structures subsequently build.

- **Incorporate Moho Mines and Fusion Reactors in your long-term base planning.** The Moho Mine and the Fusion Reactor are Level-3 structures that are built by any of the three Advanced Mobile Construction Units. They are expensive but extremely helpful for sustained metal and energy production in the middle and later stages of a game. Keep Fusion Reactors separated by at least a half-screen or more, since they level a large area if destroyed by the enemy.

- **Don't forget wind power and geothermal power.** It's easy to concentrate on Solar Collectors and Metal Extractors for resource production and forget about Wind Generators and Geothermal Power Generators. If you find yourself on a mountain, hill, or mesa, build a Wind Generator. Geothermal Power Plants are constructed by any of the mobile construction units. When placed over any of the steam vents on a planet, a Geothermal Power Plant produces 250 energy units per second. You start out with an energy and metal storage capacity of 1,000 units of each. You can increase that capacity by building metal and energy storage structures. However, because of the time and expense they take, their construction should usually be secondary to resource generation and base defense in the early part of a game.

- **Reclaim wreckage, rocks, and biomass from your potential base site.** The Commander can reclaim metal from destroyed units and structures and harvest biomass from the trees and foliage for energy (see the manual for details). You won't normally have to take either of these steps at the start of a mission or multiplayer game. On some planets, however, they come into play much sooner than others. Biomass is usually found in clumps of 250 energy units, while metal reclamation varies from a few metal units to hundreds of units for destroyed tanks and ships.

- **Detect the enemy.** Unless you come under immediate enemy attack, order your Commander to build a Radar Tower near your base. At the start of a game, this will usually give you critical information about the proximity of enemy units. The higher the ground on which you set the Radar Tower, the farther you'll be able to detect the enemy. Try to build more than one Radar Tower as soon as possible in case the first one or two are destroyed by the enemy. Remember, *Total Annihilation* uses a 3D line-of-sight model, which means there may be gaps in radar coverage—enemies can hide from your radar in gullies or behind mountains, radar is always a simple circle. Be warned—the AI rightly sees your Radar Towers as the gravest threat, and attacks them as soon as it can.

- **Use resource generators as barriers.** One way to slow down an aggressive opponent is to construct surplus energy and metal generators along the base perimeter to form a physical barrier. Your own well-placed laser, missile, and rocket towers as well as artillery units can enjoy some protection from enemy fire behind these structures, but it's important to site them so that they still have good fields of fire. Once the enemy assault is beaten back, it's not hard to rebuild the destroyed Solar Collectors, Wind Generators, and Metal Extractors.

- **Extend your base.** Spread out your base. It's not a good idea to have a small, crowded base configuration. Although an extended base that stretches out more than one or two screens may seem too difficult to defend, this base layout actually provides a measure of protection, making it difficult for the enemy to focus an assault on a specific area. Also, when your units are trying to defend a small, cramped base against attackers that have already breached the defensive perimeter, it is difficult to destroy them without collateral damage to your own structures.

Finally, by extending your base structures, you can more effectively set up fields of fire from laser, rocket, and missile towers. In the late stages of missions or multiplayer games, nuclear weapons make an appearance. If there's a nuclear strike on your base, the resulting nuclear explosion destroys more than an entire screen for buildings and/or units. (A "screen" is that portion of the map you see at one time in the main game section.) A conventional attack on one of your own Fusion Reactors can also result in a devastating nuclear explosion. If your base is constricted, a single nuclear explosion can do incredible damage.

- **Plan your base to take into account available resource production.** Knowing the production performance of your energy and metal generators will save time and effort. For example, one Geothermal Power Plant (250 energy units per second) equals a dozen Solar Collectors (20 energy units per second). The build cost is about the same between one of the Geothermal units and 12 of the Solar Collectors, but the former takes up much less room and is more durable than the Collectors. Tables 3-1 and 3-2 present the resource-production totals for various units and structures.

NOTE A Metal Storage structure stores up to 1,000 metal units. An Energy Storage structure stores up to 3,000 energy units.

Table 3-1. Metal Resource Production Totals

METAL PRODUCER OR CONVERTER	METAL UNITS EXTRACTED OR PRODUCED PER SECOND
Metal Extractor	2.0 on large metal deposits
Metal Extractor	1.0 on medium deposits
Metal Extractor	0.5 on small deposits
Metal Maker	1.0
Commander	1.0
Shipyard	0.25
Advanced Shipyard	0.5
Moho Mine	Varies with the planet, but at least three times faster than a Metal Extractor
Wrecks and some types of boulders	Varies widely

Table 3-2. Energy Resource Production Totals

Energy Producers or Converters	Energy Units produced per second
Solar Collector	20; may vary depending on the world
Geothermal Power Plant	250
Fusion Reactor	1,000
Wind Generator	Varies widely; but zero on vacuum worlds
Tidal Generator	Varies widely; usually between 15-30
Level-1 construction units and structures	Varies; about 10
Level-2 construction units and structures	Varies; about 25
Aircraft Carriers	330

Building Armies

Land-based campaigns give you a bewildering choice of army units from which to choose. The best general strategy is to think about your ground troops as having three basic types of weapons: short-range weapons that are useful only in close combat with visual contact, long-range artillery units that can fire over barriers such as hills and rivers, and anti-aircraft weapons that give air defense.

- **Upgrade your weapons quickly.** The order of battle in most missions will be to use Level-1 weapons first, followed by the Level-2 and Level-3 weapons as your construction options increase during the game.

- **Develop a standard attack formation.** As a rule, put short-range mobile weapons (those that can only hit targets within their own line-of-sight) in the front line. Put the longer-range mobile rocket, missile, and artillery units in the second line. While there is no hard-and-fast order of attack, one common Arm attack formation early in a game might include a half-dozen scout vehicles and Kbots, followed closely by a small group of light tanks, and further back by artillery and rocket Kbots. The faster, cheaper units attract most of the initial enemy fire, while the artillery and rocket units draw less initial attention, and can fire away undisturbed.

- **Have a good mix of weapons in any squads you form.** A small squad that has a variety of weapons is the most versatile. For example, a 12-unit Arm squad might contain 4 PeeWees, 2 Hammer artillery units, 1 Rocko rocket launcher, 2 Jethro anti-air units, 1 Jeffy scout vehicle, and 2 Flash tanks. This is an all-purpose Level-1 squad that provides short, long, and air weaponry as well as a scouting function and some armor.

Tables 3-3 and 3-4 present mobile and stationary army weapons, respectively, broken out by short-range, longer-range, and anti-air units. Line-of-sight weapons are short-range and can hit only targets that they can see.

Table 3-3. Mobile Weapons

Weapon Type	Unit Type	Arm	Core	Technology Level
Short-range, line-of-sight weapons	Kbot	PeeWee	A.K.	Level 1
	Scout vehicle	Jeffy	Weasel	Level 1
	Light tank	Flash	Instigator	Level 1
	Medium tank	Stumpy	Raider	Level 1
	Heavy assault Kbot	Fido	The Can	Level 2
	Fast scouting Kbot	Zipper	—	Level 2
	Flamethrower Kbot	—	Pyro	Level 2
	Lightning gun Kbot	Zeus	—	Level 2
	Crawling bomb Kbot	Invader	Roach	Level 2
	Main battle tank	Bulldog	Reaper	Level 2
	Amphibious tank	Triton	Crock	Level 2
	Paralyzer Kbot	Spider	—	Level 2
Longer range weapons	Artillery Kbot	Hammer	Thud	Level 1
	Rocket-launcher Kbot	Rocko	Storm	Level 1
	Super-heavy tank	—	Goliath	Level 2
	Mobile artillery	Luger	Pillager	Level 2
	High-trajectory rocket launcher	Merl	Diplomat	Level 2
Anti-aircraft weapons	Anti-air missile Kbot	Jethro	Crasher	Level 1
	Mobile SAM missiles	Samson	Slasher	Level 1

Table 3-4. Stationary Weapons

Weapon Type	Unit Type	Arm	Core	Level
Short-range, line-of-sight weapons	Laser tower	Light Laser Tower	Light Laser Tower	Level 1
	Heavy laser tower	Sentinel	Gaat Gun	Level 2
Long-range weapons	Plasma battery artillery	Guardian	Punisher	Level 2
	Nuclear missile launcher	Retaliator	Silencer	Level 3
	Energy shell cannon	Annihilator	Doomsday Machine	Level 3
	Plasma cannon	Big Bertha	Intimidator	Level 3
Anti-aircraft weapons	Missile tower	Defender	Pulverizer	Level 2
	Missile-defense structure	Protector	Silencer	Level 3

Building Navies

You don't have quite as many choices when building a navy. However, learning to form strong, versatile naval task groups is crucial to ruling the seas of TA. Think of your naval units as having three distinct purposes: surface guns that shoot ship-to-ship or ship-to-land, anti-aircraft guns or missiles, and torpedoes for underwater operations. Just like your ground troop squads, a naval group that contains a mix of all these weapons is the most effective. For example, a good Level-1 Core naval group should contain a Searcher scout ship that carries anti-aircraft missiles, a couple of Enforcer destroyers with surface cannons and anti-sub depth charges, and two or three Snake submarines. When building your navy, keep in mind to:

- **Build subs early and often.** An aggressive submarine force is extremely potent and tough for the enemy to combat. An enemy without a good sub force will have trouble maintaining an effective naval presence. Begin producing subs right away when you construct a Shipyard. They make good perimeter patrol and recon units, and are able to sink the enemy scout ships, cruisers, and other subs that are usually the first to arrive.

- **Protect your battleships.** Although battleships are extremely powerful, they have no defenses against subs. Make sure you use destroyers, cruisers, and sub killers alongside your battleships at all times.

- **Include anti-aircraft units in your naval squadrons and task forces.** Air power is effective against all ships with the exception of subs. Missile ships and scout ships are capable of knocking aircraft out of the air. Important: Missile ships can also fire at surface targets.

- **Recognize your ships' best uses.** Scout ships are very fast and maneuverable, but also very lightly armored. Use several scout ships to quickly explore the map. Cruisers have guns with the longest range among all the naval units. Grouped together with battleships, they are lethal against land targets. Remember the weapons each naval unit has, and plan to use ships together to complement their strengths and weaknesses. Table 3-5 lists the Arm and Core water-based units.

Table 3-5. Naval Units and Weapons

Unit Type	Weapons	Arm	Core	Technology Level
Scout ship	Anti-air missiles	Skeeter	Searcher	Level 1
Destroyer	Depth charges, surface cannons	Crusader	Enforcer	Level 1
Submarine	Torpedoes	Lurker	Snake	Level 1
Transport	—	Hulk	Envoy	Level 1
Submarine killer	Long-range torpedoes	Piranha	Shark	Level 2
Missile ship	AA missiles and rockets	Ranger	Hydra	Level 2
Cruiser	Long-range guns to target islands	Conqueror	Executioner	Level 2
Battleship	Long-range guns	Millenium	Warlord	Level 2
Light carrier	Repair and radar only	Colossus	Hive	Level 2

Building Air Forces

Building an Aircraft Plant, especially early in a mission or multiplayer game, provides you with the fastest way to find out where the enemy base is, and what is being built there. Begin by building a Construction Aircraft, giving you more construction, repair, and reclaim options. Fighters should be next; initially get at least a half-dozen in the air patrolling above your base. Bombers should be third on your construction list. Build no fewer than six or eight of them to really do damage to the enemy. Air transports can then be built, but only if there is an immediate need, such as carrying units across water or lava. If there is no immediate need, then build more fighters and bombers to make your air force as strong as possible.

- **Keep your aircraft construction going all the time.** Air units have a limitless fuel supply and limitless ammunition, but a relatively short life span. Make sure that you queue up many aircraft construction units so that those that are being destroyed can be replaced immediately. It is easy to forget the building process when you are trying to control air combat situations.
- **Build plenty of aircraft.** Aircraft are generally ineffective except in significant numbers. Although individual fighters can make a difference in air-to-air combat, you need a minimum of six to eight bombers on any attack to cause significant damage.
- **You really need Level-2 aircraft.** Do not bother building a lot of Level-1 fighters and bombers. They are not that effective. Go straight for the Level-2 production. Stealth fighters, strategic bombers, and gunships are what you need to really pound the enemy. This Level-2 rule is more important for air power than for ground and naval units.
- **Have a mixture of air-to-air and air-to-ground aircraft.** Your aircraft production should reflect a mix of weapons that includes air-to-air missiles, such as the fighter aircraft, and air-to-ground bombs, such as the bombers. When attacking an enemy base, go in first with the air-to-air fighters to clear out some of the enemy fighters on patrol there. Table 3-6 presents the Core and Arm aircraft and their weapons.

Table 3-6. Air Units and their Weapons

Unit Type	Weapons	Arm	Core	Technology Level
Air scout	No guns	Peeper	Fink	Level 1
Fighter	Air-to-air missiles	Freedom Fighter	Avenger	Level 1
Bomber	Bombs	Thunder	Shadow	Level 1
Air transport	No weapons	Atlas	Valkyrie	Level 1
Stealth fighter	Air-to-air and air-to-ground capabilities	Hawk	Vamp	Level 2
Strategic bomber	Air-to-air defenses as well as bombs	Phoenix	Hurricane	Level 2
Gunship	Hovers and fires missiles	Brawler	Rapier	Level 2
Torpedo bomber	Torpedoes only	Lancet	Titan	Level 2

Use scout aircraft with fighters to confuse the enemy anti-aircraft units. When attacking enemy bases with aircraft, try sending in scouts just ahead of fighters and bombers. Enemy AA will target the poor scouts instead of the approaching strike aircraft.

Covering the 3D Terrain

One of the most intriguing aspects of *Total Annihilation* is the way that the 3D terrain—trees, forests, hills, cliffs, mountains, rivers and oceans—dictates much of your strategy, just as in a real combat situation.

- **Use forests as barriers.** Forests provide natural barriers that stop or slow down advancing troops, especially tanks, which can be blocked by the obstacles. Units can effectively hide underneath dense forested areas, a technique especially helpful in multiplayer games—a human opponent can often be fooled in this way.

- **Seize the high ground.** Whenever possible, seize the high ground. This not only affords excellent sites for Radar Towers, but also for positioning Laser, Missile, and Rocket Towers. It is also easier to set up overlapping fields of fire for your stationary weapons when they command the area from higher ground. Artillery units can lengthen their range when firing from high ground, but remember to compensate for the changed trajectory of their shells—you can easily overshoot enemy troops as they climb toward you up the slope. However, climbing the slope also means that the enemy units will move much more slowly, buying time for your defense. Figure 3-6 provides an example of how to set up defensive structures on higher ground.

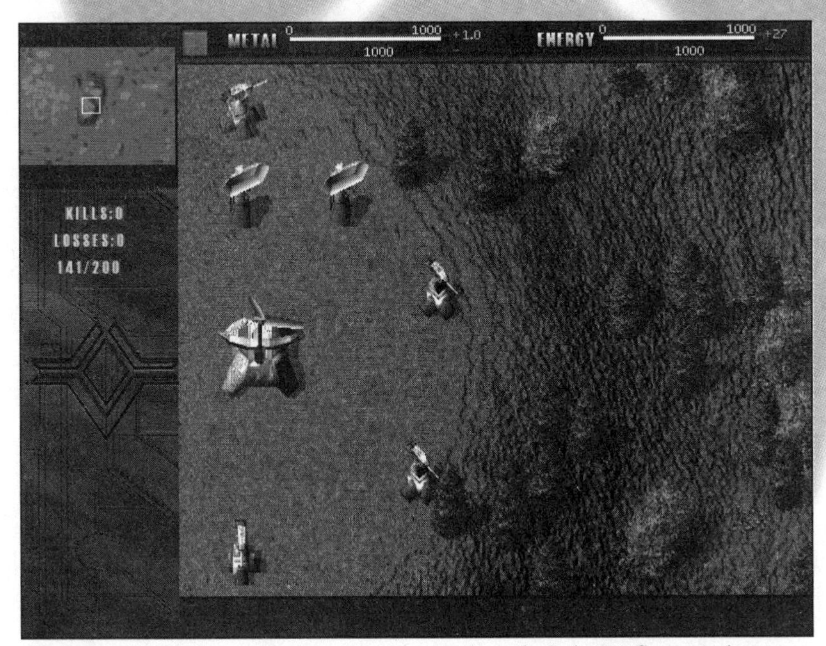

Figure 3-6: Setting up Laser Towers so that their laser fire overlaps one another is an effective defensive formation.

- **Use your amphibious units to attack.** The presence of rivers and oceans affects your strategy in a big way. It's important to be aware which units can cross bodies of water, and which cannot. For example, the Commander is capable of crossing any river and any ocean. Amphibious tanks, such as the Arm Triton and the Core Crock, can also cross rivers and oceans that are impassable by other units. The only other land units with full amphibious capabilities are the crawling bomb Kbot, the Arm Invader, and the Core Roach. Those units cannot be spotted by the enemy unless there are Sonar Stations on duty in the vicinity. When spotted, all units underwater become vulnerable to submarine attack. However, in the absence of a working enemy sonar, you may be able to mount a surprise attack against an unsuspecting enemy. A squad of amphibious tanks or a series of crawling bombs that suddenly appear from out of the water can surprise your enemy and throw them off balance. This can be particularly effective if you can time things so that your amphibious units emerge just when your other forces commence their attack.

Use the small mission map in the upper left corner of your screen to pinpoint enemy subs. If you have set up Sonar Stations around the perimeters of your base, the submarines that are within their range will show up on the mission map as colored dots. Select one or more of your own subs or destroyers, then click on one of the dots on the mission map to attack. As long as the target is within your sonar, your attack units will continue to pursue it.

- **Find the river fords.** Rivers frequently have more than one shallow area, or ford, that you can cross. They show up as lighter blue areas. Scout around crossing points carefully. Since all land units are slowed to half-speed while crossing shallow fords, well-placed stationary laser towers and enemy mobile units can cut your troops to pieces very quickly while they wade across the water (see Figure 3-7).

No-Mercy Strategies

Whether you're mounting an all-out attack or putting together a last-ditch defense, you have to understand the TA strategies that separate the real Commanders from the cannon fodder. Spend some time learning the offensive and defensive basics, and you'll soon be pounding your enemies back to the Stone Age.

Offensive Strategies

Build your offensive strategies around the strengths of the different mobile units in your arsenal. These vary greatly, depending on whether you are putting together a land, sea, or air campaign. Of course, most of the time you'll be combining elements of all three. In this section, you'll discover different approaches that can be taken by both Arm and Core. Remember, that the order in which you take these actions changes, depending on the single-player mission or the multi-player map.

Land-Based Attacks and Campaigns

Using the Arm as an example, here are the main considerations in a land-based strike against an enemy base early in a game:

Figure 3-7: Arm units are caught in the middle of a narrow river ford by Core troops waiting on the other side.

- **Get the basics started.** If you start a mission with just the Commander and a few other units, first build several Solar Collectors and Metal Extractors. Next, construct a Radar Tower so you won't be surprised by an aggressive enemy. Then build a Kbot Lab and a Vehicle Plant. Set the Kbot Lab to produce several PeeWees, a Construction Kbot, and a few Hammer artillery units, and Rocko rocket launchers. Don't worry about the Jethro anti-air Kbot at first, unless you see some evidence that enemy aircraft already exist. Set the Vehicle Plant to produce a couple of Jeffys and Flash tanks.

- **Scout first.** Send a couple of Jeffy scout vehicles and two or three PeeWees out to scout the area for resources and to find the enemy. In multiplayer games, the aggressive harassing approach is to immediately attack the enemy base with a few Jeffys and PeeWees in order to throw the enemy off balance, and to blow up a few Solar Collectors and Metal Extractors. A more conservative approach, once you've encountered the enemy base, is to get as much information as possible from your Jeffys as they race around the area, then pull them back if possible. This gives you some information about the enemy without losing any—or many—of your units.

- **Set your perimeter.** While you are building up your resources with a few additional Solar Collectors, Wind Generators, and Metal Extractors, decide how you want to protect them. Light Laser Towers are effective early in the game, but they take 2,546 energy units and 262 metal units each. That's a serious drain on your energy resources early in the game. One strategy to consider is to protect your exposed resource generators with fast-moving Jeffys, PeeWees, and Flash tanks. They are not stationary, like the Light Laser Tower, and can react quickly no matter where an attack comes from.

- **Study the terrain.** Now is the time to decide what units will be most useful. If the terrain is mostly flat and open, then Flash, Stumpy, and Bulldog tanks will move swiftly and can be a major part of your offensive punch. If the terrain is rocky, mountainous, full of forests, and rivers, then tanks will be easily bogged down. In that case, go with an offensive force with more PeeWees, Hammers, and Rockos. Start building a few Jethro AA Kbots to take along on your assault—they protect your troops from aerial attacks.

- **Keep building construction units.** Always try to build the next level of construction units and structures. For example, once Arm has acquired a Construction Kbot or a Construction Vehicle, then more powerful structures such as Sentinel Heavy Lasers and Defender Missile Towers can be built. The Construction Kbot or Vehicle can also begin building an Advanced Kbot Lab or Advanced Vehicle Plant. These structures, in turn, build the Level-2 Kbots such as the Zipper fast-attack Kbot, the Zeus lightning-gun Kbot, the Bulldog main battle tank and the Merl rocket launcher. These Level-2 mobile units are the best choices for assaulting enemy bases.

- **Understand your attack formation.** Think of the typical ground attack force as having a three-line formation. The first, leading line, is made up of fast-attack units such as Jeffys, PeeWees, Flashes, and Zipper assault bots. These units have short-range weapons and can get in among the enemy quickly. The second line is made up of middle-distance Hammer artillery units, Rocko rocket launchers, Fido assault bots, and the heavier Stumpy and Bulldog tanks. The third line, at the rear of your assault group, consists of the longer-range ground units, such as Merl mobile rocket launchers and Luger mobile artillery.

- **Concentrate fire on specific targets.** As you approach the enemy base, pick out the enemy's stationary defensive structures that do the most damage. Through concentrated fire, first knock out the heavy-hitting Gaat Gun heavy laser towers and Punisher Plasma Batteries (if they've been built). If it's early enough in a game, the main defensive structures may still be Light Laser Towers. Once you have broken down some of the most damaging defenders, concentrate on destroying Metal Extractors and Solar Collectors as well as any construction unit or structure you can find.

- **Plan for the long-term.** You must think ahead about the ultimate Level-3 structures and units that give you the edge you need to win. That means constant construction! As the game progresses, and there is no early winner, you should build the Advanced Construction Kbots, Vehicles, and Aircraft that are capable of constructing the Big Bertha long-range cannon, the Retaliator nuclear missile launcher, and the Annihilator long-range energy cannon. Your enemy will; so you'd better build them, too.

Total Annihilation is set up in such a way that you have to make difficult choices about which technologies you pour your resources into. It is not advisable to try to develop your Kbot, Vehicle, Sea, and Air units and structures to the same advanced levels simultaneously because it spreads you too thinly over too many construction projects. The result would be that your enemy would soon gain a superior advantage over you in one or two technologies, reaching the Advanced Construction Units before you do and, thus, constructing Level-3 weaponry first.

Water-Based Attacks and Campaigns

Core and Arm each have ten ships to use for the naval component of Total Annihilation, about half of the number of available ground units for each. Of these ten, seven carry weapons—submarine, destroyer, scout ship, attack sub, cruiser, battleship, and missile frigate. The other three—light carrier, transport, and Construction Ship—have specialized roles that don't include weapons.

You must learn to use the ships together in the most effective way by grouping them according to their respective strengths and weaknesses. This is the way to get started with a naval attack force on the Core side.

- **Scout first.** Once you have the basic energy resources under way, order the Commander to build a Shipyard. Then, order the Shipyard to build a Searcher scout ship and then a Snake submarine. If you are under attack, build the sub first to help defend, then build the Searcher. Send the Searcher on a scouting mission while the sub is under construction. After the sub, build an Enforcer destroyer, which can attack subs as well as surface ships. Place the Snake and then the Enforcer on patrol to protect your shipyard. By now, your first Searcher should have given you some idea of the surrounding area. The third or fourth unit created by your Shipyard should be a Construction Ship. Once that's operational, it can begin building Tidal Generators, Sonar Stations, and Torpedo Launchers.

- **Analyze your surroundings.** Is this mission or map likely to challenge your island-hopping assault skills, or is it a part of a land campaign that requires support from surface ships? The answer to that question determines your building priorities. Island hopping usually means that Envoy transport ships must be built earlier in your schedule. Early in the game, if you're coming under attack from Level-1 Arm Crusader destroyers, Lurker subs, and Skeeter scouts, your own Level-1 Snakes and Enforcers should be able to hold their own. However, you should move toward the Level-2 Construction Ship as soon as possible.

- **Build for power.** On the seas of *Total Annihilation*, it's the Level-2 ships that hold the real power. Once your Construction Ship is operational, start building the Shark attack sub, which is more effective against other subs than the Snake. The Executioner cruiser, which has the longest-distance surface guns as well as depth charges, should be next. Whether you're attacking islands or a mainland, the Warlord battleship should be constructed after the cruiser. Remember, while the Warlord has strong armor and big surface guns, it has no anti-air or anti-sub capabilities. You must protect the battleship with cruisers, subs, destroyers, and missile ships. If your enemy is concentrating on air power, make sure you have Searcher scouts, which carry missiles, and Hydra missile frigates to give air protection to your other ships.

- **Use your transports.** Core transport ships can carry 24 other units, while Arm transports can carry only 20 units at a time. Since the transports have no weapons, protect them with a couple of subs, a couple of cruisers, and a destroyer or two. A rule of thumb is to have at least four to six support ships of some kind for each transport ship.

A good transport attack strategy is to place two radar jammers on an Envoy along with 24 other Core units. The radar jammers keep your transport invisible. When you reach land, offload one of the radar jammers and the 24 attack units. The small land force is invisible to radar and your Envoy, still carrying the second radar jammer, remains invisible to radar as it leaves.

- **Build your attack force.** Submarine packs should be a part of any naval strategy you create. They are hard to find and harder to sink. And they are capable of sinking any other ship. A pack of a half-dozen or more subs can create havoc among a surface strike force or a transport convoy. So, always build plenty of subs. For land bombardment, nothing beats cruiser and battleship combos. The cruiser not only has big surface guns, but also depth charges to ward off subs. The battleship has powerful plasma cannons that are effective against surface ships and land targets alike.
- **Control attack formations.** Your naval formation should start with Snake subs and Searcher scouts. The scouts are fast and can quickly break into enemy formations. Subs soften up the lead enemy ships. Cruisers and battleships sit back behind the subs and destroyers, using their cannons to the best effect from a distance.

Air-Based Attacks and Campaigns

Air warfare is a lot of fun in *Total Annihilation,* with ten types of aircraft for each side. Four of the ten carry no weapons: Scout aircraft, transport aircraft, and two types of construction aircraft. That leaves six air units with weapons: three types of bombers, two types of fighters, and a gunship.

The effectiveness of your aircraft is largely dependent on numbers—the more units in the air, the better. Squads should have a minimum of six aircraft in order to do substantial damage. There are a variety of ways to use the aircraft. Here is a collection of ideas for a winning air strategy.

- **Scout widely around the map.** Building an aircraft plant costs a couple of hundred units more in both energy and metal resources than any of the other three Level-1 Construction structures, but there are two advantages to building this structure before the others. First, the ability to build an Arm Peeper or Core Fink scout means that you can send one or two of them out right away to find metal deposits and the enemy. Their speed lets them cover even a large map very quickly. Second, an Aircraft Plant can build a Construction VToL (Vertical Takeoff and Landing) Aircraft, which can travel swiftly to build units and structures anywhere on the map, including Metal Extractors and Geothermal Power Generators.

Order the Construction VToL Aircraft to build multiple Solar Collectors or Metal Extractors in areas of the map that have been scouted, showing metal deposits. Multiple orders can also be given to the aircraft to reclaim metal from wrecked units and structures left after a battle. In an open area of the map, away from the enemy, a Construction Aircraft can build an entire base. By first sending in a radar jammer to that area, you can frequently hide the location or size of this second base.

- **Build scouts and fighters first.** Neither Peepers nor Freedom Fighters carry much armor, but each is fast enough to make them worth building. Freedom Fighters have the advantage of being able to fight back. If you're pursuing an attack strategy that relies on air power, build at least four Freedom Fighters and three to four Peepers before sending any out to attack the enemy position. Send the Peepers in just ahead of the Freedom Fighters so that any AA units will be busy locking onto the scouts instead of the fighters.
- **Move to an Advanced Airfield quickly.** The Arm Thunder and Core Shadow Level-1 bombers are not very powerful, although they can still accomplish easy to medium objectives if used in numbers. However, their slow speed makes them very easy to knock out of the sky with even Level-1 Jethro or Crasher anti-air missile bots. The advanced air units, such as the Phoenix strategic bomber, the Hawk stealth fighter, and the Brawler gunship, are much more powerful and more difficult to destroy. Once you have built a Construction VToL Aircraft, make one of your first building projects an Advanced Aircraft Plant to give you access to the advanced air units.
- **Be creative with air transports.** Although air transports are capable of carrying only one unit at a time, what you choose to take can surprise the enemy. One strategy is to take a radar jammer to a remote location and set it down. Return to your base and pick up a construction unit of some kind, then take it to the radar jammer. Other than the radar profile of the transport as it leaves, the enemy will not know there's a new base starting. Another idea is to order your air transport to take a crawling bomb near an enemy base, then let it head toward the perimeter.
- **Send in gunships to soften AA.** The Brawler and Rapier gunships have the ability to hover over targets and fire at them for extended periods. They are much more effective in groups of a half-dozen or more. When raiding a base, soften up its AA defenses with gunships, selecting targets in a proper sequence—go after the more dangerous ones first. If your gunships can destroy most or all of the AA, they can then take their time destroying the rest of the enemy base.
- **Attack in waves.** The best formation for air attacks is to go in first with mixed Peeper scouts and either Freedom Fighters or Hawk fighters. The AA will be trying to hit the cheap Peepers and let a few of the fighters through. After the fighters have made a run or two, follow those sorties with a bombing run or two, concentrating on air defenses. Ideally, your air attacks will weaken the enemy defenses so that your ground troops will not encounter as much resistance when they follow up.

To establish tight control over your aircraft, press Ctrl plus 1–9 to assign air units to squadrons. For example, squadron one might be a group of ten mixed Peepers and Freedom Fighters, squadron two could be a dozen Phoenix strategic bombers, and squadron three could be seven or eight Brawler gunships. By jumping from one squad to another with the Alt plus 1–9 keys, controlling your air force can be much more organized.

Coordinated Attacks and Campaigns

Effectively coordinating your land, air, and sea forces is, of course, the best way to work toward ultimate victory. Each plays a complementary role to the others depending on the mission or the multiplayer options chosen. What follows is an example of a coordinated attack on an enemy base that is located fairly close to the water. In this scenario, the Core armed forces have built the basic Level-1 units and structures, plus one or two Level-2 mobile units.

- **Get your ground troops in position.** As the Core ground forces reach the halfway point to the Arm base, seven or eight Weasel scouts and PeeWees are attacking one or two Arm Light Laser Towers they have encountered next to Arm Metal Extractors. Thud artillery units and Slasher missile launchers are also helping to get rid of the Arm towers. The main body of the medium-size ground assault force consists of fifteen A.K. bots, a dozen Instigator and Raider tanks, eight or nine Thud artillery units, another eight or nine Crasher missile Kbots, and four Slasher missile launcher vehicles. Also along, providing some cover from radar, are two Spectre radar jammers. The ground units move cautiously forward to keep the slower artillery units within fairly close range.

- **Send in the ships and planes.** Before the ground assault begins, your naval and air units will be softening up the enemy base. Since the base sits fairly close to the shoreline, five of your Snake subs begin to fire torpedoes at several Arm Lurker subs and a couple of Skeeter scout ships and a Crusader destroyer on patrol. Behind your subs are three Hydra missile frigates, four Searcher scout ships, and two destroyers. You have managed to build one Level-2 Executioner cruiser, with its powerful surface guns. At the same time that the naval units are first encountering the enemy, three waves of Core aircraft begin to fly repeated sorties over the Arm base. First comes a mixed squadron of ten Fink scout planes and Avenger fighters. They begin to target Arm Light Laser Towers, Jethro anti-air units, and Hammer artillery Kbots. Immediately behind the fighters and scouts come a dozen Shadow bombers dropping their payloads onto the Arm Vehicle Plant. The Arm air force, not yet developed as much as your own, is having trouble responding to the assault with its few Freedom Fighters.

- **Start the assault.** As the first wave of Finks and Avengers fly in and the Snake subs are starting to hit the Arm naval units, the front line of Weasels, A.K. units, and Instigator tanks are encountering Light Laser Towers, two rows of Dragon's Teeth, and a half-dozen Flash light tanks. From behind the perimeter, Hammer artillery and Rocko rocket launchers are starting to fire at your forward units. About the same time, your Slashers, Thuds, and Crashers are finding targets in the base.

- **Keep the pressure on.** A few AKs and Weasels have found their way through two holes in the Dragon's Teeth barriers and are now firing at a Kbot Lab. Three of the Core Instigator tanks are in among the Arm defenders and are firing at a few Hammers and Rockos. While your artillery and missile units on the ground are barraging the base, your air force is conducting repeated strikes. Since you have divided the air units into two groups, you switch back and forth between them (press Alt-1 and Alt-2) to pick the most expensive targets you can find. In the harbor near the base, your Executioner cruiser is sitting outside of enemy range shelling the Arm base, while your Searcher scouts and Hydra missile ships are aiming missiles at decreasingly few Arm aircraft.

- **Keep producing.** While this assault has been going on, your factories have been continuing to produce more Kbots, vehicles, ships, and aircraft. You have also ordered a Construction Vehicle to build Metal Extractors on six different metal deposits you came across during the buildup to the assault.

Of course, no two battles are ever the same in *Total Annihilation.* And you will seldom have a perfect setup for the best coordinated land, air, and sea attacks.

Defensive Strategies

The best defensive strategies in Total Annihilation include stationary defensive structures with overlapping lines of fire as well as mobile units that can move swiftly to intercept enemy attacks on your base. Whether you side with Arm or Core, try these defensive approaches:

- **Set up redundant Radar Towers.** You cannot afford to lose sight of your enemy even for a short time. For defensive security, build three or four Radar Towers right away, especially against an enemy that seems to be aggressive from the start. Even if one or two Radar Towers are destroyed, you have backups that you don't have to worry about. As always, issue multiple commands at once for their construction. As a game progresses, have Construction units other than your Commander build more Radar Towers. Level-2 units build Advanced Radar Towers, which have better range.

- **Lay down Dragon's Teeth.** Almost indestructible, Dragon's Teeth can channel an attacking enemy force in just about any direction you wish. By ordering a mobile Construction unit to build multiple rows of Dragon's Teeth, you spend thirty seconds issuing orders, and come back ten minutes later to find an entire defensive pattern of Dragon's Teeth in place.

- **Build stationary laser and missile towers.** The debate over whether to use Light Laser Towers early in the game boils down to whether you find that the relatively high expense (2,546 energy, 262 metal) and the fact that they are stationary justify their effectiveness against the enemy. But if you are pursuing a strong defensive position, their use is mandatory. The same can be said for such Level-2 structures as the Sentinel heavy laser and the Defender missile tower. When used with rows of Dragon's Teeth, these structures will cause big problems for the enemy.

- **Patrol aggressively.** Patrol units can consist of almost any combination of mobile units, whether on land, sea, or in the air. An aggressive patrol philosophy means that you try to spot incoming enemies well before they get near your base. Jeffy or Weasel scout vehicles sent on extended patrols are fast enough to cover a lot of ground and can alert you quickly. The same is true for Skeeter and Searcher scout ships, and for Peeper and Fink scout aircraft.

One specialized patrol function is to set a Construction Kbot or Construction Vehicle on a straight line patrol pattern within your base and click the Repair button for that unit. As front-line troops are wounded, send them back to the patrolling Construction unit to be automatically repaired as the unit moves back and forth near them.

- **Scout in order to defend.** By using scout vehicles and/or scout aircraft to find and observe the enemy, you can frequently see what kind of construction is going on. This gives you a clue about future threats and the best defense policy. For instance, if you see an Aircraft Plant, it's time to start working on your AA defense system. Later in a game, if you spot a long-range cannon or a nuclear missile launcher before it's too late, you have at least some time to prepare defenses or stage a strike to destroy the unit. Knowing your enemy is one of the most important keys to successful defense.
- **Build wisely.** Take advantage of terrain features between your base and your enemy's base by building Light Laser Towers and positionig scout vehicles, Kbots, light tanks, and artillery units along the route that your enemy must take to attack you. These emplacements not only reduce the number of your attackers, but also serve as an early warning system and an obstacle course for the enemy's attack units.
- **Use Sonar Stations with Torpedo Launchers.** For coastal defenses, build Sonar Stations to locate enemy subs. Close by, build Torpedo Launchers that will respond as soon as the sonar detects an enemy sub. The Sonar Stations also serve to tell you if the enemy is sending amphibious tanks, crawling bombs, or the enemy Commander across the ocean floor.

When sending the Commander, amphibious tanks, and crawling bombs underwater, be aware that they are extremely vulnerable. All three can be spotted by enemy sonar. Neither the Commander nor the amphibious tanks can fire weapons when underwater; and the crawling bombs are very slow, giving plenty of time for subs to destroy them.

- **Use radar jammers extensively.** If the enemy has trouble seeing you, then it detracts from his offensive strategy. It also means he cannot target individual units and structures by using the radar image on the small mission map. The mobile radar jammers can be set to patrol across your base and also to travel with scout units that are exploring new territory. On the seas, a radar jammer that's set down on an aircraft carrier will prevent enemy radar from seeing the carrier.

Use the Guard command in the Orders menu window to attach individual units to one another or to structures that you want defended. This is one way to keep a small squad together on patrol or while scouting. If you order a radar jammer to guard a scout or a patrol, those units will remain invisible to enemy radar.

The number of strategies you will use in Total Annihilation is virtually limitless. In fact, one of the best aspects about the game is its great variety and range of play. Chapters 4, 5, and 6 provide a closer look at each of the game's units and structures, and the Arm and Core missions in Chapters 7 and 8 bring into play many of the strategies that are covered here.

Part II

The Unit Guide

Long ago the galaxy had known peace. Paradise was ruled by the hand of science, and the hand was that of the galactic governing body known as the Core.

Paradoxically it was the ultimate victory, the victory over death itself, which brought about the downfall of their Paradise and started the war that would decimate a million worlds. The process, which was called "patterning," involved the electronic duplication of brain matrices and allowed the transfer of consciousness into durable machines. Effectively it meant immortality, and the Core decreed the process mandatory for all citizens in order to ensure their safety...

(Will act like there is 100 percent radar coverage)

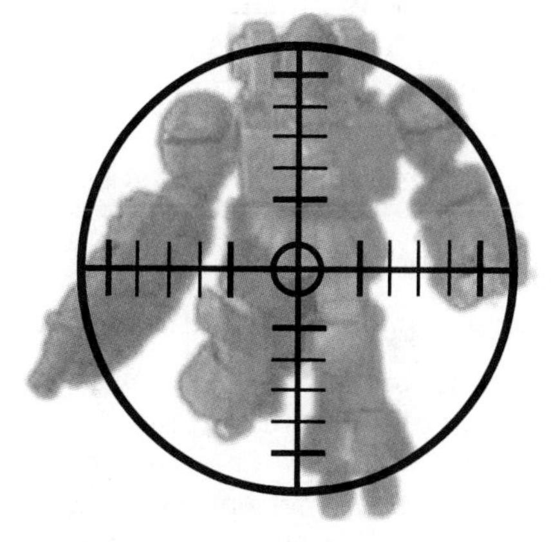

Arm and Core Common Structures and Units

Whether you start from the green forests and mountains of Arm's home planet, Empyrrean, or the harsh metal-plated sterility of Core Prime, you will be using the units and structures in this chapter to build and battle your way to ultimate victory or ignominious defeat. These are the weapons and tools that are common to both sides of the conflict, and each of them has its own role to play in your efforts. Learn them well and you will prosper; ignore them and you are the other guy's lunch.

Advanced Aircraft Plant

Type: Level-2 construction plant

Description: This structure enables you to create some of your best aircraft. For the Arm, the Advanced Aircraft Plant turns out *Hawk* stealth fighters, *Phoenix* strategic fighters, *Brawler* gunships, and *Lancet* torpedo bombers. For the Core, the plant produces *Vamp* stealth fighters, *Hurricane* strategic fighters, *Rapier* gunships, and *Titan* torpedo bombers.

Strategic use: For missions or multiplayer campaigns that require air power, build an Advanced Aircraft Plant as soon as possible. While the Level-1 aircraft units are sufficient for scouting and light air campaigns, they are nowhere near as "smart" or as effective as the Level-2 units.

See also *Sentinel, Defender, Guardian, Gaat Gun, Pulverizer,* and *Punisher*

Advanced Construction Kbot

Type: Level-2 construction Kbot

Description: This mobile factory is necessary to obtain several offensive and defensive units that are excellent long-range weapons. For the Arm, this factory turns out the *Big Bertha* long-range cannon as well as the *Retaliator* nuclear missile launcher, the *Annihilator* high-energy cannon, and the Protector nuclear missile defense. For the Core, the plant creates the *Intimidator* long-range plasma cannon, the *Doomsday Machine* high-energy cannon, the *Silencer* nuclear missile launcher, and the *Fortitude Missile Defense* nuclear defense. Two other key technologies developed by this factory are the *Fusion Reactor* and the *Moho Mine*. Note that Ctrl-F selects all factories that are immobile construction untis.

Strategic use: As a strategic warfare game, *Total Annihilation* requires that you continually upgrade your construction units and structures to take advantage of advanced weapons not available to lower-level construction units. The three advanced mobile construction units can be particularly effective in large-map missions and multiplayer games in which you wish to set up multiple bases, or bases that are closer to your enemy.

You can also order any Advanced Construction Unit to patrol a certain area or route. While on patrol, this smart unit not only automatically repairs damaged units along the way, but also reclaims metal and energy. With movement orders set to Roam, you can even make it reach and repair units some distance away from its patrol route.

See also *Advanced Construction Vehicle* and *Advanced Construction VToL Aircraft*

Advanced Construction Vehicle

Type: Level-2 construction vehicle

Description: Like the *Advanced Construction Kbot* and the *Advanced Construction VToL Aircraft*, this construction vehicle produces the long-range cannons, nuclear missile launchers, and other powerful weapons that you must acquire to achieve strategic dominance.

Strategic use: You can order any of the mobile construction units to Repair a unit that is being produced by another factory—this speeds up the unit's construction. The result can significantly increase your overall production ability. (See Chapter 3, "Winning Strategies," to learn more about this technique.)

See also *Advanced Construction Kbot* and *Advanced Construction VToL Aircraft*

Advanced Construction VToL Aircraft

Type: Level-2 construction aircraft

Description: Perhaps the most versatile of the Level-2 construction units, the Advanced Construction VToL Aircraft is particularly effective on large maps because of its ability to set up bases across water barriers and in faraway, hard-to-access locations. For example, by having this unit build an Arm *Big Bertha* or Core *Intimidator* long-range cannon or another Level-3 weapon at a distant location, you can surprise the enemy by launching an attack from an unexpected direction.

Strategic use: This is the fastest, most wide-ranging of the advanced mobile construction units. When your metal reserves are low, try sending the VToL out to reclaim metal in addition to producing other units. Its big drawback is the low speed with which it makes and repairs units.

See also *Advanced Construction Kbot* and *Advanced Construction Vehicle*

Advanced Kbot Lab

Type: Level-2 construction plant

Description: This lab produces the Kbots you will use most often. After all, they are cheap and can be churned out in large quantities without wiping out your stocks of metals. The Advanced Kbot Lab also produces advanced radar jammers and crawling bomb Kbots.

Strategic use: For those who like to put together aggressive assault strategies to keep the enemy off balance in the game, this lab is an excellent early choice. Also, building a radar jammer can help to keep your own base under wraps.

See also *Zipper, Zeus, Fido, Invader, Eraser, Thud, Pyro, Roach,* and *Spectre*

Advanced Radar Tower

Type: Level-3 radar tower

Description: This advanced tower is much more far-reaching and effective than the Level-1 Radar Tower, providing better long-range radar coverage.

Strategic use: Keeping tabs on the enemy is one of the most important elements of *Total Annihilation*. Build redundant towers so that you do not lose contact at a crucial moment. Since the advanced construction units can build this radar tower, you can place it at different points on the map quite easily.

See also *Radar Tower*

Advanced Shipyard

Type: Level-2 construction plant

Description: As with the *Advanced Kbot Lab,* this shipyard produces some of the most effective naval units, which you will use on a regular basis—attack subs, cruisers, battleships, and light carriers.

Strategic use: Most players tend to focus on land and aerial warfare at the expense of their navies. Don't make this mistake; a good navy can make victory much easier. When playing a naval mission or on a sea map, developing this shipyard quickly will result in a valuable tactical advantage early in the game. In addition, it will open up several strategic options, such as large-scale amphibious assaults.

See also *Piranha, Ranger, Conqueror, Millenium, Colossus, Shark, Executioner, Warlord,* and *Hive*

Advanced Vehicle Plant

Type: Level-2 construction plant

Description: If you are a fan of tank warfare and *blitzkrieg* tactics, the Advanced Vehicle Plant will be one of your most heavily used factories. It provides you with mobile artillery, amphibious tanks, mobile rocket launchers, and assault tanks, as well as Arm's *Spider Assault Vehicle* and Core's *Goliath* super-heavy tank.

Strategic use: Direct your Advanced Vehicle Plant's production to acquire a variety of diverse assault vehicles. Set up the plant some distance away from your base, protected by a radar jammer, and quietly prepare an attack force that will surprise the enemy.

See also *Bulldog, Luger, Triton, Merl, Seer, Jammer, Spider, Reaper, Pillager, Crock, Diplomat, Informer,* and *Deleter*

Aircraft Plant

Type: Level-1 construction plant

Description: This plant gets your air force started with basic reconnaissance, fighter, and bomber aircraft as well as an air transport. Level-1 aircraft units might not be the greatest, but they are cheap and quick to build.

Strategic use: You can use scout and fighter aircraft as inexpensive, fast patrol units. Also, plan to quickly build a *Construction VToL Aircraft* that offers great flexibility in siting the basic structures.

See also *Peeper, Freedom Fighter, Thunder, Atlas, Fink, Avenger, Shadow,* and *Valkyrie*

Aircraft Repair Platform

Type: Level-3 repair pad

Description: Capable of being built by any of the advanced mobile construction units, the Aircraft Repair Platform is a cheap way to provide aircraft repair facilities near the sites of your major air encounters.

Strategic use: Consider placing these platforms at multiple locations to lengthen the life of your aircraft, keeping them in good repair as they pound enemy forces and bases.

See also *Advanced Construction* units

Commander

Type: Level-10 Leader

Description: The Commander is central to every action you take. But this is a two-edged proposition, because he is also a liability. While extremely powerful, the Commander is easily overwhelmed by combined enemy forces if not protected with other units or defensive structures—especially in large, confusing combat situations. Remember, losing the Commander means losing the battle (if not the war). Use the Ctrl-C key to regularly check on the Commander's status.

Strategic use: Remember that part of the Commander's power is the ability to build stuff fast. Using the Repair function, the Commander can dramatically speed up any construction that is under way in any factory or mobile construction unit. (This option is discussed in detail in Chapter 3, "Winning Strategies.")

Construction Kbot

Type: Level-1 construction Kbot

Description: Mobile construction units, such as the Construction Kbot, help the Commander out by allowing multiple projects to get under way simultaneously. (The Unit Build Hierarchy for each construction unit and structure is shown and explained in detail in Chapter 3, "Winning Strategies.")

Strategic use: These mobile construction units can build a variety of mobile units and structures, but they are slower at it than the Commander. Keep this in mind when assigning production to a construction unit in time-critical situations. The Construction Kbot is more agile than the *Construction Vehicle,* so it is the right construction unit choice for difficult terrain.

See also *Construction Vehicle, Construction Ship, and Construction VToL Aircraft*

Construction Ship

Type: Level-1 construction ship

Description: Construction Ships produce *Tidal Generators, Sonar Stations,* and *Torpedo Launchers,* in addition to *Advanced Shipyards.* Like other construction units, they are defenseless against attack, except for the ability to reclaim the metal in an enemy unit—particularly effective against a scout ship. Keep them well protected behind your perimeter defenses, or by mobile units such as tanks and Kbots.

Strategic use: In any sea campaign, Construction Ships provide you with a handy mix of units and structures. Order your Construction Ships to produce Sonar Station structures along your base perimeter in order to gain extra protection from enemy submarines. Construction ships can also reclaim metal in sunken ships. This is a safer course than using the Commander to reclaim underwater where he is vulnerable to sub attacks.

See also *Construction Kbot, Construction Vehicle,* and *Construction VToL Aircraft*

Construction Vehicle

Type: Level-1 construction vehicle

Description: The Construction Vehicle is an unarmed mobile unit that builds Level-2 structures and can reclaim metal from wrecked units and structures. It can also build the same basic structures that the Commander can, thus freeing the Commander from some of those duties.

Strategic use: Construction vehicles and the other mobile construction units are also able to reclaim metal from unarmed scouts, although this technique will not work against armed units. Use Construction Vehicles and other construction units in pairs when clearing wrecks under enemy fire. They can repair one another as well as other units.

See *Construction Kbot, Construction Ship,* and *Construction VToL Aircraft*

Construction VToL Aircraft

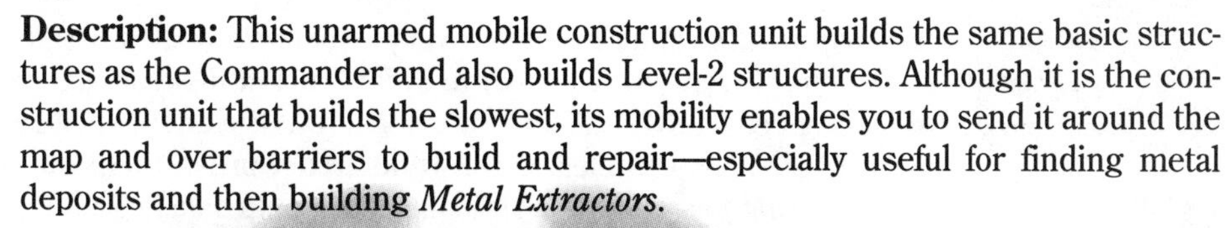

Type: Level-1 construction aircraft

Description: This unarmed mobile construction unit builds the same basic structures as the Commander and also builds Level-2 structures. Although it is the construction unit that builds the slowest, its mobility enables you to send it around the map and over barriers to build and repair—especially useful for finding metal deposits and then building *Metal Extractors.*

Strategic use: In island campaigns, the Construction VToL Aircraft is perfect for moving from island to island finding metal deposits to extract, open spaces for factories, and strategic locations for gun emplacements.

See *Construction Kbot, Construction Vehicle,* and *Construction Ship*

Dragon's Teeth

Type: Level-1 perimeter defense

Description: Dragon's Teeth are perimeter defense barriers. They are easy to place, cheap, and almost indestructible.

Strategic use: When terrain permits, Dragon's Teeth can be set in rows to block advancing enemy units, or help channel them into kill zones. Either occurrence can bring a strong assault to a stop, letting your base defense units and structures pick the enemy apart.

Energy Storage

Type: Level-1 storage structure

Description: Your energy and metal resources need to build up, and that cannot happen without storage structures that increase your storage capacity. Each Energy Storage structure can add 3,000 energy units (EU) of storage to the game's basic 1,000-unit capacity.

Strategic use: Extra storage for resources is always useful, but sometimes must take a back seat to more immediate demands. An Energy Storage structure costs 2,430 EU and 240 MU (metal units), which early in a game may take away more EUs than you would like. Early on during some missions or multiplayer games, you may not need to build an Energy Storage structure right away. But, in a campaign of any size and scope, the ability to stockpile energy and metal can make the winning difference. The question is only *when* is the best time to build storage structures, not *if* you should build them.

See also *Metal Storage*

Fusion Reactor

Type: Level-3 power generator

Description: Although they are very expensive (35,058 EU, 5,130 MU) and time-consuming (over four minutes) to build, Fusion Reactors give a tremendous boost to your energy flow—1,000 EU per second. If the enemy destroys them, the resulting nuclear blast can clear out a wide area. Spread them out about half a screen apart, so that you will not risk losing your entire base if one or more Reactors go up in flames.

Strategic use: One multiplayer strategy is to build one of the advanced construction units as early as possible, and then get going on a Fusion Reactor. Along with the *Moho Mine,* which has a similar boosting effect on metal extraction, the Fusion Reactor can make your resources flow much faster.

See also *Moho Mine, Solar Collector, Wind Generator, Geothermal Power Plant,* and *Metal Extractor*

Galactic Gate

Type: Arm and Core planet entryway

Description: These gates are the entryways onto the various planets on which Core and Arm fight their wars. In the single-player missions, their capture—not destruction—is frequently the mission goal.

Geothermal Power Plant

Type: Level-2 power generator

Description: Wherever you find steam rising from a geothermal vent, consider planting a Geothermal Power Plant. They always produce 250 EU per second. By comparison, a Solar Collector produces only 20 EU per second.

Strategic use: Place Geothermal Plants wherever you find steam vents on a planet's surface. On Core Prime, the vents are grates on the surface; on other planets, they are cracks in the earth. A Geothermal Power Plant can supply the energy requirements for an Aircraft Plant (1,370 EU), for example, in a little over five seconds; a Solar Collector would take more than one minute. Consider putting a laser tower nearby to discourage enemy raids and marauding units.

Kbot Lab

Type: Level-1 construction plant

Description: The most basic of weapon-producing facilities, the Kbot Lab provides you with an entire arsenal of weapons—lasers, artillery, rockets, and missiles—from the four Kbots it produces. It also builds the *Construction Kbot* that is required to build a Level-2 *Advanced Kbot Lab*.

Strategic use: This lab is usually the right choice for your first weapon-making facility; the *Vehicle Plant* is more expensive, and so are its products. Early in the game, you do not have a lot of resources, and whatever the Kbot Lab makes comes at a reasonable cost. In both single and multiplayer games, try ordering your Commander to build a couple of Solar Power Plants and a Kbot Lab right away. Assemble groups of Peewees or A.K. infantry and some artillery or rocket untis for backup, and then immediately start harrassing the enemy. This can throw a scare into a human opponent, who usually isn't expecting offensive enemy action so early in the game.

See also *PeeWee, Hammer, Rocko, Jethro, A.K., Storm, Crasher,* and *Thud*

Light Laser Tower

Type: Level-1 laser tower

Description: The Light Laser Towers (LLT) are among the first group of defensive weapons available when you build a base. Because of their quick, relentless laser fire, multiple laser towers are effective at helping briefly hold back attackers in the early stages of a game. That's especially true if they are sited so that two or three Towers can concentrate their fire on narrow choke points such as valleys, which enemy units can pass only one at a time. Note that the LLT stores 100 energy units; that helps it maintain firing ability when energy stocks are low.

Strategic use: Placing a few laser towers on hills considerably away from your home base can play havoc with enemies approaching your base. They give you advance warning and cut down the strength of the attacker. But, their armor is not as strong as that of the advanced laser towers.

See also *Sentinel* and *Gaat Gun*

Metal Extractor

Type: Level-1 resource provider

Description: The Metal Extractor is cheap to build (521 EU, 25 MU), but also easy to destroy. On metal-rich planets, such as Core Prime, metal presents less of a shortage problem for you than does energy. However, on most of the planets on which you will fight, metal is less plentiful than energy. Locating metal deposits and getting metal extractors going is a crucial activity especially in the early Arm missions.

Strategic use: When you place a Metal Extractor some distance away from your base defenses, try setting up a laser tower nearby to ward off inquisitive enemy units.

See also *Solar Collector, Geothermal Power Plant, Fusion Reactor,* and *Moho Mine*

Metal Maker

Type: Level-1 resource converter

Description: Metal Makers are not very efficient as they go about their task of converting energy units into metal units. But, in a pinch, they can help stave off disaster by converting energy in the absence of available metals.

Strategic use: While converting, keep an eye on metal reserves. The Metal Maker can be switched on and off, so do not run it once your metal stocks have improved. A common mistake for beginners is to put Metal Makers on ore outcroppings. Metal deposits do not affect the placement decision on Metal Makers one way or another.

See also *Metal Extractor, Moho Mine,* and *Metal Storage*

Metal Storage

Type: Level-1 storage structure

Description: Metal Storage structures and *Energy Storage* structures allow you to stock resources necessary for producing units. A Metal Storage structure holds 1,000 metal units—almost enough to build an Arm Lurker submarine (1,151 metal units).

Strategic use: On metal-rich planets, you will probably want to build a Metal Storage structure right away to provide storage for excess capacity. This is not the case nearly so often on metal-poor planets on which you seldom exceed capacity in the early building stage. But as a game progresses on a metal-poor planet, you will eventually want to have the extra storage.

See also *Metal Extractor, Moho Mine,* and *Metal Maker*

Moho Mine

Type: Level-3 metal extractor

Description: Just like the *Fusion Reactor* boosts energy production, the Moho Mine dramatically increases your metal extraction. It is expensive (8,700 EU, 1,508 MU) and time-consuming to build, but the benefit is long-term metal availability.

Strategic use: Metal resources generally run short more frequently, and are harder to secure than energy sources. Try building your construction units and structures as rapidly as possible, from lower-level to higher-level, until you get to the stage at which you have one of the three Advanced Construction mobile units that can build a Moho Mine. This is especially important if the surrounding metal resources are scarce. If you are trapped in an area limited by space or by available metal deposits, consider reclaiming one of your *Metal Extractors* and replacing it with a Moho Mine. Because of the time it takes to build, try to do this when you have stockpiled a good supply of metal.

See also *Fusion Reactor, Metal Extractor,* and *Metal Storage*

Radar Tower

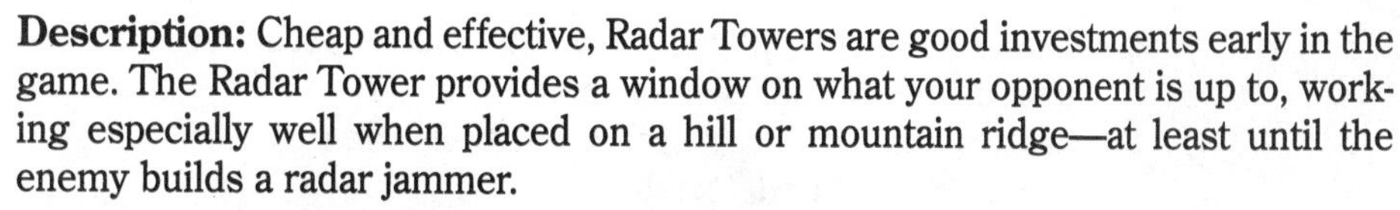

Type: Level-1 radar tower

Description: Cheap and effective, Radar Towers are good investments early in the game. The Radar Tower provides a window on what your opponent is up to, working especially well when placed on a hill or mountain ridge—at least until the enemy builds a radar jammer.

Strategic use: Always build more than just one Radar Tower. You cannot run the risk of having your radar disabled at a critical point. By clicking on a Radar Tower, a circle appears on the mini-map on your screen, showing the radar coverage radius.

See also *Advanced Radar Tower* and *Sonar Station*

Shipyard

Type: Level-1 construction plant

Description: In any mission or multiplayer map that features bodies of water, building a Shipyard early on in the game is vital to your offensive and defensive power. Not only does the Shipyard build the basic scouts, destroyers, missile frigates, and submarines, but also *Construction Ships.*

Strategic use: When building a Shipyard, consider the probable location of future naval battles and how quickly you will need to get ships there. Sometimes, it is very important to have a Shipyard launching new ships as close to the action as possible. In most cases, however, finding a secure location is more important than proximity to the enemy. Still, try building shipyards far enough from shore so that your ships do not waste time getting out of the yard.

See also *Searcher, Hydra, Enforcer, Snake, Envoy, Skeeter, Crusader, Lurker, Hulk,* and *Construction Ship*

Solar Collector

Type: Level-1 power generator

Description: The Solar Collector is one of the two basic resource generators—the *Metal Extractor* being the other one—that the Commander initially builds. Solar Collectors are cheap and quick to build.

Strategic use: Solar Collectors can act as a cheap defensive buffer if sited in a ring around a base. Just remember that once they start getting blown up, your energy production will drop in a hurry.

See also *Metal Extractor, Geothermal Power Plant,* and *Fusion Reactor*

Sonar Station

Type: Level-2 sonar structure

Description: With the substantial threat posed by submarines, Sonar Stations become a key defensive element in "water" missions and maps featuring plenty of seas. A defensive ring of these stations can prevent surprise sub attacks that otherwise may be undetectable.

Strategic use: Protect Sonar Stations with *Torpedo Launchers* and submarines against enemy sub and surface attacks when possible. They are vulnerable, and should not be exposed to attack. Note that the torpedoes launched by attack subs and torpedo launchers have a much longer range than the enemy sub's sonar. Try placing a number of cheap Sonar Stations in front and loger range structures in back. Thus you can shoot enemy subs without danger, and only lose a few cheap Sonar Stations.

See also *Torpedo Launcher*

Tidal Generator

Type: Level-2 power generator

Description: In sea missions and water-rich environments, the Tidal Generator becomes an important source of energy. This is especially so if, during an island campaign, you find that land space is at a premium or unavailable.

Strategic use: Try to build Tidal Generators in easily protected areas, even though enemy threats are not easy to pinpoint before they actually appear.

See also *Construction Ship*

Torpedo Launcher

Type: Level-2 torpedo launcher

Description: A torpedo launcher is a stationary water structure equipped with sonar and torpedoes. Effective against both ships and submarines, Torpedo Launchers are excellent perimeter defense structures on sea maps. However, their rate of fire is slow.

Strategic use: Set up Torpedo Launchers in the water along your base perimeter close enough so that their ranges overlap. Any ship or submarine that tries to go between them will attract torpedoes from both sides.

Vehicle Plant

Type: Level-1 construction plant

Description: This factory provides the basic recon vehicles and tanks that support your Kbots and aircraft in the early stages of a mission or multiplayer game.

Strategic use: One approach is to initially skip building a Kbot Lab, and immediately build a Vehicle Plant instead. The tanks and scout vehicles it makes can be quickly thrown in to harass the enemy (see the Appendix for detailed unit statistics).

See also *Jeffy, Flash, Samson, Stumpy, Weasel, Instigator, Slasher,* and *Raider*

Wind Generator

Type: Level-1 power generator

Description: This energy generator is cheap to build, and can be placed just about anywhere. Its power generation is based on the strength of the wind, which varies from planet to planet.

Strategic use: Build laser towers near Wind Generators sited beyond your defensive perimeter.

See also *Solar Collector, Geothermal Power Plant,* and *Tidal Generator*

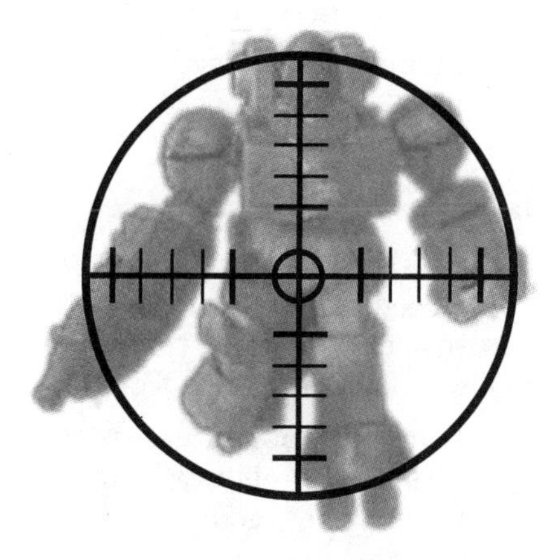

Arm Units

Your base is under attack from enemy aircraft! Quick, is it better to use a Jethro or a Hammer for anti-aircraft fire? Why are Zippers good units for hit-and-run missions? For mountain attacks, are you better off with a squad of PeeWees or a small group of Flash tanks? These are life-and-death questions for you as you lead the Arm forces. Study their strengths and weaknesses, and then prepare for battle, Commander!

Annihilator

Type: Level-3 high-energy cannon

Description: The Annihilator is an offensive weapon that fires energy shells from its three guns, and is effective as an anti-aircraft defense. Although expensive and time-consuming to build, the Annihilator is one of Arm's more powerful units.

Strategic use: Like other Level-3 weapons, the Annihilator is produced by any of the three advanced construction units. Although it does not have the extreme range of a *Big Bertha*, it has almost twice the spotting range, and its shells still pack a huge punch.

Corresponding Core unit: *Doomsday Machine*

Atlas

Type: Level-1 aircraft

Description: The Atlas air transport provides a quick way to move everything from troops to construction units around the map. It has an unlimited range. Relatively inexpensive and fast to build, this Level-1 aircraft can be used to surprise the enemy by landing troops behind the front lines.

Strategic use: On large maps, use air transports to pick up construction vehicles and deliver them to strategic points. When attacking bases, transport *Invader* crawling bombs near the enemy, then set them loose.

Corresponding Core unit: *Valkyrie*

Big Bertha

Type: Level-3 long-range plasma cannon

Description: This long-range cannon fires antimatter slivers, less accurate than plasma cannon fire, but very powerful and expensive. The antimatter slivers are about a milligram in size. It can shoot the slivers up to almost eight screens away. Be careful not to accidentally bombard your own forward units during combined assaults. It takes 1,500 energy units (EU) to fire a Bertha, so it works best when you have a Fusion Power Plant and extra energy storage.

Strategic use: To soften up well-defended Core bases, place a Bertha cannon or two within range. Use the radar on the mission map to target Core units many screens away. However, remember that the Bertha is powerless and defenseless when attacked at short range. Be sure to protect the Bertha with perimeter defenses, such as *Light Laser Towers* and *PeeWee* infantry.

Corresponding Core unit: *Intimidator*

Brawler

Type: Level-2 gunship aircraft

Description: Brawlers have the capability to hover over targets and rain down fire for prolonged periods of time. The Brawler has heavy armor and it fires powerful lasers. Brawlers have a side-to-side hovering movement that makes them more difficult to hit.

Strategic use: Offensive. When attacking an enemy base with Brawlers, try to achieve numerical superiority over enemy anti-aircraft defense units and structures. Once you have knocked out the anti-aircraft defenses, the Brawlers can keep hitting targets without further danger even if they have taken a lot of damage. Also, use the Brawler to blow away unprotected enemy *Metal Extractors.*

Corresponding Core unit: *Rapier*

Bulldog

Type: Level-2 heavy assault tank

Description: The Bulldog is a heavy assault tank, with about half the speed, acceleration, and turning rate of a *Stumpy* medium assault tank. But what the Bulldog lacks in speed, it makes up for in armor and its plasma cannon firepower. This is the Arm's main battle tank, slow but durable and powerful.

Strategic use: Bulldogs are more effective on open terrain where they can move at a sustained speed. Terrain that is hilly, mountainous, or clogged with burned-out wreckage slows the Bulldog down, making it an easy target for well-placed Core defensive units. Bulldogs work best when you use at least three or four of them together as a heavily armored attack wall that can accept enemy fire while still moving forward.

Corresponding Core unit: *Reaper* and *Goliath,* which is the largest, most powerful, albeit slowest tank in *Total Annihilation*

Colossus

Type: Level-2 light aircraft carrier

Description: This is the light aircraft carrier of Arm's fleet. The Colossus automatically repairs all aircraft units that are nearby. There is a fission power plant inside that adds to Arm's overall energy production. The Colossus also carries radar, which helps aircraft identify targets.

Strategic use: All aircraft units in *Total Annihilation* have infinite ranges without refueling. Still, keep a Colossus or two near areas where your aircraft units are engaging the enemy, so that they take advantage of the carrier's radar and automatic repair ability.

Corresponding Core unit: *Hive*

Conqueror

Type: Level-2 cruiser-class ship

Description: The cruiser is lighter than a battleship and does not carry as much armor. However, its guns have the longest range in the game, and it can enter shallower waters than a battleship. Cruisers are best at bombardment of inland targets.

Strategic use: The Conqueror is a good ship for bombarding land bases because of its long reach, and its shallow-water capability. It also has good antisubmarine defenses, including depth charges.

Corresponding Core unit: *Executioner*

Crusader

Type: Level-1 destroyer-class ship

Description: The Crusader has good anti-submarine capabilities, but is only lightly armored and does not last very long in fierce sea battles.

Strategic use: Use the Crusader to patrol areas of the sea that are vulnerable to submarine attacks. Because of its lack of heavy armor, however, do not try to use it to slug it out against a powerful enemy.

Corresponding Core unit: *Enforcer*

Defender

Type: Level-2 missile tower

Description: The Defender is a missile tower that provides anti-aircraft support. It is a very cheap Level-2 structure that takes only a brief period of time to build. The Defender can also be deployed against ground units, although it does not excel in this role. It is fairly effective against scouting vehicles, which are typically fast but lightly armored.

Strategic use: Place Defenders around your base so that their fields of fire overlap. Site them so as to offer varied firing angles.

Corresponding Core unit: *Pulverizer*

Eraser

Type: Level-2 radar jammer Kbot

Description: The Eraser is a radar jammer, and one of your most important units. You will want to build multiple jammers in order to keep the enemy from spotting all of your units on their radar.

Strategic use: Once the enemy has acquired radar, they can start targeting your units at long range. The Eraser blocks that threat, so keep jamming throughout the game. When you select an Eraser, a circle appears in the mini-map on your screen, showing the area that it jams. If you select one Eraser and press Ctrl-Z, all Erasers will be selected. This enables you to spread them out for the best coverage.

Corresponding Core unit: *Spectre*

Fido

Type: Level-2 assault Kbot

Description: A four-legged assault Kbot, the Fido is somewhat similar to a main battle tank, good enough to stand up to the enemy's main battle weapons. It features a good firing range, has fast acceleration, and performs well in rough, mountainous terrain.

Strategic use: The biggest weakness of the Fido is that it cannot take a lot of damage. For that reason, using Fidos for quick raids and guerilla-style combat is better than trying to use them in a slugging match with the enemy.

Corresponding Core unit: *The Can*

Flash

Type: Level-1 light assault tank

Description: One of your first, and best, weapons is the quick-moving Flash light tank. The speed and relative low cost of the Flash make it a good weapon for recon patrols, against light targets, and for harassing the enemy.

Strategic use: Try building a good-sized squad of Flash, *PeeWee*, and *Hammer* units, then mix in a few heavier weapons such as *Merls* and *Lugers*. Throw them en masse against the enemy. The Level-1 light units will draw initial enemy fire while the heavier units rake the enemy from a safe distance.

Corresponding Core unit: *Instigator*

Freedom Fighter

Type: Level-1 fighter aircraft

Description: The Freedom Fighter is not terribly expensive but with good flight speed and accurate firepower.

Strategic use: Try building a couple of these and station them on a permanent patrol across your front lines. Their spotting range supplements your radar, and they can intercept enemy strike and reconnaissance aircraft. Whenever the enemy's radar jammers make targeting your big guns difficult, fly a few Freedom Fighters right over the enemy base for spotting purposes.

Corresponding Core unit: *Avenger*

Guardian

Type: Level-2 stationary plasma cannon

Description: The Level-2 stationary plasma battery is an artillery unit that is equally effective against ground and sea targets. The Guardian has strong armor, so it can survive a pounding.

Strategic use: Place a number of Guardians along a shoreline. They can trade shots with good results even with battleships. However, they are very expensive, so do not build them until your economy is booming.

Corresponding Core unit: *Punisher*

Hammer

Type: Level-1 artillery Kbot

Description: The heaviest hitter among Level-1 Kbots, the Hammer can deliver significant damage to the enemy. Its short range is balanced by firepower that is adequate against most units.

Strategic use: In the early stages of a game, try producing a squad of mixed PeeWees, Flash tanks, Rockos, and Hammers, and then send them on a raid against an enemy base. This harassing maneuver can disrupt the enemy's production.

Corresponding Core unit: *Thud*

Hawk

Type: Level-2 stealth fighter

Description: The Hawk is a very effective stealth fighter aircraft, able to fire two-missile salvoes. Its profile does not show up on radar, and it is faster than a Freedom Fighter.

Strategic use: If you steer your production towards acquiring the Hawk early, you can build a few of them before your enemy is expecting to see a Level-2 fighter. Its sudden appearance can be a surprise that makes your enemy alter plans because of a perceived threat.

Corresponding Core unit: *Vamp*

Hulk

Type: Level-1 transport ship

Description: In most sea missions and on multiplayer maps that feature large seas, Hulk sea transports constitute an important part of every invasion force. They have the capacity to transport just about anything, but are highly vulnerable, so make sure they are surrounded by escort ships equipped with working sonar.

Strategic use: The Level-1 sea transport is a crucial element of island campaigns. Also, by moving construction units to remote locations, the Hulk can help you set up hidden bases.

Corresponding Core unit: *Envoy*

Invader

Type: Level-2 crawling bomb Kbot

Description: The Invader crawling bomb, which creeps slowly but steadily toward its target, can be used in a variety of ways. You can set the bomb to crawl to a remote location and detonate, or you can set it to explode following a five-second delay.

Strategic use: The Invader is very effective on water maps. The first time an enemy notices it is when it crawls out of the water. You can also have air transports take crawling bombs to enemy bases. However, if a crawling bomb is intercepted by the enemy and is destroyed, the blast radius is much smaller.

Corresponding Core unit: *Roach*

Jammer

Type: Level-2 mobile radar jammer

Description: This mobile radar jammer blocks radar signals, just like the *Eraser*.

Strategic use: Build several Jammers and have them patrol round your base so that the enemy radar is totally blocked. Also, include a Jammer in small assault groups so that they stay undetected until visual contact.

Corresponding Core unit: *Deleter*

Jeffy

Type: Level-1 scout vehicle

Description: The Jeffy is a fast scout vehicle that is cheap, and takes a very short time to produce. It is very effective as a recon and patrol vehicle, and has the firepower to destroy undefended structures such as metal extractors. However, an enemy hit does a lot of damage, so don't try slugging it out.

Strategic use: Early in a game, use Jeffys to find metal deposits and search for the enemy's perimeter. Later in a game, use the Jeffy's extended visual range to good effect by having it patrol across your front lines.

Corresponding Core unit: *Weasel*

Jethro

Type: Level-1 anti-air missile Kbot

Description: The Jethro is only lightly armored and has a short firing range. However, you will want to build a few just in case the enemy is employing aggressive air tactics.

Strategic use: Even though the Jethro does not do much damage to land units, try arranging them so that in addition to anti-aircraft protection, they can also pitch in against land attacks.

Corresponding Core unit: *Crasher*

Lancet

Type: Level-2 torpedo bomber

Description: This torpedo bomber is effective against ships and submarines, especially when used in groups. Lancets do not have sonar, so anti-sub sorties have to be coordinated with other, sonar-equipped units.

Strategic use: Try attacking enemy missile ships with groups of Lancets. Missile ships are generally powerful units, but not in the AA department.

Corresponding Core unit: *Titan*

Luger

Type: Level-2 mobile artillery

Description: The Luger is an effective mobile artillery unit that fires its shells accurately at targets as far as two to three screens away. It does a lot of damage to whatever it hits, too.

Strategic use: There is not much armor on a Luger, so don't have it wade into the thick of things during a land-based assault. It is most effective when it sits back, and bombards the enemy from a distance.

Corresponding Core unit: *Pillager*

Lurker

Type: Level-1 submarine

Description: The submarine is one of the most effective sea units in *Total Annihilation*. Difficult to spot, the Lurker is relatively fast and its torpedoes are deadly. Most aircraft will not detect it.

Strategic use: Although a sub can withstand some damage, its real power is in its stealth and its firepower. Be aware, however, that the reload time for a sub's torpedo tubes is far from short.

Corresponding Core unit: *Snake*

Merl

Type: Level-2 mobile rocket launcher

Description: The Merl mobile rocket launcher fires unguided missiles at ranges up to about two screens away.

Strategic use: The Merl is vulnerable, so avoid exposing it to enemy fire. The best use is to have it sit back and target enemy structures on the other side of rivers, mountains, and other obstructions.

Corresponding Core unit: *Diplomat*

Millenium

Type: Level-2 battleship-class ship

Description: The Millenium battleship is the most powerful of the sea units, effective against other ships as well as land units—especially land units stationed on islands. The plasma cannon does a lot of damage.

Strategic use: Battleships are not effective against submarines; they have no sonar, and also no anti-aircraft weapons. This means you need to provide a suitable escort of other ships capable of ASW and AA duties. Battleships have strong armor, however, so they can survive attacks for a while.

Corresponding Core unit: *Warlord*

Peeper

Type: Level-1 scout aircraft

Description: The Peeper is a scout aircraft that easily evades anti-aircraft fire, unless you try to turn it sharply while within enemy AA weapon range. The Peeper slows sharply in turns, and becomes vulnerable. Peepers are cheap and take only a short time to build.

Strategic use: Try producing a dozen Peepers and then launch them with a few fast fighters mixed in. While the anti-aircraft units are targeting the scouts, the fighters can hit enemy targets undisturbed.

Corresponding Core unit: *Fink*

PeeWee

Type: Level-1 infantry Kbot

Description: The PeeWee is the "grunt," the infantry Kbot that's the cheapest to build. But PeeWees are a good bargain—they are fast, maneuverable in mountainous terrain, and pack twin Energy machine guns.

Strategic use: Don't underestimate the usefulness of PeeWees. Although they get chewed up quickly by Core forces, when cleverly used en masse they can rapidly climb many tough ridges and attack defending units from several sides simultaneously. Also, use them as temporary perimeter sentries if your radar system is not operational, or is of limited use because of terrain.

Corresponding Core unit: *A.K.* (albeit an A.K. fires a light laser rather than twin Energy machine guns)

Phoenix

Type: Level-2 strategic bomber

Description: The Phoenix strategic bomber is very effective against enemy bases. Not only is its bomb payload more powerful than the *Thunder* Level-1 bomber, but it also has defensive armament against aircraft.

Strategic use: Because the Phoenix has strong armor and an air-to-air response capability, you can take the bomber in on bombing runs through tough anti-aircraft fire. However, exceptionally strong air defenses will knock the Phoenix out, so make sure you have scouted the intended flight path before you undertake a major bombing run.

Corresponding Core unit: *Hurricane*

Piranha

Type: Level-2 attack submarine

Description: The Piranha is a submarine-killer attack sub, equipped with guided long-range torpedoes. Although the Piranha can attack surface ships, its main role is to destroy enemy subs. Its sonar has a long range.

Strategic use: The long range of the Piranha's guided torpedoes enables you to keep the attack sub out of the line of fire and still have it destroy enemy subs at a distance.

Corresponding Core unit: *Shark*

Protector

Type: Level-3 nuclear missile defense

Description: The Protector is a nuclear missile defense unit that is a vital link in your defense against nuclear threats. Its accuracy is almost 100 percent when an incoming nuke is headed directly at a Protector site. It drops slightly in accuracy as the angle of attack widens, although a single Protector does have a coverage umbrella of just under four screens in radius. By clicking on the Protector, a circle will appear showing what is protected.

Strategic use: The secret behind an effective Protector defense is to build plenty of them—at least one for each expected incoming nuke. If you do not, enemy missiles will get through. Note that after you have built a Protector, you must select it and build missiles, which, of course, take metal, energy, and time to build.

Corresponding Core unit: *Fortitude*

Ranger

Type: Level-1 missile frigate

Description: The Ranger missile ship can do double duty because it is equipped with guided missiles that can bring down aircraft, and also with rocket launchers that are effective against surface ships and land units.

Strategic use: The Ranger is versatile enough to be a threat when used by itself, not only in conjunction with other missile ships. But it is best combined with a destroyer, cruiser, battleship, and light carrier.

Corresponding Core unit: *Hydra*

Retaliator

Type: Level-3 nuclear missile launcher

Description: The Retaliator is the nuclear missile launcher that is expensive and takes time to produce. However, it can destroy everything within a one-screen radius of where it strikes—flattening everything. It is ineffective against bases that are spread out over many screens. The nuclear missile launcher is available in multiplayer games, but not in single-player missions.

Strategic use: One aggressive strategy is to build a Retaliator as soon as possible. However, don't forget about building base defenses strong enough to withstand an early attack! A nuclear first strike can cripple opponents, especially those unaware of the Retaliator's presence.

Corresponding Core unit: *Silencer*

Rocko

Type: Level-1 rocket launcher

Description: This rocket launcher works well in the early stages of a game, supplying medium- to long-range support along with the *Hammer's* artillery, while your *PeeWee* infantry and *Flash* and *Stumpy* tanks handle the short-range combat.

Strategic use: Position your Rockos behind your base perimeter defenses to provide fire support without exposition to danger. Because of their range, Rockos will frequently begin firing before your front troops engage. Be careful with those rockets to avoid friendly fire casualties when your units are right up against the enemy.

Corresponding Core unit: *Storm*

Samson

Type: Level-1 anti-air missile launcher

Description: A Samson surface-to-air missile launcher is mobile, as is the *Jethro*. But, it provides a more powerful anti-aircraft defense.

Strategic use: To provide better protection against air attacks, set your Samsons on permanent patrol around your base. Definitely build more than one!

Corresponding Core unit: *Slasher*

Seer

Type: Level-2 mobile radar jammer

Description: As a mobile radar unit, the Seer can take up position just about anywhere. This gives you an opportunity to move your radar where it will reveal most about the enemy. The Seer can also be set on a patrol route, which makes it harder to target by the enemy, and provides greater radar coverage.

Strategic use: Terrain affects radar range in a big way. As you spread out your base, try placing a Seer on the highest ground you can find near your base. If space allows, order the Seer onto a patrol route, so that it is not a motionless target.

Corresponding Core unit: *Informer*

Sentinel

Type: Level-2 heavy laser tower

Description: The Sentinel is a heavy-duty version of the *Light Laser Tower* (LLT). It can take more punishment than the LLT and boasts a longer range of fire.

Strategic use: This is an excellent weapon for base defense, especially if you can position multiple heavy lasers so that their fields of fire overlap to catch approaching enemy units in a crossfire.

Corresponding Core unit: *Gaat Gun*

Skeeter

Type: Level-1 scout ship

Description: The seaborne equivalent of a Jeffy scout land vehicle, the Skeeter is fast, but very lightly armored. Its primary purpose is to seek out the enemy as well as search for land masses suitable for occupation.

Strategic use: Use the Skeeter on far-flung patrols to quickly give you a sense of where the enemy is. While you are building your base and accumulating your resource reserves, Skeeters can be scouting the map for you. Just be ready to pull them back if they suddenly encounter enemy units. They will not last long in a fight.

Corresponding Core unit: *Searcher*

Spider

Type: Level-2 assault Kbot

Description: The Spider assault vehicle is a specialized mountain unit. Its laser fire actually stuns enemy units (instead of destroying them) to temporarily paralyze hard-to-reach enemy units.

Strategic use: The main use of Spiders is to paralyze mobile units so that the Commander can capture them. It is difficult to capture moving units.

Corresponding Core unit: None

Stumpy

Type: Level-1 medium assault tank

Description: The Stumpy is a medium assault tank, stronger and slower than a *Flash* light tank, but faster and with weaker armor than a *Bulldog* main battle tank.

Strategic use: Stumpy and Flash tanks work well together in the early part of the game. The Stumpy is not expensive, and has adequate armor plus a powerful plasma cannon for good offensive/defensive qualities. Its biggest drawback is similar to the Bulldog's—the Stumpy is clumsy enough to get bogged down in narrow valleys and among dense wrecks and ruins..

Corresponding Core unit: *Raider*

Thunder

Type: Level-1 bomber aircraft

Description: The Thunder is a relatively slow aircraft that does not have the air-to-air defensive capabilities of the *Phoenix* strategic bomber. However, it can be built quickly and inexpensively, making an aggressive air campaign right at the start of the game a realistic option.

Strategic use: Ensure that you make the Thunder's bombing runs straight. Anti-aircraft fire will destroy a Thunder almost immediately if it starts to turn, for turns slow it down sharply. Always execute turns well outside AA fire range.

Corresponding Core unit: *Shadow*

Triton

Type: Level-2 amphibious tank

Description: The Triton is a basic light tank that is totally amphibious, allowing it to hop from island to island, crossing bodies of water that defeat other vehicles. It is not particularly well armored, but can be a part of an island assault or an assault across a deep river.

Strategic use: Produce several Tritons and then launch them against an enemy island as early in the game as possible. The enemy will not see them unless sonar is established in the area to which they are headed. When they emerge at the enemy location, support them with aircraft and nearby ships.

Corresponding Core unit: *Crock*

Zeus

Type: Level-2 lightning-gun Kbot

Description: Like the *Zipper*, the Zeus has no direct corollary on the Core side. While very powerful, the lightning gun requires that the Zeus be close and within the line of sight of targeted units.

Strategic use: A good close-quarters slugger, the Zeus works best in situations that do not require long-range supporting fire.

Corresponding Core unit: None

Zipper

Type: Level-2 fast-attack Kbot

Description: Squads of Zippers are particularly good at raids and guerilla-style warfare—getting in, hitting the target, and then quickly getting out.

Strategic use: Don't waste Zippers in close-quarter assaults and sieges if you can avoid it. Try to treat them like light cavalry—make them appear unexpectedly, create havoc, and then vanish. In small squads, they can easily penetrate behind enemy lines and yet offer significant firepower.

Corresponding Core unit: None

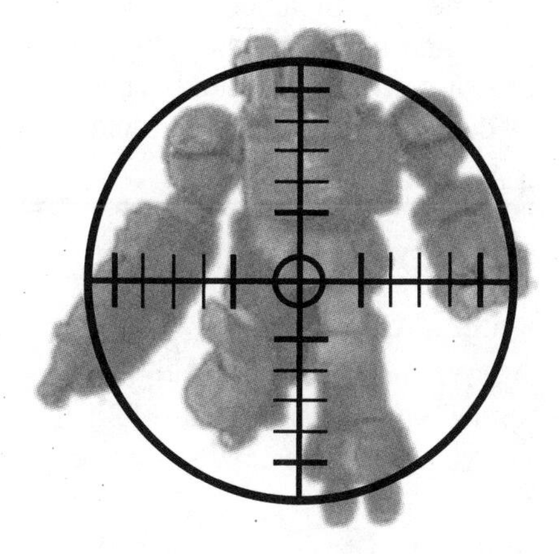

Core Units

The mighty armed forces of Core await your command. From A.K. infantry to Weasel scout vehicles, the units and structures in this chapter will take you to a stunning victory over Arm—if you understand how and when to use them. This is your alphabetical reference guide to Core, including unit type and description, strategy tips, and the corresponding Arm unit or structure.

A.K.

Type: Level-1 infantry Kbot

Description: The mainstay of Arm infantry, the A.K. Kbot is an inexpensive and versatile land unit. It handles most types of terrain well, has a respectable spotting range, and is fast enough to be employed as a recon unit. However, the AK's light laser is a weaker weapon than the twin Energy guns mounted on Arm's PeeWee.

Strategic use: Despite its light armor, the A.K. is a good choice for raids on Arm bases early in the game. Accompanied by *Weasel* scout vehicles, it can quickly knock out metal extractors and solar collectors before the enemy has a chance to build base defenses. Later on, the AK's limited firepower relegates it to secondary roles; because of its low cost, it's useful as a sacrificial goat—a unit to draw enemy fire.

Corresponding Arm unit: *PeeWee*

Avenger

Type: Level-1 fighter aircraft

Description: The Avenger is a basic fighter aircraft that is built by the Level-1 Aircraft Plant. Not as powerful as the Level-2 Vamp stealth fighter, the Avenger is relatively inexpensive and can be used for patrolling the battlefield as well as air-to-air combat.

Strategic use: Primarily patrol and recon tasks. Light armor and armament mean the Avenger isn't the best choice for intercepting enemy aircraft, especially if Level-2 fighters are available. However, continue using the Avenger on search-and-destroy sorties even after more sophisticated aircraft become available. In addition to intercepting light enemy forces in the field, the Avenger is good at destroying isolated enemy Metal Extractors that aren't protected by AA defenses.

Corresponding Arm unit: *Freedom Fighter*

The Can

Type: Level-2 armored assault Kbot

Description: The Can is a heavily armored artillery Kbot. Equipped with a powerful plasma cannon, it excels at hitting enemy structures at long range; each hit causes significant damage. Its low speed makes it less than ideal for targeting enemy vehicles. The Can is also equipped with a short-range laser for close combat purposes that does plenty of damage.

Strategic use: The Can has a huge number of hit points and has a short-range weapon—usually used defensively where metal can be recovered if it is destroyed. Group three or four Cans together to bombard an enemy base from outside the range of return fire. The Can's powerful guns are also a good choice when you want to target an exposed enemy Commander, or a structure vital to the enemy's war effort.

Corresponding Arm unit: None

Crasher

Type: Level-1 anti-air missile Kbot

Description: This is Core's first anti-aircraft weapon. Although relatively slow, it can patrol your base perimeter and defend it from incursions by hostile aircraft, especially early in the game. Later on, more sophisticated AA defenses become a necessity.

Strategic use: Include six or more Crasher units in your base defense, and any attack force that you are sending against the enemy. Crashers provide a measure of AA defense against enemy aircraft attempting to strike your task group; place them in the flight path of enemy aircraft with "Hold Position" movement orders.

Corresponding Arm unit: *Jethro*

Crock

Type: Level-2 amphibious tank

Description: This amphibious tank can give your enemy a nasty shock when it emerges from under the water and attacks an enemy base. Sonar Stations will reveal its presence, however, so when sending Crocks out, include a submarine escort to keep enemy subs at bay.

Strategic use: In island campaigns, send squads of four or five Crocks at intended targets. Time their attack with the arrival of your navy and air force—remember that an attack by combined forces is much more effective.

Corresponding Arm unit: *Triton*

Deleter

Type: Level-2 mobile radar jammer

Description: An ECM (electronic counter-measures) unit, the Deleter jams enemy radar within a small area. Its jamming radius is short, however; don't count on a single Deleter concealing the presence of a large, spread-out group of units. It can be deployed as part of a mobile task force, or to conceal solitary structures such as metal extractors built on a metal deposit.

Strategic use: Select the Deleter, click on the Guard command from the Orders menu, and the Deleter will stay with whatever unit you select. For example, have a Deleter guard the Commander, and the Commander will move around the map protected from radar by the Deleter. Similarly, add a Deleter to any strike group you're sending out—it will help keep your moves secret.

Corresponding Arm unit: *Jammer*

Diplomat

Type: Level-2 mobile rocket launcher

Description: The Diplomat is a mobile missile launcher whose missiles have a considerably longer range than those fired by the Level-1 Slasher. The Diplomat's warheads are predictably much more powerful than the Slasher's; however, it is vulnerable, and should be provided with a defensive screen of hard-core combat units.

Strategic use: Diplomats are an invaluable addition to your arsenal, particularly when you've got good radar coverage. Include a half-dozen Diplomats in major base assaults. Their long range enables them to hit the enemy base from a distance, while your strike force mixes it up at close quarters.

Corresponding Arm unit: *Merl*

Doomsday Machine

Type: Level-3 high-energy cannon

Description: The Doomsday Machine is equipped with a cannon that fires explosive energy shells. Although expensive to build, the gun is extremely powerful and very effective. It becomes a linchpin of your base defense the moment it's available.

Strategic use: Include a battery of Doomsday Machines in your base defense system. They can drop shells in the midst of approaching enemy forces while the attackers are still too distant to fire at your base!

Corresponding Arm unit: *Annihilator*

Enforcer

Type: Level-1 destroyer-class ship

Description: The Enforcer is the most versatile Core naval unit. It's equipped with sonar and depth charges to help you find and destroy submarines. It also has deck guns for short-range ship-to-ship combat. However, its guns have neither the long-range distance nor the power of Core's Executioner cruiser-class or Warlord battleship-class naval units. The Enforcer is only lightly armored, making it an easy target for Arm cruisers and battleships.

Strategic use: Use the Enforcer to accompany battleships, which don't have sonar and are vulnerable to subs. The Enforcer is also a good choice for anti-submarine warfare (ASW) patrols, spotting and stopping enemy subs before they can cause mischief.

Corresponding Arm unit: *Crusader*

Envoy

Type: Level-1 transport ship

Description: The Envoy is a transport ship that can carry up to 24 units at a time, 4 more than the Arm's Hulk transport. The ship is invaluable in island-hopping missions in which you need to expand your territory. Predictably, the Envoy transport is very vulnerable to attack by both enemy ships and aircraft, so always provide it with an escort—at least when it's full!

Strategic use: Obvious—this baby's used to carry units across bodies of water. Form your transports into convoys escorted by several submarines and destroyers. You can also load a radar jammer on board—that will keep your convoy off enemy radar screens.

Corresponding Arm unit: *Hulk*

Executioner

Type: Level-2 cruiser-class ship

Description: The Executioner is a cruiser with ASW capability—it is equipped with depth charges as well as strong artillery, equally effective against both land and sea targets. The cruiser's plasma cannon has the longest range among naval guns.

Strategic use: The Executioner's shallow draft allows it to get closer to land targets than other Level-2 ships; it's a good choice for land bombardments. The Executioner carries no anti-aircraft weapons. For this reason, provide it with an escort of Hydra missile frigates and Searcher scout ships.

Corresponding Arm unit: *Conqueror*

Fink

Type: Level-1 scout aircraft

Description: As a Level-1 aircraft, the Fink is Core's best long-range scout early in the game. Although unarmed, it's fast and consequently difficult to hit. A couple of Finks can quickly scout out most of the battlefield, providing you with valuable intelligence. However, Finks have very light armor and are easily lost over bases protected by AA weapons.

Strategic use: Recon, patrol, and sacrificial goat. Note that when the Fink makes a turn, it slows down, making it an easy target for enemy AA fire. When planning its patrol route, make sure all the turns are made over empty land or ground occupied by friendly units. Several Finks sent in just ahead of a squadron of fighters will temporarily draw AA fire away from the fighters.

Corresponding Arm unit: *Peeper*

Fortitude Missile Defense

Type: Level-3 nuclear missile defense

Description: This is the only really effective defense against nuclear missiles. The defense system is expensive, but late in a long game it pays to have several of these structures protecting your base. Try to build at least one Fortitude for every enemy nuke launcher; having any less may mean some enemy nukes could get through.

Strategic use: Defense against nuclear attacks. Space out several Fortitudes in a line across your base, about a half screen apart. If an enemy nuke's trajectory happens to fall in line with one of the Fortitude launchers, the odds of knocking it out of the sky are almost 100 percent.

Corresponding Arm unit: *Protector*

Gaat Gun

Type: Level-2 heavy laser tower

Description: The Gaat Gun is a powerful two-barreled laser tower that is a valuable component of your base defense system. As a Level-2 structure, the Gaat can be built by any of the mobile construction units. Be aware that the Gaat needs a supply of energy to fire its powerful lasers.

Strategic use: You'll use the Gaat Gun primarily in advanced base defense because of its power. However, because the mobile construction units can build it anywhere, in missions and multiplayer games when you need to consolidate your hold on an area (for instance, when setting up a new base), the Gaat Gun is a good choice. It's much more rugged structure than the Light Laser Tower, and its twin lasers provide strong firepower..

Corresponding Arm unit: *Sentinel*

Goliath

Type: Level-2 super-heavy tank

Description: This is the only super-tank in the game. (Arm doesn't have one.) It can be very effective during major base assaults. Although slow, this Level-2 armored unit can provide invaluable support, especially when the opposition's tough.

Strategic use: The Goliath can take a lot of damage. Use it to head your assaults against enemy bases. However, it's very slow, about half the speed of a Raider medium tank. It can be difficult to keep the Goliath with the rest of your land units during a long drive. In addition, the Goliath's low speed and maneuverability mean it does poorly in terrain strewn with obstacles such as rocks and wreckage.

Corresponding Arm unit: *None*

Hive

Type: Level-2 light aircraft carrier

Description: Aircraft of all Levels can land on this light carrier. It automatically repairs landed air units. There's onboard radar as well, making it a particularly useful ship in an invading task force.

Strategic use: As part of a naval task group. It's best deployed together with other naval combat units, such as battleships and cruisers. Single Hives may also be deployed as repair depots for combat aircraft—planes will return to a nearby Hive automatically. This can be very helpful when conducting aerial offensives across bodies of water. The Hive produces 330 energy units and is the only Level-2 energy-producing unit on the water.

Corresponding Arm unit: *Colossus*

Hurricane

Type: Level-2 strategic bomber

Description: This is the Core's most powerful bomber. It boasts laser anti-aircraft defenses, and can cause dramatic damage to enemy bases. The Hurricane is much more powerful than the Level-1 Shadow bomber; however, it should still be employed in groups, not individually.

Strategic use: Use this aircraft to strike enemy bases, and large concentrations of enemy units. Send Hurricanes against selected targets in successive waves of two or three at a time. If Fink scout aircraft go in just ahead of the bombers, some anti-aircraft defenses will target the scouts instead of the bombers.

Corresponding Arm unit: *Phoenix*

Hydra

Type: Level-1 missile frigate

Description: The Hydra is basically a floating AA weapons platform, although it does have a symbolic laser gun for surface targets. The Hydra's surface-to-air missiles, or SAMs, provide valuable AA protection for other ships such as battleships, which otherwise would be defenseless against attacking aircraft. This ship is only lightly armored, and won't survive much damage, so it's a good idea to include several Hydras in every naval task force. They are a valuable addition—the missiles can be used against surface targets, and they have long range.

Strategic use: In addition to including them in naval task groups, put Hydras on patrol in the approach paths of enemy aircraft targeting your base. Its missiles can knock down quite a few of the enemy planes before they can close in on the target.

Corresponding Arm unit: *Ranger*

Informer

Type: Level-2 mobile radar jammer

Description: The Informer is a mobile radar unit that lets you deal with one of the main faults of stationary radar: static coverage. Move it anywhere to get a clear picture of enemy activity in any area of the map, taking care not to run it into enemy sentries and patrols. On very large maps, especially, the Informer can be used to discover distant enemy concentrations.

Strategic use: The Informer is great at gathering intelligence about enemy moves in faraway areas. In addition, it works well in the sentry role; send the Informer on an extended patrol route back and forth along your entire base perimeter. You'll get a continually updated picture of enemy activity in all the surrounding areas.

Corresponding Arm unit: *Seer*

Instigator

Type: Level-1 light assault tank

Description: The Instigator can be a particularly valuable weapon early in a game, especially when used in squads of four to six tanks in open, vehicle-friendly terrain. Mountains and forests limit the Instigator's maneuverability, which is its greatest advantage; its quick-firing laser doesn't do that much damage. It can also serve as a good mobile sentry, patrolling your defensive perimeter.

Strategic use: Recon, patrol, and small scale offensive actions. Instigators are relatively cheap to build (887 energy, 110 metal). Build a half dozen of them early in a game, and use them as a hit-and-run squad. When guarding a perimeter, this kind of squad responds quickly to raids on your base.

Corresponding Arm unit: *Flash*

Intimidator

Type: Level-3 long-range plasma cannon

Description: The Intimidator is one of the most powerful weapons in the game: A Level-3 structure that can fire shells up to ten screens away. Very expensive to build, it can only begin to make a major difference late in the game, when energy and metal reserves are high enough to allow its full scale production.

Strategic use: Long range bombardment. Use some of your Weasels to spot distant enemy units and structures hiding from your radar. You can target them with the Intimidator by clicking on their radar blips in the small map window in the upper left of your screen. However, do not count on knocking them out with a single shot—the Intimidator is one of the most inaccurate weapons in the game.

Corresponding Arm unit: *Big Bertha*

Pillager

Type: Level-2 mobile artillery

Description: The Pillager is a Level-2 mobile artillery unit that's an excellent choice for base bombardment, and for lobbing shells into large groups of approaching enemy units. Its long range allows it to send shells over hills and other obstructions.

Strategic use: Mostly offensive, in assaults and raids on enemy bases. When using the Pillager during a base assault or a large-scale battle, line up a half dozen or more, if possible, and have them concentrate on one big target at a time.

Corresponding Arm unit: *Luger*

Pulverizer

Type: Level-2 missile tower

Description: The Pulverizer is armed with an anti-aircraft missile launcher that's much more accurate and powerful than the Slasher mobile SAM launcher, but being a structure, it provides AA protection only over a fixed area. As a Level-2 structure, it's the main anti-air unit for Core, but doesn't have much effect on ground units.

Strategic use: AA base defense. If your opponent is deploying plenty of aircraft, build Pulverizers as soon as you can—it provides much better AA defense than Level-1 structures and units. Spread Pulverizers throughout your base so that they can fire at attacking aircraft from different points, and at different angles.

Corresponding Arm unit: *Defender*

Punisher

Type: Level-2 stationary plasma cannon

Description: The Punisher offers the best shoreline defense against enemy ships. Expensive to build (7,585 energy, 1,887 metal), the Punisher has the heaviest armor of any land-based unit or structure, including the Goliath super-heavy tank.

Strategic use: Because of the Punisher's heavy armor and powerful medium-range cannon, try placing the Punishers between the inner and outer rings of base defenses. Its artillery shells can soften up approaching ground troops, and the Punisher itself can act as a temporary physical barrier because of its heavy armor.

Corresponding Arm unit: *Guardian*

Pyro

Type: Level-2 flamethrower Kbot

Description: These flame-throwers are unique to the Core, and make great hit-and-run raiders. Their speed is moderately fast, and their continuous stream of flames will take a quickly mounting toll on most enemy units.

Strategic use: Both offensive and defensive; invaluable in tackling large groups of enemy units. A squad of four or more Pyros makes a very good force to attack the enemy Commander with. Also, try keeping a squad of Pyros independent of your main forces, using them as a strike team against enemy Kbots. The Pyro is not as effective against vehicles.

Corresponding Arm unit: None

Raider

Type: Level-1 medium assault tank

Description: The Raider has the best combination of armor, firepower, and maneuverability among Level-1 Kbots and vehicles. However, it's slow enough to be easily surrounded and destroyed on its own by three or four PeeWees. Use the Raider in a squad with other Raiders, Instigators, and Kbots for best results.

Strategic use: Mostly offensive. Early in a game, when assaulting an enemy base, concentrate the fire of half a dozen Raiders on dangerous base defenses, such as Arm's Sentinel heavy lasers and Guardian artillery units.

Corresponding Arm unit: *Stumpy*

Rapier

Type: Level-2 gunship aircraft

Description: With its ability to hover over targets, continuously firing its rockets, the heavily armored Rapier is particularly good against ground targets. Note: its rockets are unguided and thus may miss fast units; but they do heavy damage to an entire area.

Strategic use: Gunships are good at attacking undefended or lightly defended enemy Metal Extractors, Wind Generators, and Solar Collectors. When attacking a base, focus at least a half-dozen or more Rapiers on the anti-aircraft units and structures first. With their heavy armor and hover ability, the Rapiers are the right choice for knocking out enemy AA defenses from the air.

Corresponding Arm unit: *Brawler*

Reaper

Type: Level-2 heavy assault tank

Description: Core's main battle tank is heavily armored and comes with a deadly plasma cannon. It's a slow unit, so don't use it in hit-and-run raids.

Strategic use: In major offensives and base strikes/assaults. In open, flat terrain, a squadron of Reapers can effectively combat light ground units. In mountainous areas, however, and when hemmed in by wreckage, Reapers get bogged down and become easy targets for faster vehicles and aircraft.

Corresponding Arm unit: *Bulldog*

Roach

Type: Level-2 crawling bomb Kbot

Description: The crawling bomb can be sent to blow up at a specific, distant location; or it can be set to explode on a five-second fuse. If it's hit and blows up in an unplanned fashion, the resulting explosion is much weaker. When it self-destructs, it destroys anything within a radius of about three-quarters of a screen.

Strategic use: This is a Kbot take on the army sapper. When used in numbers, Roaches can play havoc with the enemy, destroying vital structures (in the single player mode, it can also be successfully deployed against groups of units). A Roach can also be loaded onto an air transport and, given good timing, can self-destruct right over the enemy base. If the transport is shot down, however, the loss of aircraft and bomb is an expensive experiment.

Corresponding Arm unit: *Invader*

Searcher

Type: Level-1 scout ship

Description: The Searcher is a lightly armored scout ship with a good turn of speed. Send out a couple of Searchers as early as possible on missions or multiplayer maps that have large bodies of water. Although they can't take much damage, they can spot the enemy and move in to attack in a blink of an eye. What's more the Searcher is the only Level-1 ship equipped with AA weaponry.

Strategic use: Use the Searcher as a fast patrol boat and AA escort as well as a scouting ship. Its deck guns can cause some damage to enemy units on land, since it can come right up to the shore, shortening the range.

Corresponding Arm unit: *Skeeter*

Shadow

Type: Level-1 bomber aircraft

Description: This is Core's Level-1 bomber, not particularly fast and without air-to-air defenses. However, its relatively low price makes it a good choice for harassing runs against enemy bases early in the game. Once AA defenses have been built up, the Shadow is easy to bring down.

Strategic use: This is a light strike aircraft; it may be deployed against an enemy base early in the game, but later on, its strike capability limits it to attacks on isolated structures and stationary units. When attacking a base with AA defenses, order Avenger fighters to precede the Shadows to distract AA fire from the bombers. The Shadows' light bombs don't do much damage—it takes several hits before a building is noticeably affected.

Corresponding Arm unit: *Thunder*

Shark

Type: Level-2 attack submarine

Description: An attack submarine, the Shark is primarily a sub killer. It has long range guided torpedoes, better speed, and longer sonar range than the Level-1 Snake submarine.

Strategic use: Hunter-killer sub. Set a couple of Sharks on a patrol route along your perimeter. The Shark does a good job of supporting the stationary Torpedo Launchers, and is best used at extreme long range. Do not send Sharks off singly on offensive patrols; group them in packs of three or more and keep them moving for maximum efficacy. Ordinary subs have a hard time hitting them at all if they are on the move.

Corresponding Arm unit: *Piranha*

Silencer

Type: Level-3 nuclear missile launcher

Description: This is Core's nuclear missile launcher, a Level-3 structure that fires long-range missiles.

Strategic use: Nuclear strikes against enemy bases/large troop concentrations. Build more than one Silencer—in fact, if you can only afford it, build plenty. You can only count on inflicting damage with your nukes if as you have more Silencers than the enemy has missile-defense systems.

Corresponding Arm unit: *Retaliator*

Slasher

Type: Level-1 anti-air missile launcher

Description: The Slasher is Core's mobile AA missile launcher. Although not very powerful, this is the best early defense against enemy airpower. It's not particularly effective against ground troops, but can be deployed in that role if needed.

Strategic use: Mobile AA defense. Set several Slashers on permanent base patrols. Plan patrol routes so that they cover your entire base. Slashers can be assigned to guard certain units, such as the Commander, to provide protection from air attacks.

Corresponding Arm unit: *Samson*

Snake

Type: Level-1 submarine

Description: Core's submarine is one of the most useful and effective units in the game. Invisible to the enemy until Sonar Stations are set up, the Snake is a good perimeter-defense unit, especially for sinking enemy subs. It has sonar, powerful torpedoes—a single one sinks a Piranha—and cannot be knocked out quite that easily (two Piranha fish).

Strategic use: This is a very versatile, relatively inexpensive unit. Build as many Snakes as your economy will allow. In force, they can dominate the seas. Have them hunt in packs, rather than alone, to counteract the slow reload time for their torpedoes.

Corresponding Arm unit: *Lurker*

Spectre

Type: Level-2 radar jammer Kbot

Description: The Spectre jams enemy radar within a short radius. It's the Kbot equivalent of the Deleter. As with the Deleter, the Spectre's mobility means that you can order it to guard another mobile unit. The radar jammer accompany its charge, wiping it off enemy radar screens.

Strategic use: Same as Deleter's, with one difference—the Spectre Kbot handles rough terrain better than the Deleter vehicle. Remember you can use mobile radar jammers to hide moving troops on both land and sea. Place a Spectre on board a Hulk sea transport unit along with attack units for commando-style raids and surprise landings.

Corresponding Arm unit: *Eraser*

Storm

Type: Level-1 rocket launcher

Description: The Storm is a good base defender, and a strong though slow attack unit. Its heavy armor lets it stand up well in furious battles. It's best deployed behind attacking front-line A.K. infantry and Instigator tanks—its rockets have a very respectable range.

Strategic use: Another very versatile unit, equally at home in both defense and offense. Groups of three or more Storms maximize their effectiveness. When the action starts, this helps compensate for the Storm's relatively slow reload time. Six Storms can take on almost everything—destroyers included.

Corresponding Arm unit: *Rocko*

Thud

Type: Level-1 artillery Kbot

Description: The Thud is Core's Level-1 artillery Kbot, and a good weapon early in the game. It's capable of indirect fire over obstacles such as hills, water, lava pits, and other obstructions. The Thud has good armor for a Level-1 unit, although it's not very fast.

Strategic use: Both offensive and defensive. Ideally suited for early-game offensive actions, when not much weaponry is available.. Because it's cheap to produce, you can create attack squads that include from four to six Thuds even for these early attacks. In base defense, Thuds work well when deployed in support of structures such as the Light Laser Tower.

Corresponding Arm unit: *Hammer*

Titan

Type: Level-2 torpedo bomber

Description: The Titan torpedo bomber is very effective against subs, especially when used in squadrons of three or more at a time. However, the Titan doesn't carry sonar. You'll need to use Sonar Stations and other sonar-carrying units or structures to help the Titan find its targets.

Strategic use: Keep Titans flying over waters that are "covered" by your sonar. For example, order several Titans on permanent patrols over water beyond the outer perimeter of your base but within your Sonar Stations' range. They will automatically attack subs that your sonar picks up.

Corresponding Arm unit: *Lancet*

Valkyrie

Type: Level-1 air transport

Description: Although it can only carry one unit at a time, the Valkyrie air transport is very effective at dropping Core units into places where the enemy doesn't expect them.

Strategic use: The Valkyrie's limited cargo capacity makes it best suited for unorthodox transport tasks. For example, a Valkyrie can transport a construction mobile unit to an isolated corner of the map to start a second base of operations. Or, it can carry a crawling bomb toward a target and set the bomb off directly above the target.

Corresponding Arm unit: *Atlas*

Vamp

Type: Level-2 stealth fighter

Description: Core's stealth fighter is invisible to enemy radar and features powerful air-to-air missiles. The Vamp is the best Core fighter aircraft.

Strategic use: This is your best interceptor. To maintain better control over your stealth fighters, group a half-dozen or so into one squadron by selecting them all and then pressing the Ctrl plus one of the 1-9 keys. By subsequently pressing the Alt key plus corresponding number key, you select those aircraft as a unit no matter where on the map they may be.

Corresponding Arm unit: *Hawk*

Warlord

Type Level-2 battleship

Description: This is the most heavily armed of Core's naval units. However, its use is limited to surface targets on both land and sea. It has no sonar, so it can't find or sink subs; it also has no AA defenses. For that reason, it's a good idea to keep the Warlord accompanied by Shark sub killers, Hydra AA platforms, and Executioner cruisers.

Strategic use: Shore bombardment and naval combat against surface vessels. The Warlord is particularly effective at bombarding enemy bases. Best deployed as part of a larger task force, and protected by cruisers, subs, and sub killers, the Warlords are capable of quickly reducing a base to a smoking wreck.

Corresponding Arm unit: *Millenium*

Weasel

Type: Level-1 scout vehicle

Description: The Weasel scout vehicle has several uses early in the game. Because of its speed, this is a good unit to harass enemy Commanders trying to build their bases. The Weasel also makes a good unit to have positioned near Metal Extractors and Solar Collectors early in the game. They can respond quickly to fast-attack units that try to get into your base.

Strategic use: Patrol, recon, and light strike. Use Weasels on patrol around the perimeter of your base. They can engage and slow down attacking enemy units well outside your base perimeter. They're also the best land vehicles for quickly scouting out metal deposits on the map.

Corresponding Arm unit: *Jeffy*

The Mission Guide

There were many who were unwilling to toss aside their bodies so casually, many indeed who regarded patterning as an atrocity. They fled to the outer edges of the galaxy, where they banded together to form a resistance which became known as the Arm. War began, though it was never officially declared by either side. The Arm developed high-powered combat suits for its armies, while the Core transferred the minds of its soldiers directly into similarly deadly machines. The Core duplicated its finest warriors thousands of times over. The Arm countered using cloning. The war raged on for over four thousand years, consuming the resources of an entire galaxy and leaving it a scorched wasteland...

+DOUBLESHOT

(Will double the damage of all the weapon fire across the board)

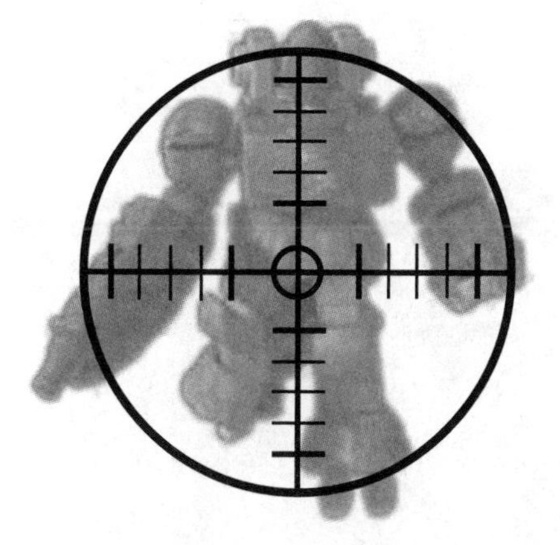

Arm Missions

The final war between Arm and Core starts among the green slopes and forests of Arm's home planet, Empyrrean. Core invaders have set up bases from which they plan to conquer the entire planet. Some terrain is hilly, thick with trees, and broken by rivers—favoring rugged Kbots that can climb steep mountain walls and artillery units that can fire over hills and across streams. Other areas are more open and level, providing good land for swift-moving scout vehicles and lumbering tanks. As Arm fights back, the action shifts to other planets, including Thelassean where submarines, destroyers, battleships, and cruisers become the weapons of choice for the Arm and Core navies. In all your missions, you must build your energy and metal resources carefully to be able to afford the Kbot labs, vehicle and aircraft plants, and shipyards that are the foundation for your armies, navies, and air forces.

Mission 1:

A Hero Returns

Difficulty rating: Easy

Objective: Your simple goal in this first mission is to move near the Galactic Gate near the top of the map.

Starting forces: 5 PeeWee Kbots, 2 Jeffy scout vehicles, 1 Hammer artillery Kbot, 1 Rocko rocket launcher, 2 Flash light tanks, 1 Stumpy medium tank

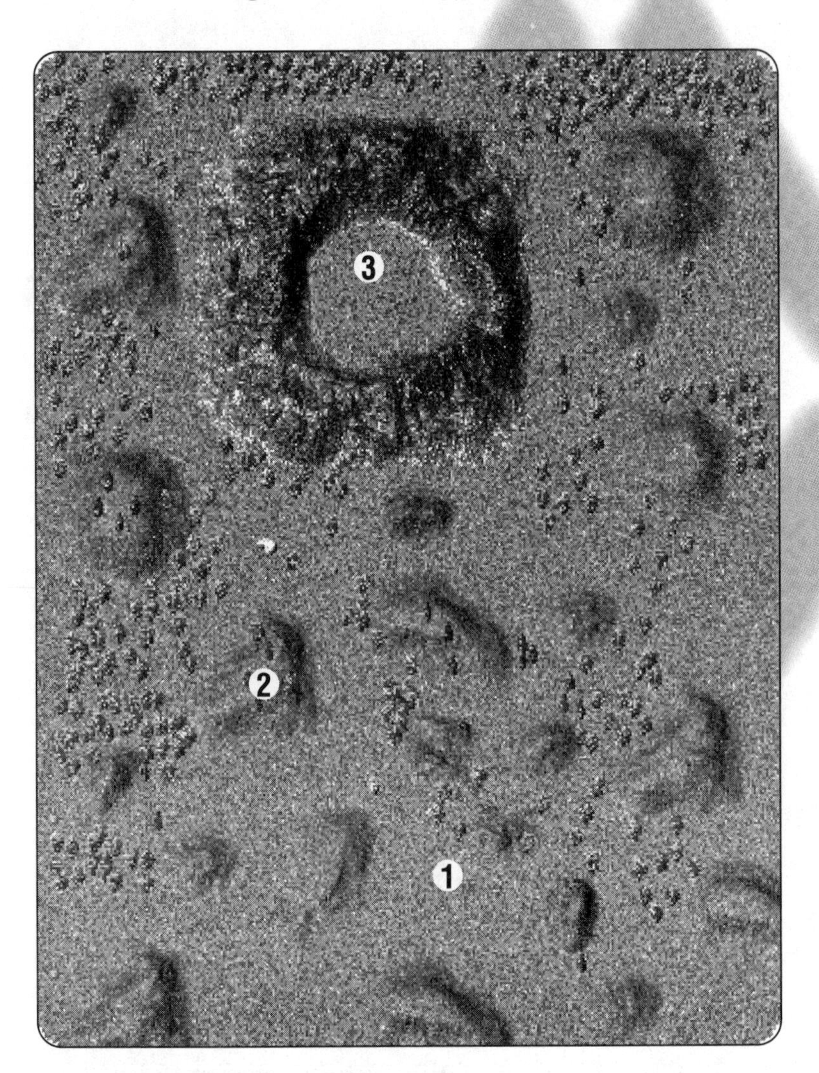

Mission Briefing

There's nothing but search-and-destroy in this initial mission. Roving Core units are between you and the Galactic Gate in a crater at the top of the map. This is your chance to practice maneuvering your troops against small squads of the enemy. The hunting is easy.

How to Win

- **Group your units.** At the starting point (1), press Ctrl plus 1–9 in combination to create individual squads. For example, try forming a squad with a couple of PeeWees, plus a Rocko or Hammer, and a tank. You don't have to do this to win this mission, but it's excellent practice for later missions when you need to control squads quickly.
- **Direct your squads.** Head either west for a clockwise cleanup march around the map or east for a counterclockwise route. Either way is fine and provides a systematic way to sweep the map.
- **Attack the Core land units.** To the northwest of your starting point is a hill where you'll find a Storm rocket launcher (2). Try coming at it fast using a two-pronged attack with your PeeWees on one flank and your tanks on the other. Use your Rocko rocket launcher and Hammer artillery bot from a distance. A couple of AKs and Weasels will get involved, but it won't take long to take care of them all.
- **Defend against Core Weasels and A.K. infantry.** Your troops will quickly gain the attention of patrolling Weasel vehicles and A.K. Kbots. There is another Storm just to the east as well. Concentrate the fire from your squads on one or, at most, two targets at a time. Concentrated fire is always more effective.
- **Sweep the map!** Use this same approach with your squads to take on all Core units you run into. Ignore the Galactic Gate at the top of the map (3). Once you have cleared the last Core unit, the mission is over.

Mission 2:

Core Kbot Base, Destroy It!

Difficulty rating: Easy

Objective: Build a base, including a Kbot lab. Then, cross the river to the west with a force strong enough to destroy a Core Kbot lab and all defending units.

Starting forces: Commander, 2 PeeWee Kbots, 2 Rocko rocket-launcher Kbots, 1 Hammer artillery Kbot

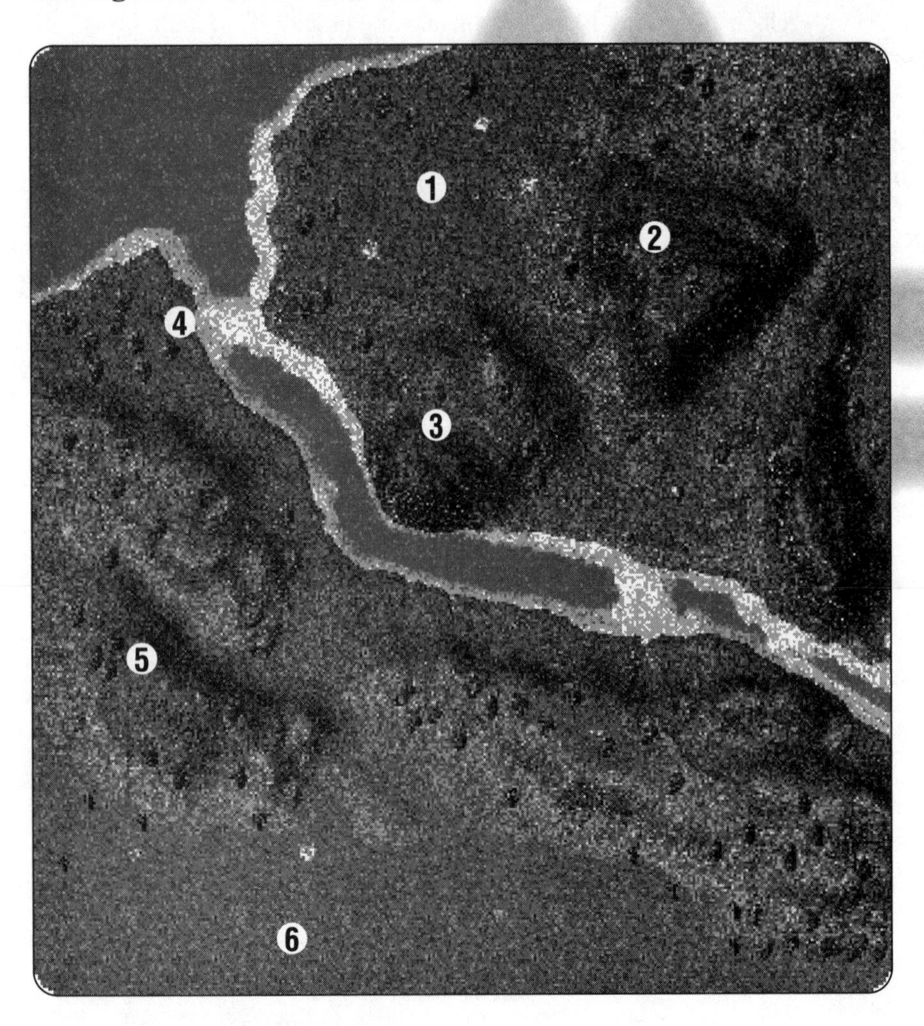

Mission Briefing

This introductory mission enables you to get familiar with establishing a base and a defensive perimeter, building a Kbot lab, and assaulting a Core base. Core units are not overly aggressive. The Core base is lightly defended by three well-placed laser towers and about two dozen Kbots, mostly AKs, and a few Storm rocket-launchers and Thud artillery bots.

How to Win

- **Build your base at your starting point (1).** Order your Commander to set up three metal extractors on the three metal deposits there; then build two or three solar collectors.

- **Prepare for Core A.K. infantry.** A few Core units will approach you from a ridge (2) and from across the river (4). Send a PeeWee and a Rocko to the riverbank and a PeeWee, Rocko, and Hammer to the base of the ridge to defend those positions while your Commander is building energy and metal generators.

- **Build a Kbot lab at your base (1).** Order the lab to start cranking out an assortment of PeeWees, Rockos, and Hammers. Don't bother building anti-air Jethro Kbots in this mission, unless it is for practice in maneuvering them.

- **Command the heights.** Have your Commander build two Light Laser Towers (LLTs), one next to each Ford at the hilltop that overlooks the river (3). Any Core units that approach that point from south or north will come under the LLT's laser fire. A steady stream varying between five and ten AKs are patrolling just east of the hill along a narrow north-south valley. They may stray into your perimeter.

- **Cross the river.** There are two shallow points along the river, one near the southeast corner of the map and the other just to the west of your base (4). The south crossing is fairly well protected by Core AKs and laser towers, which may open fire before your units are out of the water. The passage west of your base (4), however, is only lightly defended, and you will find a good staging area for your growing army once you have made it across the river. You may also try a simultaneous attack at both crossing points. A decoy attack at one crossing point draws Core troops, allowing your main attack to encounter less opposition.

- **Attack the Core base.** The Core Kbot lab is located at the southwestern corner of the map (6). Before you get there, you should destroy a Core laser tower (5). To maximize your firepower, attack any laser tower, such as this one, from more than one angle at a time. If you have been building your PeeWees, Rockos, and Hammers all this time, you should have a good force ready to wade into the outlying defenders and then the base. You can advance your forces straight along the river to take out defenders or turn west and south to destroy the base and then the remaining Core units.

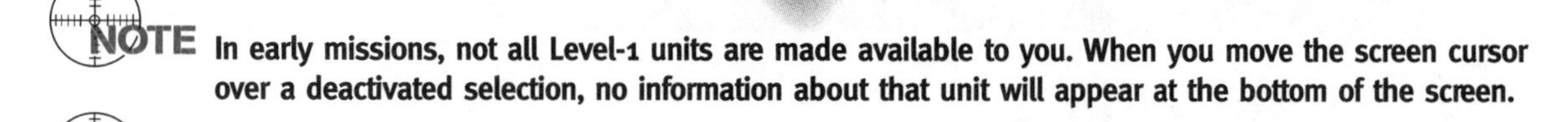

NOTE In early missions, not all Level-1 units are made available to you. When you move the screen cursor over a deactivated selection, no information about that unit will appear at the bottom of the screen.

TIP Practice issuing multiple commands to the Commander by choosing a unit in the Build selection box, such as a Solar Collector. Then, holding the Shift key down, place the build cursor over one or more locations on which you want to build those units. This enables you to have the Commander build multiple units while you're busy with other duties. Remember that you can also line up a production queue in your Kbot lab—just click repeatedly on the unit production icon in the Build menu.

Mission 3:

Spider Technology

Difficulty rating: Easy

Objective: Rescue three Spider Kbots isolated near the top of the map. Core wants them destroyed. Bring them back to your base near the southeast corner of the map, and move at least one of them behind the Dragon's Teeth barrier to win the game. You don't have to destroy all Core units to win the mission.

Starting forces: Commander, 2 Rocko rocket launchers, 3 Hammer artillery units

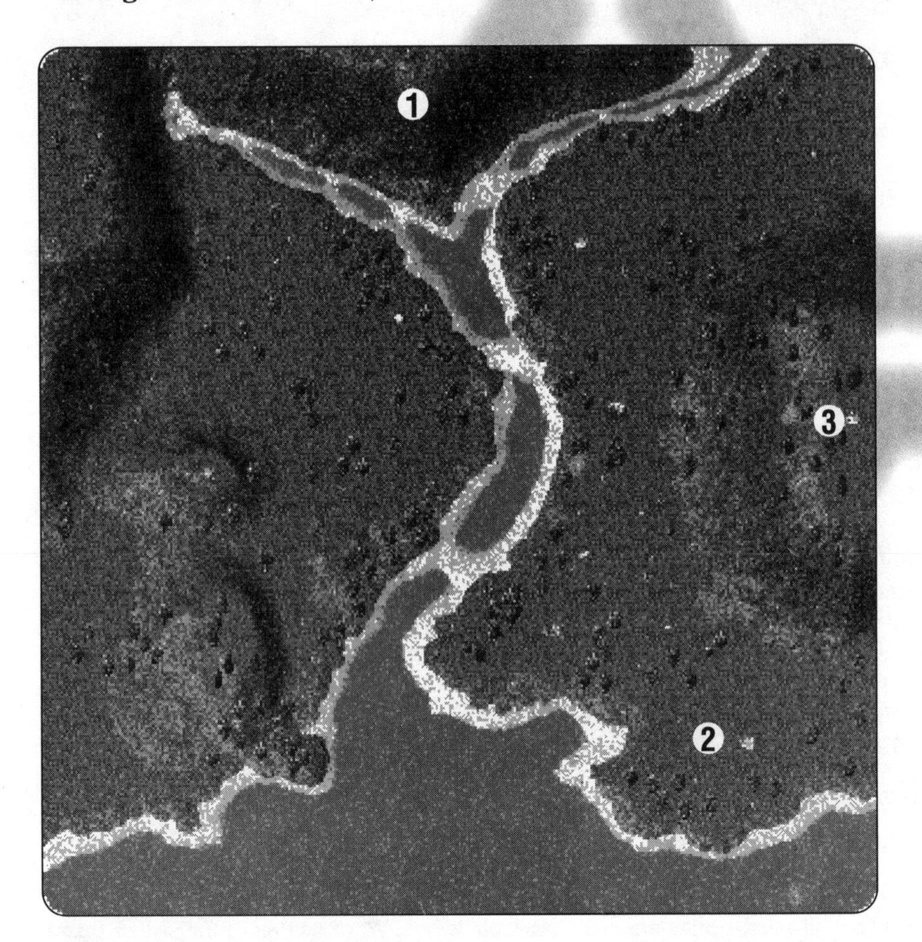

Mission Briefing

There is no Core base in this mission, just roaming patrols of Core A.K. bots, Thud artillery, Storm tanks, and Weasel scout vehicles. More than two dozen of them take up the western half of the map, across a north-south river. Another couple of dozen are to your north between your troops and the Spiders. Some of them patrol back and forth at a river ford. You must build a Kbot Lab, get enough strength to head north with a raiding party, and shepherd at least one of the Spider bots back to your base to be successful.

How to Win

- **Take care of the Spider Kbots.** Select the three Spider Kbots (1). Move them as far north on the screen as possible to prevent a passing Core unit from spotting them early in the mission. While they're selected, press Ctrl-1 to form them into a squad that will respond when you simultaneously press Alt-1. This will simplify selecting them again when you need to head them south.

- **Start your base.** Order your Commander to build three Solar Collectors and a couple of Metal Extractors at the starting position (2). Then, immediately begin building a Kbot Lab there and set it to build at least five PeeWees, four Hammers, and four Rockos. Before long, a Core Thud artillery Kbot will wander south toward your base. At about the same time, an A.K. or a Weasel is likely to find your Spiders (1). Remember that your Spiders can paralyze an enemy unit, but not destroy it. You can keep an enemy unit paralyzed for a short time, but keep your eye on the Spiders' health by pressing the tilde (~) key to show their health bars.

- **Move the Spiders and your troops.** Once the Spiders are discovered, you have to move swiftly north with what troops you have on hand. There is a ridge to the east above your base (3) with four or five Thud artillery units and a couple of Storm tanks. Stay off that ridge for now. Press Alt-1 to select the Spiders and head them down the cliff wall toward the Arm base. At the same time, have your Commander and a half-dozen PeeWees, several Rockos, and several Hammers move north toward the approaching Spiders. Get at least one of the Spiders behind the Dragon's Teeth barrier, and you have met the winning conditions will have been satisfied.

NOTE **A key to quick victory is to be able to form a protective north-south corridor with your troops to allow the Spiders to move quickly south. This is a point when having the Spiders selected as a squad will facilitate their movement through the battlefield, keeping them separated from the fighting troops.**

TIP **You can build a Vehicle Plant if you wish, although it is not necessary for this mission. The Kbots have enough firepower to handle Core in this mission. Also, it is possible to win this mission without engaging many of the Core troops across the river.**

Mission 4:

Core Contamination Spreads

Difficulty rating: Easy

Objective: Continuing to fight back against the Core invasion of Arm's home planet, Empyrrean, you must destroy all Core units on the map, including a base containing a well-defended Vehicle Plant.

Starting forces: Commander, 1 Zeus, 2 Rockos

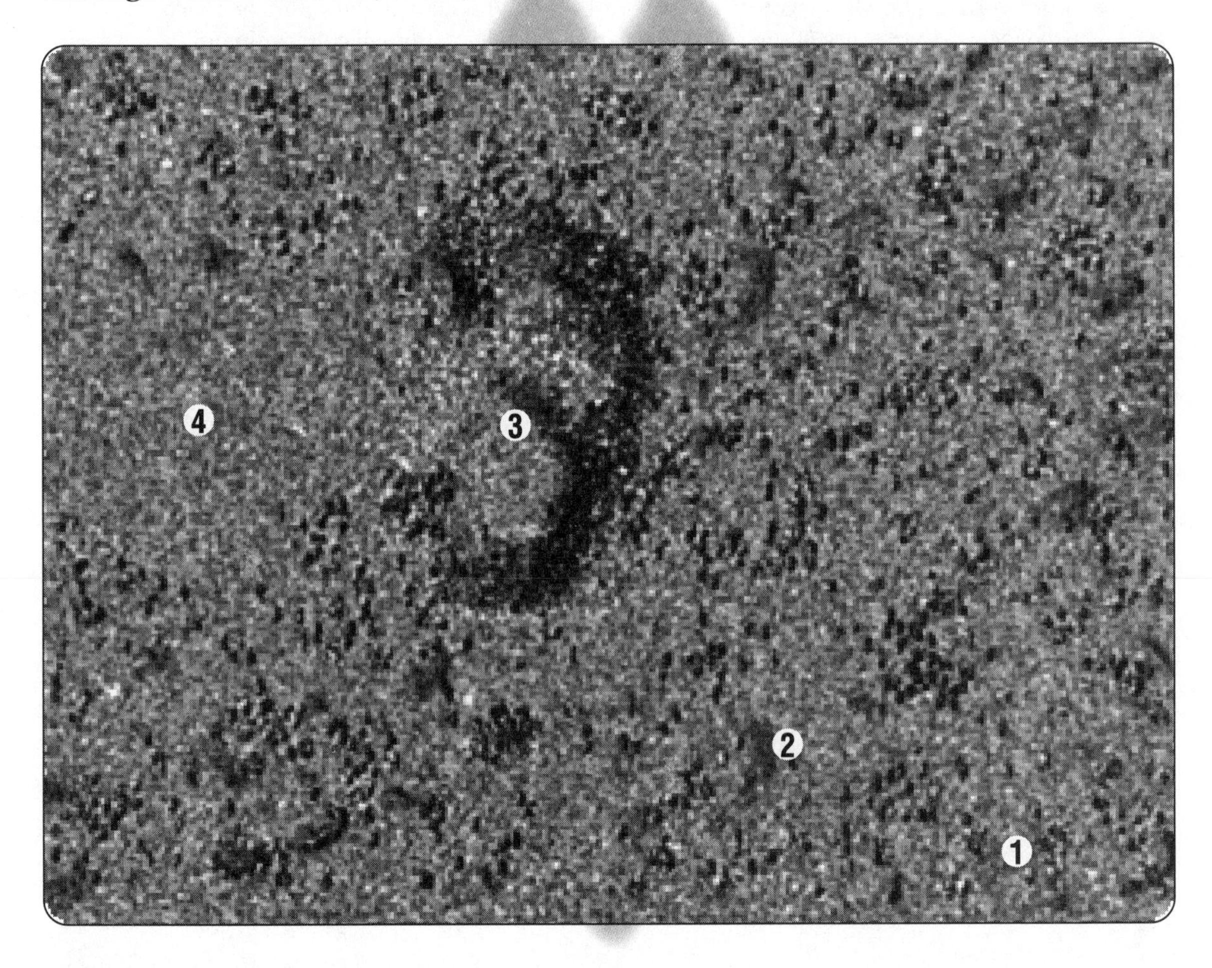

Mission Briefing

Beginning in the southeast corner of the map with several Arm units, your Commander must construct a base and prepare to lead forces against a Core base on the west edge of the map. Patrols of mixed Core units are to your north, directly west, and in the center of the map. The primary lesson to learn in this mission is to maintain productivity and protection at your base while assaulting a distant Core base.

How to Win

- **Start building a base where you begin the mission (1).** Almost immediately, defend against two Raider tanks from the north. After they have been destroyed, build a Radar Tower in the same area to get a fix on your enemies. Then build a Kbot Lab. Several Core Thud artillery and Instigator tanks will attack from the north. Several Weasels arrive from the west. Your Zeus and Rockos can handle the intrusions while the Commander carries out the building projects. It's important to continue an active defense of your base throughout the game, since such attacks will occur in waves.
- **Begin Kbot Lab production quickly.** Build a half-dozen PeeWees and several Hammer artillery and Rocko rocket launchers for patrol duty on the west and north perimeters of your base. A Light Laser Tower is also helpful on the west perimeter to take care of fast-moving Weasel scout vehicles. Make sure that one of the first orders is to build a Construction Kbot that can soon build an Advanced Kbot Lab.
- **Look to the hills.** In the middle of the map are two hills, one directly above the other (3). The lower of the two hills is a mesa that contains Core resource generators and two or three Light Laser Towers. You are preparing to move a force in that direction to capture the hill, then assault the Core base directly west (4). To get ready for that, once the Kbot Lab is complete order the Commander to build a Vehicle Plant. Keep the Kbot Lab churning out PeeWees, Hammers, and Rockos for base protection. When the Construction Kbot is completed, order it to start on an Advanced Kbot Lab. When the Vehicle Plant comes on line, order it to build several Flash and Stumpy tanks and Jeffy scout vehicles. Keep producing those.
- **Head west.** Form a small strike team consisting of the Commander, a half-dozen PeeWees, six or seven Hammers and Rockos and several Flash light tanks. Head due west from your base to a small hill (2) containing a Core Radar Tower and one or two Light Laser Towers. The Commander can capture one of the LLTs without taking a lot of damage. The easier course is to have your troops destroy the LLTs and then order the Commander to capture the Radar Tower. Control your attack so that your troops don't shoot the Radar Tower.
- **Order the Advanced Kbot Lab to begin production,** creating Zipper fast-attack bots, Fido assault bots, and a couple of Zeus lightning-gun bots. Wherever possible, have your Commander reclaim metal from wrecks as you go along. The Construction Kbot should also reclaim metal at any opportunity. Core Thuds, Weasels, and Raiders will continue to attack your base, aiming for the resource generators and construction plants. Their numbers are small, however.
- **Attack the hill (3).** Use a force of PeeWees, Flash tanks, Hammers, and Rockos to head west toward the two central hills. The west side of the map is thick with Core units, including Instigators, Thuds, Storms, Weasels, Reapers, and the Pyro flame-throwers. Once you have attacked and destroyed the Light Laser Towers on

the hill (3), form a defensive perimeter and prepare to repulse Core Weasels, Storm rocket launchers, and Thud artillery coming from the west. Keep cranking out replacement forces back at the base and sending them to the newly captured hill.

- **Consolidate your attack forces.** As Fidos and Zippers become available, send them to the hills you've just taken. Add in some Stumpy medium tanks, as well. The remainder of the campaign consists of keeping the pressure on against successive waves of Core units. Once the attacks on your forces become less frequent, you may have to search the map to find the last remaining units. Set up a Radar Tower on the central hill to help with that. The mission ends when you destroy the last Core unit and structure.

It's tempting to over-extend your Commander in this mission, especially when attacking the twin hills (3). The fire-power of multiple Light Laser Towers and small groups of Pyros, AKs, and Instigators can quickly overwhelm the Commander.

Mission 5:

The Gate to Thalassean

Difficulty rating: Easy

Objective: Destroy a Core ground force guarding a KBot Lab and a Vehicle Plant, in order to capture the Galactic Gate that Core has used to gain access to Empyrrean. All Core units and structures must be destroyed, and the Commander must capture the Gate for Arm. The Gate must not be destroyed.

Starting forces: Commander and a group of Fidos, Jeffys, Zeus, Lurkers, Skeeters, Tritons, Bulldogs, and Zippers.

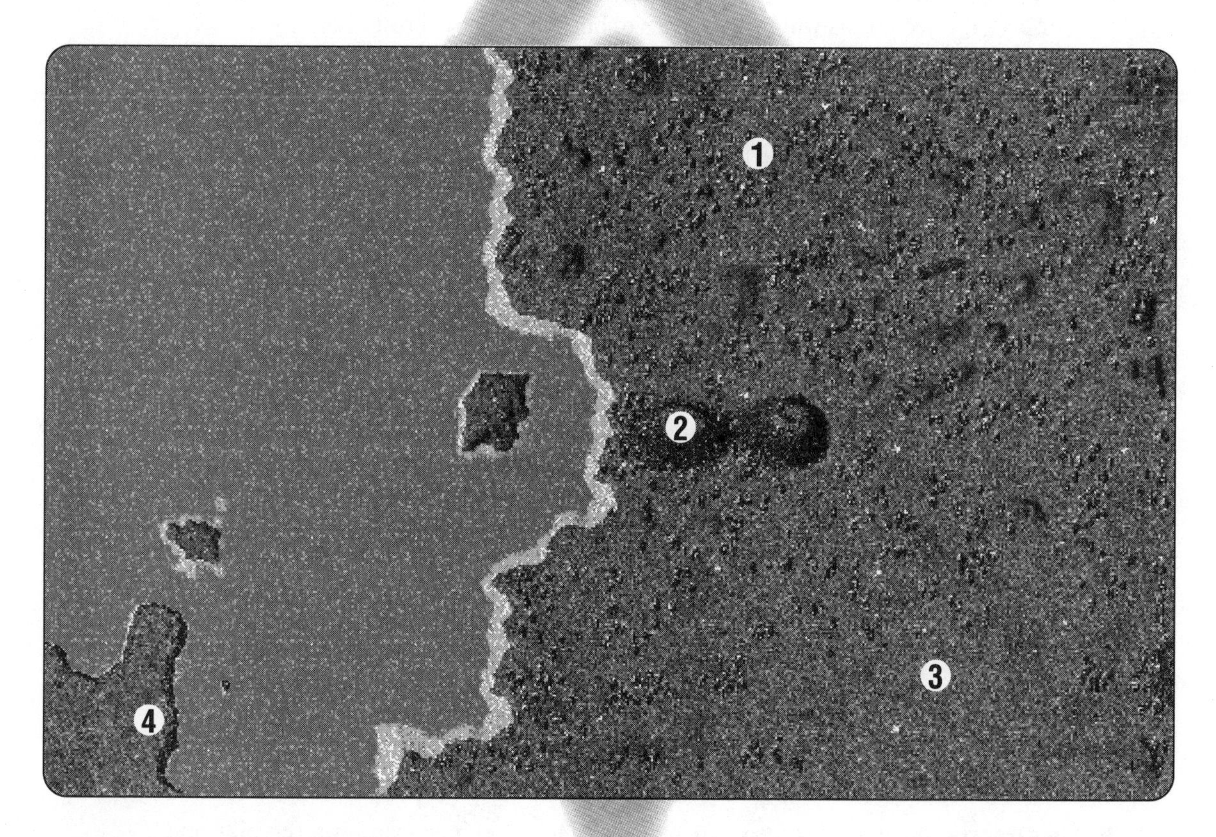

Mission Briefing

Core's remaining forces on Empyrrean have established a base south of your starting position taking up most of the eastern half of the screen. They protect the Galactic Gate through which Core emerged on Thalassean. The Gate is on a small peninsula in the southwest corner of the map. This is primarily a ground campaign that includes a water-based assault using Triton amphibious tanks at the end of the mission. You will move south against Core ground forces, taking over territory in stages. Then, you'll attack the peninsula and capture the Gate.

How to Win

- **Construct a base near the top of the map (1), close to your starting point.** Begin building Metal Extractors, Wind Generators, and a few Solar Collectors. Establish a perimeter facing south with Fidos, Zippers, Jeffys, Zeus, and the two Bulldogs. As you build your base, Thud, A.K., and Storm units will begin to attack in several small waves. The Commander should first build a Kbot Lab, followed by a Vehicle Lab. Have the Kbot Lab start constructing PeeWees, Rockos, and Hammers. Build Jeffy scout vehicles and Flash tanks with the Vehicle Plant.

- **Secure the northern area, then expand in stages to the two hills to the south (2).** Core forces will be aggressive, but not overpowering. Leave your sea units—the Skeeters, Lurkers, and Triton amphibious tanks—where they are at first as you initially build your land forces. As soon as the Kbot Lab and Vehicle Plant are running, build a Construction Kbot and a Construction Vehicle and have them start an Advanced Kbot Lab and an Advanced Vehicle Plant. Use PeeWees and Jeffys on the outer ring of your base defenses, with Flash, Zipper, and Zeus units close to them. Just behind that outer line, place Hammers, Rockos, and the two Bulldog tanks.

- **Build an Advanced Vehicle Plant and Advanced Kbot Lab.** Your goals with these plants are to have the Advanced Vehicle Plant construct Triton tanks for the peninsula assault later on, and to have the Advanced Kbot Lab build more Zipper, Zeus, and Fido assault bots. Core will continue to send Thud, Storm, and Instigator units toward your base from the south. Your two Skeeter scout ships can harass the Storm rocket launchers on the two hills near the center of the screen, but keep them moving back and forth to avoid the rockets.

- **Construct Guardian plasma cannon.** As your forces fight back the Core attacks, move in increments further south until you can attack the two hills you'll find about halfway down the map. The Bulldog and Flash tanks can lead the short-range charges, bolstered by Zippers and PeeWees, and backed up by Fidos, Hammers, and Rockos. When you've gained the hills, have either of your mobile construction units build a Guardian plasma cannon on top of the leftmost hill. Keep moving your ground troops around and in front of the hills to prevent Core artillery from targeting the heights.

- **Destroy remaining Core ground troops.** When you have captured the hills and built your Guardian, you will have broken the back of the Core defenses. They will still try to attack, but the Guardian and your troops on the hills should be able to repulse their counterattacks without much difficulty. There are a Core Kbot Lab and Vehicle Plant near the southeast edge of the map (3). Your Commander can capture these, but you don't need their production to win.

- **Send Tritons to wipe out the Galactic Gate defenders.** As you are mopping up remaining Core units in the east, assemble your Triton tanks into two strike groups. By now, your Advanced Vehicle Plant should have built eight to ten Tritons. Move them east to the water. Your two subs can lead the way toward the southwest corner of the map, followed by your Skeeters, and your Tritons. The peninsula (4) you find is packed with Gaat Guns, Pulverizers, Crashers, and Thuds, so the attack is not easy at first. Order your subs to sink the one Searcher scout ship patrolling near the base. The Skeeters can provide some covering fire as a distraction, but they won't last long. Order the Tritons to simultaneously attack the peninsula from the west side and the east side—three or four per side. There isn't much land space on which to come ashore at the peninsula, so make sure you space the Tritons out to have them all surface at about the same time—not one after another.

- **Concentrate fire on the Pulverizers and Gaat Guns.** As the attack begins, have your Commander positioned underwater near the peninsula. It will take two or three waves of Tritons to take care of the Core defenders. As the Core defense is slowly overwhelmed, bring your Commander up to the shore to help finish. It is very important that none of the tanks target the Galactic Gate itself. If it is destroyed, you lose your chance to capture it and take the war off world. Finally, order the Commander to capture the Gate, and you've swept Core from Empyrrean.

Mission 6:

Beachhead on Thalassean

Difficulty rating: Medium

Objective: Your Commander has just stepped through a Galactic Gate to Thalassean, a windy planet largely covered by water. Secure the island on which the Commander lands, then withstand the attacks of Core naval units. You must destroy all Core units in this mission to win. This is the first step in driving Core from Thalassean in a future mission.

Starting force: Commander

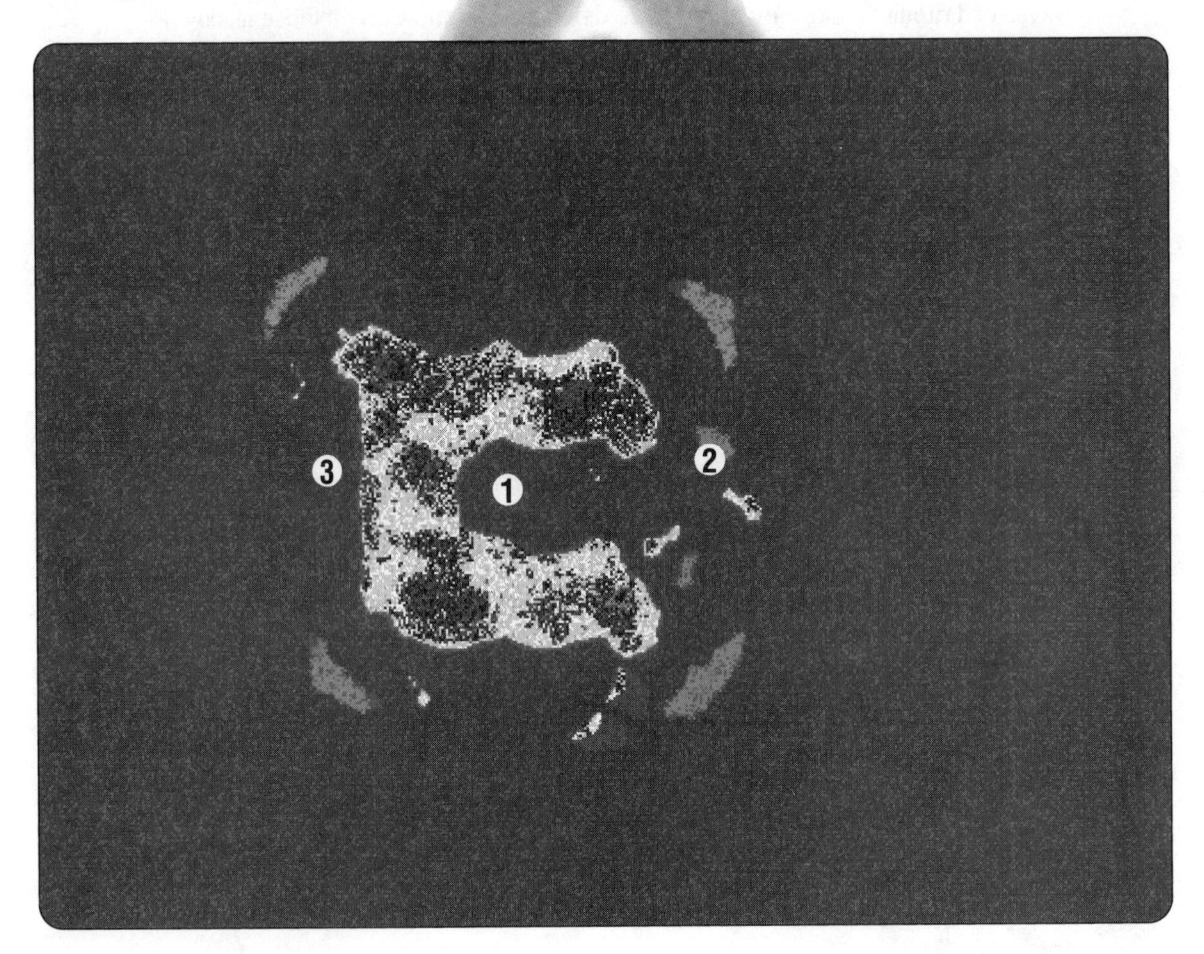

Mission Briefing

This is primarily a siege mission in which your Commander must hold the island, building a Shipyard and a Kbot plant to generate ships, artillery Kbots, and Guardian plasma cannons to repulse the naval attacks. Be ready for immediate defensive measures when the Commander steps through the Gate.

How to Win

- **Have the Commander shoot the Core welcoming party of AKs.** Try not using the Disintegrator Gun, then reclaim the metal A.K. remains. Build three Metal Extractors and three Wind Generators. Remember that this is a windy planet. You will have to watch for one or two Core Searcher scout ships in the harbor. Have the Commander destroy them. A forest fire may result from your A.K. battle. There is not much metal on Thelassean, so order the Commander to reclaim metal from wreckage.

- **Get power resources up and running.** Once resource generators are going, build a Shipyard in the protected harbor (1). Order the Shipyard to build two Lurker submarines, followed by a Construction Ship, a couple of Crusader destroyers, and then more subs. There still remain a couple of AKs on the island—either capture or destroy them. You must keep building ships as fast as possible.

- **Prepare for the onslaught.** Core naval units will come at you from several directions, particularly from east and west. Put a couple of subs at the mouth of the small harbor (2) until you can get your Construction Ship there to build a couple of Torpedo Launchers. The Construction Ship can also reclaim metal from sunken ships. Don't risk using the Commander for this dangerous job. The Commander is slow and has no defenses under water. Build a small fleet of Lurkers and Crusaders, plus a couple of Skeeter scout ships to be able to counterattack against Core ships.

- **Destroy Core Snake subs and Enforcer destroyers.** These Core units are patrolling just outside the harbor. They will be aggressive. Keep at least two subs near the mouth of the harbor at all times to prevent Core ships from entering. Move the Commander over to the west side of the island (3) to build a Kbot Lab. You need to build six to eight Hammer artillery units to target Core surface ships that will come in to destroy Arm forces on the island. The Hydra missile frigates are the most deadly, but the Enforcers can cause damage as well. You'll also want to build a Construction Kbot that can start creating Guardian stationary plasma cannons along the western shoreline. The Guardians are excellent choices for island defense.

- **Take subs and destroyers to the west side of the island.** As your navy grows, dispatch a small squad of ships, including two or three subs and two destroyers, around the north side of the island to the west coast and set up patrols there.

- **Build an Advanced Shipyard.** As soon as the Advanced Shipyard is constructed, build a couple of Piranha attack subs and two Conqueror cruisers. The cruiser's long-range guns will help against surface ships, and the Piranhas are very effective against Core subs.

- **Keep your units mobile and aggressive.** Core will run out of ships eventually, and the attacks will slow down and then stop altogether. You may have to send out your ships to hunt down the last one or two Core units. Your strategy should be to keep the Hammers busy, moving around the island in response to Core naval attacks. When the Hammers' health drops to half-strength or less, have the Commander or Construction Kbot repair them. Have at least two Guardian cannons pounding Core surface ships; and be very aggressive with your subs, especially when you get the Piranhas.

Mission 7:

The Defense of Larab Harbor

Difficulty rating: Medium

Objective: Defend Larab Harbor and your crucial Moho Mine from a series of Core naval and air attacks. There's little metal on Thelassean, and the Moho Mine must be intact when the onslaught ends for you to continue the war against Core.

Starting forces: An unfinished harbor base with Shipyard; Dragon's Teeth protect the shoreline in front of the Moho Mine, Jethros provide some air cover, and a Guardian plasma cannon sits next to the Moho Mine.

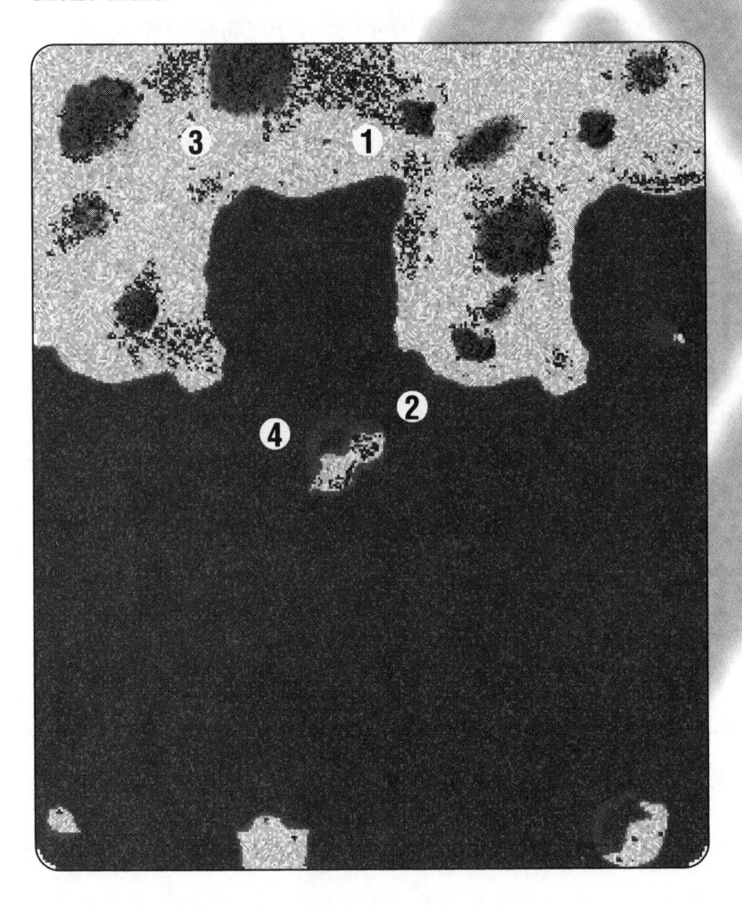

Mission Briefing

A large Core fleet is south of your position, sending waves of naval and air units. Expect Crock amphibious tanks as well. The key to this mission is to produce enough naval units to withstand the onslaught by sea and enough anti-air cover to knock out the Core planes before they destroy the Moho Mine (1). Continually reclaiming metal and repairing the Moho Mine are crucial to victory. You are under much more time pressure in this mission to build and deploy units and structures before you're overwhelmed.

How to Win

- **Prepare for an immediate Core attack.** A Core Enforcer destroyer and Hydra missile frigate will arrive almost immediately (2). Searcher scout ships will follow, and then a squadron of Shadow bombers will begin laying down clusters of bombs at the west end of your base (3). Your first move should be to relocate your Ranger missile ship slightly south to avoid being a stationary target when the Hydra arrives. Also move your Skeeters and Crusader toward the Core naval targets (2). Move a couple of Jethros and a Samson to the west end of the base for better anti-aircraft fire against the Shadows.

- **Order the Shipyard to produce a Construction Ship and several Lurker subs.** You must hurry to produce subs that can get to the southeast mouth of the harbor before more Core ships arrive. The Construction Ship, when completed, should immediately begin to build an Advanced Shipyard to produce Piranha attack subs, Ranger missile ships, and Conqueror cruisers as soon as possible. Order the Commander to repair the Moho Mine from any bomber damage, then have him reclaim metal and start to build a Vehicle Plant. The Vehicle Plant will supply you with Samson anti-air missile trucks initially, then a Construction Vehicle that will build Defender missile towers and Guardian plasma cannons to repel air and sea attacks, respectively.

- **Order your Construction Ship to reclaim metal from underwater wreckage.** The Construction Ship should then set up several Torpedo Launchers at the harbor opening, protected by subs while this is going on. This is a tricky part of the mission because of the recurring Core naval attacks. The Commander should build a few more Solar Collectors or Wind Generators and reclaim metal. When the Commander ventures into the water to reclaim metal, The Construction Vehicle should be kept close to the Moho Mine for repairs while it builds a couple of Guardians and Defenders.

- **Build two more Construction Ships to reclaim metal.** The point when you do this can vary, depending on how successful you've been at beating back repeated Core attacks. You must maintain the energy and metal levels sufficiently high to allow the Advanced Shipyard to build the more expensive attack subs, missile ships, cruisers, and battleships you need to stop Core. The Construction Vehicle should be producing anti-air units and repairing damages on those that exist.

- **Remember that your main goal is protection of the Moho Mine.** Do not launch ships to attack Core on the open sea. Core has a very large fleet, but they do not all attack at once. You must be prepared for successive waves, so trying to launch an offensive is foolish. Have a Construction Ship build Torpedo Launchers at both harbor openings (2 and 4).

- **Group your defenders near the Moho Mine.** Crock amphibious tanks will enter the harbor and head for the Moho Mine. If you have your subs and Torpedo Launchers in place, they may not reach the beaches. If they do, however, the Dragon's Teeth will block them long enough for you to focus fire from Hammer,

Jethro, and Samson units. If your Commander is within a short distance of the Moho Mine, this might be a good time to use the Disintegrator Gun—but don't expose the Commander if he or she is less than fully healthy.

- **When the onslaught ends, so should the mission.** Attacks will slowly trail off and then stop. By now, you should have at least a couple of cruisers, several destroyers, a couple of missile ships, and six to ten Lurker and/or Piranha subs remaining. If the mission does not end, it is safe at that point to hunt out any remaining Core ships. Core does not continue to build forces, so there are no factories to destroy.

If you build subs fast enough and position them just outside the southeast corner of the harbor, it is possible to block up the entranceway with wreckage. This can make it difficult for more Core surface ships to come into the harbor from that direction.

Mission 8:

The Gate to Tergiverse IV

Difficulty rating: Hard

Objective: Build a naval strike force to attack Core forces across several heavily defended islands. Have your Commander capture the Galactic Gate that leads to the planet Tergiverse IV. You must not destroy the Gate.

Starting forces: Commander and a small force on an island base at the south of the map. Base contains a Shipyard and a small group of Jethro anti-air Kbots and Hammer artillery Kbots, along with several Lurker subs, a handful of Skeeter scout ships, a Crusader destroyer, and a Ranger missile ship.

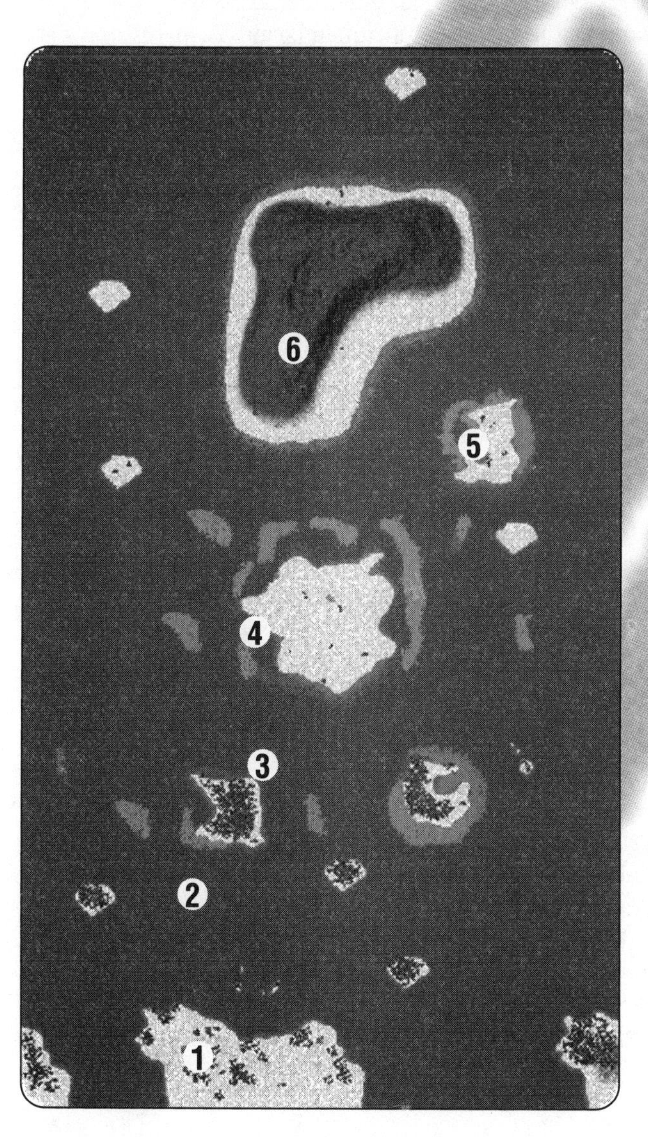

Mission Briefing

This is a prolonged naval-assault mission in which you must build your base to withstand repeated Core naval and air attacks while, at the same time, you prepare to expand your navy for an assault on several Core islands. You build your navy to Level-2 strength, then expand in a series of island-hopping moves. There are three key islands (4, 5, 6) for you to take over. On the final assault (6), your troops must not blow up the Galactic Gate by accident. This is a long and rigorous mission. Save your game position frequently.

How to Win

- **Build a Construction Ship.** Start building it right away, giving secondary orders to the Shipyard for several Lurker subs. You aggressively build up your navy to succeed. The other priority is building a Radar Tower. Begin energy and metal generation on the island. Metal is scarce here; you'll have to reclaim metal from every sunken ship that you can reach as this mission unfolds. You'll spend its first part defending your base from both aerial and naval attacks coming in several waves. While the Construction Ship is being built, arrange your Lurker subs, Skeeters, Crusader, and Ranger to patrol close to your base, between points 1 and 2. Order the Construction Ship to set up Torpedo Launchers in the same area-at least three. Have your Commander build a Vehicle Plant so that you can generate Samson mobile missile launchers to go along with the Jethros on your main island. Also build a Construction Vehicle that can later make Guardian plasma cannons and Defender missile towers for base defense.

- **Expand slowly, using islands as buffers against naval attacks.** A buffer of four small islands offers some protection from naval assaults. Concentrate your defenses among the three channels between the four islands. Order the Commander to walk over to the island directly west of point 2, and then build a Radar Tower. After the Construction Ship has completed the Torpedo Launchers, order it to build an Advanced Shipyard just south of the first Shipyard. Keep the first Shipyard busy building subs, destroyers, and scouts, and a couple of Hulk transports.

- **Build a Guardian on the island at point 3.** When you add Level-2 Piranha attack subs, Ranger missile ships, and Conqueror cruisers to your navy, start your preparations for an assault on the center island (4). As you're preparing for this, your Torpedo Launchers and subs may detect and attack six or seven Crock amphibious tanks that were launched from the center island (4). The Dragon's Teeth on your shoreline will help the eight to ten Flash and Stumpy tanks and Samson mobile missile launchers you should maintain as a base defense force. After a couple of hours, you should have a sizable naval force with a variety of Level-2 ships, and good anti-air cover from Jethros. Your territory should have expanded to include the island at point 3. To help with this, Core Torpedo Launchers can be taken out by having your destroyer shell them while staying just out of reach. Have a Hulk transport take a Construction Vehicle to the island at point 3, and begin building a Guardian long-range plasma cannon that will be used against the island at point 4.

- **Assault and capture (4).** Your first big assault should contain several Conquerors, a couple of Millenium battleships, several Rangers, and a handful each of Lurkers, Crusaders, and Skeeters. If your Guardian and the cruisers and battleships have been shelling the island at point 4, then the assault won't be as tough. A lot will be going on at the same time, however, so don't forget to use the minus (-) and plus (+) keys to slow things down or speed things up as necessary. Have your Hulks bring along a dozen anti-air units, such as Jethros and Samsons, to help fight off what's left of the Core air force.

- **Use the island (4) as a staging area.** You'll be on the receiving end of significant artillery shelling from the islands at points 5 and 6. Don't overlook the smaller island (5), which contains a couple of Gaat Guns and Pulverizers. One option to help secure the main island is to have an Advanced Vehicle Plant at your original base that cranks out Triton amphibious tanks. A Hulk can take six of them to your staging area just before the final big push.

- **Control your final assault.** The real danger as you begin your final assault is that your ships will bombard the Galactic Gate by accident, destroying it and any chances of victory just as it is close. Just around the Gate are a few Pyro flamethrower bots and a Pulverizer, Radar Tower, and Wind Generator. By now, you should have either walked the Commander over to island 4 or carried it there aboard a Hulk to capture the Gate. A Guardian cannon on the staging-area island is effective, but direct its fire so that it doesn't hit the Gate. By the time the Commander comes ashore to capture the Gate, almost all of the Core forces should be neutralized. If there are one or two Pyros around, the Commander can handle them himself.

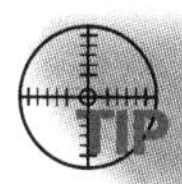

Always keep a Construction Ship with your fleets. They can repair the big ships when they're damaged, and they can continually reclaim metal from sunken ships.

Mission 9:

The Hydration Plant

Difficulty rating: Medium

Objective: Build an aircraft plant, then use your growing air force to neutralize Core's air power and weaken its ground troops. Your Commander must capture the Core Hydration Plant to win this mission. The Hydration Plant must not be destroyed.

Starting forces: Commander

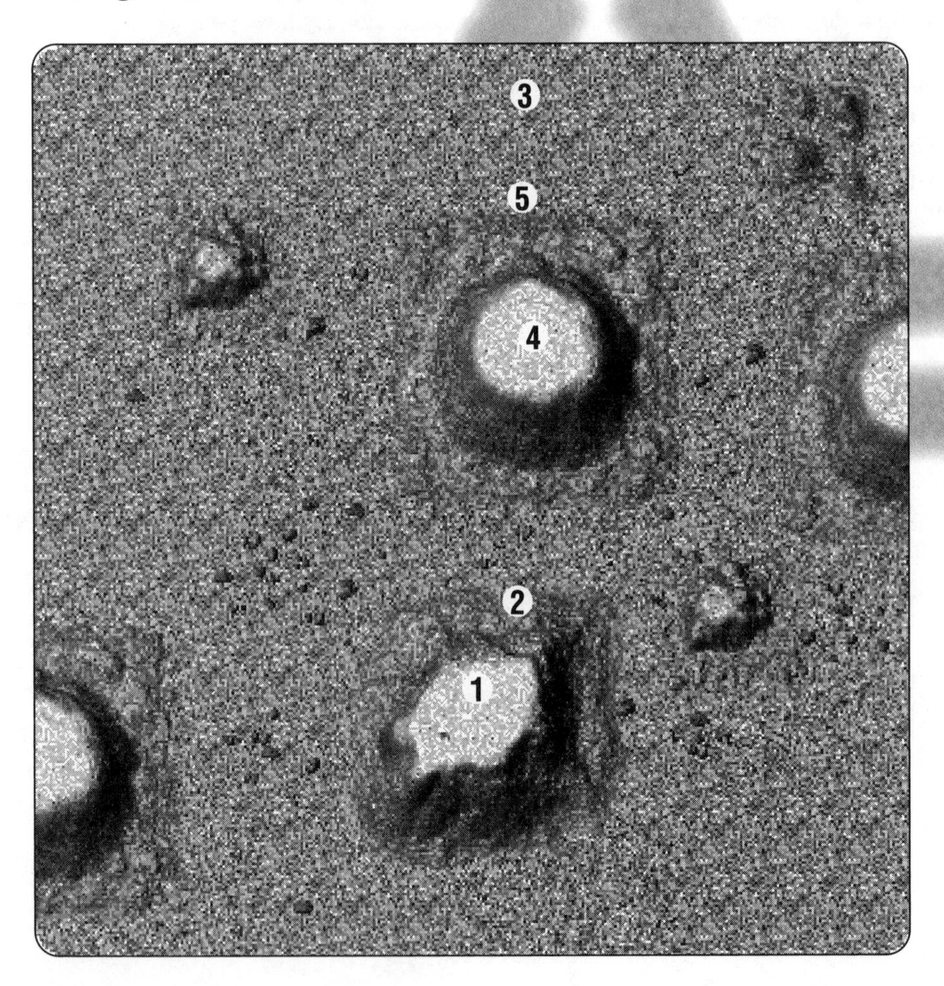

Mission Briefing

This mission introduces Arm air power, and requires you to use aircraft to beat back Core combined air and ground forces. Your Commander begins alone, and must capture Core equipment and build an air base from which to launch Arm attacks. The mission begins on a high butte that Core troops cannot climb. This is a straightforward mission that enables you to learn how to command air units.

How to Win

- **Fight back, then capture.** As the mission begins, two Pyros are attacking your Commander. Shoot them, and then capture the Core Radar Tower and Metal Extractor there. Set up a Radar Tower on the butte and then immediately begin building an Aircraft Plant there as well. Build two Light Laser Towers, one at the south side of the butte and the other on the north side.

- **Build Freedom Fighters and begin patrolling.** Core Avenger fighters will begin to attack your position. The Light Laser Towers will help to ward them off until you get planes into the air. When the first Freedom Fighter is ready, set it patrolling around the top of the base in a tight pattern by clicking on the Patrol button and then, with the Shift key depressed, set the turning points of the patrol route you want it to fly. Have the Commander repair the Light Laser Towers, Metal Extractor, and energy from damage caused by Core aircraft. Your Laser Towers will frequently be firing at Core ground troops at the base of the north and south sides of the butte (2).

- **Launch an air attack against Core aircraft on the ground.** Build Freedom Fighters and then Thunder bombers. Keep the fighters flying on patrol around your base. When your air patrols grow larger, the Core aircraft will begin to diminish. But to wipe them out completely, put together an attack force of at least six to eight Freedom Fighters and a half dozen or more Shadows, then send them to the northern edge of the map (3), where they'll find Avengers still on the ground. Bomb and strafe them until they're all destroyed. In the meantime, keep turning out aircraft, including a couple of Atlas air transports.

- **Walk or fly the Commander to point 4.** Your air force will begin to thin out Core ground troops after a while. But it's still not safe to have the Commander walking too freely among Core troops. Put the Commander on an Atlas and fly over to a butte just north of your base (4). There may be a Light Laser Tower there unless your air force has destroyed it. The Commander can quickly take care of it, and then capture the two Solar Collectors there. Below that butte, just to the north, is the Hydration Plant, surrounded by Dragon's Teeth.

- **Land the Commander next to the Hydration Plant, then capture it.** You can fly the Commander down to the Hydration Plant or, if you are feeling daring, you can walk the Commander down there. There will be some ground troops in the area, but your air force should have knocked out most of them. Capture the plant, and the mission is a success. You don't have to destroy all Core troops to win.

Control your air units better by grouping them into small squads. Use the Ctrl plus 1–9 keys to assign a number to several small groups. Once a squad is selected, then anytime you wish to select them again, use the corresponding Alt plus 1–9 keys to choose them. When you have a lot of aircraft flying, this is the best way to redirect and recall them quickly.

Mission 10:

The Bromid Maze

Difficulty rating: Easy

Objective: Rejoin several isolated Zipper fast-attack Kbots with your Commander, build a base, and then destroy all Core forces on the map to secure Tergiverse IV under Arm control. There is a Core Kbot Lab in the northeast corner of the map (4).

Starting forces: Commander, Zeus, Hammer, and 2 Spiders in south center of map (1); 4 isolated Zippers are in the northwest (2)

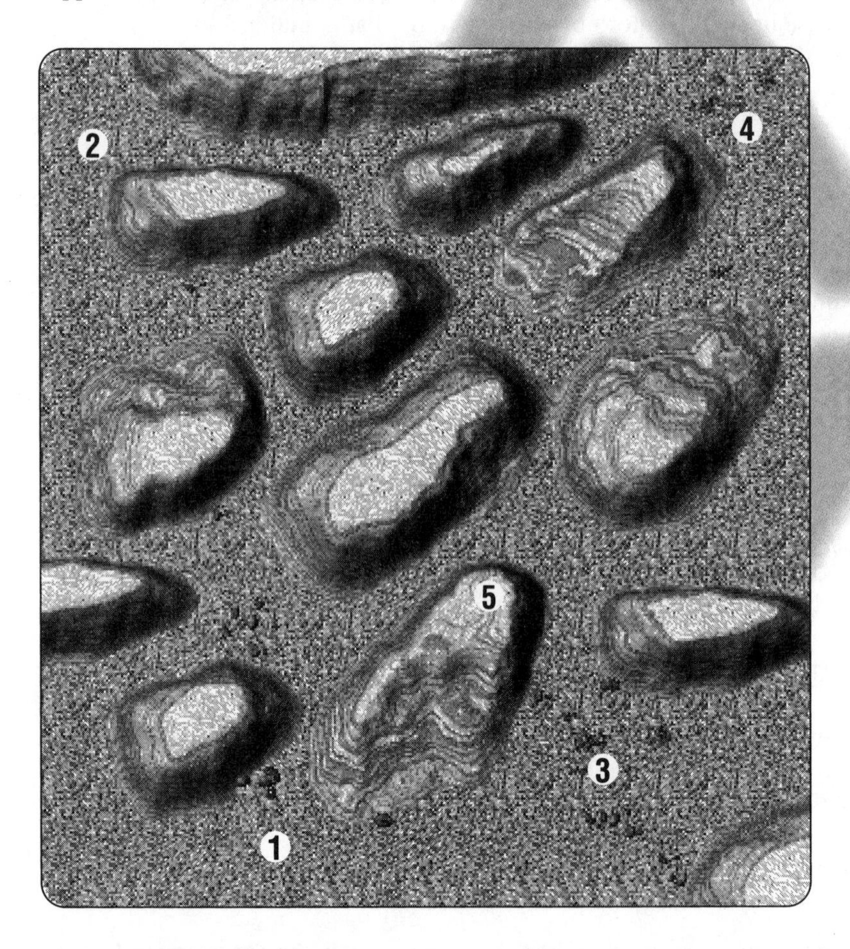

Mission Briefing

Order your Zippers back to your main group. Your small force then needs to seek a good place to the east to set up a base. Develop Kbot, Vehicle, and Aircraft plants in order to assault the Core base in the northeast corner of the map. Core air and ground attacks will come periodically, but you should have little trouble getting established.

How to Win

- **Order Zippers south.** When the mission begins, order the four Zippers in the northwest corner (2) to head straight south next to the west edge of the map. When they encounter a rock outcropping halfway down, move east long enough to get around it, then straight south again. They should move east along the bottom of the map until they rejoin the main group (1).

- **Move your team east to set up a base.** To the east of your group is an open area (3) protected by two mesas. Move your team there, then build a Radar Tower halfway up the rock (5). You will fight off a few Core ground units and several Avenger aircraft, but nothing very serious. Build an Aircraft Plant right next to the south side of the rock (5) to protect it from Core long-range artillery. The Commander will need to reclaim metal from rocks in the area in addition to building a couple of Metal Extractors.

- **Build a Kbot Lab and a Vehicle Lab.** When your Aircraft Plant is finished, order it to build a Construction Aircraft and a 6 Freedom Fighters. You must get Freedom Fighters patrolling above your base asap. They also serve as your eyes to see the Core base. Once the aircraft construction is under way, have your Commander begin a Kbot Lab and then a Vehicle Lab. Core ground and air attacks will come from the northeast.

- **Use Spiders to paralyze Core units, then capture them with the Commander.** When small Core ground units enter the area, it is possible to have one or both of your Spiders paralyze them long enough for the Commander to capture them. This is a good way to bolster your forces early in the game. Begin to make recon runs with your aircraft over the northeast corner of the map. Press the T key to track one of your aircrafts and see what it uncovers as it flies.

- **Build a Guardian above your base (5).** Don't try to move your forces until all three of your construction facilities are making units. Build at least two construction bots. The Construction Aircraft can search the west side of the map for metal deposits to extract and for rocks to reclaim. A Construction Kbot or Construction Vehicle should move to the top of the sheltering rock (5) and begin to build a Guardian plasma cannon. When completed, it will do significant damage along almost all of the enemy base's outer perimeter.

- **Attack the Core base from the south and southwest.** The forces protecting the Core Kbot Lab and surrounding base are a mixed bag. Crasher missile Kbots, Pyro flamethrowers, and Raider tanks patrol along the narrow canyons. By using the radar map to target your Guardian's fire, you can eliminate many of them. There's a Core Punisher plasma cannon atop a rock just southwest of the Kbot Lab (4). By splitting your ground troops into two forces, simultaneously sweep up the eastern edge of the map and along the northern valley just to the west of that. The valleys are narrow, so line up tanks and PeeWees first, followed by covering artillery. Keep your Commander out of the fight until you have destroyed the Punisher.

There's not much metal in the Bromid Maze. Have your Commander and Construction bots reclaim metal from rocks as well as wrecked vehicles.

Mission 11:

The Gate to Barathrum

Difficulty rating: Easy

Objective: The Galactic Gate of Barathrum lies at the east end of a giant gulch. Destroy all Core forces and capture the Gate, which is at the eastern-most end of the gulch. The Gate must not be destroyed.

Starting forces: Commander, 2 Brawler gunships, 2 Jethros, 2 Zippers, 1 Zeus, 1 Fido

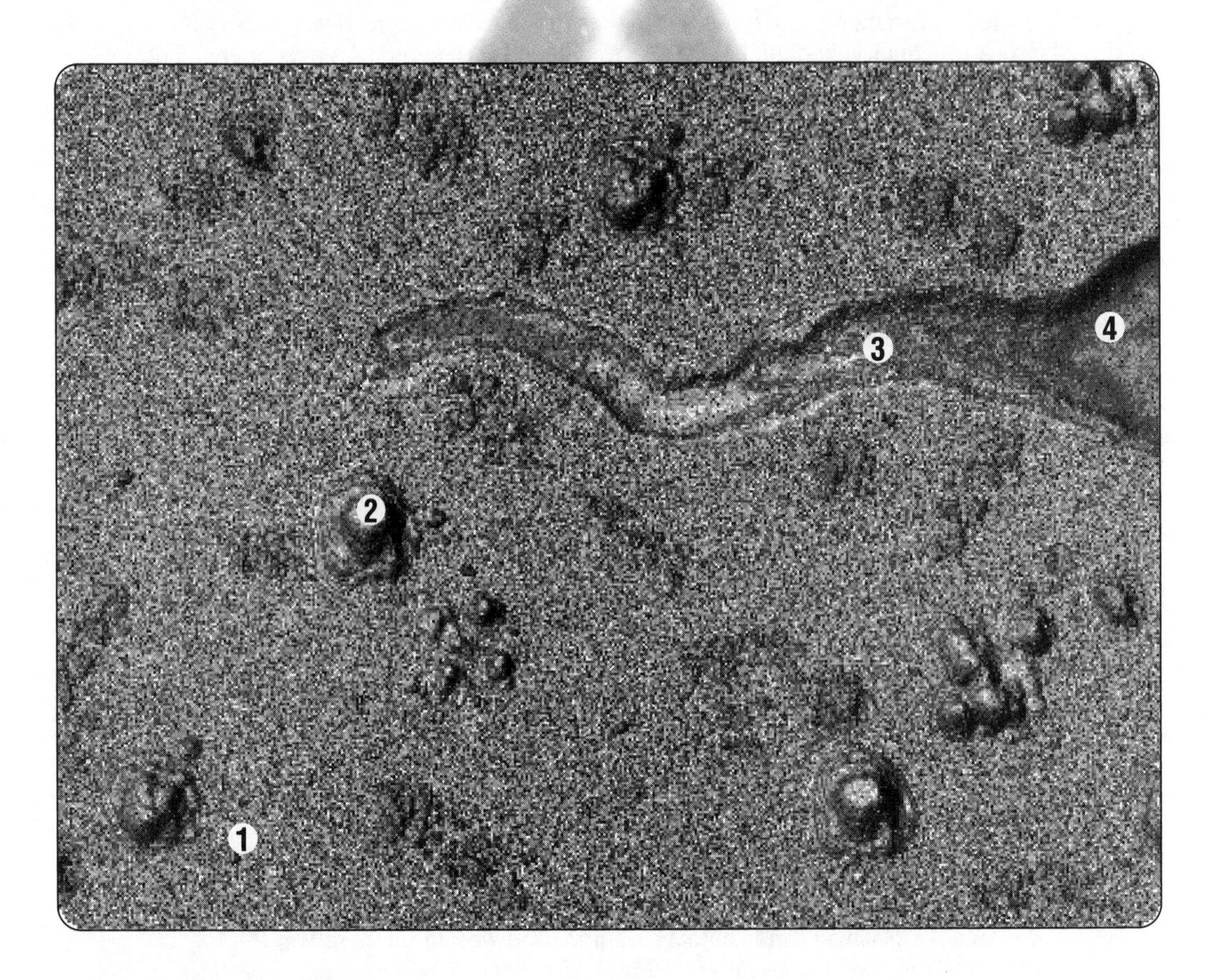

Mission Briefing

There is plenty of energy in this mission, but metal is hard to come by. Construct a base and slowly build your forces to attack the Core base on the east edge of the map (4). Core forces are not aggressive until you begin to attack. This is a good mission in which to practice controlling the accuracy of air strikes and long-range artillery. The mission is not terribly difficult, but management of metal is crucial.

How to Win

- **Start your base (1).** Start the usual energy and metal resource generation at the point at which you open the mission (1), then construct a Vehicle Lab followed by a Radar Tower. Set the Radar Tower on a hill just to the northwest of point 1. Core forces may send a few Avenger aircraft at first, but there is not much pressure during the early stage of the mission. In addition to building Metal Extractors, order the Commander to reclaim metal from rocks in the area. When the Vehicle Plant comes online, first order it to build a Construction Vehicle, then a half-dozen Flash tanks and a half-dozen Samson anti-aircraft missile vehicles.

- **Head for the skies.** Construct an Aircraft Plant near the Vehicle Plant, but leave some room for maneuvering so that new units can be placed on the base perimeter quickly. When it is finished, order it to build seven or eight Freedom Fighters and a half-dozen Thunder bombers. Slowly move your Jethros, Zippers, Zeus, Flash tanks, and Fido forward toward the large butte (2), extending your perimeter. Order your Construction Vehicle to build a Geothermal Power Plant at a steam vent next to the southwest edge of the butte. This should take care of most of your energy generation. Order the Commander to build a Kbot Lab, and then order it to build a Construction Kbot and some PeeWees and Hammers. When the Construction Vehicle has finished building the Geothermal Power Plant, order it to the top of the rock at point 2 to build a Guardian plasma cannon. By now, your perimeter should be pushed out to just beyond point 2.

- **Bombard the Core outer perimeter.** Order your growing air force to patrol in a circle that includes a point just beyond the butte (2). You must protect the Construction Vehicle from attack by placing Samson anti-aircraft vehicles around the base. Keep your Commander scouting for wrecked bots, metal deposits, and rocks to replenish your metal resources. While the Guardian is under construction, have the Commander build a Radar Tower at the base of the butte. When completed, the Guardian can be targeted to hit a variety of Core targets north and east of the butte.

- **Take your attack to the gulch.** It is now time to use your aircraft to soften up the Core defenses in the gulch. There are twin Pulverizer missile towers (3) on either side of the gulch, with twin Gaat Guns farther along to the east on either side of the gulch. Order several Freedom Fighters to carry out flybys of that area to see where the Galactic Gate is located. Freedom Fighters, followed by Thunder bombers, can take out the Pulverizers. That is also the best way to destroy the Gaat Guns and the Punisher plasma cannon that is located just to the west of the Galactic Gate (4). Make sure that your air strikes do not include the Gate itself. Control the aircraft by forming them into squadrons by pressing the the Ctrl and 1–9 keys.

- **Carefully advance against the enemy base.** Air power will take care of most of the defenses. However, you will have to bring a ground force up toward the Gate to take care of four Reaper tanks and other nearby ground troops that are too close to the Gate to be safely destroyed by aircraft. Don't bring up your artillery to shell the Reapers because you will also hit the Gate. At this stage, carefully pick targets, then concentrate the fire of units that have line-of-sight weapons—PeeWees, Zeus,

Zippers, and Jeffys. Your Commander can take part in the ground assault once the Punisher and Gaat Guns are gone. But don't use the D-Gun wildly, because the blast area may destroy the Gate. When the Commander does stroll in to capture the Gate, almost all Core forces should have been destroyed.

If metal resources prove to be too much of a problem, build a Construction Aircraft that can search all over the western half of the map for metal deposits and rocks to reclaim.

Mission 12:

Barathrum!

Difficulty rating: Hard

Objective: Establish a base on Barathrum, build your forces, and launch an assault that will capture Core's Moho Mine in the northeast corner of the map (6). The mine must not be destroyed.

Starting forces: Commander

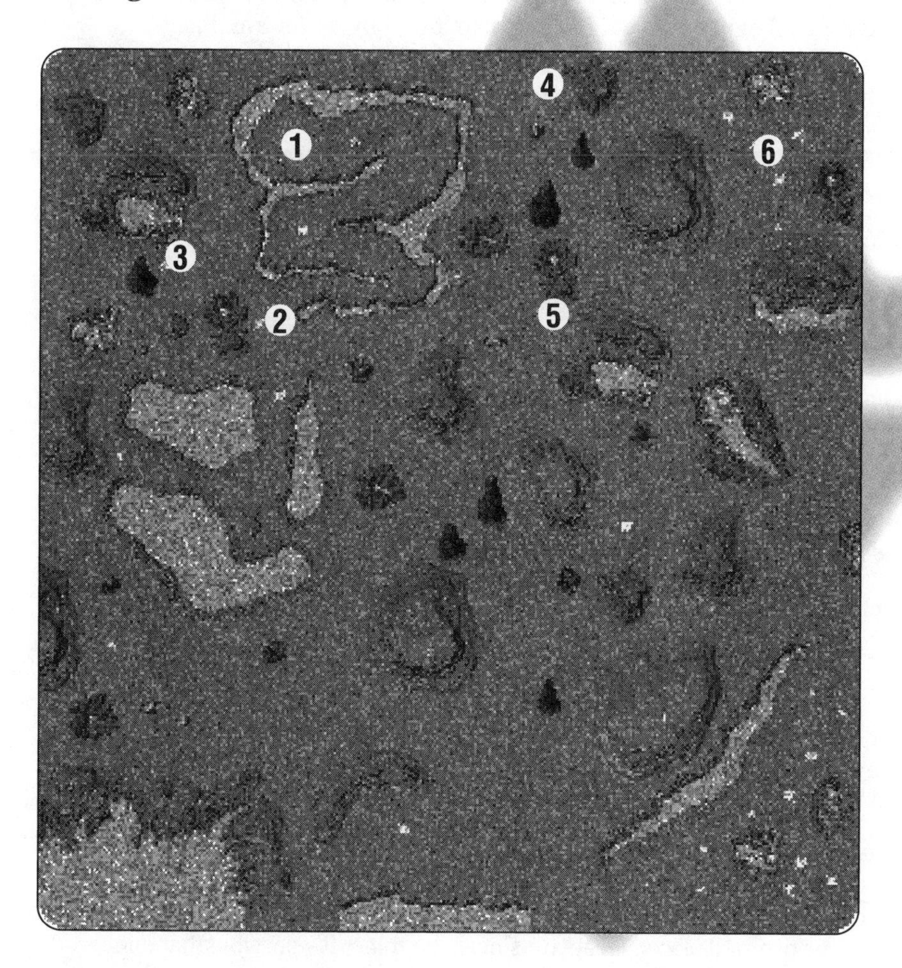

Mission Briefing

Prepare for an extended slugfest! Your Commander steps alone onto Barathrum (1) in a maze of lava flows. Core has an extensive base in the south, including an Aircraft Plant and an Advanced Vehicle Plant. Your goal is to capture a Core Moho Mine in the northeast corner of the map. The Mine is hidden from radar by a Deleter and well protected by Gaat Guns, Pulverizers, and Thuds. You will have to build substantial forces before you can try and take it. Core will send waves of ground and air troops. Metal is plentiful on Barathrum, so plan to build and rebuild as the onslaught continues.

How to Win

- **Follow the lava-lined path.** Move your Commander down the circuitous path where you start (1). You will find a metal deposit to use, and farther on there is a Core Light Laser Tower. You can order the Commander to capture the Tower, although he will take substantial damage doing it. Otherwise, use the D-Gun to destroy the laser.

- **Build a base in the northwest.** You have a few minutes before Core sends in some Weasel scouts and then a couple of air attacks. Find more metal deposits for your Metal Extractors, and then begin to build a Kbot Lab, followed by an Aircraft Plant. Don't forget to build a Radar Tower, as well. You will need Jethro anti-aircraft units, as well as Hammers and PeeWees from the Kbot Lab. Also, build a Construction Kbot. Once the Aircraft Plant is up and running, build a couple of Peeper scouts to scour the map for you. Order a Construction Aircraft and a half-dozen each of Freedom Fighters and Thunder bombers.

- **Build and rebuild.** Core will regularly send attacking units, including Weasels, Thuds, Slashers, and Storms. By air, expect both Avenger fighters and Shadow bombers. Establish an air defense with Jethros, and order your Construction Kbot to build several Defender missile towers around your base (3). Order patrols of Freedom Fighters to circle the perimeter of your base as added air protection. As the mission continues, order both your Construction Kbot and your Construction Aircraft to build, respectively, an Advanced Kbot Lab and an Advanced Aircraft Plant.

- **Prepare for a Core assault.** Your growing air force can begin to target the Gaat Guns and Thuds that are just to the west of the Moho Mine (6). You can send your Commander along the top of the map to help destroy some of the defending units there. But make sure the Commander only stays long enough to destroy one of the Gaat Guns near point 6, then heads back to the base. Core will respond to these attacks with a big assault from the south. Your Advanced Kbot Lab should be supplying you with Zippers, Fidos, and a few Zeus units. In addition, build an Eraser radar jammer to cut down on your radar profile. The Advanced Aircraft Plant can supply you with a few Brawler gunships, which can hover near targets that they are attacking. A half-dozen of these can help to diminish Core forces. Continue to have your Construction Kbot build Sentinel lasers for base defense.

- **Go after the Gaats.** The Core attacks will finally peter out, but not without an extended period of intense battle. When you notice a slowdown, use your air force to scout the remaining Core forces to the south. It is now time to go in for the Moho Mine (6); that means destroying one or two well-placed Gaat Guns near the mine. It's possible that one of them may have been destroyed, if you brought your Commander in for the guerrilla attack mentioned earlier. Attacking from points 4 and 5, use line-of-sight, short-range weapons—such as those from Zeus, Zipper, PeeWee, and Fido units—for any targets near the mine. Control their fire by selecting the units as a group and then picking out the individual targets you want to destroy. The Moho Mine must not be destroyed.

Barathrum has many rock-like nodes scattered across the planet. They contain significant amounts of energy that your Commander can reclaim to replenish energy levels.

Mission 13:

Landown's Interface

Difficulty rating: Hard

Objective: Find a way over the extremely high wall known as Landown's Interface, a natural rift running east-west that was created by shifts in Barathrum's planetary crust. Set up a base, then attack the large Core base to the north of the rift. You must destroy all Core elements.

Starting forces: Commander, 4 Jethros, 1 Zeus, 4 Zippers, 1 Fido

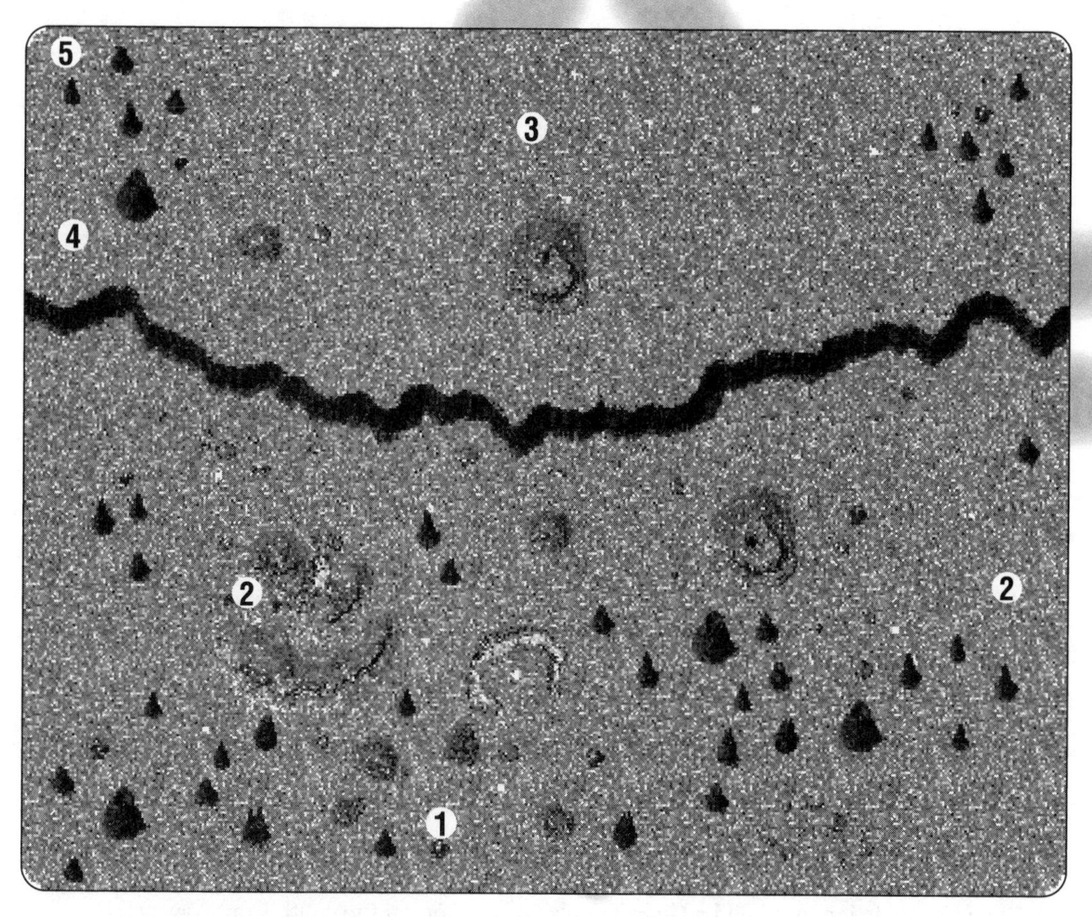

Mission Briefing

Landown's Interface cannot be successfully scaled by ground troops. You must establish a base near the point at which you begin the mission (1), build your resources, then construct Atlas air transports that will carry construction units to the northwest corner (5) of the map. You must set up a base there, and build your forces to defeat a large ground army being built by Core (3). Success requires a strong air force and a sustained buildup over an extended period of time. Expect heavy fighting once you're established on the north side of the Interface.

How to Win

- **Set up a well-fortified base (1), including an Aircraft Plant.** Core will send in Avenger fighters almost immediately. There is plenty of metal for your buildup, and the energy nodes that dot the landscape should be tapped by the Commander whenever possible. To the east of your base are rocks that also add to your metal resources. Send a Construction Aircraft to two steam vents (2) to build one or two Geothermal Power Plants. Use Jethros and, later, Samsons to offer some protection for the plants from air attacks. They are far enough away from Landown's Interface to be safe from the Core Gaat Guns and Pulverizers that dot the wall.

- **Anticipate Core's buildup.** North of the Interface, Core is assembling a huge land force consisting of Reapers, Instigators, Slashers, Weasels, The Cans, Crashers, and Pyros—just about anything that moves (3). The faster you move, the fewer units you have to contend with. Have your Aircraft Plant keep building Freedom Fighters, Thunder bombers, and a half-dozen Atlas air transports. You will use the Atlas to ferry units over the wall. Use Freedom Fighters to get glimpses of where the gun emplacements are. Order a Construction Aircraft to build an Advanced Aircraft Plant. You will need Hawks, Brawlers, and Phoenix bombers to help overwhelm the enemy later in the mission.

- **Destroy the far-west Gaat Gun.** Mounted on the Interface wall, at the far west, is a Core Gaat Gun (4). Use Freedom Fighters and Thunder bombers to destroy it. At this time, also intensify your air attacks on the main area of Core's buildup (3), targeting gun emplacements. Once the Gaat Gun is gone, it's easier to sneak Atlas air transports back and forth, bringing Construction units to build a base.

- **Build up air forces in the south and land forces in the north.** Once across the Interface, order your mobile Construction unit to build a Kbot Lab, then a Vehicle Lab. Your goal is to produce as many anti-air Jethros and Samsons as possible, mixing in some PeeWees and Rockos as well as Flash and Stumpy tanks. Try to avoid being drawn into large battles until your ground forces grow muscles. Air attacks by Avengers and Rapiers will continue to be a problem for a while.

- **Pound with air units, drive with ground units.** With your new base growing, Core suddenly finds itself facing a two-front war. Your air units sweep up from the south across the Interface. Your ground units are pushing east from the northwest corner. Core has had time to build a large ground force, even though its air power will by now have dwindled. Prepare for a long series of attacks followed by consolidating gains. By having a Construction unit build a Guardian plasma cannon on the south front—away from shorter range Pulverizers—you can shell the Landown heights from the south.

It is possible to sneak a Construction Aircraft to the very northwest corner of the map early in the game. Send the aircraft from your base (1) due west to the edge of the map. Then, fly the aircraft all the way to the top left corner of the map, hugging the map's west edge the entire way. Once there, start building a Kbot or Vehicle Plant. You must keep your troops up there on Return Fire so that they do not start shooting and give themselves away too soon. This approach can speed up the start of your offensive in the north.

Mission 14:

The Heat Increases

Difficulty rating: Hard

Objective: Build your forces to sufficient strength to assault a well-entrenched Core stronghold and capture the Galactic Gate. The Gate must not be destroyed.

Starting forces: Commander, 4 Fidos, 4 Zippers, 2 Jethros

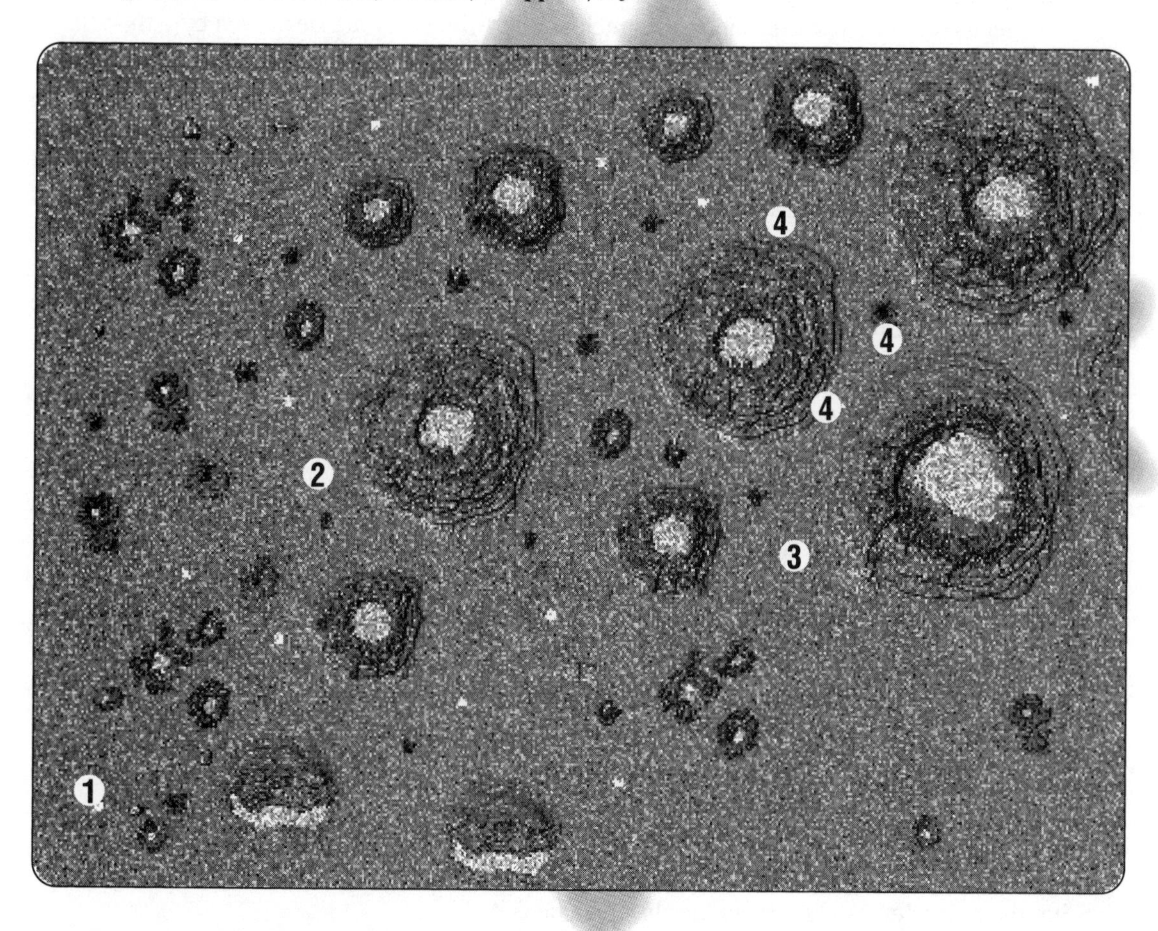

Mission Briefing

This mission is a tank commander's nightmare. Core has dug in on the east side of the map with three Punisher plasma cannons (4) and plenty of supporting Gaat Guns, Pulverizers, Reaper tanks, and other ground units. The relatively flat landscape, interrupted by lava pits, is easily defended against attacking forces. There are also Rapier and Avenger fighters. They are all protecting the Galactic Gate (5) that you must capture. Core introduces some two dozens of its Roach crawling bombs, many of which start to head in your direction when the mission begins. You will use combined air and ground forces to chip away at the defenses so that the Commander can capture the Gate.

How to Win

- **Stomp out the Roaches.** As soon as the mission opens, have the Commander begin to build Solar Collectors, Metal Extractors, and a Radar Tower. Then order a Kbot Lab and a Vehicle Plant. While this is going on place several Fidos and Zippers in a line along a perimeter in front of the base (1). About two dozen Roach crawling bombs are spread out in the area to the north and northeast (2). Use the radar signals to spot the crawling bombs and have your perimeter units shoot them before they get too close. A crawling bomb can destroy half a screen when it self-destructs, so shoot them before they get too close. Their explosions are much weaker when they are destroyed by your fire. A couple of Light Laser Towers will help get rid of them.

- **Establish aerial defenses and recon.** For the first half-hour or so, get used to the steady stream of explosions and screen-rocking that occurs when a Roach is destroyed. During this period, complete the Kbot Lab and the Vehicle Plant and start building a Construction Kbot and a Construction Vehicle. Then order the Commander to build an Aircraft Plant. Core Avengers will attack, but not in large quantities. You have time to build a solid force of Kbots, vehicles, and aircraft during this period.

- **Destroy the Punisher plasma cannons.** Air power is the best way to destroy the Punishers, Pulverizers, and Gaat Guns guarding the Galactic Gate. You can control your air strikes more accurately than you can artillery barrages; and you can't afford to accidentally blow up the Gate. Target the Fusion Power Plant next to the northernmost Punisher (4) with bombers and fighters. When a Fusion Power Plant is destroyed, it takes out everything within a two-screen radius. That means that the northernmost Punisher will be destroyed as well.

- **Watch out for Rapiers.** When Core Rapiers start to attack, use your air defenses to keep them from effectively targeting the Commander. As you prepare for your assaults against the Core stronghold, build as many Stumpy and Bulldog tanks as you can. Near point 3, there are two Gaat Guns surrounded by Reaper tanks. Use your air power to knock out at least one of the Gaat Guns.

- **Go to your Merls.** Build an Advanced Vehicle Plant and an Advanced Kbot Lab. Start constructing Merl rocket launchers to help remove the Core Pulverizers, Gaat Guns, and Reapers. Take a force of Merls, Bulldogs, Zippers and Fidos to point 3 to blow away the southern flank of Core defenses. At the same time, keep your air force, now including Phoenix strategic bombers and Hawk stealth fighters, pounding the other defenses approaching the Galactic Gate.

- **Control the final assault.** As with any mission in which you must capture a Galactic Gate, use air power and line-of-sight ground troops to focus your fire away from the Gate itself. If you have been successful in knocking out the Fusion Power Plant in the north, then a southern approach to the Gate is best. If you have not destroyed the plant, then approaching from the north is more time consuming, but better prevents accidentally destroying the Gate.

Don't try a strong ground attack, such as a tank rush, until your air force has removed one or two of the Punishers. Their shots are very accurate and chew up ground units in a hurry.

Mission 15:

Rougpelt

Difficulty rating: Easy

Objective: Your Commander steps onto the planet Rougpelt alone and must capture a Core Advanced Radar Tower. A wounded Arm Zipper is near the Galactic Gate when the Commander arrives.

Starting forces: Commander, Zipper

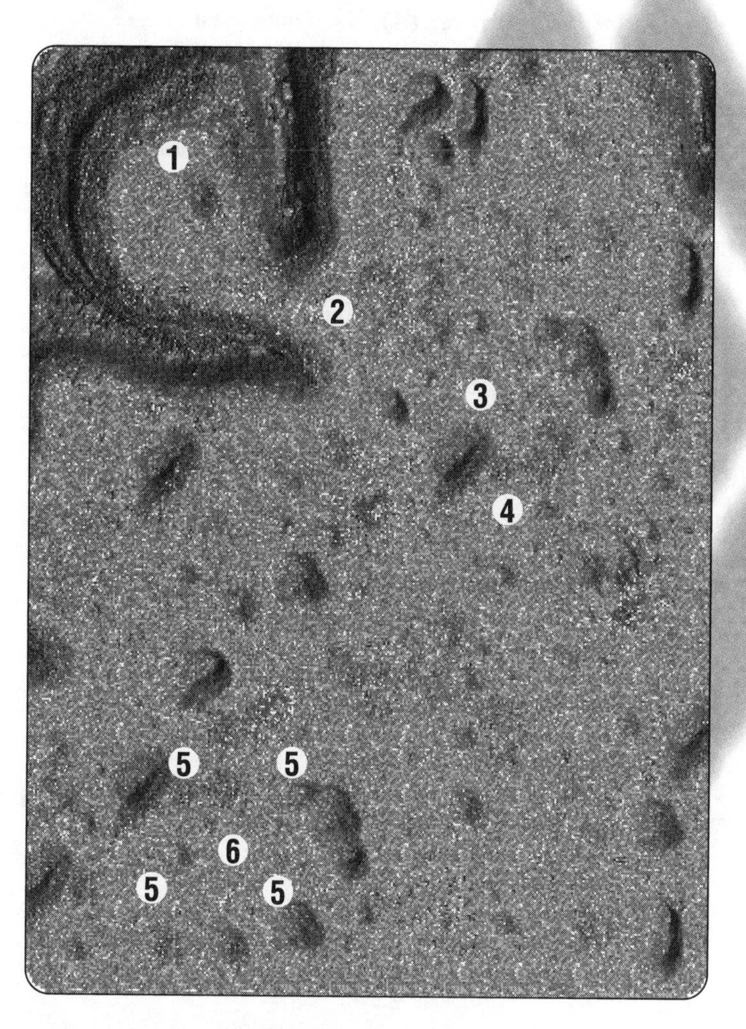

Mission Briefing

This mission is a change of pace. Your Commander steps through the Galactic Gate (1) onto Rougpelt to find a damaged Zipper as the last remaining member of an Arm advance team. The Commander must capture an Advanced Radar Tower in the south (6). Roaming Core units are in the way. You don't have to destroy all of the Core units to claim victory in this mission.

How to Win

- **Shoot the AKs and repair the Zipper.** As your Commander steps onto Rougpelt, a damaged Arm Zipper will come toward the Galactic Gate. Order the Zipper behind the Commander. Two or three AKs will be following the Zipper. The Commander can use the laser or the Disintegrator Gun on all three. When they are out of the way, repair the Zipper and move them both east to the mouth of the small canyon in which they are standing. Build a Radar Tower there to spot enemy troops.

- **Move to two Solar Collectors (3) and a Radar Tower (4).** Head southeast of your position toward two Core Solar Collectors (3). A couple of Core Weasels will confront you. Your Commander and can handle them easily. Next, capture one or both of the Solar Collectors to supplement energy reserves. Just beyond the Solar Collectors, there's a Core Radar Tower (4). Try to destroy nearby Core units before approaching it. You want to capture it, not blow it up by accident. Keep the Zipper back so that it doesn't get trigger-happy. Once the Tower is captured, all the units to the south will be revealed on the radar map.

- **Destroy Core units on the way south.** The Core forces are not too numerous—a Reaper, some AKs, and a few Thuds, Storms, and some Roaches. Have the Commander and Zipper head south toward the Advanced Radar Tower. Or, you can leave the Zipper on guard duty at the Laser Tower and send the Commander on his own. If interrupted along the way by a Reaper or another of the Core units, use the Commander's D-Gun or laser, and keep moving.

- **Blow up four Light Laser Towers near the Advanced Radar Tower.** Surrounding the Advanced Radar Tower are four LLTs (5). You must destroy all of them before trying to capture the tower. Otherwise, the remaining LLTs will open fire on the newly captured Advanced Radar Tower.

- **Capture the Tower.** Once the four LLTs are destroyed, order the Commander to capture the Advanced Radar Tower and accomplish the mission goal.

The spider-like biomass scattered around Rougpelt provides a good source of extra energy for the Commander. That's important, because the D-Gun uses a lot of energy.

Mission 16:

Stockpile at the Abutment

Difficulty rating: Medium

Objective: Set up and protect a base in the south, while building air and ground forces for an assault on the Core forces north of the long east-west Abutment. Destroy all Core mobile units; capture or destroy all Core structures.

Starting forces: Commander, 3 Zippers, 2 Fidos, 1 Zeus

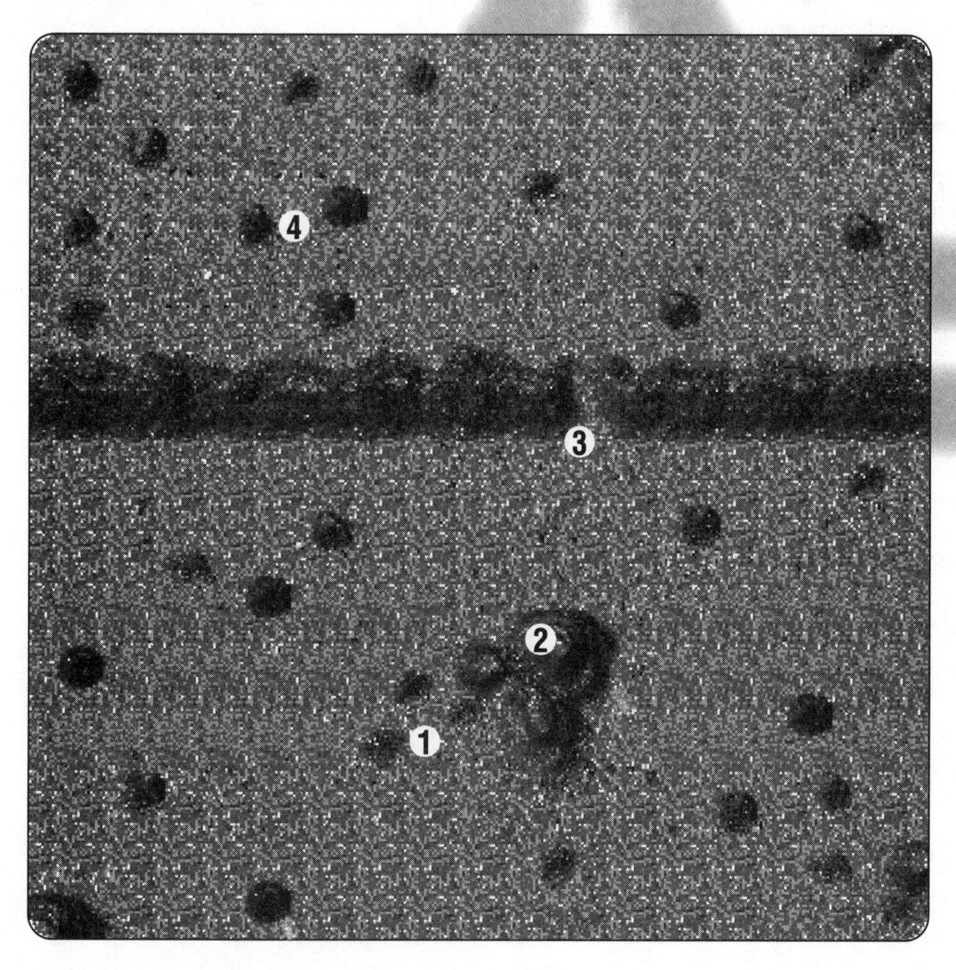

Mission Briefing

Core has established a large base north of the long east-west abutment. There's only one ground passage (3) to the other side, and it's heavily guarded by Pulverizers and a Punisher, plus nearby Diplomat missile launchers. Build a base (1) in the south, then construct a strong air force to attack over the Abutment. Air power will soften up enemy forces at the entrance sufficiently to bring troops through. There's also an open area in the northeast where you can build a second base, if needed.

How to Win

- **Plan for air protection first.** Your Commander and his small squad start out next to a large butte that will give you partial protection from Core air raids, and occasional ground attacks by Core AKs, Raiders, and Cans. Attacking ground units will come through a narrow opening (3) in the Abutment wall. Start by building a Vehicle Plant in order to construct six Samson AA vehicles, then a tank force of a dozen Flashes or Stumpys. You will also want to build a Construction Vehicle early in the mission to construct several Defender missile towers—they work well against Avenger and Vamp fighters and Rapier gunships. Your Commander should reclaim energy from the spider-like life forms, and metal from rocks.

- **Build a strong air force.** Start building an Aircraft Plant to get your air force under way. In addition to a Construction Aircraft, you will want to build six or more Freedom Fighters to patrol above your base. The Construction Aircraft will be used to build an Advanced Aircraft Plant that, in turn, will construct at least six to eight Brawler gunships, six to eight Hawk stealth fighters, and eight to ten Phoenix bombers for your assault on Core.

- **Bomb the ramparts with your Phoenix aircraft.** When you have constructed a squadron of stealth fighters and Phoenix bombers, start them on runs against the twin Pulverizers and the Punisher that guard the pass through the Abutment (just north of point 3). Keep building aircraft to replace casualties. Continue to pound the pass in the Abutment while you bring ground troops forward. Don't storm the pass until your air force has destroyed all or most of the defensive structures near point 3.

- **Build Spiders to stun Core structures during your assault.** Order your Advanced Vehicle Plant to build seven or eight Spiders. Include them in your ground forces when you go through the Abutment pass. By launching them at a Pulverizer or a Gaat Gun and paralyzing the enemy gun quickly you will make it easy to destroy the enemy structure. Once your air force has cleared the heights of the Pulverizers and the Punisher, send in stealth fighters and strategic bombers to hit the Diplomat rocket launchers (4) near a Moho Mine and a Geothermal Power Plant. Then follow that with six to eight Brawlers that will hover above the Diplomats and Crasher anti-air units, keeping them under fire.

- **Capture when you can.** Keep your ground forces out of harm's way until most of the air-attack action has shifted to point 4. When you do go through the Abutment pass, try to move fast with Zippers, PeeWees, and Flash tanks leading. Keep Brawlers firing at enemy ground troops. If the opening starts to get clogged with wrecks, have a Construction Vehicle reclaim the metal. Your goal is to destroy all mobile units, not necessarily all structures. The Commander can capture Solar Collectors, Metal Extractors, and other structures as your forces move farther into Core territory.

- **Hunt remaining mobile units.** Core doesn't have any factories in this mission, so your continual attacks will eventually whittle down the enemy. By the time you make it through to the north side of the Abutment, you should have a significant superiority in numbers.

For an interesting variation, have an Atlas transport bring an Eraser radar jammer to a spot on the north side next to the eastern edge of the map. Leave it there, and then shuttle a few tanks and a Construction Kbot or Vehicle over to the jammer to start an eastern front.

Mission 17:

Fortress at Brooban's Isle

Difficulty rating: Hard

Objective: Core is building a Silencer nuclear missile launcher. From your small base in the south of the map (1), build a strike fleet and an air force that can assault the Core fortress on Brooban's Isle, so that the Commander can capture the Silencer nuclear silo. The Silencer must not be destroyed.

Starting forces: Commander, 3 Jethros, 1 Zeus, 1 Shipyard, 1 Crusader, 1 Skeeter, 1 Construction Ship

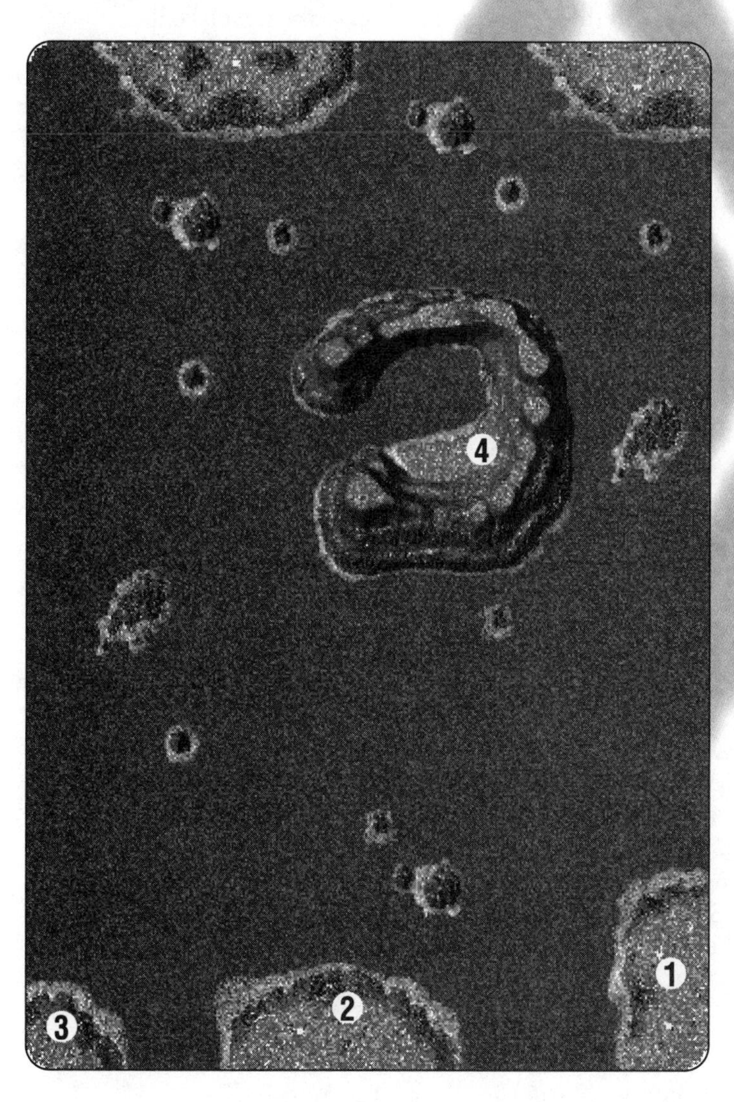

Mission Briefing

Prepare for a massive naval assault. You must build a strong navy and air force that can neutralize three Punisher plasma batteries on Brooban's Isle (4) and a Core fleet nearby as a step in capturing the Silencer nuclear silo on the east side of the island. A Deleter there jams your radar. There are additional strong Core forces on the two islands at the very top of the map. You will first expand to two nearby islands for more space plus additional energy and metal resources.

How to Win

- **Build an Aircraft Plant and several Lurker subs.** After that construction is under way, begin fortifying your position by ordering your Construction Ship to build a Sonar Station, followed by a couple of Torpedo Launchers. Core Avengers and Finks will make runs on your position, but your AA Jethros can handle them initially. Next, Core Searcher scout ships will arrive to attack your Shipyard and other ships. Crusader and Skeeter if the Torpedo Launchers are not ready.

- **Construct an Atlas transport.** When finished, carry the Commander or a Construction unit to the island directly to the west (2) and, later, to the next island (3). You will need to clear rocks and energy biomass from the islands to make room for your factories and your armed forces staging areas. Set up Solar Collectors and Metal Extractors on all three islands. Core Enforcers will attack from the sea. Order Lurker subs to patrol in front of your Shipyard and the next island (2).

- **Concentrate on naval units first, then on aircraft.** Core has Titan torpedo bombers and Rapier gunships patrolling Brooban's Isle. A couple of Warlord battleships are in the lagoon of the island. Executioner cruisers and Shark attack subs will repeatedly launch probing attacks. You'll also face combined sorties by Warlords and Hydra missile frigates. Finally, Crock amphibious tanks will also attack. Build an Advanced Shipyard and produce Piranha attack subs, Ranger missile ships, Conqueror cruisers, and a couple of Millennium battleships. Build a Construction Aircraft and start construction on an Advanced Aircraft Plant.

- **Battleships and cruisers to the attack!** Millenniums and Conquerors are the ships with the most powerful surface guns in your navy. Keep them patrolling near your islands as you build your forces to target the Punishers on the main island. Surround the cruisers and battleships with Lurker and Piranha subs and with Rangers to protect them from Core Rapiers and Avenger aircraft. Your Advanced Aircraft Plant must produce Lancet torpedo bombers in addition to Hawks, Phoenix, and Brawler aircraft. The torpedo bombers will be especially helpful against the Core cruisers and battleships.

- **Gain air superiority.** Your growing air force will soon gain air superiority as your production outlasts the existing Core aircraft. Order your Phoenix bombers to first destroy the Punisher on the southernmost ridge of Brooban's Isle. This will allow naval units to get closer to the island. Use your bombers and stealth fighters to attack the two Punishers on the east side of the main island. A naval bombardment might accidentally destroy the Silencer silo between the two big guns. If you do use the cruiser and battleship on the Punishers, control their targeting precisely.

- **Be careful with the Commander.** Rapier gunships will repeatedly attack your Commander. Keep the Commander back from the main assaults, and always provide the Commander with good AA protection—put him next to missile towers, and accompany him with Samson anti-air missile trucks and/or Jethro anti-air Kbots when moving. Order an Eraser radar jammer to guard the Commander. Keep one or two Construction Ships near your cruisers and battleships to facilitate repairs when the warships take damage.

- **Attack the northern islands.** The top half of Brooban's Isle is covered by the northern Punisher cannons. Your air force should methodically attack the Punishers on both islands, as well as any ships that are still in that area. If your naval strength is up to par, your battleships and cruisers can also participate by shelling both islands. However, make sure your air force hits those positions first. Bring your Commander to the island to capture the missile silo only when the four Punishers have been destroyed, Core Brawlers have been neutralized, and your navy rules the waves.

Having trouble finding room for all your factories on those three small islands? This is a good mission in which to order a mobile Construction unit to reclaim the metal in an existing Kbot Lab, Vehicle Plant, or Aircraft Plant in order to make room to build the advanced versions of each.

Mission 18:

Vengeance!

Difficulty rating: Easy

Objective: Core has decided to execute some of your Arm troops. While you cannot stop the execution, you can take a measure of revenge by wiping out all the Core forces on the map.

Starting forces: Commander and a sizable attack force of 8 Hammers, 8 Rockos, 10 PeeWees, 4 Jethros, 6 Fidos, and 1 Advanced Construction Kbot

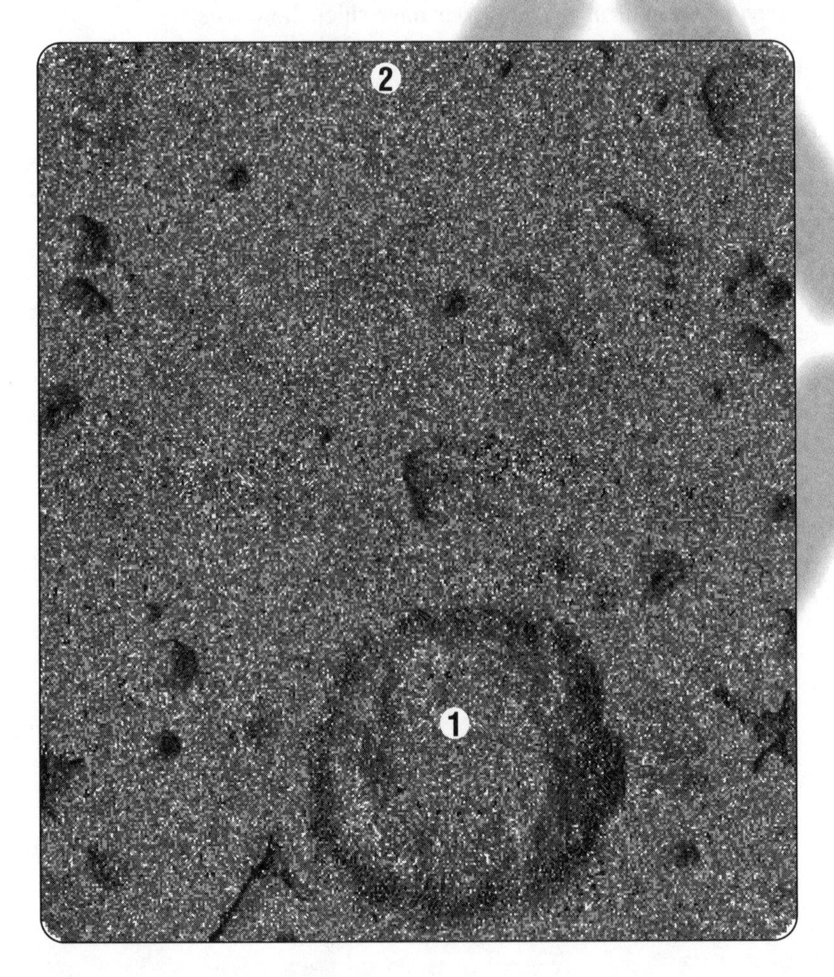

Mission Briefing

An eye for an eye and a bot for a bot. Core AKs, Pyros, and Cans open the mission by executing about 20 Arm PeeWees that are surrounded in the south part of the map (1). Your superior force is in the north (2). You can either wait for the Core troops to move toward you, or you can head straight south to take revenge. Either way, your superior force should make quick work of them.

How to Win

- **Start with your forces in formation.** The Hammers, Jethros, and Rockos are on the back row (2), with Fidos and PeeWees toward the front. Stay in position and wait for the Core troops to come. They will be led by AKs that your artillery and rocket troops will target as they come into artillery range. By splitting your starting formation right down the middle into two groups, you can envelop the approaching Core from two sides, then move forward.
- **Shoot AKs, Weasels, and Storms first, then slower Raiders, Reapers, and The Cans.** As the Core forces arrive, they will be spread out over a long line, with faster units arriving well before others. Your units will make quick work of them. Then, when the slower Core forces finally get near, your artillery and rockets will once again begin picking them off before they can reach you.
- **After the melee, head south for the Core Construction Kbot.** There is one more little housekeeping chore for you after you've destroyed the attack force. Head south to point 1, where the executions took place, and shoot a Construction Kbot there. You may encounter one or two slower Core units along the way.

At the moment the mission begins, hit Ctrl-S to select all the PeeWees on the screen, and immediately begin clicking to move them north. By repeatedly ordering them north to keep them from trying to fight back, you can save three or four of them. There's nothing in between them and your main force. Then, you can start your revenge after saving twenty percent of the doomed PeeWees.

Mission 19:

The Motien Ramp

Difficulty rating: Hard

Objective: Core has retreated to the ancient earthworks called the Motien Ramp on the planet Rougpelt. You must build a strong base, assault the Core base, and capture the Galactic Gate that leads to the enemy's home planet, Core Prime.

Starting forces: Commander, 1 Construction Kbot, 1 Merl, 2 Samsons, 2 Fidos, 1 Invader crawling bomb, 1 Radar Tower

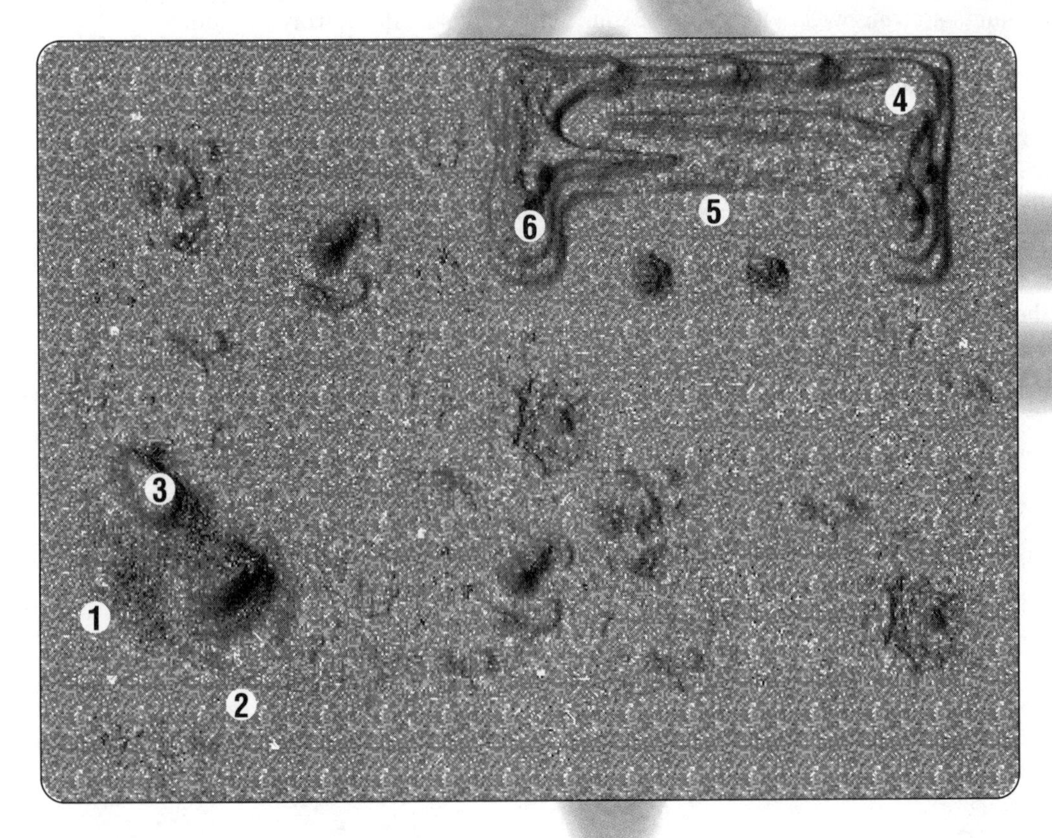

Mission Briefing

Core has a powerful ground force at its base in the northeast, led by Reaper and Raider tanks. There are four Rapier gunships that try to target your Commander, two Vamp stealth fighters, and eight Kbots. Core's long-range Intimidator cannon can reach your small force with its shells, once Core has discovered your base. Fortunately, the Intimidator is wildly inaccurate. Unfortunately for you, it doesn't *always* miss. Build an air and ground force that can first provide protection from the Rapiers and Vamps. As early as possible, put together an air strike to destroy the Intimidator. The landscape is perfect for tank warfare, so concentrate on your armored units more than usual. Be careful not to destroy the Galactic Gate (4), which is in the far northeast corner. The Commander must capture it.

How to Win

- **Seek cover behind the mesas (1) just northwest of your starting position.** Arrange your Samson anti-aircraft missile trucks and Merl rocket launcher along the south end of those mesas. Two Rapier gunships will be the first Core units in your area, and they will patrol over that same area, just south of your position. There are metal deposits north and south of your base. Order the Commander to build Solar Collectors and Metal Extractors. Then build an Aircraft Plant as close behind the mesa as possible to protect it from Intimidator fire later on. Order the Construction Kbot to build a Kbot Lab right next to it. A Construction Aircraft to scout out metal deposits should be your first aircraft. After building it, start producing Freedom Fighters to patrol over the base.

- **Build a Radar Tower, a Defender missile tower, and a Sentinel.** Have the Construction Kbot build a Radar Tower on top of the highest mesa near you (3), followed by a Defender missile tower and then a Sentinel heavy laser. A few minutes after the Rapiers have made several patrol passes, some AKs, Weasels, and a Diplomat rocket launcher will appear just below the front of those mesas. Your Sentinel, Fidos, and Zippers can take care of them. Just out of visual range is the Diplomat. Send the Zippers out to blow it up before it causes trouble with its missiles. An Eraser radar jammer will be a big help here.

- **Build an Advanced Kbot Lab and an Advanced Aircraft Plant as soon as possible.** Order the Commander to build a Vehicle Plant to start turning out Flash and Stumpy tanks. Also, produce a Construction Vehicle to begin building the Advanced Vehicle Plant. Don't attempt an advance before you have built plenty of Level-2 Kbots, vehicles, and aircraft. As soon as any of your troops move anywhere near the Core base, the Intimidator starts firing shells onto and around your base—so, don't let any of your aircraft stray over or near the base early in the game.

- **Pump out Brawlers and Merls.** The gunships and the mobile rocket launchers are effective against the ground troops that Core will send out against you. Core does have a Kbot Lab and a Construction Kbot, so you can't sit back forever and build a fortress or you will face much larger Core forces than you will if you move more quickly against them. When you have a tank force of at least ten Stumpys or, better still, Bulldogs, advance towards the Core base leading with tanks and a half dozen each of Zippers, Fidos, and Rockos. Provide continuing air cover with six to eight Brawlers and follow with four Merls. Include at least two radar jammers, either Erasers or Jammers, one near the front of your column, and the other in the rear. Also, include a Construction unit for repairs enroute, and two Seer mobile radar units to help sight enemy targets.

- **Send Hawks and Phoenix bombers to destroy the Intimidator.** As your force starts the advance, send a half-dozen Hawks and seven or eight Phoenix against the Intimidator in the center of the enemy base (5). It's protected by Gaat Guns and Diplomats, as well as a couple of Punishers, so prepare to take casualties. As you get close to the Core base, try to have the Merls target the lead Gaat Gun (6). There are

Raiders and Reapers stationed at the Core base, but some will already have been destroyed in forays against your base, and by your air strikes.

- **Prepare for a surgical strike.** You must not destroy the Galactic Gate (4), so keep your tanks, Fidos, Zippers, and other ground units together in a single group, focusing everyone's fire on selected targets. It destroys them quicker, and prevents uncontrolled fire. Direct your air force the same way, with a pre-selected squad (Ctrl plus 1–9) of fighters, another squad of bombers, and a third of Brawlers. There will be a lot going on at once—don't forget to use the minus (-) key to slow down the action if need better control. The closer you get to the Galactic Gate, the more tightly you have to control your units. Don't bring in the Commander until late in the assault, and make sure that there are no Core Brawlers still flying when you do.

Position the Invader crawling bomb directly in front of the twin mesas in front of your base. Place a PeeWee directly in front of it to draw fire. When the AKs and Weasels come into radar range, select the Invader and hit Ctrl-D. Five seconds later, the Invader blows itself up. If your timing is right, it will take out three-quarters of a screen and several of the attackers.

Mission 20:

Dump

Difficulty rating: Medium

Objective: Lead a small squad of Arm troops through the labyrinth of Core's garbage moon, Dump. Destroy all Core elements.

Starting forces: Commander, 1 Zeus, 2 Fidos, 6 Zippers

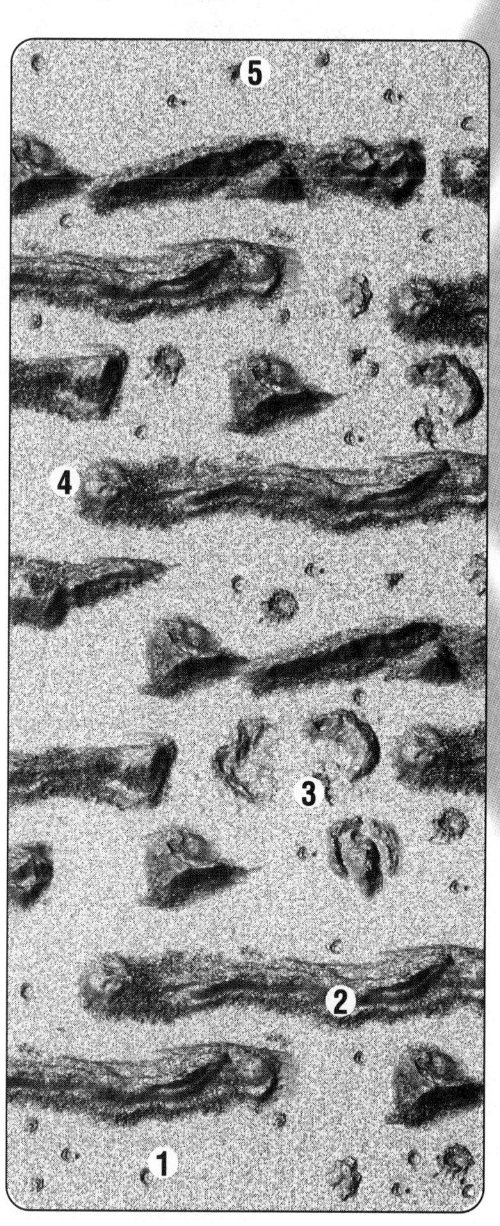

Mission Briefing

The Galactic Gate from Rougpelt has led to Core Prime's garbage can moon, Dump. The map is a series of switch-back trails with Core troops pocketed in a half-dozen places. This mission is complicated because of the twin presence of Diplomat mobile rocket launchers and Goliath super-tanks in the top third of the map. The Diplomats fire rockets over the switch-back hills with deadly effect. Core's forces are only at half-strength, however, which means they are easily destroyed.

How to Win

- **Rescue a Jeffy and build a Vehicle Plant.** At your starting point (1) a Core Construction Kbot will wander into your group. Your Commander can capture the Kbot if you immediately give all your units orders to Hold Fire. This capture will speed up your construction efforts a great deal. Whether or not you capture the Kbot, send the Commander to point 2 to capture a Jeffy scout vehicle that the Core has captured. It is stuck trying to climb a ridge. This Jeffy, once captured, will be your scout. Build several Metal Extractors and Solar Collectors for the resources you need. Then, build a Radar Tower on the rock ledge just above you to the north, then begin a Vehicle Plant. If you have captured the Construction Kbot, order it to build an Advanced Kbot Lab, and then start building Fidos and Zeus Kbots.
- **Prepare for the Core welcoming parties.** At point 3, there is a Core Radar Tower protected by three Instigator tanks and five A.K. Kbots. At point 4, there are nine AKs that are within range of a Diplomat just behind the next hill. Two Goliath tanks, two Reaper tanks, and another Diplomat are just to the east. At the top of the map (5), you will find three more Goliaths, three Reapers, and a couple of Diplomats.
- **Merl rocket launchers and Bulldog tanks make a good antidote to Core's forces.** When you have a force of mixed Kbots and tanks—about 12 to 15 units—move forward with the captured Jeffy out in front for recon. Instigators and AKs will meet you near point 3. If you can destroy them without blowing up the Radar Tower, do so. Then bring the Commander up to capture it. Before you reach point 4, put four or more Bulldogs out front, followed by Zippers and Fidos. Bringing up the rear should be at least three Merls. Have a Construction Kbot behind them so that it can reclaim metal if the narrow trails become blocked.
- **Blast past the AKs.** The AKs can slow you down and give the Core Diplomats, Goliaths, and Reapers a chance to converge on you. Send the tanks through the AKs and on to the Core armored units just beyond. Keep the Merls close enough to target the Diplomats and Goliaths above point 4. The Goliaths are tough, and you will need to keep resupplying your troops from your base. Keep your Commander safely back, out of Diplomat range.
- **Overwhelm Core with your numbers.** This mission is easy to win if you simply keep producing units fast, and continuously resupplying your troops at the front. Core has no factories on Dump, so a war of attrition works in your favor. Match the Diplomats with your Merls and send many more Bulldogs than there are Goliaths, and you will sweep the moon clean.

Caution **The biggest danger in this mission is over-committing your Commander within range of the Goliaths and Diplomats. It's possible for a strong player to win this mission with fewer forces than outlined in the relatively conservative approach outlined above. However, the risks are higher for your Commander if you try that because you will have to use him more aggressively, thus exposing him to more attacks.**

Mission 21:

Welcome to Core Prime

Difficulty rating: Medium

Objective: The Commander steps onto Core Prime, the metal planet that Core calls home. Capture what structures you can, and then build a base strong enough to destroy a rapidly growing Core force on this map.

Starting force: Commander

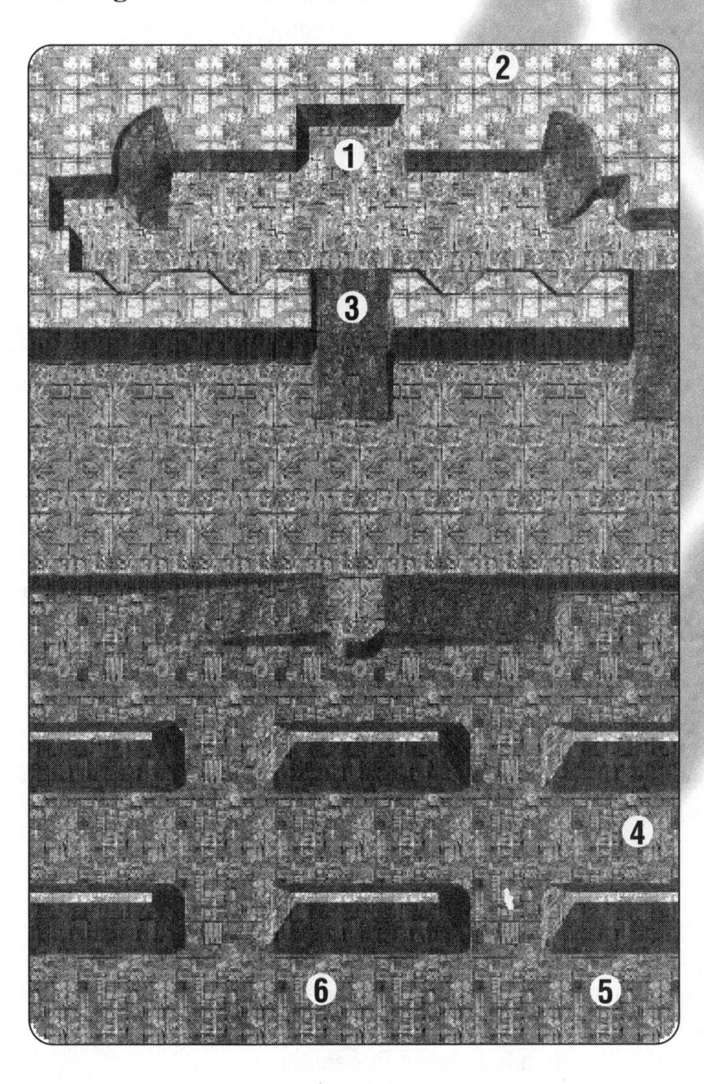

Mission Briefing

This mission is another slugfest, one in which Core grows stronger fast—it has an Aircraft Plant, a Kbot Lab, a Vehicle Plant, and several Construction Kbots itching to start producing. The Commander starts near the northern edge of the battlefield, (1) next to the Galactic Gate. Behind him (2) are Core Solar Collectors, Metal Extractors, and a roaming Core Construction Kbot. Capture as many of the Core resource generators as possible, then begin building a base along the northern edge of the map. Your base will spread east and west along this northern boundary. You are left in peace at first, so build as much as you can—either start building a tank force, an air force, and then strike against Core and its factories as soon as the strike force's ready; or focus on setting up strong air defenses that include Level-2 aircraft. If you go for the defensive option, you also need some big guns, including several Big Berthas. The first strategy is riskier, and results in a quick resolution. The second strategy is safer, and leads to a drawn-out conflict. Both are a lot of fun.

How to Win

- **Capture and build.** Immediately move your Commander to the walkway behind him, and capture the Solar Collectors and Metal Extractors around point 2. Build a Radar Tower while you're up there—it will reveal enemy units around you. There is a Construction Kbot that can also be captured, but you will have to pin it against a wall to stop it from moving. Begin building a Kbot Lab, then an Aircraft Plant, then a Vehicle Plant.

- **Focus on the center.** Core ground attacks don't start immediately. When they do, they follow a path from the south straight up the middle of the screen through point 3, headed directly for the Galactic Gate. As the first PeeWees, Hammers, and Rockos emerge from the Kbot Lab, position them out in front of the Gate between points 1 and 3. Order your Vehicle Plant to build Flash and Stumpy tanks, as well as Samson air-defense trucks. Make sure that you include a Construction Kbot, a Construction Vehicle, and a Construction Aircraft among the first units you build. You must be able to build Level-2 mobile units and structures quickly.

- **Start an air force, fast.** Start off with Freedom Fighters, getting them into the air patrolling east and west in front of your base as soon as each is produced. Send one or two on long recon missions, using the T key to track them. Fly over points 4, 5, and 6 to see, respectively, the Core Aircraft Plant, Kbot Lab, and Vehicle Plant.

- **Construct Guardians, then Big Berthas.** The first ground attack that comes at you consists of around six AKs. It's followed by two more waves of AKs. The third wave also includes Instigator tanks and Weasel scouts. Next you'll be visited by a Slasher missile launcher, another group of AKs, and four Raider tanks. All of them try to knock out the Galactic Gate. Begin pushing your perimeter out towards point 3, protecting the gate, but close enough to be supported by your artillery on the walkway above and behind the Gate. One of your primary goals isto get some Level-2 structures under way—specifically several Sentinel heavy lasers, Guardian cannons, and Defender missile towers. By having your mobile construction units build advanced factories, you can also move to the Level-2 mobile units fairly early. You want a couple of Eraser and/or Jammer radar jammers along the back wall to help keep your factories and big cannons there out of the reach of Core radar. Build at least one Advanced Construction unit, so that Big Berthas and Advanced Radar Towers are an option.

- **Bomb the factories.** The Core attacks are sporadic, giving you time to really push your building capabilities. Get an Advanced Aircraft Plant up and running so that you can produce Phoenix strategic bombers, Hawk stealth fighters, and Brawler gunships. Start grouping them into squadrons by pressing Ctrl plus 1–9. This enables you to target them and reroute them very easily once they are airborne. When you have at least a half-dozen Hawks and a half-dozen Phoenix, launch a bombing run against the Core Aircraft Plant (4). Your new goal is to disrupt and then cripple Core's production capacity. Throughout the mission, keep your Commander busy helping the Construction units build faster, and reclaiming metal from nearby metal pipes.

- **Push for a Moho Mine and a Fusion Reactor.** Once you have an Advanced Construction unit, build a Fusion Reactor along the back wall (2), and then a Moho Mine. During this construction period, it helps if you have at least two Guardian cannons that can hit the forward Core troops as they advance towards point 3.

- **Time for the Tank Rush!** Your air force and your long-range guns should relentlessly pound Core's units within the range of your Advanced Radar Tower. All of this time, hold all your ground forces in defensive positions in front of the Galactic Gate. If you build a large force of Bulldogs and Stumpy tanks, followed by Kbots and Merl rocket launchers, you should have a very strong force when you attack. Be aware, however, that in this mission Core is in a building frenzy. The longer you wait, the more Core forces will face you. Divide your large ground force into three or four strong, mixed groups and send them straight down the middle of the screen through point 3. Direct your columns at the Aircraft Plant first (4), preceding their arrival with Phoenix bombing runs and Big Bertha shells. The large metal barriers near the south edge of the screen limit the long-range cannons' effectiveness. The fighting along the south edge of your game screen will be crowded and fierce. Leave a defensive force near the Galactic Gate to take care of any Core counter-attacks near the top of the game screen. Keep the pressure on, destroy the factories, and then sweep your remaining ground troops around the battlefield methodically destroying any remaining Core units and structures.

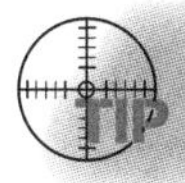

When you have production capability that includes having three or four construction units in addition to the Commander, pool their resources on large projects such as Moho Mines, Fusion Reactors, and Big Berthas. The Commander builds at 300 work units per second, while Level-1 construction units build at 100 work units per second and Level-2 construction units build at 200 a second. When you put three or four of them together on a building project, their work-unit production numbers are *added* to one another.

Mission 22:

Battle for Coordinate 6551:447

Difficulty: Medium

Objective: A massive Core storage energy and metal facility lies to the north of your starting point across two channels of water. You must destroy or capture all of the storage structures and destroy all Core mobile forces.

Starting forces: Commander, 4 Zippers, 1 Zeus

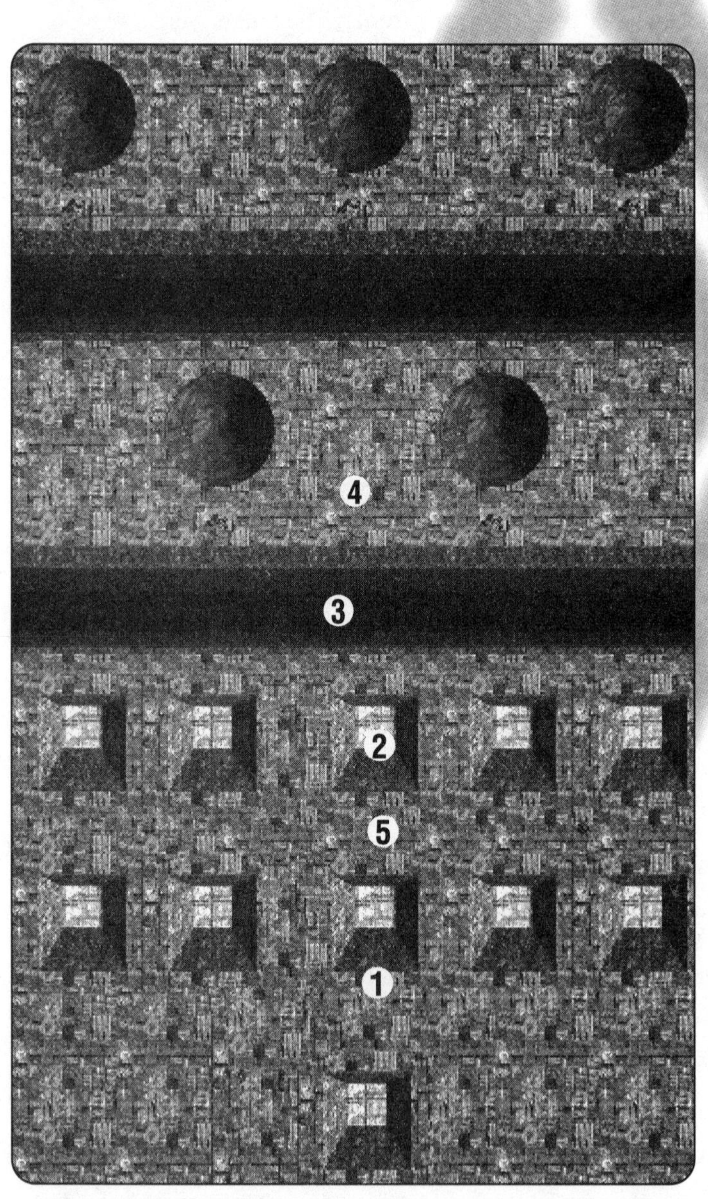

Mission Briefing

Your small force must build a base that can strike at Core defenses across two narrow channels of water. An Aircraft Plant to pump out fighters and bombers is your first move. Also, build long-range cannons that can target the Core Pulverizers and Slashers that protect the storage structures.

How to Win

- **Set up radar, establish resource generators, and build an Aircraft Plant and a Vehicle Plant (1).** Core forces will not attack during the early phase of the game, giving you time to get your resources and your base started. Move your Commander forward to one of the raised platforms (2) to set up a Radar Tower. Just beyond the platforms, in the channel at point 3, are two Searcher scout ships and a Core Lurker sub. Build an Aircraft Plant and then a Vehicle Plant behind one or two of the platforms (1). With each of them, first build a construction unit, then start pumping out Freedom Fighters and Samson anti-air missile trucks, respectively. Core only has six Avengers and two Rapiers in its air force, so the Samson trucks can help knock them down when they appear a bit later.

- **Start air recon, then destroy two Searchers in the first channel (3).** Your radar should show three Pulverizers just across the channel at point 4. To the left and right of the Pulverizers are six Slasher missile trucks—three to a side. This is a good anti-aircraft front line, and you want to destroy as many of them as possible before your air force starts going in. Have one or two of your Freedom Fighters try an aerial recon, hitting the T key to track them. You'll get heavy enemy anti-air fire. With the Construction Vehicle you built, start working on a Guardian cannon near point 5; or, you can use the Construction Aircraft on top of the nearest platform to build the Guardian. In either case, have your Commander add his building speed to the task. Once the cannon is build, put some Samson anti-air trucks nearby and start pounding the Pulverizers and Slashers. Order the Aircraft Plant to build a couple of Atlas air transports.

- **Build Big Berthas to soften up the defenders.** Order your Construction Vehicle to build an Advanced Vehicle Plant. When completed, build a Jammer and put it near the Guardian. Start the Advanced Vehicle Plant on constructing an Advanced Construction Vehicle. You should start that plant on building a Big Bertha as soon as possible. Put the Big Bertha near the Jammer. By now, your air force should have six to eight Freedom Fighters. Order your Construction Aircraft to build an Advanced Aircraft Plant. You'll want the Hawk fighters, Phoenix bombers, and Brawler gunships for your assault later.

- **Destroy it all or capture as much as you can?** The center of the map, in between the two channels, contains 39 Core Solar Collectors. Some of them may be destroyed in the barrage from your Guardian and Big Bertha cannons. Order your Vehicle Plant to build a half-dozen Triton amphibious tanks. When they're built, send them over the first channel at the same time. The Core sub may sink one or two. Once most of the resistance on the first island is neutralized, have an Atlas carry the Commander over and capture as many of the Solar Collectors as possible. Don't go too far north, however, because there are Pulverizers on the far side of the second channel.

- **Capture the Moho Mine and Fusion Reactor (6).** Your air force should now be in full control of the skies. Send in Hawks and then Brawlers to destroy the

Pulverizers just passed the second channel. There's an Enforcer destroyer in the second channel, but your air force can destroy it quickly. A Lurker sub also is in the second channel, so don't send the Commander walking across. As resistance diminishes, use an Atlas to carry the Commander across the second channel. Then, capture all of the remaining resource generators and storage structures, including the Moho Mine and Fusion Reactor (6).

As an alternative approach, build a Kbot Lab, then a Construction Kbot, and then an Advanced Kbot Lab so that you can build Fido assault bots for firing across the channel and Invader crawling bombs to cross the channel and blow up Pulverizers and Slashers.

Mission 23:

Crossing Aqueous Body 397

Difficulty: Hard

Objective: Core has a heavily defended seaport on Core Prime that you must destroy. Build a base, then a strong naval and air force to attack the enemy ships and gun emplacements on the far shore. Destroy everything.

Starting forces: Commander, 1 Zeus, 2 Fidos, 1 Triton, 2 Peepers, 1 Crusader, 1 Lurker, 1 Sonar Station, 1 Torpedo Launcher

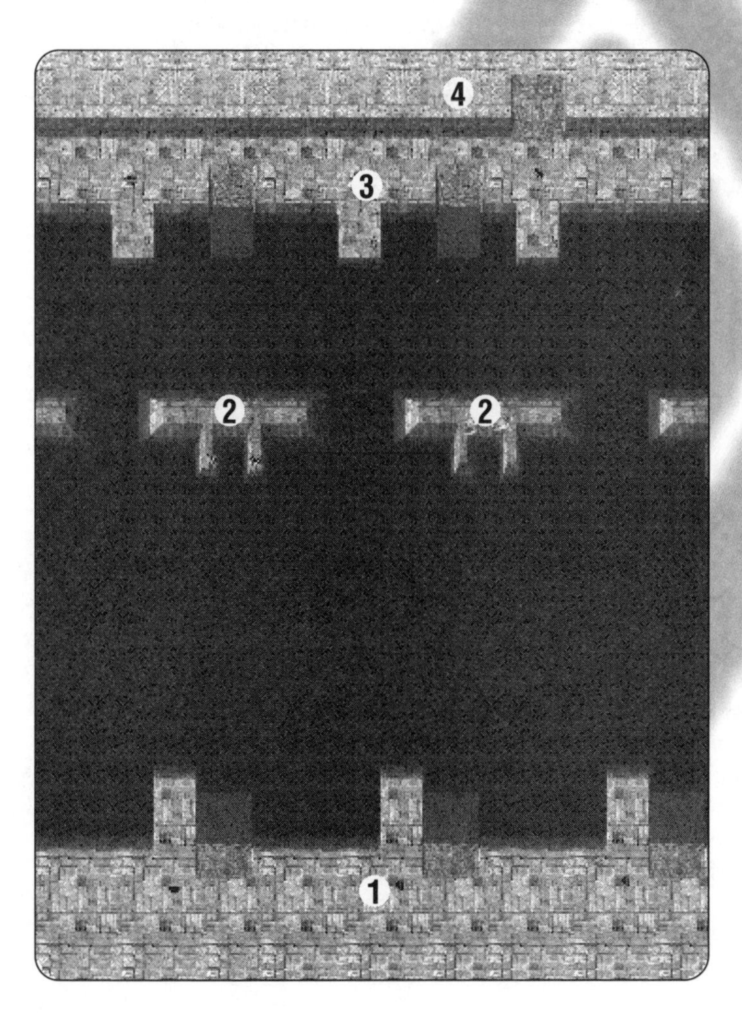

Mission Briefing

This is a huge naval and air assault mission that will take awhile to accomplish. First, build a base with anti-air missiles and subs. Then, construct a fleet of ships and a squadron of fighters and bombers to attack the Core islands (2) and knock out the Gaat Guns and Pulverizers there. Build a Big Bertha cannon to help soften Core's defenses. Include one or two Colossus light carriers for mobile radar and aircraft repair. Reduce Core's emplacements to rubble with air power, your ships' surface guns, and more cannon on the islands.

How to Win

- **Build a Shipyard, a Vehicle Plant, and an Aircraft Plant.** Once you've established your resource generators, the key early in the game is to start construction on all three of these technology paths. The naval units will be your primary force; the air units will provide essential support; the Vehicle Plant's Jammers will block enemy radar, and its Triton amphibious tanks will be a part of your landing force. While Core's small air force can be bothersome, it's the large enemy navy that will cause you the most trouble.

- **Build a Construction Ship and a Construction Vehicle.** Since building to Level-2 and Level-3 technologies is crucial in this mission, build several construction units, and help speed up the building process by combining their efforts on individual projects. Don't send ships and planes to the Core stronghold until you've gotten up to Level-2 factories. Your appearance there will trigger the Core navy's offensive earlier than if you stay home and build your base for awhile. Put your Lurker sub and Crusader destroyer on patrol in front of the dock above point 1. Core has a Hive light carrier, a couple of Snake subs, an Executioner cruiser, a Hydra missile frigate, and a Construction Ship—all between points 2 and 3. There are a couple of Searcher scout ships south of point 2 that will start to harass you right away. Also at point 3 are 14 Crock amphibious tanks that will start coming at you in waves after about a half-hour of play.

- **Build an Advanced Shipyard and an Advanced Vehicle Plant.** Several waves of Crock amphibious tanks will approach, but your Torpedo Launcher and subs should blow them up before they reach land. Get your advanced construction plants going. Your Commander and a Construction Ship should reclaim metal from sunken ships whenever possible. Build at least one Advanced Construction Vehicle and begin building a Big Bertha on the pier near point 1 to start taking out the Gaat Guns on the islands, and then on the main Core base. Place a Jammer next to your Big Bertha to hide it from Core radar. Place several Luger mobile artillery units and two Defender missile towers nearby, and three Skeeter scout ships just offshore.

- **A battleship, two cruisers, and a light carrier are among your next construction projects.** There's a lot of units you need to build—the Big Bertha, the Millenium battleship, Conqueror cruisers, and Colossus light carriers—so order your Advanced Construction Vehicle to build a Moho Mine, and then a Fusion Reactor. Your Commander and one or two other construction units can help speed up the building project. The Colossus will be used as a repair pad for aircraft in your assault on Core's base. Have your Aircraft Plant build an Atlas transport, and then order the transport to take a Jammer onto the Colossus when it's finished. This gives protection from Core radar, and still lets you have a spot on deck for aircraft repair.

- **It's naval assault time!** After you have a Moho Mine and a Fusion Reactor, your Big Bertha can start regular bombardment of enemy targets. Target the islands first (2), destroying the four Gaat Guns and one Pulverizer. Then hit Core's Doomsday Machine (4). Send out twelve Triton amphibious tanks, split into two groups of six, from positions to the left and right of your base. Direct them to come ashore at the two ramps on either side of point 3. Then, send a naval task force toward the islands, consisting of a Millenium, two Conquerors, four Lurker subs, two Piranha attack subs, and three Ranger missile ships. By now, your Advanced Aircraft plant should have produced at least a half-dozen Brawlers and the same number of Hawk and Phoenix aircraft. That's the bare minimum. Build more if you can afford it. Include the Colossus for radar and aircraft repair, and a Construction Ship for ship repair during the naval engagement about to start.

- **Keep the Bertha shooting along the waterfront (3) as your navy moves in.** You'll need to split your ships among two of the three passageways next to the islands. Have your subs out front to destroy the Sonar Stations, then simultaneously send a battleship through the opening between the two main islands, and a cruiser and a missile ship through each of the other island openings. Bring the remainder of your flotilla through as your Hawks, Phoenix, and Brawlers target enemy Cans and Punishers. Keep your Construction Ship next to the battleship and a cruiser. Their guns, along with the Bertha, should be grinding the Core defenses down quickly. Mop things up, and you're on your way to Mission 24.

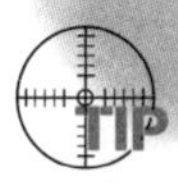

The longer you build your base and your armaments without engaging Core directly in the waters close to their base, the longer it takes Core to become agitated. So build like mad before you go on the offensive.

Mission 24:

Breakthrough to Central Consciousness

Difficulty: Medium

Objective: Within the massive central computer at the heart of Core Prime, your Commander and a small force must build a base and then break through heavy defenses to access the Central Plaza Dome. Your Commander must climb to the top of that Dome, and all Core forces have to be destroyed.

Starting forces: Commander, 5 Zippers, 3 Fidos, 1 Zeus

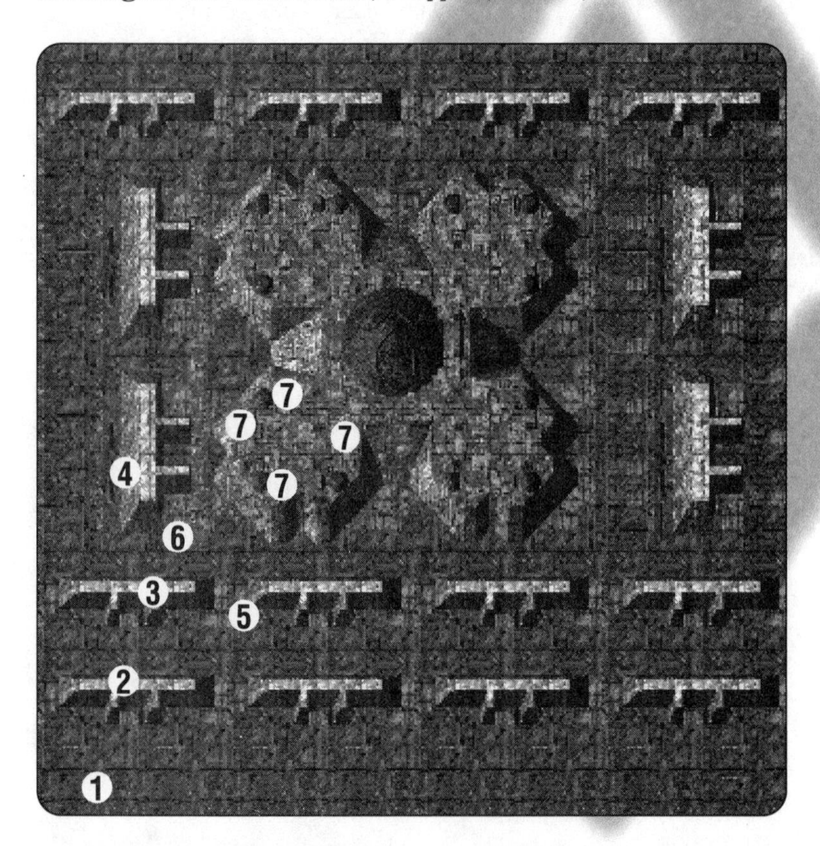

Mission Briefing

This mission is a step-by-step campaign by your combined ground and air forces to methodically destroy an entrenched Core defensive position. It's not difficult, but it does take time and a lot of building to get to the Level-3 weapons. Your Commander must stand atop the Central Plaza's Dome (8), which means destroying all of the many Core defenders that surround it. Pulverizers and Gaat Guns are located on all sides of the Dome, as shown on just one of the sides (7). There are also Cans dotting the landscape.

How to Win

- **Use the walls for protection as you build your base.** There are two parallel corridors toward the south end of the map. The walls along those corridors, broken by several gaps, offer protection from Core. Begin by moving your troops to the southwestern corner of the map (1) and start building resource generators and then a Kbot Lab and a Vehicle Plant. Have the Commander set up a Radar Tower at point 2.
- **Build a large ground force.** Two Pyros are patrolling the second corridor. Your Zippers and Fidos will shoot them when they reach the west wall. Start producing a Construction Kbot, then PeeWees, Hammers, and Rockos—six of each. Have the Commander start an Aircraft Plant near the same point (1). Build a Construction Aircraft first, so that it can start building projects on top of the steep raised platforms on top of the walls. When the Construction Kbot is completed, order it to build an Advanced Kbot Lab right away. Similarly, when the Construction Aircraft is ready, build an Advanced Aircraft Plant. With the Vehicle Plant ready, order it to build a Construction Vehicle, then five or six Samson missile launchers in case there are air attacks. When the Construction Vehicle is ready, start it building an Advanced Vehicle Plant that, when completed, should start on an Advanced Construction Vehicle. You should have little or no interference from Core during this building phase. Get to Level-2 technology as quickly as possible.
- **Advance your Radar Towers.** Move your growing body of troops out between points 2 and 3. Order the Commander to build a Radar Tower at point 3. At the same time, have a few Fidos, Hammers, and Rockos go to point 6. They can destroy Gaat Guns located at each of the points marked 7. Your goal right now is to get three or four Merls built by your Advanced Vehicle Plant, and to bring them to point 5 where they will begin to target the radar blips at point 7. Order the Advanced Aircraft Plant to start cranking out a dozen Hawks, six Phoenix and ten Brawlers. This will take time and resources, but you should have little interference.
- **Bring forward your Merls.** As the Merls begin to launch missiles, have the Commander set up another Radar Tower, this one at point 4. The improved radar coverage will provide your Merls with more targets. Core has four Rapiers patrolling to the north. Set up several Sentinel laser towers and Defender missile towers between points 3 and 5. By this time, your Advanced Construction Vehicle should be completed. Order it, together with the Commander to build Solar Collectors and Metal Extractors until there are at least a dozen of each along the southernmost wall. Order the Advanced Construction Vehicle to build a Moho Mine, followed by a Fusion Reactor. Solicit help from the Commander and the other construction units.
- **It's time for Big Bertha.** The Advanced Construction Vehicle, aided by the Commander and a few other construction units, will start on a Big Bertha, which will end up near point 6. Have some Samson missile launchers nearby. Now, with a large Level-2 air force ready and some of the Pulverizers and Gaat Guns silenced by the Merls, launch your air force on repeated runs up the western side of the map above points 4 and 7. The rest of the mission should follow a pattern of advancing radar, moving up more Merls to target stationary guns, and go on strafing and bombing runs. Slowly, but surely, you will sweep Core from the map.

Caution **Avoid rushing too quickly against the gun emplacements. They're set up to have overlapping angles of fire that can quickly wipe out a squad of your Kbots. Take the time to blast them with the Merls and with your aircraft, then move your ground troops forward.**

Mission 25:

Core Prime Apocalypse

Difficulty: Hard

Objective: Build a very powerful ground and air force that can fight its way through seven lines of Core troops stretched horizontally across the top half of the map. Destroy all of the Core forces, including their Commander, and walk the Commander to the top of the Dome (2) to win ultimate victory.

Starting forces: Commander, Construction Kbot, Construction Aircraft, Construction Vehicle, Merls, Zippers, Spiders, Bulldogs, Fidos, and PeeWees.

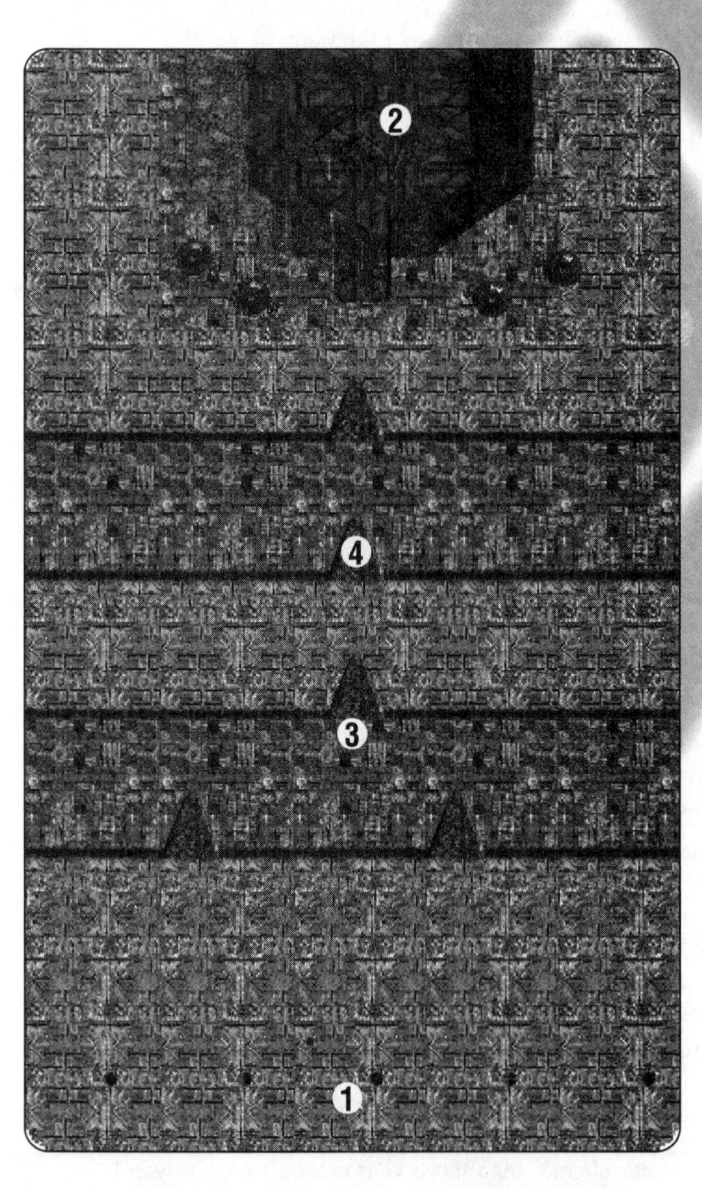

Mission Briefing

Welcome to the big show. This is the ultimate confrontation between Arm and Core. Virtually every kind of ground and air unit has been included on both sides. Prepare for a relentless and lengthy series of assaults against your position while you build your base near the southern edge of the map (1). When you have built a solid Level-2 army and air force, you are ready to launch the final attack against Core. Merls are a key to your long-range success, as is a Big Bertha or two.

How to Win

- **Immediately pull your forces back to the south, away from the Core front line (3).** Your troops are not yet ready for a slugging match with Core. Pull everything back toward the southern map boundary (1). Make sure that your Merls, construction units, and the Commander are closest to the southern edge for their protection. Set up a Radar Tower right away to give you more preparation time for the Core attacks that are soon to come.

- **Build Solar Collectors, Wind Generators, and Metal Extractors.** Unlike other missions, you start with three mobile construction units. Put them to use right away building resource generators, including Geothermal Power Generators on several steam grates.

- **Defend against Roach crawling bombs, then Slasher missile launchers, Raider tanks, Thud artillery, and Rapier gunships.** The attackers come at you in small waves every few minutes. Arrange your Kbots along a front perimeter, then have a line of artillery units, and then the Merl missile launchers. Your construction units and the Commander should be building as fast as possible.

- **Start building advanced construction plants.** The Level-2 construction plants will build most of your assault force, so plan to build advanced Kbot, vehicle, and aircraft plants before any forays into Core's defenses. While those are being built, have at least one construction unit free at all times to build several Sentinel laser towers, Guardian cannons, and Defender missile towers. Rapiers will continue to attack periodically, joined by Vamp stealth fighters. The first hour or two of play will consist of fighting off Core attacks while building your forces. Build a Big Bertha shortly after one of the advanced construction plants builds an advanced mobile construction unit. Have several of your construction units combine their building speeds to construct at least one Moho Mine and one Fusion Reactor.

- **Prepare for a counter-attack.** When your Bertha cannon starts to hit Pulverizer emplacements, it will trigger several more Rapier attacks as well as tanks and Pyro flame-thrower assaults. Reapers and Cans will follow soon after their attacks, so you must continue to build and rebuild your missile and rocket towers, as well as several Guardians. Have one of your construction units patrol just behind the length of your front line. It will automatically repair any of your units that's nearby. Build Jammer radar jammers and place them next to the Big Bertha and the Guardians.

- **Send in the fighters and bombers.** Once the Big Bertha has knocked out a number of Pulverizer missile towers, your aircraft will have an easier time striking Core defenses. Concentrate on your aircraft construction once you get the Level-2 Advanced Aircraft Plant. You will want about eight to ten Hawks, an equal number of Phoenix bombers, and six to eight Brawler gunships to get started on your attack runs. Keep the plant pumping out new aircraft.

- **Plan a Bulldog tank rush, with supporting Fidos, Zippers, and Zeus Kbots.** Keep several Merls trailing the main attack force—close enough to target their rockets, but far enough back to avoid Pulverizer and Gaat Gun fire. The rest of your extended assault will continue in this manner, with ground troops thrusting forward to point 3 and then point 4, while aircraft give supporting fire, and one or two Big Berthas pound the Core defenders. You will have to destroy just about everything before you take the Dome. Make sure the Core Commander is destroyed when your own Commander walks to the top of the Dome to victory.

Core is more aggressive than in most earlier missions. (After all, it *is* their final stand.) You won't be able to build your factories and your defenses without continuous fighting. Set the Unit Orders button for your front-line tanks, second-line missile launchers, and rocket launchers to Hold Position or Maneuver so that they won't pursue retreating attackers back to the Core front line. Keep your defenses together during the early, defensive stage of the mission.

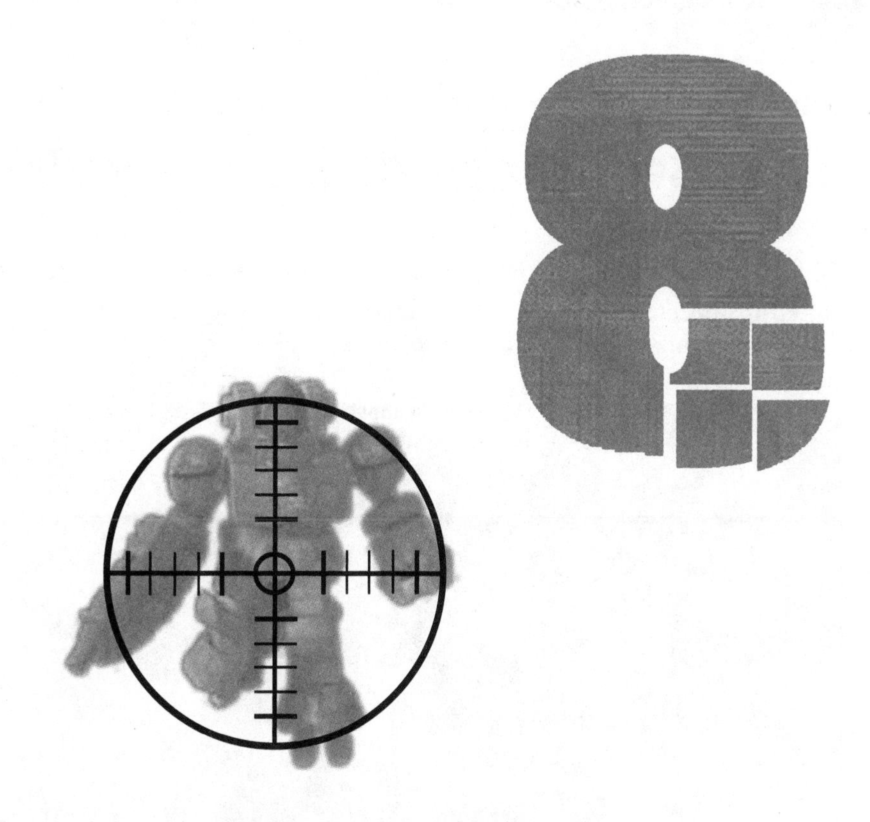

Core Missions

The first Core missions are played out on Core's metal home planet, Prime. Each battlefield is a labyrinth of narrow metal canyons; completing the missions depends on how fast you can find your way through the maze. Fields of fire tend to be constricting, and a few metal wrecks can quickly block an advance. After you successfully fend off the Arm offensive, the action shifts to other planets that feature largely Terran terrain, complete with woods and large bodies of water. You will quickly discover that using combined arms is absolutely essential to success. Careful resource management is a must in every mission, but particularly so in those that begin with your forces under Arm attack. Consider building a Kbot lab first, and then monitor energy and metal levels as you build units while expanding your base.

Mission 1:

The Commander Reactivated

Difficulty rating: Easy

Objective: Destroy all Arm forces in the area, rescuing your deactivated Commander.

Starting forces: Commander (near the northwestern corner of the battlefield), 4 AKs, 2 Storms, 3 Weasels, 1 Instigator, 1 Raider (near the southeastern corner of the battlefield)

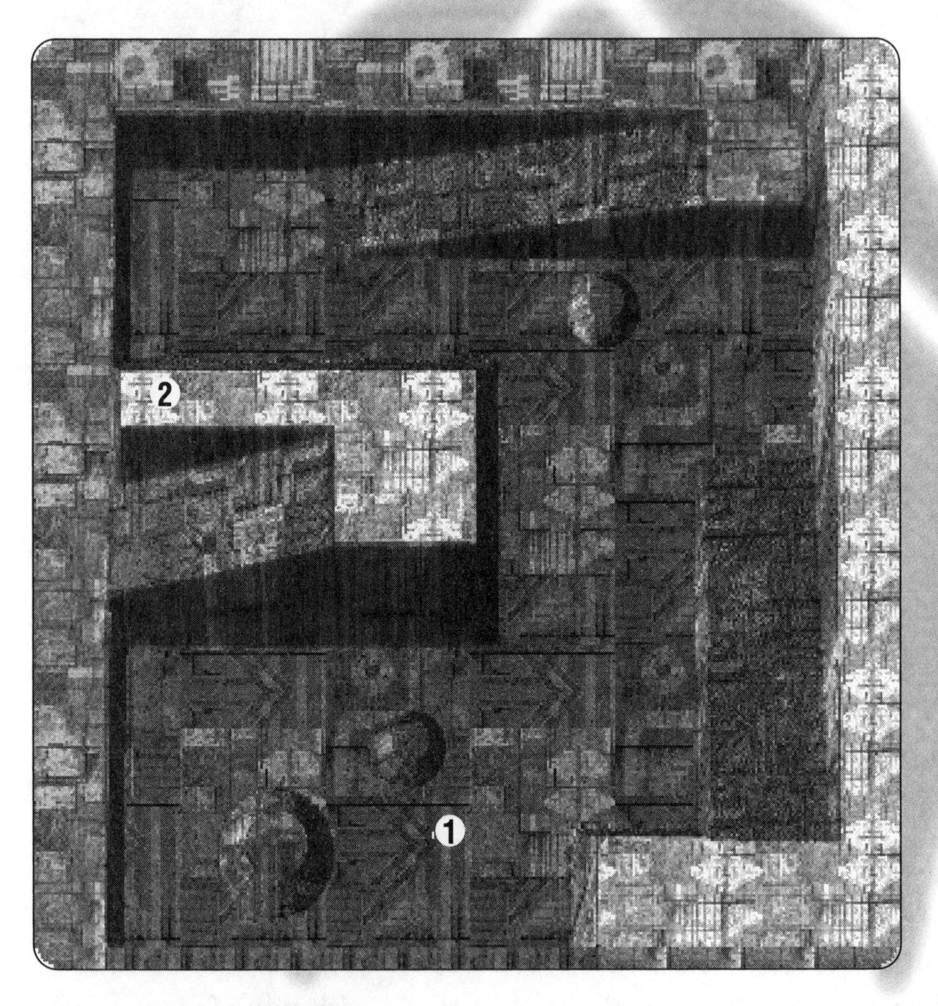

Mission Briefing

Your Commander is alone and deactivated (point 2 on the map), although not under attack by Arm troops. The Core force that will be rescuing him is far away, and harassed by light enemy units (point 1 on the map, and the first thing you see). This mission's easy. Since the Commander has no attackers, move your rescue force forward and make a slow but steady circuit of the map destroying all Core troops. Your Commander is present, but not involved.

How to Win

- **Move the rescue force.** The Commander is not in danger, so activate the rescue force and use this mission to practice moving your troops. You will shoot three Jeffys as soon as you begin. Your units will run into more Jeffys almost immediately, but should deal with them easily. As you make a circuit of the battlefield with your troops, a single Stumpy tank patrolling near the northwestern corner of the battlefield is likely to be your most persistent opponent.

- **Continue to sweep the ramps and ledges with your troops.** Have the rescue force climb the ramp and run westward along the ledge at the northern edge of the battlefield. There may be a couple of light Arm units skulking around the exit ramp from the Commander's ledge, but they present minimal threat.

- **Mop up remaining enemy units.** It's quite possible that almost all enemy units will have been destroyed by the time you link up with the Commander. If not, set the remaining units to roam—there may be the odd PeeWee or Jeffy that escaped your attention. Destruction of the last enemy unit brings the mission to a successful end.

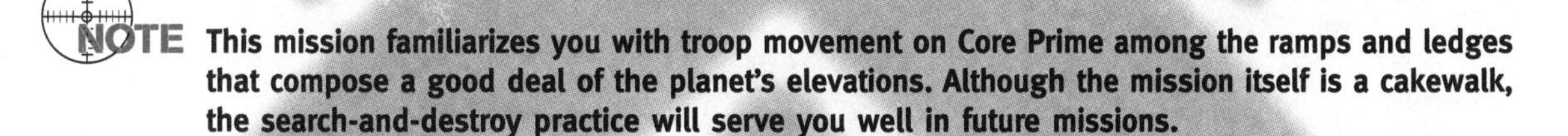

NOTE **This mission familiarizes you with troop movement on Core Prime among the ramps and ledges that compose a good deal of the planet's elevations. Although the mission itself is a cakewalk, the search-and-destroy practice will serve you well in future missions.**

Mission 2:

Vermin

Difficulty rating: Easy

Objective: Build a base that features a Vehicle Plant, and—you guessed it—destroy all Arm presence in the area.

Starting forces: Commander, 2 AKs, 1 Storm in the southeast

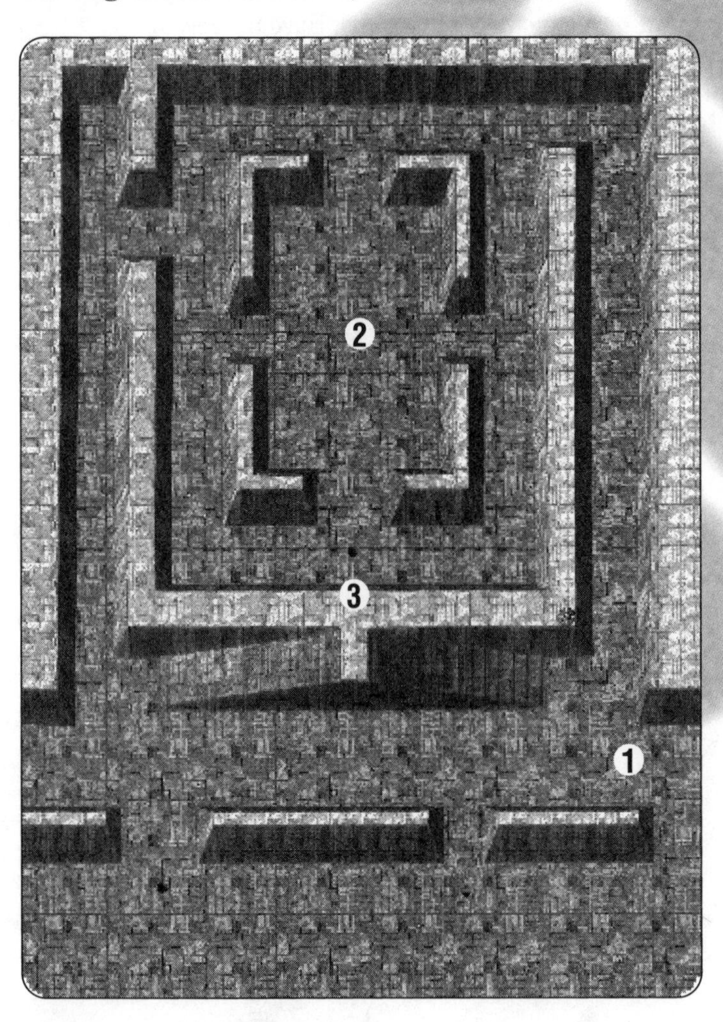

Mission Briefing

Not unlike the legendary Minotaur, the enemy base is contained in the center of a puzzle—like a labyrinth. Consult the map. You start at point 1; the enemy base is at point 2. Each of the four points of entry into the enemy base is guarded by a Light Laser Tower, with supporting Hammers. You can duke it out with those guys, but you will have to do it with just a Vehicle Plant. You cannot build any other factory. This calls for tank and missile vehicles.

How to Win

- **Build and defend.** Build up your base while fending off early attacks, mostly by small groups of determined PeeWees. Energy tends to be in short supply; make sure you have enough Solar Collectors. Build a Vehicle Lab and produce a number of Instigators and Weasels for base defense. Monitor energy and metal levels carefully as you proceed. If you have lots of energy and metal, a few Raider tanks can make base defense even easier.

- **Send out a couple of weasels north and west to scout.** While all this building is going on, your base defense force should have expanded enough to allow an offensive foray. Clear the area northwest of your base of enemy presence (scattered Kbots) near point 3. Build Instigators and Raiders as fast as possible. There are LLTs guarding the approaches to the enemy base, plus their supporting units (mostly Hammers).

- **Hunt down enemy units.** With no radar available and no Level-2 weapons, you must depend on your Weasels, Instigators, Raiders, and Slashers to carry the day. Move forward, step by step, with your tanks and your Commander to sweep the map.

NOTE **This mission teaches you to use your Commander in concert with your tanks. Practice selecting your tanks in squads with the Ctrl and 1–9 keys.**

Mission 3:

Ambush!

Difficulty rating: Easy

Objective: Destroy not only Arm units harassing Core transports on Thoroughfare 405, but any and all Arm units in the battle area.

Starting forces: Commander, 2 Storms; also half a dozen Valkyries on Thoroughfare 405, as well as a Level-1 Construction Vehicle and several Construction Kbots. The Thoroughfare 405 units are beyond your control, but their destruction impacts your score.

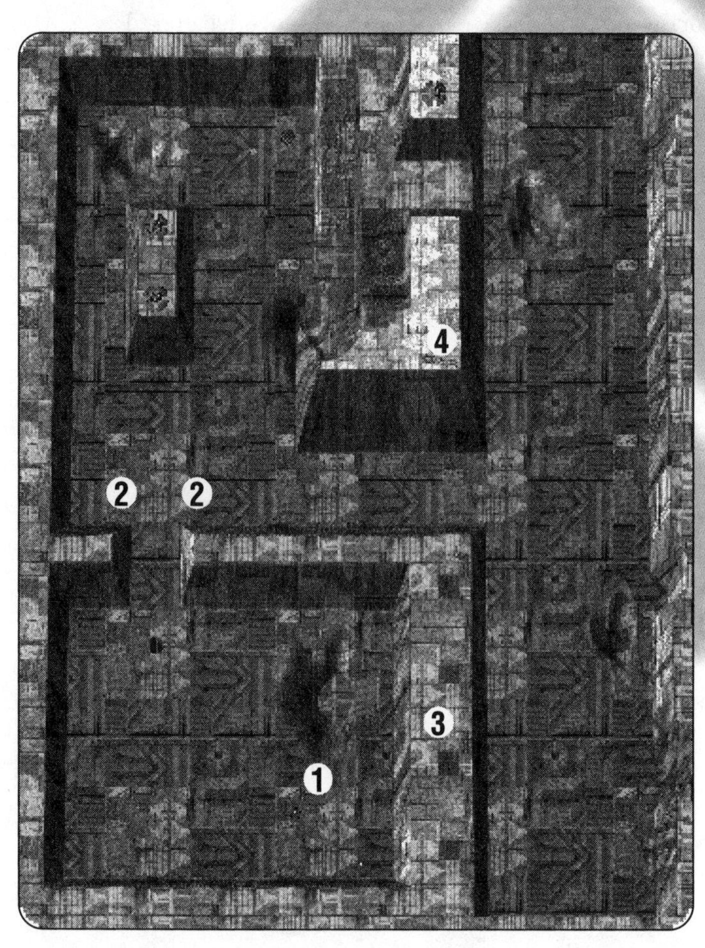

Mission Briefing

The enemy does not have a base in this mission—just bands of marauding units. Some of these are perched on the two ridges marked 3 and 4 on the map. Others roam at will; some of them may stray into your base. Enemy forces are composed almost exclusively of Kbots—PeeWees, Rockos, Hammers; you also have the capability to produce several Level-1 vehicles.

How to Win

- **Build your base and protect it from early enemy incursions.** Start building immediately around your starting point. Remember to leave lots of space between "active buildings," such as the Kbot Lab and Vehicle Plant; storage and resource-producing facilities may be squeezed together. Beware the ridge immediately to the east; if you build within spotting range of the Arm units perched on its top, you'll put your structures under enemy fire. Additionally, enemy activity includes individual PeeWees and small groups of Kbots (PeeWee plus Rocko or Hammer, two PeeWees and a Rocko) waltzing into your base and starting to shoot up everything in sight.
- **Break out of your starting area.** Build a small base defense force of AKs and Storms even as the Commander is working on the Vehicle plant. When the Vehicle Plant is ready, build several Instigator tanks—they are better at dealing with Hammers than your Kbots, and there are two Hammers guarding the exit from your base area (2). Support the Instigators with Kbots when nearby Arm units launch a series of weak counterattacks.
- **Clear the heights of enemy units.** The two ledges marked 3 and 4 on the map are home to a mix of Arm Kbots—Hammers and Rockos. Use AKs as spotters for your Storms and Thuds. Ledge 4 is inaccessible, and your units will have to fire from below. Ledge 3 can be stormed, though not without casualties. Beware of wrecks halting your advance up the narrow access ramp.
- **Mop up remaining enemy units.** Take personal command of a small squad while setting the other units to Roam from the Orders menu. The mission ends only when the last enemy unit is destroyed, and this includes guys lurking half off-screen on both ends of Thoroughfare 405.

NOTE **This is still one of the "learning" missions. Its main lesson is learning how to direct long-range rocket and artillery fire onto raised ledges from the ground below.**

Mission 4:

Enough Is Enough

Difficulty level: Medium

Objective: Intelligence reports indicate that this is the location of Arm's entry to Core Prime through a Galactic Gate. Destroy all of Arm's forces and have your Commander capture the Gate. The Gate must not be destroyed.

Starting forces: Commander, 2 Raider tanks, 2 Pyro flamethrowers

Mission Briefing

Your very small force must build a Kbot Lab and a Vehicle Plant while fighting off roving squads of Rockos, PeeWees, and Flash tanks. When your ground force is sufficiently strong, move forward to destroy Core forces, including Light Laser Towers and a Defender missile tower. Be careful not to destroy the Galactic Gate (5), which your Commander must capture to win the mission.

How to Win

- **Build Solar Collectors and Metal Extractors near the point where you begin (1).** In the southwest corner of the battlefield, build the resource generators and then a Kbot Lab, followed by a Vehicle Plant. Next, have your Commander place a Radar Tower near point 1. In the Kbot Lab, begin building Rocko rocket launchers, Thud artillery units, and A.K. Kbots. In the Vehicle Plant, first produce a Construction Vehicle, followed by six to eight Instigator tanks.

- **Fend off four Rockos and several Flash tanks.** Four Rocko rocket launchers will approach from the north on a patrol. They may send a few shots your way, but will keep marching east. Wait until their return, when you have some Kbots produced to join your initial Pyros and Raider tanks. Your Commander can also help knock them out with his D-Gun. A few Flash tanks will also come by, but by this time you should have your Kbot Lab and Vehicle Plant humming with new bots.

- **Order the Construction Vehicle to build an Advanced Vehicle Plant.** Your main goal in having an Advanced Vehicle Plant is to build four or five Diplomat mobile rocket launchers. They will be placed behind the front line of your assault force to target Arm gun emplacements. Also, build an Informer mobile radar unit and then several Reaper heavy assault tanks.

- **Keep your troops moving toward the Gate.** Arm Jethros and Stumpys, located in the northeast corner of the battlefield, will patrol south in the corridor to the east of points 3 and 4. By now, you should have a force that is superior to Arm's defenders. But you must be careful not to accidentally destroy the Galactic Gate as you move closer to point 5. There are two LLTs and a Defender missile tower just south of the Gate. Your artillery and Diplomats should be able to destroy them before you reach the top of the ramp above point 3. Most of the Arm defenders are Level-1 Kbots and vehicles, and won't be able to stand up to your forces. Just make sure that over-zealous units don't hit the Gate.

This mission is easier if you don't rush forward to points 2, 3, and 4. Build your forces first, and then methodically begin to move forward while destroying each Arm emplacement as you go.

Mission 5:

Barathrum!

Difficulty rating: Medium

Objective: The briefing says, destroy Arm guards at the Gate. "Guards" includes the whole Arm base—destroy everything and everyone belonging to Arm.

Starting forces: Commander

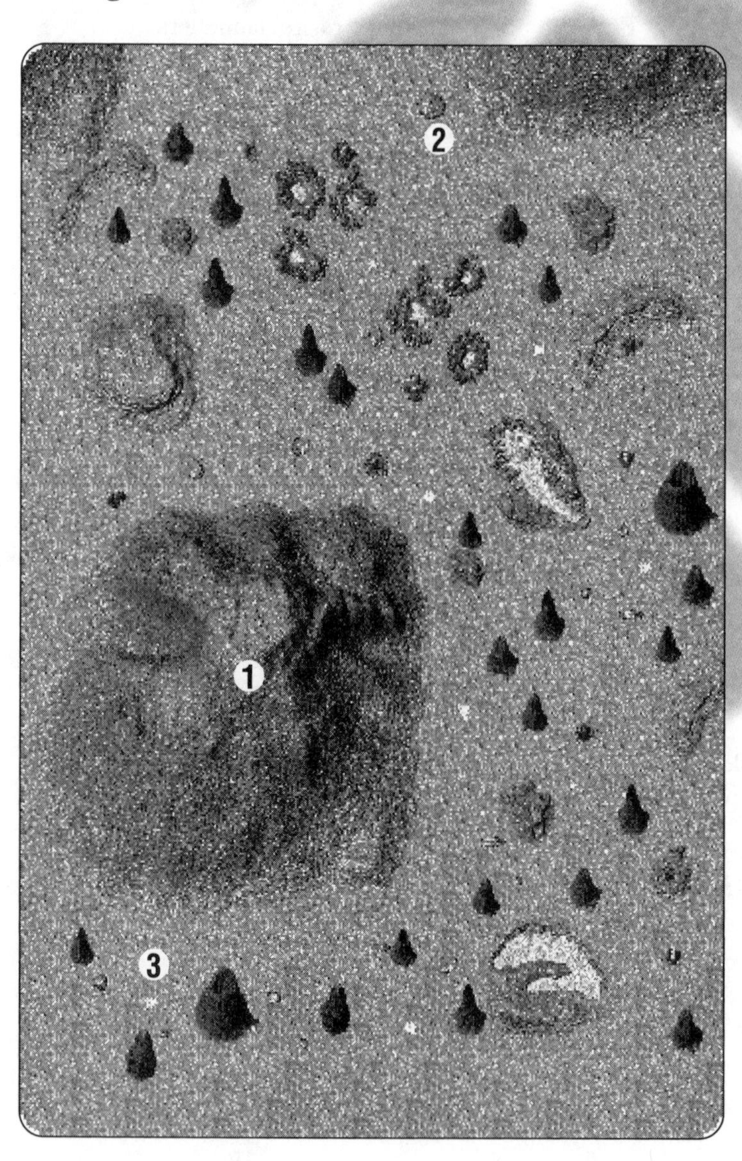

Mission Briefing

You start this mission perched atop a hill, next to the Gate, alone (1). Arm has a base to the northeast (2); you have one Commander. In spite of this inauspicious beginning, if you set up things right from the start—locate your base correctly and make the right kinds of units—this mission can turn out to be relatively easy. Air power makes its debut in this mission. Although you can, at a pinch, accomplish this mission without building an Aircraft Plant, things are much easier if you do.

How to Win

- **Run and build.** The first thing you want to do is put maximum distance between yourself and the enemy. Run the Commander straight south, with a slight tilt to the east, and set up base near the southwestern corner of the battlefield (3). That area features a metal deposit, and several rocks you can reclaim to speed things up. Start by building a Kbot Lab, so that you can begin to turn out units at a moment's notice. Follow with a Metal Extractor atop the deposit, and a Solar Collector.

- **Careful expansion.** Reconnoiter west with your Commander, keeping to the southern edge of the battlefield. You should quickly locate another metal deposit and several rocks. Metal is very short in this mission; constant reclamation from rocks and wrecks is essential. Back at the base, build a series of Crashers (enemy planes may appear early) and some Storms, possibly Thuds. Because of the metal shortage, it is better to build Kbots until you accumulate a resource reserve; Kbots cost less metal. Include a Construction Kbot on the building list.

- **Build a good army and air force.** Arm will start attacking as soon as you start expansion. These attacks—consisting mostly of Rockos and Hammers— will be cautious, and you should have no trouble holding your own. Build a couple of Light Laser and Punisher Missile Towers if you feel pressed. Arm aircraft will make repeated runs over the western part of your territory; put a strong squad of Crashers there—they will also help greatly with Arm ground attacks. Keep reclaiming metal! This will let you quickly build the metal-costly Vehicle and Aircraft Plant, and proceed to construct Slasher missile launchers and four to six Avengers. Put the fighters on patrol runs along your front lines, where they can intercept Arm Aircraft. Throughout this period, you may be harassed by heavy Arm Kbots equipped with long-range weapons. A platoon of quick-moving Instigators can greatly help in dealing with these annoying attacks.

- **Seize the initiative.** After you acquire an air force, Arm attacks are very easy to contain. Focus on building up your army— you should assemble a strike force of about 20 mixed bots (Storms, Crashers, and Thuds, plus Level-2 Kbots if you feel like playing with serious weaponry). To do things the easy way, build a Level-2 Vehicle Plant and turn out several Diplomats. Include other vehicles in the mix if you want to—Instigators and slashers work particularly well. Wait for the next Arm attack, defeat it, and counterattack in force.

- **Hit the Arm base.** Your counterattack should carry you right into the enemy base. It is fairly spread out in the northeastern part of the battlefield; its defenses consist of LLTs and Sentinels. Diplomats are invaluable in dealing with these—you may want to pull your guys back, build a couple of well-placed Radar Towers, and just let the Diplomats pummel everything red on the radar map.

- **Clean up.** After the Arm base defenses are down. you can either continue sending Diplomat missiles into structures while decimating counterattacking Arm units, or advance with your Kbots to quicken the end. If you do the latter, watch out for friendly fire casualties because of the trigger-happy Diplomats!

NOTE **Your Galactic Gate, isolated on its hill, is a target of an early Arm attack. Don't fret if you lose it—you can still win this mission.**

Mission 6:

The Cleansing Begins...

Difficulty rating: Medium

Objective: What, you don't know? Wipe Arm out.

Starting forces: Commander, 1 Crasher, 1 Fink

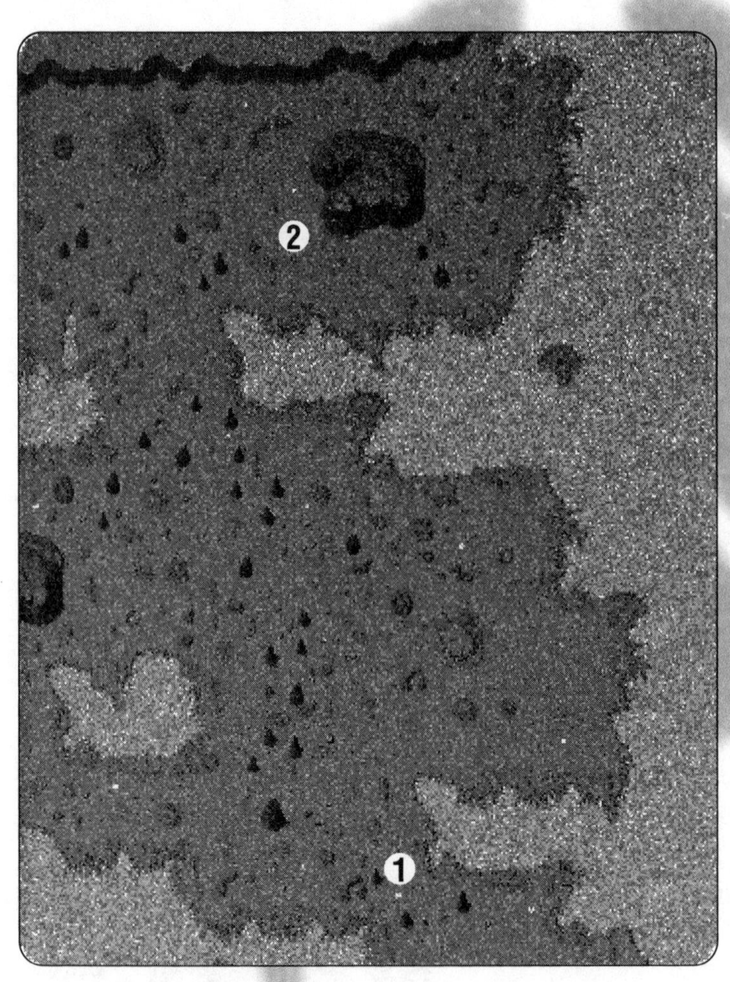

Mission Briefing

This mission is similar to Barathrum!, and this makes things easier. The geography is helpful too: Your Commander won't have to run anywhere—you can start setting up your base at your starting point (1). Also, the battle takes place on a peninsula, which means a narrow front, and smaller chances of enemy forces outflanking yours. The Arm base is close to the northern edge of the battlefield (2), just like in the previous mission. It does not contain an Aircraft Plant; once you have destroyed attacking Arm bombers, that is it for enemy air attacks. You may not need an Aircraft plant of your own.

How to Win

- **Lotsa nanolathing going on.** Build right where you start. Build Metal Extractors and energy generators. Build a Kbot Lab—you may even want to build it first, if you know how to manage resources well, because you will quickly come under attack from Arm aircraft. Build a standard AA squad of Crashers (six to seven Kbots), and deploy them in the flight path of Arm aircraft. Remember to repair damaged structures if necessary.

- **Use the Fink.** The Fink scout plane you are given at the start of this mission is extremely useful. At first, have it patrol east to west a little north of your base—this will warn you of Arm attacks, and save you the considerable energy costs of a Radar Tower at a time when every energy unit is precious. As soon as you have got a few Crashers, send the Fink on recon flights east, west, and north of your base. It will locate several metal deposits, energy nodes and geothermal vents. Use them.

- **Defend and build up your base.** Arm quickly starts to send waves of Kbots at your base, including Zeus and Fido class units. Just like in the previous mission, a line of Crashers and Storms is the perfect choice for handling this threat—their long firing ranges help a lot. You will find it helpful to bolster your base defense with a couple of defensive structures—a couple of LLTs, or preferably Heavy Laser and Punisher Towers. Remember to repair damaged units, and you will find that your army is growing very fast. While all this is taking place, build a Vehicle Plant (if you haven't already), a Construction Vehicle, and an Advanced Vehicle Plant. You want those Diplomats again.

- **Counterattack**. After you have beaten off a few Arm attacks, they will begin to dwindle. You can now switch to offensive thinking, and build a series of Diplomats plus several Reapers. When your force is assembled and ready, wait for the next Arm attack, and launch a counterattack. This ensures you will be faced with a weak Arm base defense force—Hammers, PeeWees, and the odd Fido. The defensive structures—LLTs, Sentinels, and Defenders—are more of a problem. Employ the classic Diplomat tactic: advance in stages, building Radar Towers as needed, then use the radar map to demolish enemy structures from a distance.

- **Hunt them down.** Sometimes the mission does not end after you turn the Arm base into smoking ruins; this means there is still an Arm unit or two lurking somewhere. Sweep the battlefield till you find them—planes help.

NOTE **This mission confirms Diplomats and radar are a winning combination. Note that they will only automatically fire at defensive structures; you have to actively target them on other buildings.**

Mission 7:

Pulling the Noose Tight

Difficulty rating: Easy to Medium

Objective: Capture Arm's Moho Mines, destroy everything else.

Starting forces: Commander, 2 Weasels, 1 Pyro

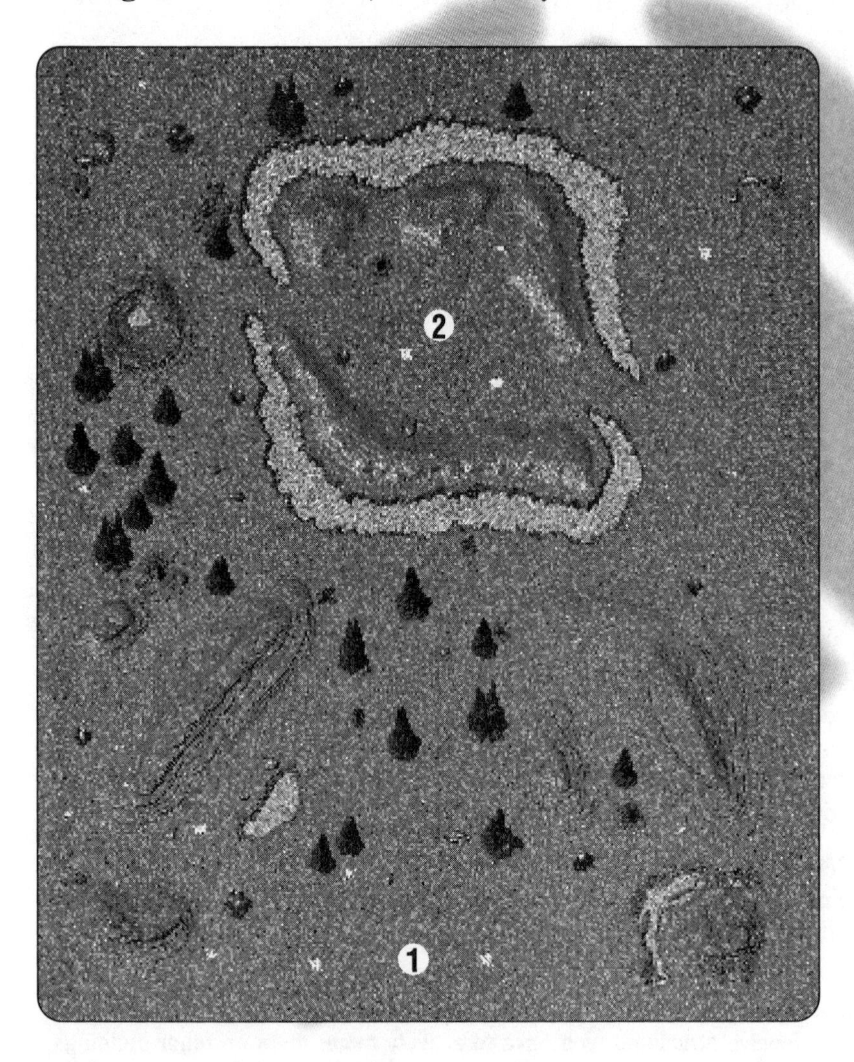

Mission Briefing

Once again, you start in the south (1), and the Arm base is to the north (2). This time, the enemy base is protected by a lava moat—the only access is through narrow land bridges in the east and in the west. And once again, you should build right where you start. This mission is very generous in terms of resources. What's more, the enemy is strangely subdued, letting you build your base in peace.

How to Win

- **Grow while the growing's easy.** The area around your starting point abounds in resources. There are four geothermal vents and five metal deposits, including those a little further away but still within easy reach. You should start by building the usual basics—extractors, energy generators, and Kbot Lab—and the usual half a dozen Crashers. Then build a Construction Kbot and end any energy problems (rapid expansion causes these) by having it build a couple of Geothermal Power Generators. your commander will have built all the Metal Extractors you need in the meantime.

- **Build a base assault force.** Absence of any meaningful Arm activity means you can start building a base assault force almost immediately. You need an Advanced Vehicle Plant first; set production to Reaper tanks and Diplomats. It's also good to build a strong squad of Crashers and Storms, possibly also Thuds, to take care of defensive needs and to aid in the upcoming offensive. Wait until you have assembled a dozen Reapers and half a dozen Diplomats.

- **Attack with a pincer movement.** Do not approach the enemy base from the south; you will have to follow the lava moat to the land bridges, and Arm's Defenders will have a party. Divide your army into two strike forces consisting of Reapers, Storms, and Crashers, and send them along the eastern and western edges of the battlefield. When they reach positions near the land bridges into the Arm base, move your Diplomats in from the south. You do not want to destroy the Moho Mines by accident—don't target the diplomats using the radar map unless you are sure the target is not a mine. The Diplomats will fire on their own on all enemy combat structures and units the moment they are spotted by your strike forces of Reapers and Kbots. Order both strike forces to attack simultaneously, and make sure the Diplos target the Defender towers first—they are the greatest danger.

- **Capture the Moho Mines.** After all the enemy units and defensive structures are destroyed, send the Commander in to capture the Mohos. Make sure you destroy or capture all other Arm structures, too.

NOTE **You have a great opportunity to practice executing a pincer movement, and coordinating a simultaneous attack on both wings—the enemy opposition is not that fierce, and you can make mistakes and still be forgiven. These tactics will be very useful both in the missions to come, and in multiplayer games.**

Mission 8:

The Gate to Aqueous Minor

Difficulty rating: Medium

Objective: Capture the Gate, and wipe out all other Arm structures and units.

Starting force: Commander, 2 Pyros, 1 Crasher

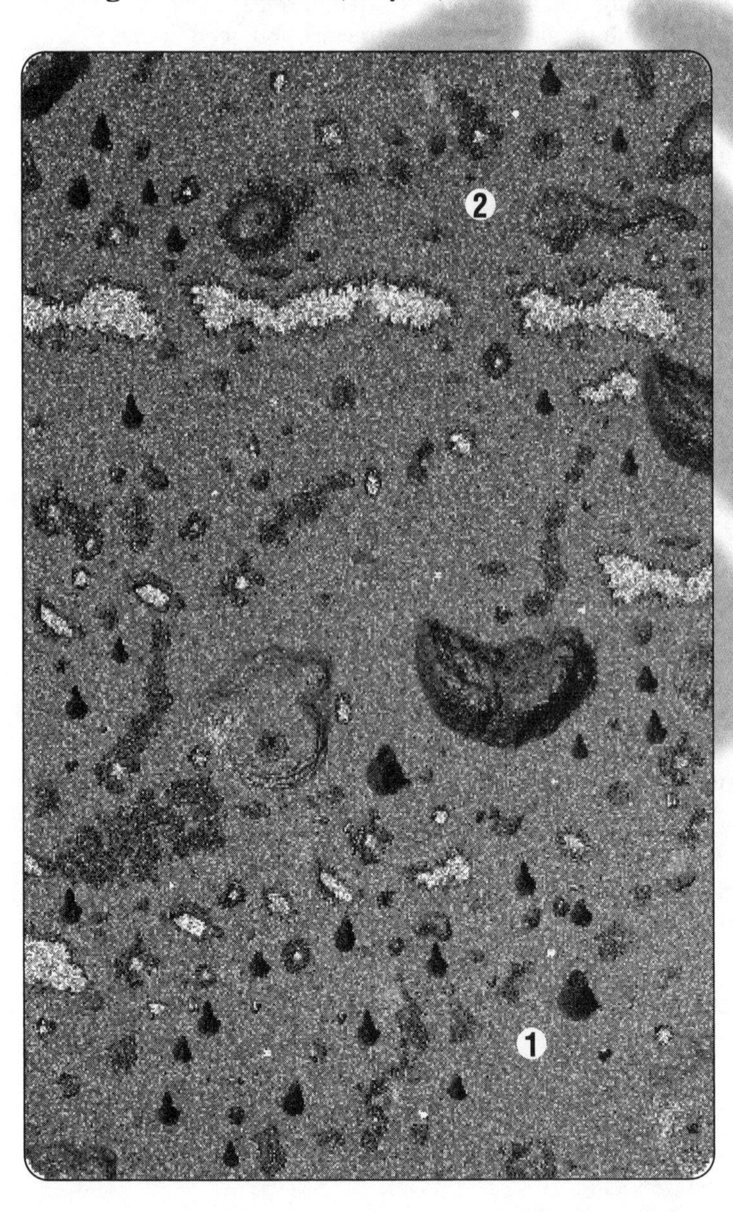

Mission Briefing

This mission is noticeably tougher than the previous one, even though Arm forces do not include aircraft. The enemy will be much more active and aggressive than in the preceding missions, while you will only have a small force with your Commander to start with (1). The strong enemy base is, as usual, in the northern part of battlefield, half-hidden behind a partial lava moat (2). This time, the lava runs from east to west, across the whole battlefield. There are three land bridges over which you can cross into the enemy base; two are narrow, one is wide enough to permit the use of heavier vehicles. For the first time, Arm will deploy heavy Bulldog tanks in base defense.

How to Win

- **Build under fire.** Once again, your Commander has to establish a base in face of enemy activity. It helps if you set up your base a little east of your starting point; Arm forces are not as likely to venture into the southeastern corner of the battlefield. Set up the standard base structures—Kbot Lab, extractors, generators—and start production with the usual half a dozen Crashers and Storms. the enemy does not use aircraft in this mission, but the Crasher's long reach greatly helps in base defense. Build a Construction Kbot as quickly as you can without jeopardizing defense. Use it to help out the Commander with base setup, to repair damaged units, and especially to build two Geothermal generators over the vents in the southeastern part of the battlefield. These will solve all your energy problems.
- **Hunting resources.** The quick pace of this mission means you will be under pressure to provide enough resources for all the necessary construction. Arm attacks on your base always come from one particular direction, one at a time. Given a base defense force of heavier Kbots supported by a couple of LLTs, possibly Gaat Guns if you can afford them, you will manage to beat off threats while scouting the neighbourhood in another direction. Build extractors on all deposits you find, and reclaim all the metal and energy you can!
- **Capture the mountain.** There is a mountain east of the center of the battlefield. Securing it, and building a Radar Tower on top will reveal most of Arm's defensive positions on your radar map—then you can take them out with Diplomats. First, however, you have to build the kind of army that will allow you to push your front lines north of the mountain, and hold them there. You have to build an Advanced Vehicle Plant in order to get Reaper tanks and those invaluable Diplomats. Depending on your battlefield abilities, build 10-20 Reapers and half a dozen Diplomats. Additionally, build up to 10 Instigators. Supported by your combat Kbots, these vehicles will let you hold Arm at bay.
- **Bombard and storm.** The Galactic Gate you have to capture is located almost exactly in the center of the enemy base. You can target Diplomats on structures lining the lava moat with the knowledge you'll be destroying Defender and Light Laser Towers, not the Gate. After you clear Arm's outer defenses, you will be ready for the main assault. It is best that you throw the Reapers onto the middle of the three land bridges—it's the broadest. Push with Instigators on the left wing, in the west, and keep the Diplomats busy. The enemy defenses are strongest to the east, slightly weaker in the west. the enemy defense force consists of Zeus, Hammer, Rocko, and Jethro bots, as well as a number of Bulldog tanks. Your skills as a commander of armor will be put to a tough test—support your tanks with Crashers and Storms whenever possible.
- **Clean up and capture the Gate.** Pockets of enemy resistance will still exist even after you have broken through the lava moat barrier and destroyed the main Arm defenses. Clearing the bridges of metal wreckage is a priority—otherwise, you will find it difficult to send reinforcements as necessary. Make sure you have cleaned out Arm units before you send in your Commander to capture the game—Bulldogs are heavy hitters!

NOTE **Arm Bulldogs pack a powerful punch, and should be neutralized quickly—break their heavy armor by targeting them with many units at the same time.**

Mission 9:

The Purgation of Aqueous Minor

Difficulty rating: Medium to Hard

Objective: Build a naval base, defend it, then destroy all of Arm's navy in the area.

Starting force: Commander

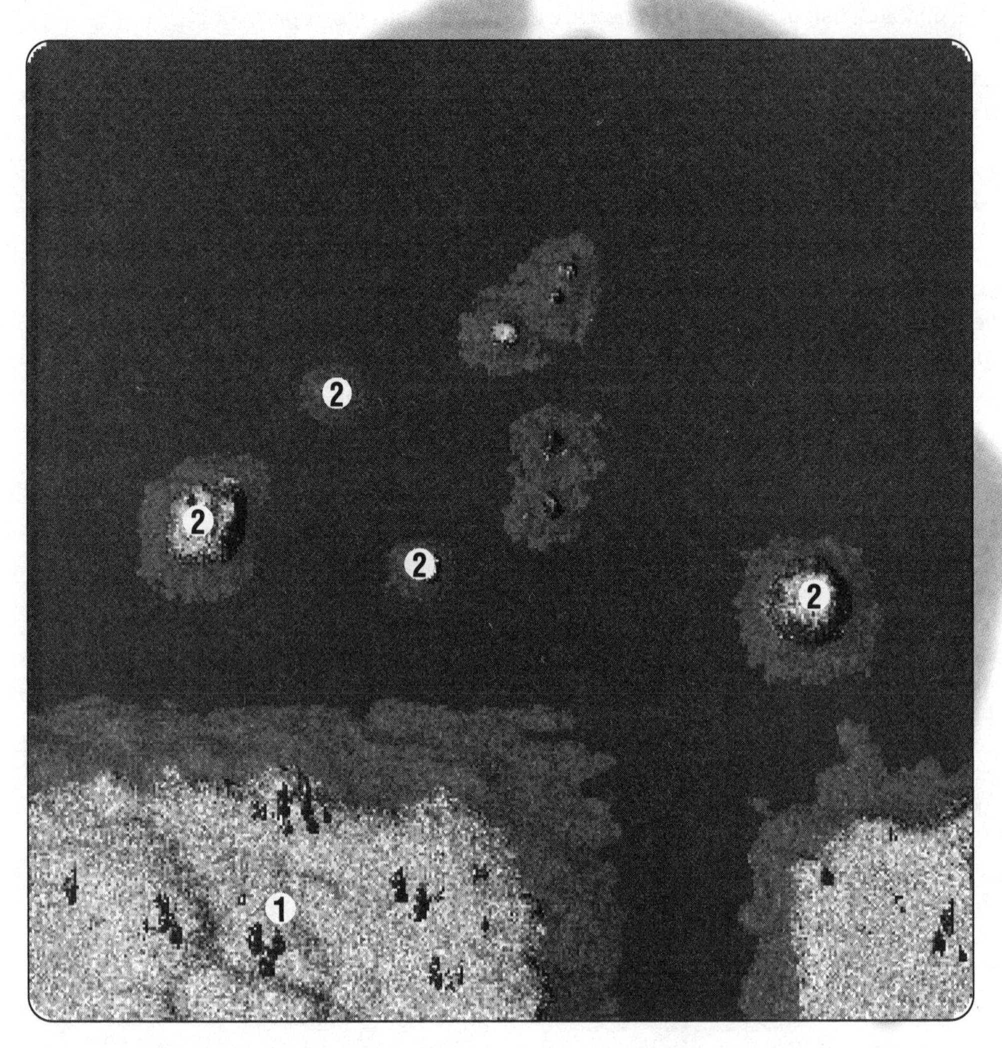

Mission Briefing

This is the first mission in which you get to play with ships. Before you do, however, you will have to build a ground force that can keep Arm ships at bay while your navy's being born. Arm has also built defensive structures (2) on the islands north of the land mass on which you start (1). You have to destroy these structures along with the enemy navy to complete the mission.

How to Win

- **Shoot and Hide.** The mission opens with your Commander near four PeeWees. Disintegrate the PeeWees. Build the basics—Kbot Lab, extractors, energy generators. Begin weapons production with half a dozen Storms. Then, build a Construction Kbot.

- **Build long-range weaponry.** There are four metal deposits and a geothermal vent on the island. Build the appropriate structures—they will be quite safe from Arm ships, which tend to target combat units. The attacking Arm navy consists of Crusaders and Rangers. Build a Vehicle Plant and order it to make Slashers and a Construction Vehicle. Attack the Arm ships offshore with six to seven Slashers even as you are building an Advanced Vehicle Plant. This will let you make Diplomats, four or five of which—together with Slashers—will be enough to keep the Arm navy at bay when you start your Shipyard. The Arm ships tend to be stationary if not bothered by submarines; this makes them easy to hit by the Diplomats.

- **Build your first navy.** Do not attempt building the Shipyard before your Slashers and Diplomats sort out the attackers—if you do, you will have to rebuild it. Start on the Shipyard only once you have beaten off three or four naval attacks. A navy costs plenty of metal, so you may want to build a Construction ship along with your first Snakes and Enforcers. Use it to reclaim metal from sunken Arm ships—a single Ranger nets you 1,800 units of metal! Remember to keep Slashers and Diplomats ready while your navy's being born; even though Arm has stopped attacking in earnest, it still has combat ships out there, and they may come nosing around. Once you've got the Shipyard and the metal, build a navy composed of several Snake subs and a flotilla of Enforcer-class destroyers, possibly also Hydra frigates.

- **Search and destroy.** Use Snakes to find the remaining enemy ships—you may have to wait with attacking them until you have dealt with the Arm structures (plasma cannon, laser towers) on the islands to the north. Attack these structures with your entire destroyer battle group—don't send single ships! This way, you won't lose any. Once you have destroyed all the structures and the remaining Arm ships (a couple of Crusaders, Skeeter class scouts) the mission is complete.

NOTE **Ships are expensive to build, but pretty easy to sink—as you will see when your Storms open up on the Arm Crusader. Remember that when leading your destroyers against Arm plasma cannon.**

Mission 10:

The Gauntlet

Difficulty rating: Medium to Hard

Objective: Simple—take a transport through the narrow straits known as the Gauntlet. That involves building a base, a Shipyard, an Advanced Shipyard, and a lot of ships.

Starting force: Commander

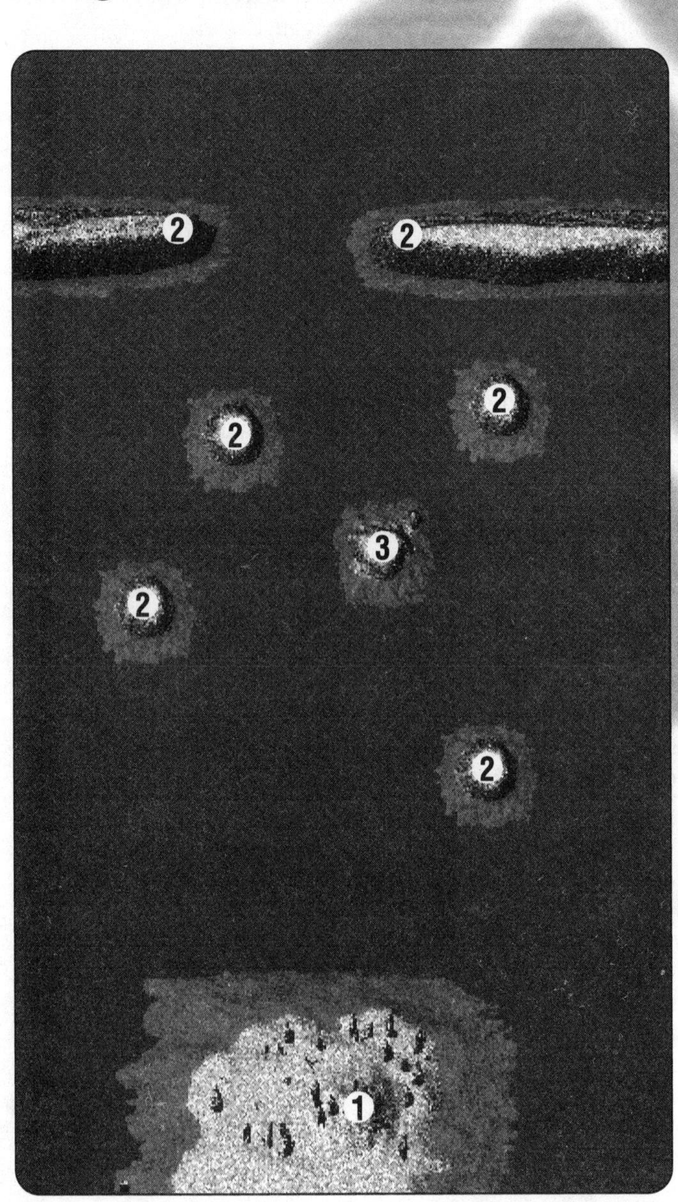

Mission Briefing

This is another naval mission. Your lone Commander is stuck on an island at the southern edge of the battlefield (1); fortunately, it takes a while before Arm's roving destroyers make an appearance. In order to take a transport successfully through the Gauntlet, you must destroy a sizable Arm naval force plus defensive structures scattered on the islands between you and the Gauntlet, and on both sides of the waterway (2).

How to Win

- **Build wisely.** Although your Commander is not under attack when this mission opens, you will have a difficult time building your base because of the very limited space. What's more, in addition to energy generators and metal extractors you will have to build a Kbot Lab too—you don't have enough time to build a Shipyard and a navy before the first Crusader starts bombarding your positions. You need a strong squad of Crashers and Storms to deal with this threat. While building, remember that if necessary you can demolish structures later on by reclaiming their metal, and building new structures in their place.

- **Create a navy, kill Piranhas.** Once Crashers and Storms protect your base from enemy attacks, build your Shipyard. Start your navy by commissioning half a dozen Snake submarines, several Enforcer destroyers, and a Construction Ship—use it to reclaim metal from the shipwrecks. Start with submarines—there are about five Arm Piranhas lurking in the nearby waters, waiting for ships to torpedo. However, your Snakes can deal with them, as long as you keep building new subs. After the Piranhas, and once you've got enough metal, build an Advanced Shipyard, and enlarge your navy by Hydra missile frigates, Executioner cruisers and a Warlord battleship or two, if metal reserves allow it. Each of the islands scattered between you and the Gauntlet features strong Arm defenses—a pair of Sentinels with a Guardian or a Defender.

- **Demolish Arm's island defenses and Torpedo Launchers.** Attack the island fortifications with your whole surface navy simultaneously, while your subs ambush any enemy ships trying to intervene. Reconnoiter north with your subs to get an idea of each island's location—you don't want your ships to get fired at from an island while they're bombarding another. Beware the Arm Torpedo Launchers to the north—there are four in total, two on both sides of the entrance to the Gauntlet, and two further out south to the east and west respectively.

- **Build an Advanced Radar Tower on the middle island.** Build an Advanced Kbot Lab, then a Level-2 Construction Kbot and ship it to the middle island on the map (3). Build an Advanced Radar Tower there. This will immediately uncover all the Arm forces on the radar map—with the exception of a group of Piranha and Lurker subs south of the entrance to the Gauntlet. Use the radar map to target the Torpedo Launchers and the defensive structures guarding the Gauntlet with your long-range naval weaponry. This may provoke the Arm subs to attack your surface force—keep your Snakes ready for this eventuality. If the Arm subs choose to stay concealed, the simplest thing to do is to force them into action by running a couple of Searcher scouts across the Gauntlet entrance, then attack them with your Snakes. Build new Snakes to maintain a pack of six subs at all times—they will come in handy later against another group of Arm ships.

- **Open up the Gauntlet.** The Arm naval force north of the Gauntlet consists of a Conqueror class cruiser and several Ranger missile frigates, and their firing ranges are better than those of your ships. But now you have advanced radar, the Arm ships are almost defenseless: You can start hitting them with your long-range weaponry while staying unseen. There is a chance the Arm fleet will sail towards yours in an attempt to fight back; let your surviving Snakes lay in ambush south of the entrance to the Gauntlet. Torpedoes and missiles will make short work of the last Arm ships.

- **Put the Commander to sea.** Load the Commander onto a transport and take him on the required cruise. That's it.

The Level-1 Snake submarine is your savior in this mission. Build plenty of these units; they're better value than the Level-2 Shark.

Mission 11:

Isle Parche

Difficulty rating: Medium

Objective: Capture the Arm Zeus Kbot. This involves wiping out a strong base on another island.

Starting force: Commander

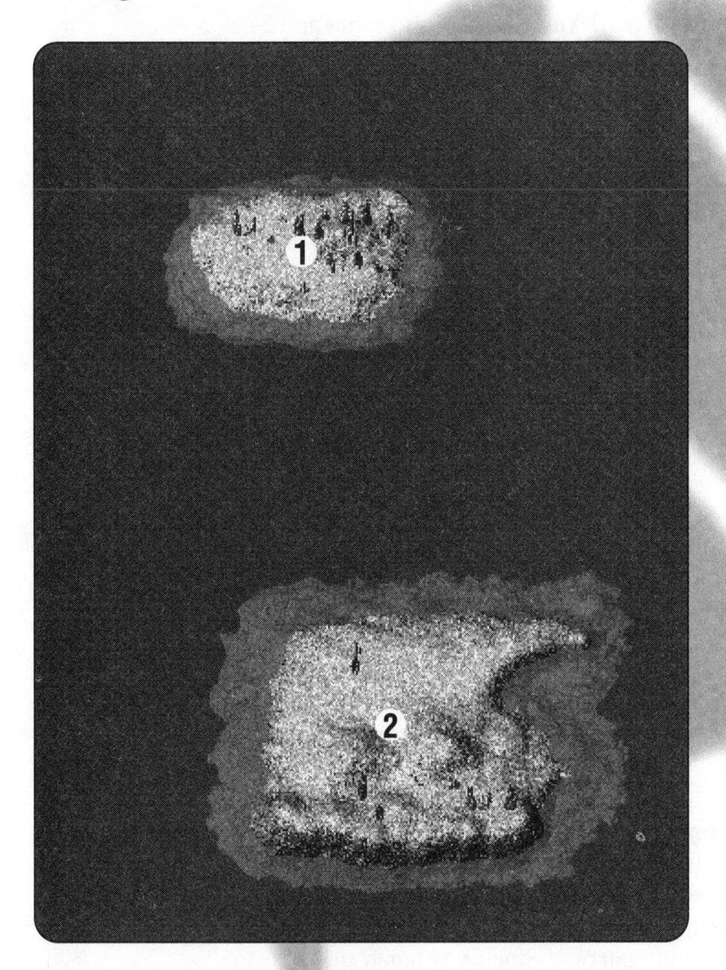

Mission Briefing

This is another naval mission, but with a twist. You must capture Arm's Zeus Kbot. You start on an island in the north (1); Arm forces occupy an island to the south (2). The Arm island sports formidable defenses—it is protected by a chain of Torpedo Launchers, plus a navy that includes Millenium battleships. You will also have to plan smartly to use the limited space available in the best way possible. Tear down Level-1 structures and build Level-2 Moho Mines and Fusion Plants in their place; you will need them to meet the cost of building a series of Level-2 warships. An Advanced Radar Tower will go a long way towards securing victory. Avoid destroying the Zeus near point 2.

How to Win

- **Build and rebuild.** Plan your base wisely; there's little space, and much to be built. Start by setting up the basics (resource generators, Kbot Lab), then build a Construction Kbot and a half-dozen Storms when resources allow—you will need them later. Order the Construction Kbot to build two Fusion Plants, reclaiming the metal from old Solar Collectors. Follow up by replacing extractors with a Moho Mine.

- **Build and rebuild, part two—the Naval Yard.** The Moho mine and Fusion Plants will provide you with the resources you need to quickly build—and rebuild—the Shipyard. Yep, the moment your Commander gets his feet wet (he has to wade into the shallows in order to build the Yard), he will come under fire from Arm Crusaders and Lurker subs. Keep your Storms on the shore to target Arm destroyers—the Lurkers cannot hit the Shipyard, only destroyers can. The Arm subs are a very real threat to your Commander, though.

- **Build and rebuild, part three—the Snake pack.** Eventually, your Storms will knock out the threat to your Shipyard. The Arm subs tend to come and go, providing time windows in which you can build in relative peace. Be persistent, and build enough Snake subs to wipe out the Lurkers. A Construction ship should be next, to reclaim metal from shipwrecks and build a Level-2 Shipyard. You need a task force of Hydra missile frigates, and Executioner cruisers or Warlord battleships (if you can afford them).

- **Radar Power.** While your fleet is being assembled, you should build an Advanced Kbot Lab (demolish the old one with your Construction Kbot), and then a Level-2 Construction Kbot. Use it to erect an Advanced Radar Tower. The radar map will sprout red spots as you uncover Arm Torpedo Launchers and the remaining Arm fleet: two Millenium battleships and a Crusader east of Arm's island. There are several Lurkers there too, so do not send in your surface force blindly: Bombard all targets from a safe distance, protecting your precious capital ships with a screen of Snakes. If Arm subs don't show their hand, send in a Searcher followed by your subs to provoke them.

- **Shore bombardment made easy.** After all the Arm ships are sunk, the mission becomes very easy. Continue demolishing Arm structures and units with the help of radar-directed gun and missile fire. You must not destroy the Zeus. Your Commander must capture it. Moving units may be hard to target; if necessary, build a transport and send over an execution party of Storms to finish the job.

If your Fusion Plants are providing a big energy surplus, build a Metal Maker and switch it on when feasible. Although inefficient, it will change idle energy into much-needed metal.

Mission 12:

A Traitor Leads the Way

Difficulty rating: Medium

Objective: Move the Zeus Kbot to the Galactic Gate and order your Commander to capture the Gate.

Starting forces: Commander, 1 Zeus Kbot

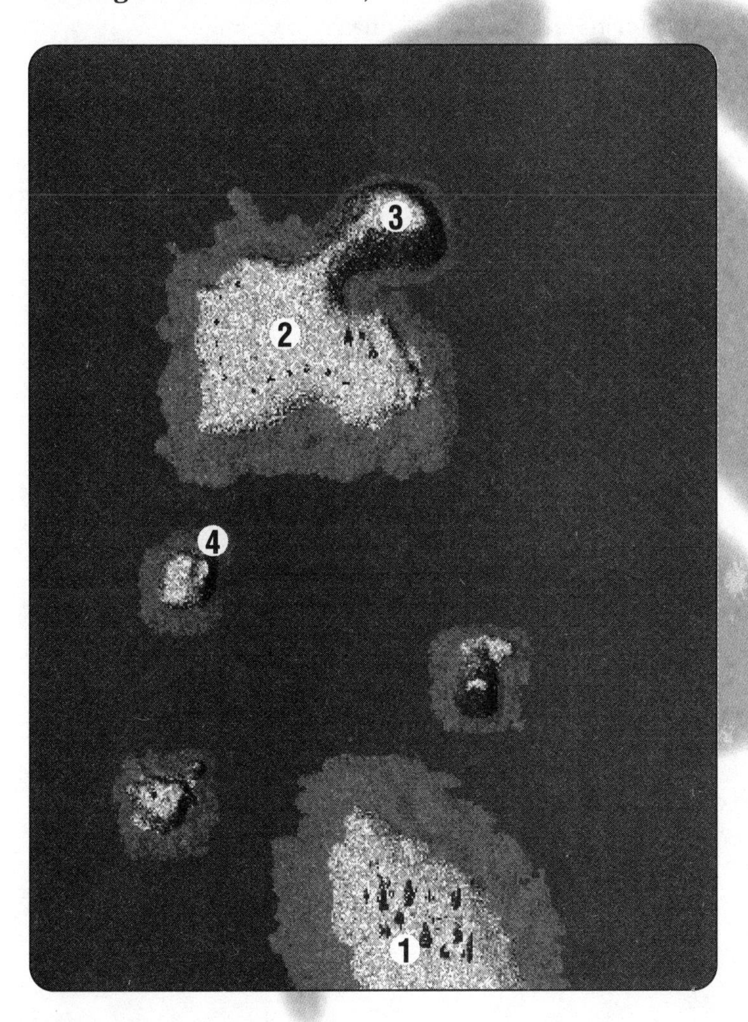

Mission Briefing

This is yet another island mission in which building an Advanced Radar Tower pays big dividends. You start in the south (1); the Arm base is on the island north (2), with the Galactic Gate located at the tip of the peninsula jutting north (3). After securing control of the waters between you and Arm, build the radar on one of the little islands (4). This will reveal Arm positions, and allow easy completion of this mission. The Hydra frigate/Advanced Radar is an unbeatable combination—as long as you don't target the Galactic Gate! Deliver your Zeus to the Gate, and then capture the Gate.

How to Win

- **Conserve real estate.** Like in the preceding mission, there is a space problem, and there are aggressive Arm Crusaders to make things more difficult. follow the usual drill and build the basics, then turn out half a dozen Storm Kbots to deal with the destroyers. Then proceed to build up to Level-2 structures, and replace your extractors and energy generators with Moho Mines and Fusion Plants.

- **Shipyard one, Shipyard two.** The Storms will also come in handy if your Commander comes under Crusader fire while building the Shipyard. Comission half a dozen Snakes—keep three near the Shipyard for defense, and send the others out to the north to deal with roving Crusaders. The little island to the west of yours has no Arm defenses; it has a metal deposit instead. Make sure you build a Moho Mine there, too—you will need to acquire a transport for your Advanced Construction Kbot. This will provide the metal supply you need to proceed to an Advanced Shipyard, and a series of warships: Warlords and/or Executioners. Combine those with Enforcers and Snakes from your Level-1 Shipyard to form an invincible naval task force. Keep your Zeus constantly repaired.

- **Conquer the islands.** Your next step should be to occupy the two remaining islands, to the north of yours. Both feature Arm defensive structures—Sentinel and Guardian towers. Slightly to the north of these islands and to the sides are two Arm naval groups—there are two Millenium battleships in each, guarded by two Lurker subs. Be ready for them as you send your fleet against Arm's islands—they may intervene. If they don't, engage and destroy them upon dealing with the Sentinels and the Guardians. Remember to protect your surface ships with your subs.

- **Set up Advanced Radar.** Once the islands are safely in your hands, send an Advanced Construction Kbot to the northwestern one, and build an Advanced Radar Tower. You'll immediately see the remaining Arm forces. Target everything in turn at long range, with the exception of the solitary red dot at the northernmost tip of Arm's island. that's the Gate you have to capture to win this mission!

- **Final Rites.** Your fleet should obliterate everything apart from the Gate. If there are any Arm survivors, your Commander D-Gun should be good enough. Transport the Commander and your Zeus to the Arm island, and capture the Gate.

Mission 13:

Rougpelt

Difficulty rating: Easy

Objective: Capture Arm's Advanced Radar Tower.

Starting force: Commander

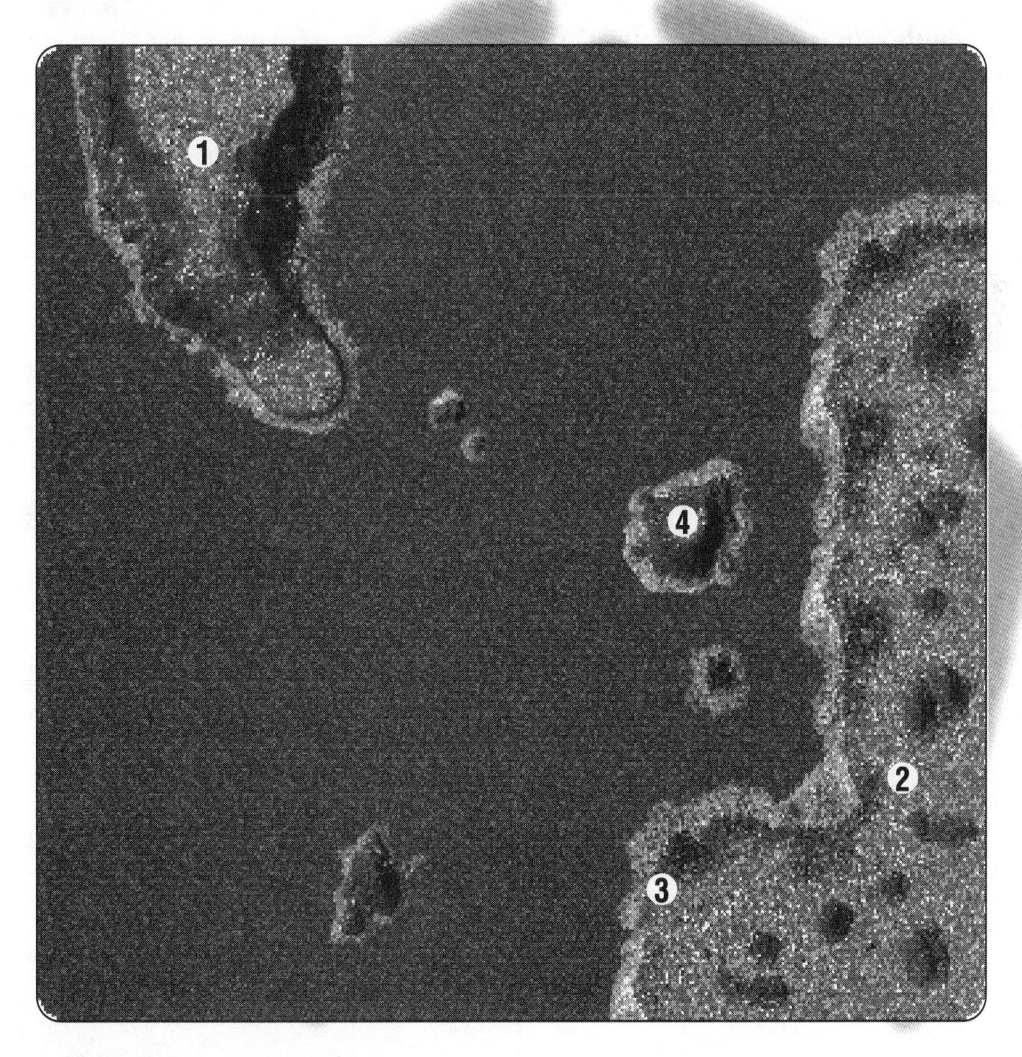

Mission Briefing

In this mission, your Commander becomes a commando. You have to destroy whatever is moving, and capture whatever isn't. You start on a peninsula (1), and have to cross the water to the land mass to the southeast. There, you'll have to destroy a variety of opposing Arm units, capture a Kbot Lab (2), destroy a LLT (3), and finally—to win the mission—capture an Advanced Radar Tower (4).

How to Win

- **Draw the D-gun.** Your Commander begins this mission under fire from two Zeus bots. Destroy them quickly; they're dangerous. Capture the Wind Generator to the east, then proceed to locate and capture the Atlas transport mentioned in the briefing; it's parked on your peninsula. Fly directly east and disembark the Commander on the northern end of the land mass you'll sight.

- **Proceed south with caution.** March the Commander south, but be cautious; you will encounter two Hammers guarding another Wind Generator in short order. They are easy pickings for your Commander's D-Gun if you are fast enough; capture the Generator to provide enough energy for the D-Gun. The third Wind Generator you will capture is a bit further south; this one is guarded by two Zippers. Proceed south and you'll come across an Arm Kbot Lab defended by a Hammer and a PeeWee. Kill the enemy Kbots and capture the Lab; it will come in useful in a little while. Don't build anything just yet, as it will use up the energy the Commander needs to fire the D-Gun.

- **Destroy and capture.** The coast curves westwards; follow it, keeping an eye out for the Arm LLT located at point 3. Blast it with your D-gun, and the mission is practically complete. Let the Commander saunter back to the Atlas while building a single Jethro bot in the captured Lab; use the Jethro to shoot down an Arm scout flying back and forth over the Lab. Then transport the Commander in the aircraft to the northernmost of two small islands to the west, and capture the Arm Radar Tower located there. That's it!

Mission 14:
Scouring Rougpelt

Difficulty rating: Hard

Objective: Kill the garrison defending the Arm base, capture the buildings, and beat off the counter-attack.

Starting forces: Commander,4 Storms, 2 Crashers, 1 Pyro, 2 Weasels, 2 Slashers, 2 Raiders, 1 Reaper

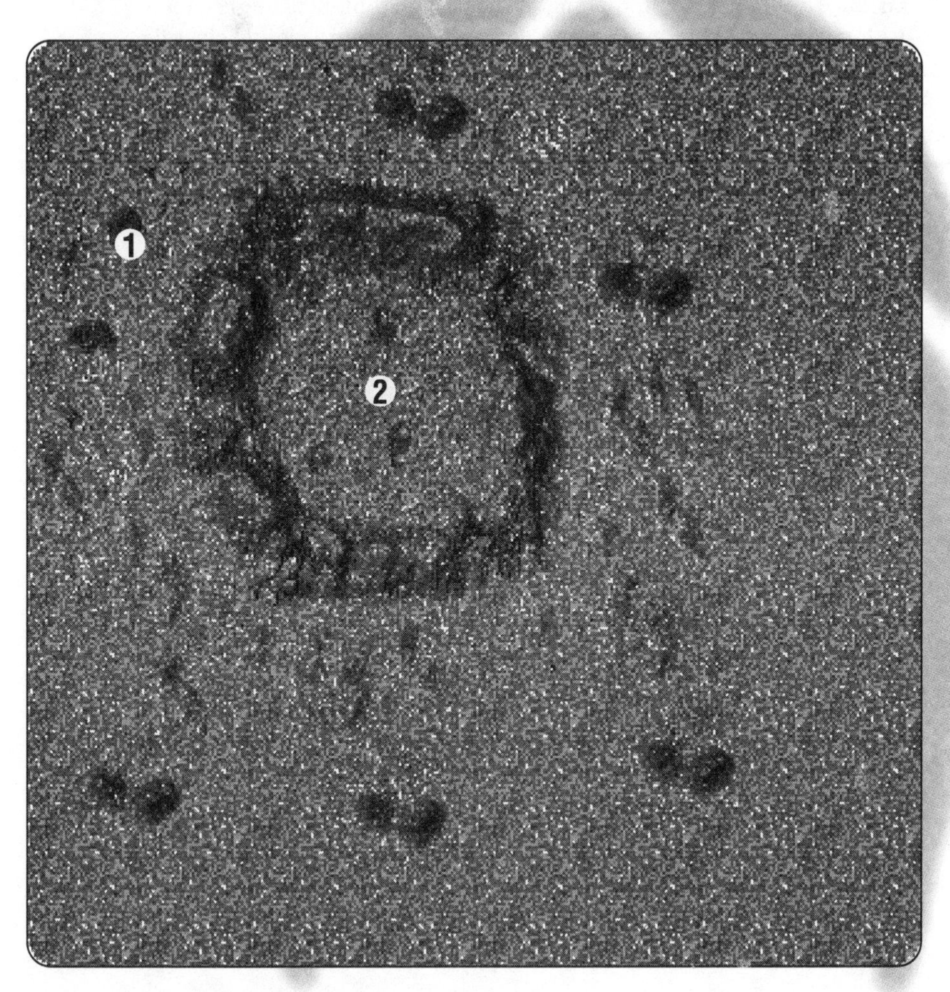

Mission Briefing

This is a mission with a twist. Defeating the Arm garrison defending the base to the east and capturing the defenseless buildings is not very hard. Beating off the subsequent Arm counterattack *is* hard. You will encounter Merl missile launchers for the first time; they are the Arm equivalent of your Diplomats—you know what that means, by now. Once you have destroyed all the attacking Arm units, the mission is yours.

How to Win

- **Capture the enemy base.** You are given a sizeable starting force for a good reason. The Arm base immediately to the east is defended by four Sentinel towers and a garrison of Kbots—six Zippers. Tackle the Sentinels one by one, taking out the Zippers as they come within range. Capture all the enemy buildings save for the Sentinels.

- **Build and rebuild.** The Arm base, unfortunately, does not contain a single Metal Extractor—just Metal Makers. There are metal deposits near your original starting point; send the Commander back there and build extractors while reclaiming extra metal from the Metal Makers. Use the captured Kbot Lab to turn out a selection of heavy bots; if metal reserves allow you to do so, construct a Vehicle Plant, and build a series of Instigators. These quick and nimble tanks can greatly help you defeat the coming Arm counterattack. You should also build several Guardian Towers with an Arm construction Kbot, courtesy of the captured Lab, and a Radar Tower.

- **Fight for your life.** The Arm counterattack, when it comes (you have a time window of several minutes) is truly vicious. Merl and Samson missile launchers are accompanied by Stumpy tanks. Use the Guardians to take out the Merls and your mobile forces to deal with the rest of the attackers. This will be a difficult fight, and a lot depends on how quickly you set the captured base in running order, and your quick reflexes on the battlefield. However, once you have destroyed all the attacking Arm units, the mission's won.

Mission 15:
Xantippe's Abyss

Difficulty rating: Easy

Objective: Capture Arm's Big Bertha cannon and use it to destroy the Annihilator in the northern part of the battlefield.

Starting forces: Commander

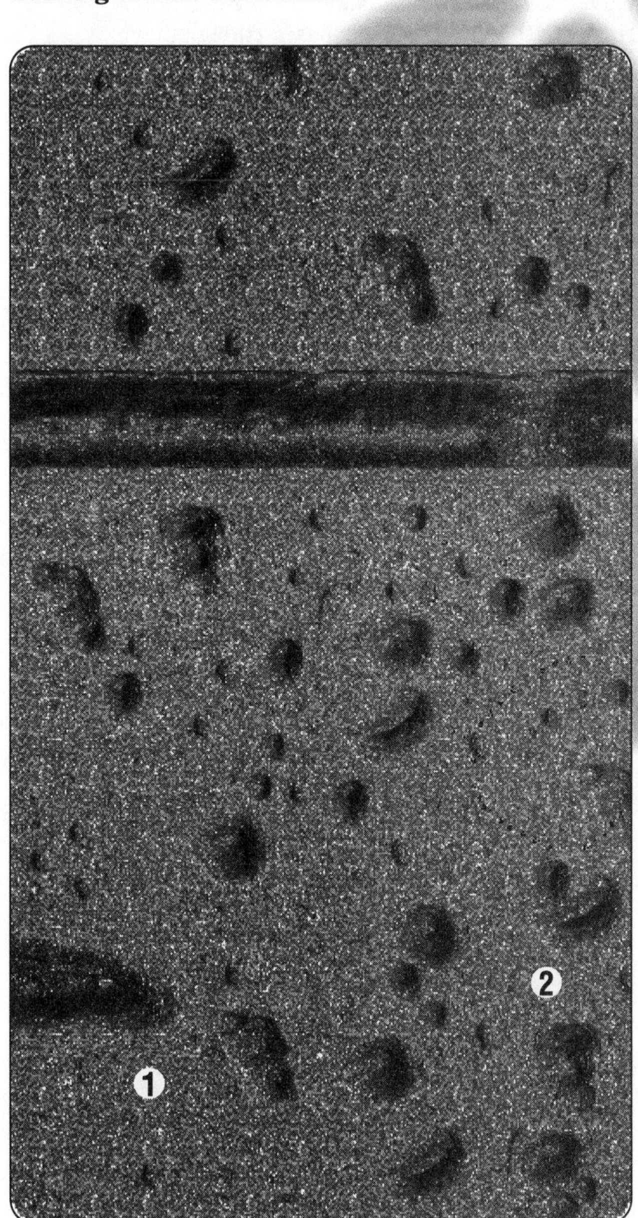

Mission Briefing

There is a Big Bertha located northeast (2) of where you start (1). It is defended by two Sentinel towers, but getting them is easy. The real problem lies in the fact that the Annihilator you are supposed to destroy is behind an impassable gorge in the northern part of the battlefield. You will have to build an Advanced Radar Tower to hunt it down, and that means quite a lot of building has to be done.

How to Win

- **Destroy the two Sentinels, get the Bertha.** Direct the Commander east of the starting point; when you are next to the eastern edge of the battlefield, turn north. Use the D-Gun on the Sentinels—they will open fire on your Commander, but fortunately the Big Bertha will not.

- **Building time.** Reclaim the Dragon's Teeth barriers nearby and start building. build a Kbot Lab, Construction Kbot, Advanced Kbot Lab, Advanced Construction Kbot, and finally an Advanced Radar Tower to the north of your base. The northern part of the radar map will come alive with red dots. These are Arm's Samson and Merl missile launchers; one of them is the Annihilator you have to destroy. You can build an Aircraft Plant, a Fink scout, and pinpoint the Annihilator; or you can simply wipe the red dots off the map one by one.

- **Keep your distance.** Don't get too close to the enemy units, or the Merls will start to rain missiles down on your units. The Big Berthas outrange the Merls easily. Keep shooting from a safe distance, and the Arm units won't even shoot back. Once you have wiped out all the dots, it's over!

Once you start hammering the enemy units in the north, the Merls may make threatening moves southwards. All they will achieve is getting stuck in the gorge; don't get nervous.

Mission 16:

Departing Rougpelt

Difficulty rating: Hard

Objective: Capture the Galactic Gate. It's right in the center of a big Arm base, so naturally you'll have to destroy everything and everyone else first. Destroy all Arm Spiders.

Starting forces: Commander, 4 AKs, 1 Thud, 1 Pyro, 1 Can, 1 Construction Kbot

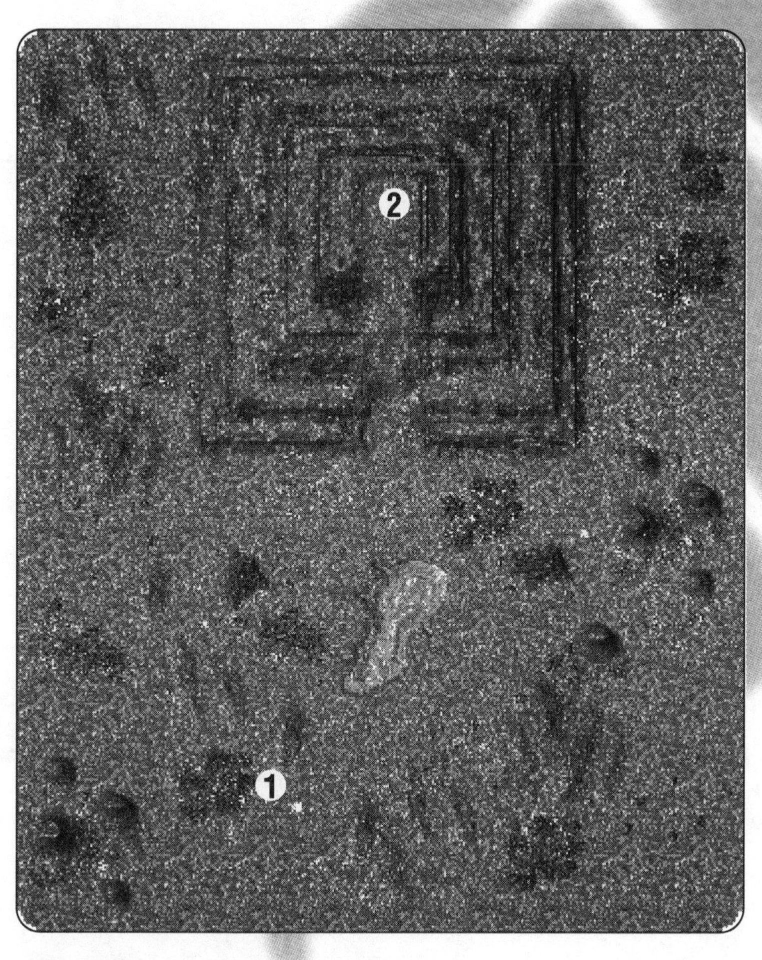

Mission Briefing

The Galactic Gate is inside an Arm fortress (2). Sentinel and Guardian Towers are supported by a large mobile force containing the dreaded Merl missile launchers, Bulldog and Stumpy tanks, and an assortment of Kbots including Fidos, Hammers, and Rockos. You will come under almost instant attack from Arm bombers, too. Your abilities will be truly tried—you will have to build a base under very difficult conditions, defend it successfully against Arm attacks, and assemble an assault force that can deal with the formidable Arm defenses.

How to Win

- **Run and build.** When the mission starts (1), run—preferably southwest, where you will find more metal deposits. Build the basics and quickly turn out a dozen or even more Crasher and Storm Kbots for base defense. Make sure you have plenty of Crashers—your budding base will be promptly attacked by Arm Phoenix bombers and Brawler gunships. They are not easy to shoot down, and they'll stay overhead until you destroy them—or they destroy you. Watch out for Arm Spider Kbots trying to sneak in!
- **Defend and scavenge.** The Brawlers will return, so make sure your AA defenses are strong. You can concentrate on building them up—no Arm ground forces are going to bother you at this stage. Once you have dealt with the Brawlers, the Arm airborne threat is over—the enemy does not have an Aircraft Plant, just a number of bombers and gunships. Keep reclaiming whatever metal you can; there's a lot of construction work coming up.
- **Advanced construction.** You need an Advanced Radar Tower, which means a lot of building: Construction Kbot, Advanced Kbot Lab, Advanced Construction Kbot. You will also need an Advanced Vehicle Plant for its Diplomats and Goliath Tanks, plus a number of light Instigators. Fortunately, Arm tends to leave you alone at this stage, and the biggest problem you are likely to have is managing your resources right.
- **Advanced radar.** You should crown all this construction work by building an Advanced Radar Tower north of your base. It will instantly reveal Arm defenses and units scattered all over a big, pyramid-like structure. The Gate you need to capture is at the very summit. Pummel everything else with your Diplomats. There will still be quite a lot Arm units left even after intensive bombardment. This is where the Instigators and Goliaths you built earlier come in.
- **Assault the Arm base.** Lead the ground attack against the Arm base with the quick Instigators, following with the Goliaths. The defending Arm units include Bulldogs and Stumpys, and there still might be the odd Guardian or Sentinel you have not taken out. Lead your armor in a decisive manner, concentrating your fire on the enemy units and structures, one by one. The Bulldogs are tough, and you may want to let your Diplomats join in—just make sure your own units don't get hit, too.
- **Capture the Gate.** Eventually, Arm resistance will cease. Scout around with your Instigators; when you are sure the area is clear of the enemy, send in the Commander to capture the Gate.

Mission 17:

The Lost Isle

Difficulty rating: Very Hard

Objective: Destroy all Arm presence in the area, but especially the carriers. This involves cleaning Arm out from a series of islands—this battle is fought over an archipelago.

Starting force: Commander, 2 Thuds, 2 Storms

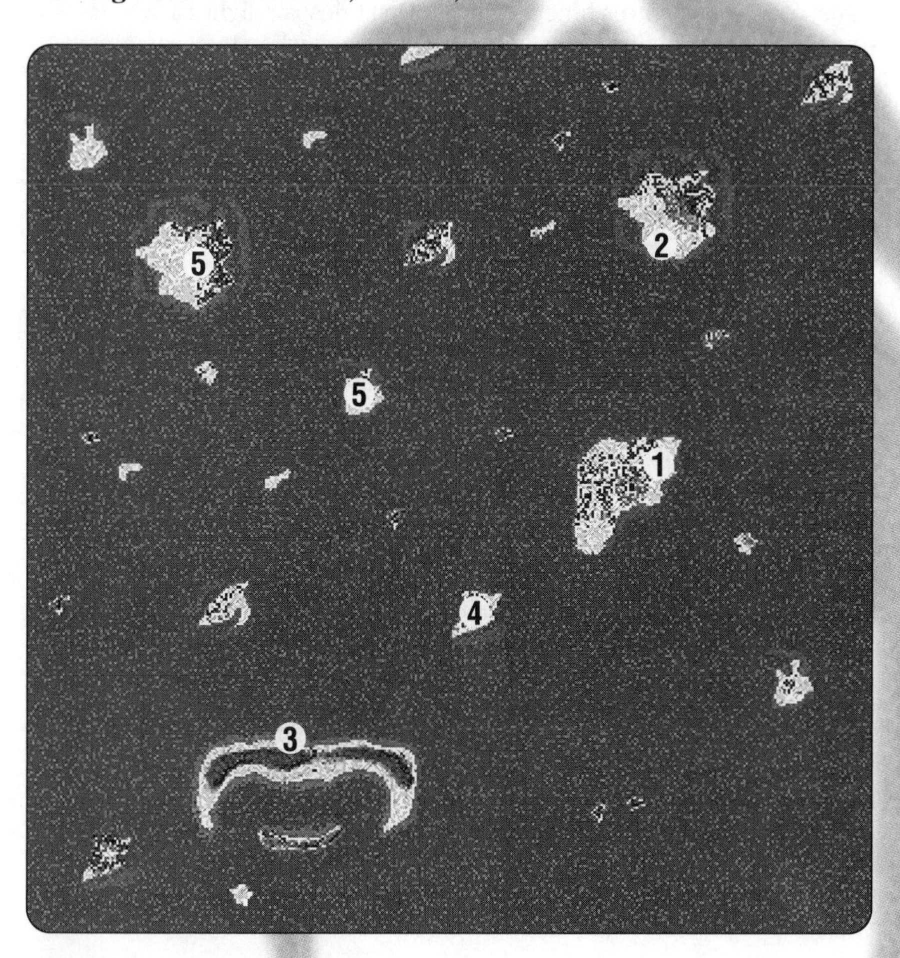

Mission Briefing

You have one island to start with (1); Arm has four (2, 3, and 5). In addition to a formidable navy, expect to encounter a powerful air force (Brawler gunships and Lancet torpedo bombers). Numerous Sentinel and Defender towers and Piranha subs complete the Arm lineup. You will need a Level-2 Intimidator plasma cannon and Advanced Radar Towers along with Rapier gunships, Executioner cruisers, and Hydra frigates. Prepare for an all-out slugfest which can only be won by combining the operations of your navy and your air force.

How to Win

- **Build basics, then rebuild them.** You begin this mission on an island in the eastern part of the archipelago. Move fast—get Extractors and Solar Collectors going along with a Kbot Lab. Turn out a series of Crashers and Storms as your first defense against Arm naval attacks by scouts, destroyers, and cruisers. As if this wasn't enough, Triton amphibious tanks will repeatedly come crawling out of the water on the northeastern shore of your island. The naval missiles raining down on your base may destroy most of your structures time and again. Don't despair. fight back the best you can—yes, Crashers and Storms can even sink cruisers when they come within range—and patiently rebuild what you have lost, keeping an eye on your energy and metal reserves. Don't neglect to build a Construction Kbot along with the combat units, and have it construct several plasma cannons along the northern and eastern shores of your island. These cannons will help considerably in defeating Arm naval attacks.

- **Advance to Level 2.** You need to build Level-2 structures and units a.s.a.p. to cope with the enemy. This will put a strain on your resources; replace your first-generation extractors and collectors with Fusion Plants and Moho Mines. An Advanced Radar Tower will reveal the positions of Arm's ships, and allow you to pick them off with your plasma cannon. Once you have started building Level-2 Intimidator towers, you are safe enough to start on your Shipyard. This will bring Arm destroyers and cruisers swarming round once again. you can trick them—they will try to target the Commander, and if you walk him underwater, your combat units will be able to pick off the attacking ships while they still fruitlessly try to kill your Commander. In this mission, Arm subs are used in purely defensive roles, and your Commander is safe as long as he is hiding in your coastal waters. Build a series of Snake subs in your Shipyard, but don't wait too until acquiring a Construction ship and an Advanced Shipyard. You really need its Hydras and Executioners.

- **Destroy the Arm stronghold to the north**. The island north of yours features four Sentinels, a pair of Guardians, a Shipyard, and a whole fleet stationed behind it. Your Advanced Radar will let your plasma cannon do a lot of the dirty work, but sooner or later you will have to send in your navy. Include a screen of snakes to protect your surface ships from Arm Piranhas. The Shipyard on the north coast of the Arm island is defended by half a dozen Lurkers—your Snakes are in for a tough fight. Fortunately, Arm's surface navy in this neighborhood can be picked off with long-range weaponry using the radar map.

- **Attack southwest next.** A crescent-shaped island near the southwestern corner of the battlefield features another Arm stronghold. The procedure is exactly the same as with the previous one; the southwestern island also features a Shipyard on its far shores, out of reach of your plasma cannon. Once again, a pack of Lurker subs guards the adjacent waters. Wipe out all Arm units and structures, and turn your attention to the small isle halfway between your base and the crescent-shaped island (4). Take a Level-2 Construction Kbot there, and set up another Advanced Radar Tower. This will reveal Arm units and structures to the northwest. Don't send your Construction Kbot aboard a transport until you can provide an escort of fighters;

Arm aircraft are nearby. This, naturally, necessitates another expense: an Aircraft Plant. Build a Construction Vtol and an Advanced Aircraft Plant next; you will need Level-2 planes and gunships. Notice the red dots moving quickly over the islands to the northeast? These are Arm's Brawlers and Lancets.

- **Turn northwest and destroy the Arm air force.** By that time, it will become obvious you are slowly gaining the upper hand. Don't get too cocky and send off your navy to deal with the Arm forces to the northwest; the enemy planes will cut your ships to pieces. Make sure you have over half a dozen Rapiers first. then send your snakes towards the enemy. For some reason, Arm pilots become excited and try to hit the Snakes even though they cannot—capitalize on this and have your Rapiers knock down the Brawlers, who most probably will keep trying to get your subs. Get the Brawlers first and the Lancets second. Although the Arm torpedo bombers can hit your subs, it takes them a long time to sort their bearings; if you attack them first, the Brawlers will come after your gunships. This way, you can deal with the Lancets without any Brawlers interfering—they will all be shot down first.
- **Go for the final kill.** Once the Arm air force ceases to exist, it is time to wipe the enemy off the two islands to the northwest. Both islands feature Aircraft Plants, Sentinels, and Defenders. Avoid losses—recall your aircraft, and send in the navy. Using radar, target the red dots one by one and destroy them with your ships. Congratulations, you've made it!

Keep constantly an eye on the radar map and pick off any red dots you see with your plasma cannon.

Mission 18:

Slolam Pilago

Difficulty rating: Medium

Objective: Destroy everything belonging to Arm. You must destroy the Fusion Power Plant hidden at the bottom of a crater.

Starting forces: Commander, 3 Fink scout planes

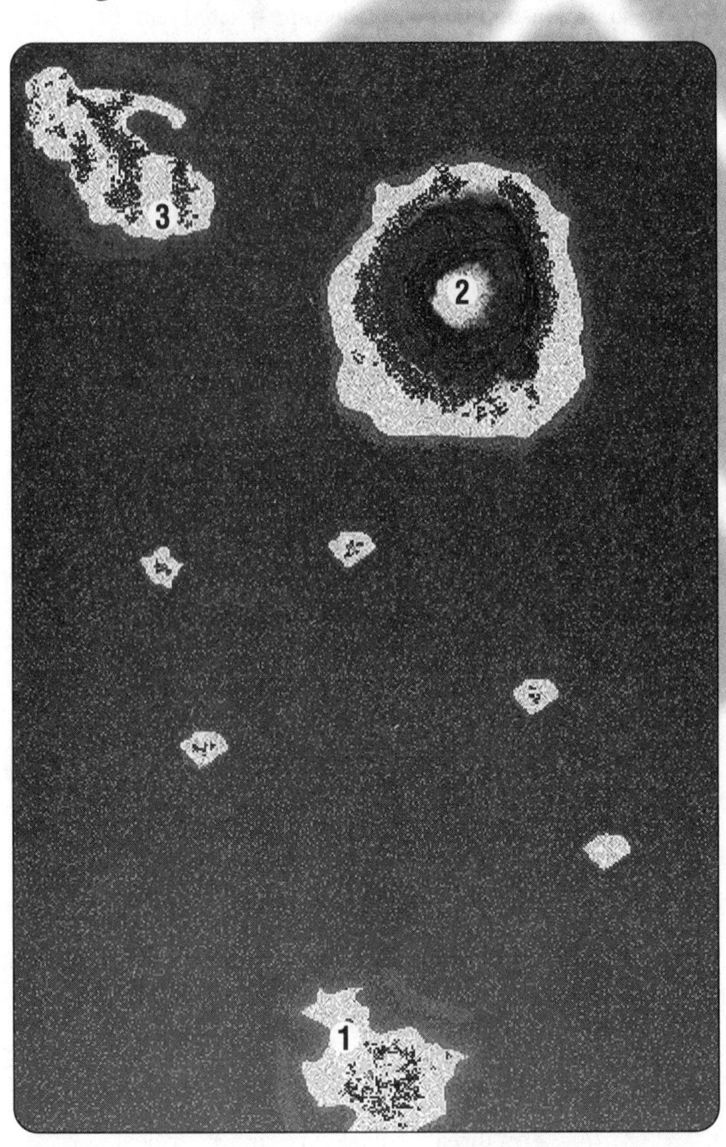

Mission Briefing

You begin this mission on yet another tiny island in the southern end of the battlefield (1). Arm occupies two islands to the far north and northwest. The Fusion plant is on the round island directly to the north (2); the one to the northwest (3) is home to seven to eight Brawlers. The Fusion plant is protected by a Guardian and three Sentinels. Destroy it with bombers.

How to Win

- **Think small.** There is very little space available for construction on your island—much of it is covered in jungle. Fortunately, for once your Commander can go about setting up a base without being fired on. Build the basics, including a Construction Kbot, reclaim the Kbot Lab, and build an Advanced one. When you get your Level-2 Construction Kbot, exchange extractors and generators for Moho Mines and Fusion plants. The energy surplus provided by the Fusion plants makes it feasible to build Metal Makers, thus supplementing the production of the Moho Mines. This enables you to proceed with the task of building a powerful fleet. Reconnoiter the battlefield with your Finks, but be careful not to let them stray too far north, or they will be shot down.

- **Shipyard blues and Slashers.** Once you get going on the Shipyard, you will come under attack by Arm subs. To solve this problem you need—Slashers! Yes, these missile Kbots can actually sink Arm Lurker subs. You need to force the Slashers to fire at the spot from which you see torpedoes emerge even though you cannot see the subs—press the A key or click the Attack option on the control panel. You should have a line of Slashers dropping missiles in an arc next to each other. Do this right, and you will be rewarded by exploding Lurkers appearing seemingly out of nowhere. Keep this up until your shipyard is complete, and you have managed to pump out several Snakes. With these, you can complete the destruction of the Arm submarine threat.

- **Build a navy.** Your next step should be to build a Construction ship, and a Level-2 Shipyard—you will need advanced warships in this mission. Commission up to 5 Warlord battleships and a similar number of Hydra missile frigates. While this goes on, get your Level-2 Construction Kbot to erect an Advanced Radar Tower on the northern shore of your island. As usual, Advanced Radar will make things much easier.

- **Target practice.** You will see clumps of red dots pop up on your radar map—four to each of the five little islands between you and the big Arm-held islands. These four-dot sets represent Arm defenses—three Sentinels and a Guardian. Use your battleships to target the Arm structures one by one, starting with the nearest ones. Keep going until you have destroyed all the defenses on the five small islands.

- **Push forward.** Once you have completed the stage, send your fleet out to clear roving Arm Crusaders from the seas around the little islands. Then ferry the Level-2 Construction Kbot to the northernmost island, and build another Advanced Radar Tower. This will reveal both the fusion plant you are after as well as the Arm planes on the far northwestern island. Don't go after the Fusion plant until you have eliminated the Arm air force and the remaining Arm navy (several Crusaders and Conqueror cruisers). Send battleships and subs against the Arm navy, and Hydras against the planes. Hit them hard with everything you have; no more than one or two aircraft should make it off the ground, and when they do, they will be no match for the Hydras.

- **Destroy the Fusion plant island.** With the Arm threat neutralized, move your fleet in to destroy the defenses and the Fusion plant. It is the red dot plumb in the center of the island. The Sentinel towers are no match for your Warlords and Hydras.

Mission 19:

The Vebreen Fleet

Difficulty rating: Medium to Hard

Objective: Your Commander and the accompanying fleet control an island in the path of an approaching Arm armada. You must not let the enemy ships pass.

Starting forces: 3 Searchers, 4 Snakes, 1 Enforcer, 1 Hydra, 1 Warlord, 1 Construction Ship, Construction Kbot, 2 Punisher plasma cannon

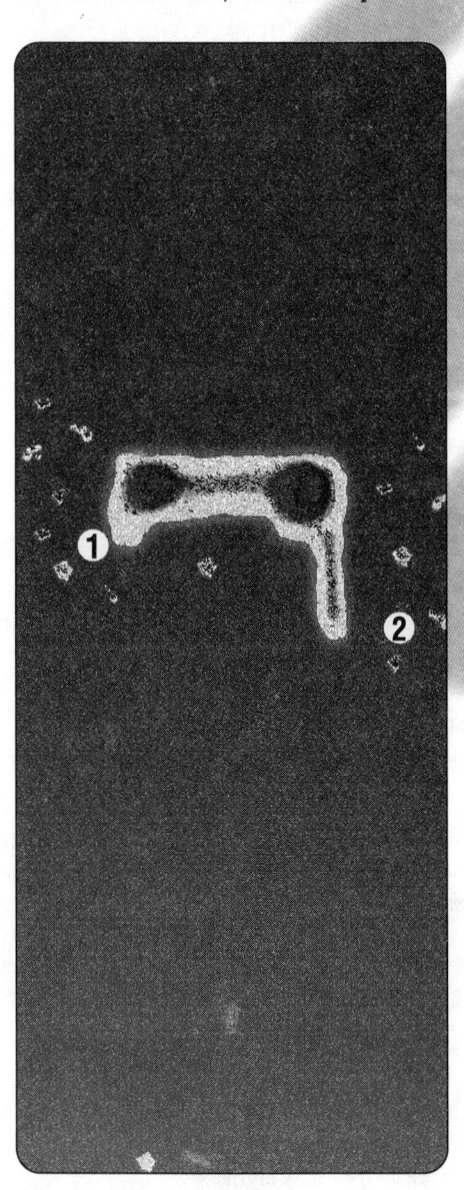

Mission Briefing

The Arm fleet headed your way is a powerful one. It features several Colossus carriers with Brawlers aboard, and these can be real trouble. Fortunately, the enemy lineup is missing a vital link: Submarines. Rely on your sub force to tear the enemy apart. It will not be very easy—you are up against five battleships, three cruisers, half a dozen destroyers, and three missile frigates plus Colossus carriers and Hulk transports to boot. Split your navy into two task groups and position them at opposite ends of your island (1, 2) to intercept the enemy ships.

How to Win

- **Build fast to survive.** Your fleet is outgunned, and you need to add ships to it fast if you are to win this mission. The Arm task force coming your way is composed of almost all the ships Arm can build and some it cannot—it also features a Warlord battleship! However, the Arm leaders have neglected to include subs in this armada. Get a Shipyard pumping out Snakes—double-quick. You will need more than a dozen subs to deal with the Arm naval threat.

- **Deploy your forces wisely.** Although it seems impossibly risky in face of such daunting odds, you should split your fleet in two. Send each half to the side of your island—one to the west, one to the east—making sure that each group contains two Snakes. Add new Snakes to each group as your Shipyard builds them.

- **Sink the carriers.** You have very little time; still, you should assemble a large pack of snakes at each end of your island. The first wave of Arm ships consists of a mix of Hulk transports and Colossus light carriers. Target the carriers first—if they launch their Brawlers, you will be in big trouble. You have to sink the carriers fast! There is no time to build adequate AA defenses.

- **Sink the rest of the armada.** With the Brawler threat removed, your subs should carry the battle. Keep your Shipyard building new Snakes, and immediately direct them to join your two groups. Your surface ships should stay behind the subs, out of harm's way, joining in whenever possible along with the plasma cannon on the island. There are no magic tricks to be employed; if you have learned how to command ships well, you'll win; if not, you'll lose.

When enemy ships are fired on by your surface fleet, they will ignore the snakes. Deployed in groups of six, Snakes can quickly tear even the most powerful enemy ship apart.

Mission 20:

The Gate to Aegus

Difficulty rating: Hard

Objective: Wipe everything belonging to Arm off the map—except the Galactic Gate, which you should capture.

Starting forces:. Commander, 4 Searcher class scout ships, 1 Snake sub

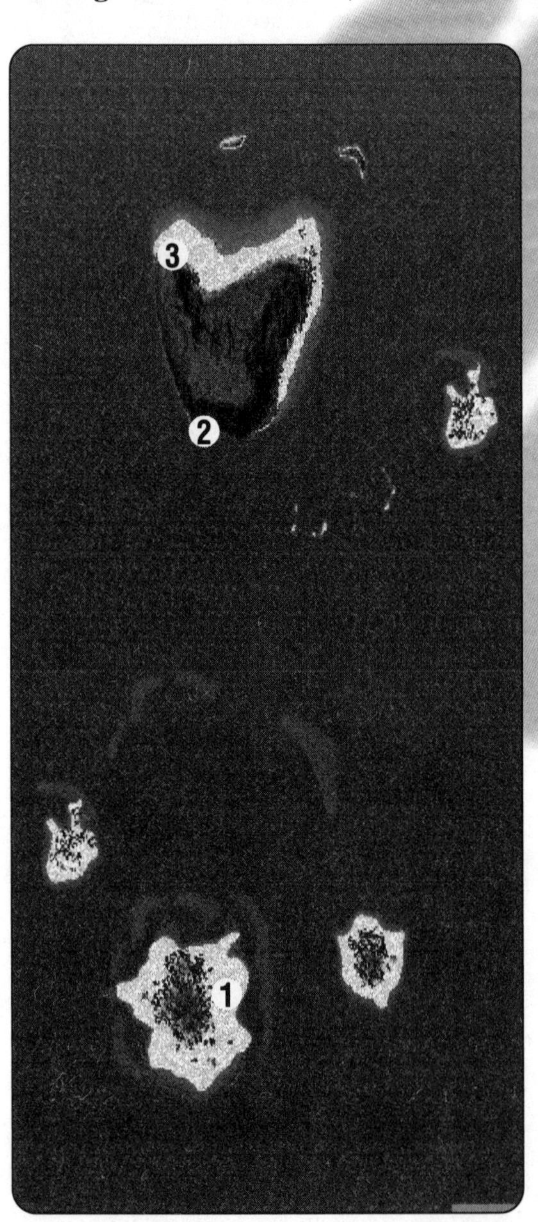

Mission Briefing

This mission starts on an island that is bigger than what you are used to (1). A large island some distance away to the north contains the Arm base (2) and the Galactic Gate you must capture (3). Arm defenses include six Defender towers, two Guardians, and a Merl launcher. Use Advanced Radar to your advantage—it will pick off the enemies from a distance.

How to Win

- **Make every second count.** When this mission starts, build the basics including half a dozen Storms for defense against any Arm naval threats.Proceed with the construction of defensive structures, including Level-2 Punisher plasma cannons and Pulverizer missile towers. Build three of each on the northern coast to assist in repulsing the four or five Triton tanks that will invade there. At one point or another during this mission, these structures will also help to deal with four Brawlers and three Lancets that Arm sends forth.
- **Radar rules once again.** Once the plasma cannon and the missile towers are in place, your next priority is an Advanced Radar Tower. This involves, as you know, going through with the construction of an Advanced Kbot Lab and a Level-2 Construction Kbot. Build a shipyard either concurrently, or right after you acquire the Advanced Radar. Site the Shipyard on the southern shore of your island—it will be under attack from Arm Lurkers a precious few moments later than it would have been when located to the north. This slight delay can let you get an extra Snake or two built in the meantime, which greatly helps in countering the Lurker threat. Keep all your ships south of your island and the yard; then enemy subs will go directly after the Shipyard without bothering about your ships. They will be so intent on the yard they might well ignore your Snakes. Capitalize on that.
- **Advanced construction.** The Advanced Radar Tower is the first Level-2 building you erect. Consequently, have your Advanced Construction Kbot complete a Fusion Plant and Moho Mines to replace the Level-1 extractors and generators. This boosting of your supply in resources allows you to build a Level-2 navy without acute metal and energy shortages. Of course, first you need to build a Construction ship, and a Level-2 Shipyard.
- **Advanced navy.** Once the Advanced Shipyard is ready, commission five Hydras and another five Executioner cruisers. Your powerful radar will have revealed many red dots. Send your ships after the four stationary dots encircling the southern shore of Arm's island—these are enemy Torpedo Launchers. To the east, you will see a small island; it contains an Arm Moho Mine and a Defender tower. Destroy these, too. Proceed to target structures on the main Arm island. There is a chance you may get lucky and destroy the small but powerful Arm air force—four Brawlers, three Lancets—that is parked on the ground. If not, your Hydras will have to shoot them down when they finally attack your ships.
- **Merciless shelling.** Do not relax your guard if everything has been going well; the Arm island sports formidable defenses. They include six Defender towers, two Guardians, an Annihilator, plus a Merl launcher and an Eraser Kbot. This last unit may give you a headache when active—you will have to lead your ships to the shore, where they will have to trade fire with the strong Arm defense. Don't shoot at anything in the northwestern part of the island—that is where the Galactic Gate is located.
- **Execution.** Once you have wiped out most of the opposition and just two to three red dots remain, get your Commander onto the Arm island. With a Fusion Plant in your base, you can keep the D-Gun firing almost continuously with no fear of an energy shortfall at a critical moment. Capture the Gate, and the mission is complete.

Mission 21:

Aegus . . . Empyrrean's Guardian

Difficulty rating: Medium

Objective: On Aegus, the moon orbiting Arm's home planet Empyrrean, reunite two separate Core forces, build a base, and then attack Arm forces guarding the Galactic Gate that leads to Empyrrean. You must capture the Gate.

Starting forces: Your forces are split between a dozen or so mobile artillery units in the southeast and, in the northeast, your Commander with a force of tanks and rocket launchers.

Mission Briefing

This mission enables you to use your skills as a tank commander, with missile and artillery backup. The flat, open terrain of Aegus is perfect for your armored units. You will first consolidate your forces, build up a strike force of ground troops, and then slowly advance on the Arm position. Destroy all of Arm's units and capture the Galactic Gate.

How to Win

- **Consolidate your troops in the northeast (1).** The only crossing point for your armored vehicles over the long north-south ridge is at the very north end of the battlefield. To rescue your long-range artillery units in the southeast, send units from the north, including your Commander, fighting their way down through Arm troops to a Dragon's Teeth barrier (2). Have the Commander D-gun the Dragon's Teeth so that you can bring your long-range artillery through the passage to the north.
- **Set up a Radar Tower and build a Kbot Lab and a Vehicle Plant.** Your first job is to establish radar to get a fix on any nearby enemy units. Follow that with a Kbot Lab and a Vehicle Plant. Send your Commander all the way to the south end of the rift to find an Arm Moho Mine (3) that you should be able to capture, unless it has been blown up during the opening firefight. You don't have the option to build an Aircraft Plant in this mission, so your ground troops must carry the day. Build toward an Advanced Vehicle Plant and an Advanced Kbot Lab as soon as possible.
- **The Arm Galactic Gate is in a crater (4).** Next to it is an Annihilator long-range cannon that you must destroy without destroying the Gate itself. Attacks start with a Zeus Kbot from the south, followed by Fidos and Jeffys. Metal is scarce, so have construction units and the Commander reclaim metal from wreckage. Build up your ground forces to include at least six Reaper tanks and three Goliath super tanks. Also construct three more Diplomat mobile rocket launchers. From your Advanced Kbot Lab, build a half-dozen of the tough Can assault Kbots and Pyros. Keep whittling away at the waves of Arm forces that come at you, but wait until your ground forces have at least a half-dozen or more of each major unit type that you will use for your offensive. The Diplomats and the tanks are most important.
- **Approach the crater, using your Diplomats to pinpoint the Arm Annihilator.** Lead your tank charge with your Reapers and Goliaths, accompanied by Cans and Pyros. Follow them with your Diplomats, guarding at least one of the Diplomats with an Informer mobile radar unit. Send several Weasel scout vehicles ahead to the southern entrance to the crater. Get at least one of them inside the entrance to reveal exactly where the Annihilator is. Once you spot it, zero in on it with your Diplomats. By now, the Arm forces will be noticeably weaker because of your attacks.
- **Head west beyond the entrance to the crater.** There are Arm forces on the other side of the crater. Destroy them before you take your forces inside the crater. Throughout this drive, continually direct your units' fire so that they don't start shooting at the Gate itself. Once the outer Arm units have been destroyed, send your Commander into the crater to capture the Gate.

NOTE **In missions, unless a unit has been set to a Unit Order other than the default, Roam/Fire at Will, it's supposed to try to destroy any enemy structure. However, sometimes the AI redirects those priorities and it may not automatically open fire at non-combat structures.**

Mission 22:

A Big Empyrrean Welcome

Difficulty rating: Medium

Objective: Capture the Big Bertha south of your starting point.

Starting forces: Commander, 2 Pyros, 1 Construction Kbot

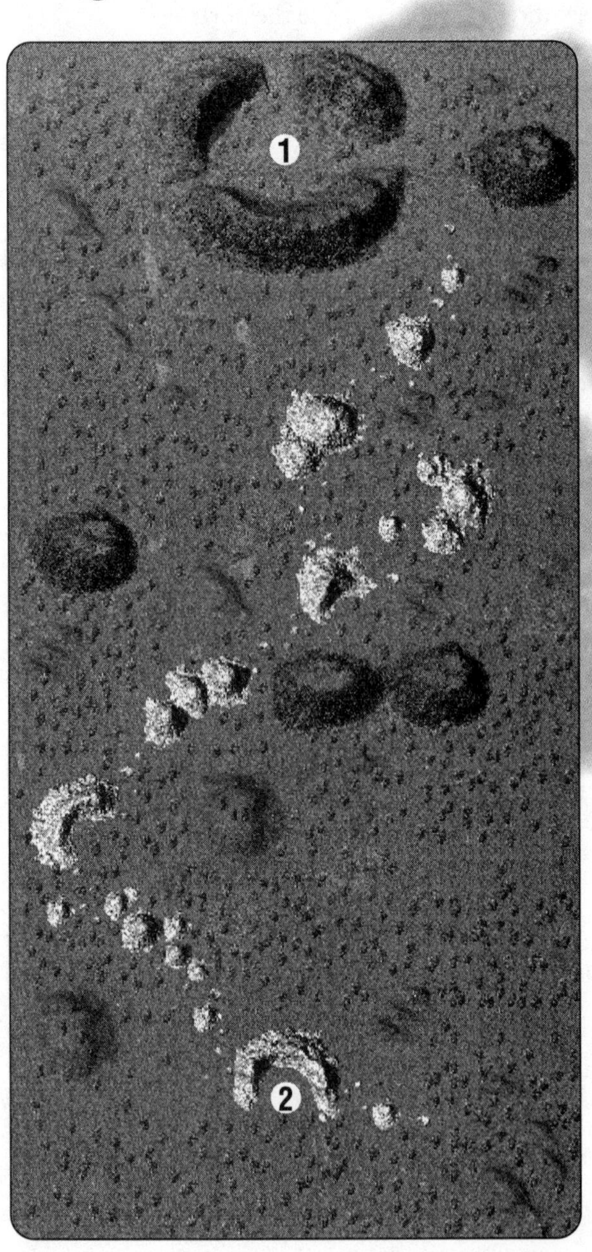

Mission Briefing

You start this mission inside a big crater in the northern part of the battlefield (1). This is good, since the crater conceals your guys from the wicked Big Bertha in the south (2). That's the gun you have to capture—but unlike the Berthas you had to capture previously, this cannon actually fires on your units. Its shells are powerful enough to cut your mission short with one lucky hit—be careful! Remember to build energy generators so that your Commander can use the D-Gun at will.

How to Win

- **Find a good site for Solar Collectors.** The crater is a nice starting point, even though three Zippers attack from three sides the moment the mission begins. However, you cannot build Solar collectors there; as soon as you leave—and you must, to capture old Bertha—other Zipper bots will enter from the side and demolish your energy generators. These are absolutely essential to the success of your mission, so you have to build them elsewhere. Go northeast and build a complex of Collectors in the northeastern corner of the battlefield; they will be out of Big Bertha's range, and seemingly out of the Zippers' area of interest. This is because the Arm Zips are divided into two groups; each seems to be responsible for one side of the battlefield. If you build in the northeast and then march south, you will encounter the two teams of three Zippers each that are responsible for patrolling the eastern half, and your Collectors will be safe; the western Zippers don't cross over into the other half of the battlefield.

- **Zigzag south.** You have to go south to get the Bertha, but you will have to dodge its shells on the way. Lead your units in a zigzag; this throws off the big cannon's aim—it takes a long time to retrain its sights on targets that change position in the horizontal plane. This means it will shoot much less often. It will not be a cakewalk, because in addition to the big shells you will have to deal with several Zippers and Hammers along the way. Try to handle them with a Pyro while the rest of your group marches on; but don't forget to send the Pyro on after it has finished torching enemy units.

- **All you need is luck.** To some extent, the success of this mission depends on luck—if two cannon shells crash into your Commander, he's had it. Keep that Construction Kbot nearby for emergency repairs, and keep going. the Bertha is not distracted by your other units—it will always target the Commander. As you get near the big gun, watch its barrel, and keep your commander one step ahead of its moves. Remember the Bertha has trouble re-targeting on the horizontal plane—keep zigzagging. when you get to the cannon, immediately run the Commander behind it and start capturing it—it is a process that takes some time, but the Bertha takes even longer to turn around. Watch out for enemy Kbots arriving to intervene—put the Pyros to good use. Of course, you should be keeping them in good repair as well; remember you have also a Construction Kbot. If it seems like the Bertha will manage to turn around and nail your Commander, stop the capturing process and move him again, putting him exactly behind the cannon, and ordering him to capture it again. You should only have to do it once before he completes the task, and the mission.

Mission 23:

The Fortress Falls

Difficulty rating: Hard

Objective: Attack a powerful Arm base and destroy all units. What else?

Starting forces: Commander, 2 Finks, 3 Pyros

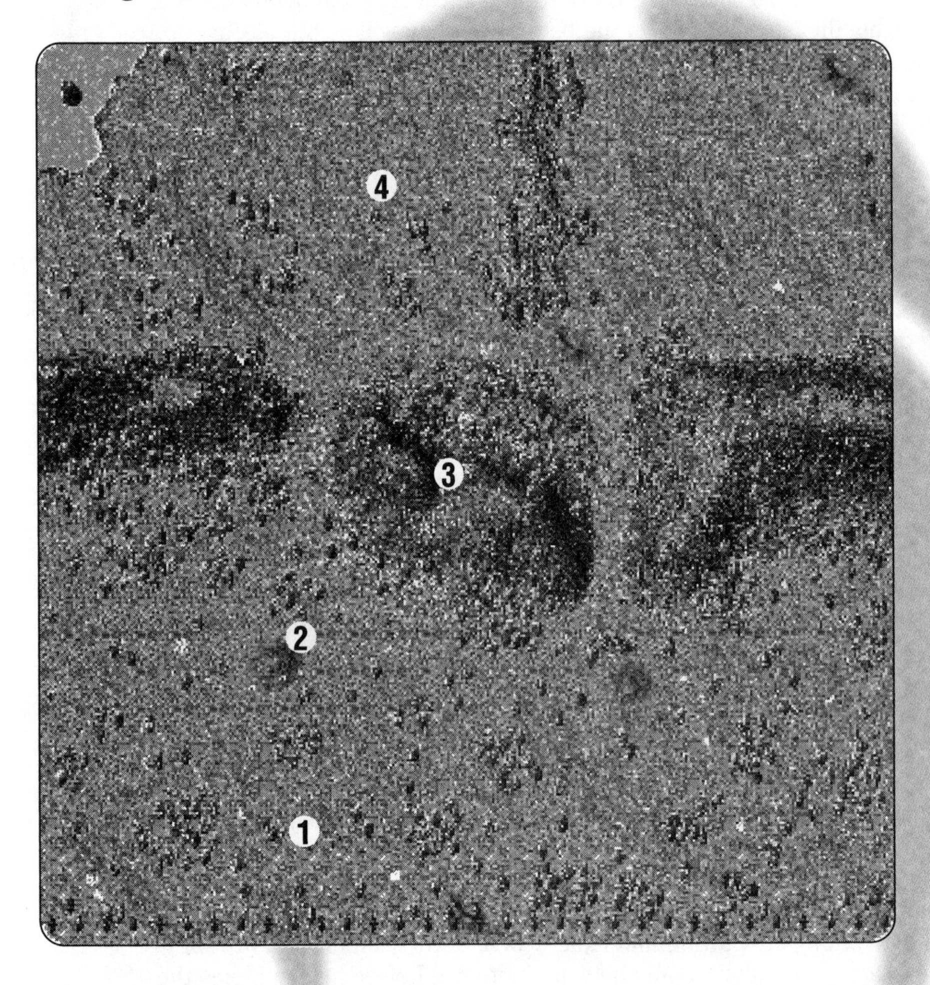

Mission Briefing

One of the most difficult missions you will face, this is an air and ground assault against an extended Arm base spread across three rolling hills and taking up almost the top two-thirds of the battlefield. Arm has a large air force and well-entrenched defensive positions, including a Millenium battleship in the very northwest corner. Fortunately, they don't attack right away, giving you time to build a base, ground troops, and an air force in the southwest section of the battlefield. After digging in and outlasting Arm attacks, you will lead your army forward to topple the fortress. You'll be playing this mission for awhile—save the game frequently!

How to Win

- **Keep your Finks on the ground and your Commander busy building.** Arm has a very strong force in this mission, and you must build air and ground defenses while you are also putting together a large assault force. Build a Kbot Lab, a Vehicle Plant, and then an Aircraft Plant in the southwest corner where you begin (1). Arm Peeper aircraft will fly over your position, but keep your own Fink scouts on the ground for now. Set up a Radar Tower to keep an eye out for Arm troops heading south.

- **Metal resources are to the east and west.** Build anti-air defenses—Crashers and Slashers. As soon as you can, build a Construction Vehicle or a Construction Kbot, construct several Pulverizer missile towers and Gaat Gun heavy lasers. Set their Unit Orders to Return Fire rather than Fire at Will. You don't want to excite Arm unnecessarily until you are stronger. As quickly as possible, build towards having mobile construction units, then advanced construction plants. You will need the Level-2 and Level-3 weapons to ultimately dig Arm out of its emplacements.

- **Prepare for Zippers and Brawlers.** When you do get the attention of Arm, it will most likely be announced by a half-dozen Zippers patrolling east to west just north of your position. They will be followed by several Brawler gunships, so have your air defenses ready. Fidos will attack you next from the northeast. Note that once you do begin to move your forces north to start battling the Arm forces for the hills, you will immediately be attacked by waves of Arm units including Merls, Bulldogs, Lugers, and Rockos.

- **Build for awhile, then move forward to point 2 and dig in.** When you have built a force that includes at least eight to ten Reaper tanks, four or five Diplomats, more than a half-dozen Cans, and the same number of Pyros and AKs, your ground forces are ready to move forward to point 2. But you must also have air support in the form of six to eight Rapier gunships and Vamp stealth fighters. This takes awhile, but once you have unleashed Arm's response you will be in for a long, hard series of firefights.

- **Keep the Diplomats targeted.** Keep them targeted by having an Informer mobile radar unit accompany them as they move forward. Don't try to overrun the hills in front of you right away. This is a good position from which to use the Diplomats to destroy Defender and Sentinel guns that are positioned on the hills. You will slowly begin to see fewer attacks and, as your Diplomats hit home, fewer big laser and missile emplacements on the hills. Keep your factories in the southwest building and replacing the units which are cut down by Arm's forces.

- **Take the hills and extend the advance.** As you pound the hills with artillery and aircraft, keep bringing up replacements from the factories behind you. It will most likely take at least a couple of hours of fighting before you can storm the hills and begin setting up an assault from the hilltops. As your attacking force moves slowly forward, have one or two construction vehicles finding metal deposits in the south to keep the flow going. At the same time, begin building a Moho Mine and then a Fusion Reactor. Don't push forward to the north (4) of the hills until your energy and metal reserves are strong. Build at least one Intimidator next to the hills, so that you can start shelling the remaining Arm forces. Don't be impatient and try to rush Arm at this point. It will take quite a while to fight your way through to the top of the battlefield. Slowly, you will wear away the Arm forces.

In the missions, you can seldom go wrong digging in and producing resources and units while you are left alone. Remember, in this game—as in real life—gaining a superior force in numbers is sometimes the key to victory.

Mission 24:

Surrounded and Pounded

Difficulty rating: Hard

Objective: Stabilize your precarious position on top of a mesa in the center of the battlefield. Build a base to survive the onslaught of a large Arm force. Destroy all Arm elements.

Starting forces: Commander, Mobile Artillery, 1 Construction Kbot, 2 Crashers, 1 Pyro, 3 Thuds, 1 Slasher, 1 Diplomat, 2 Storms, 1 Can

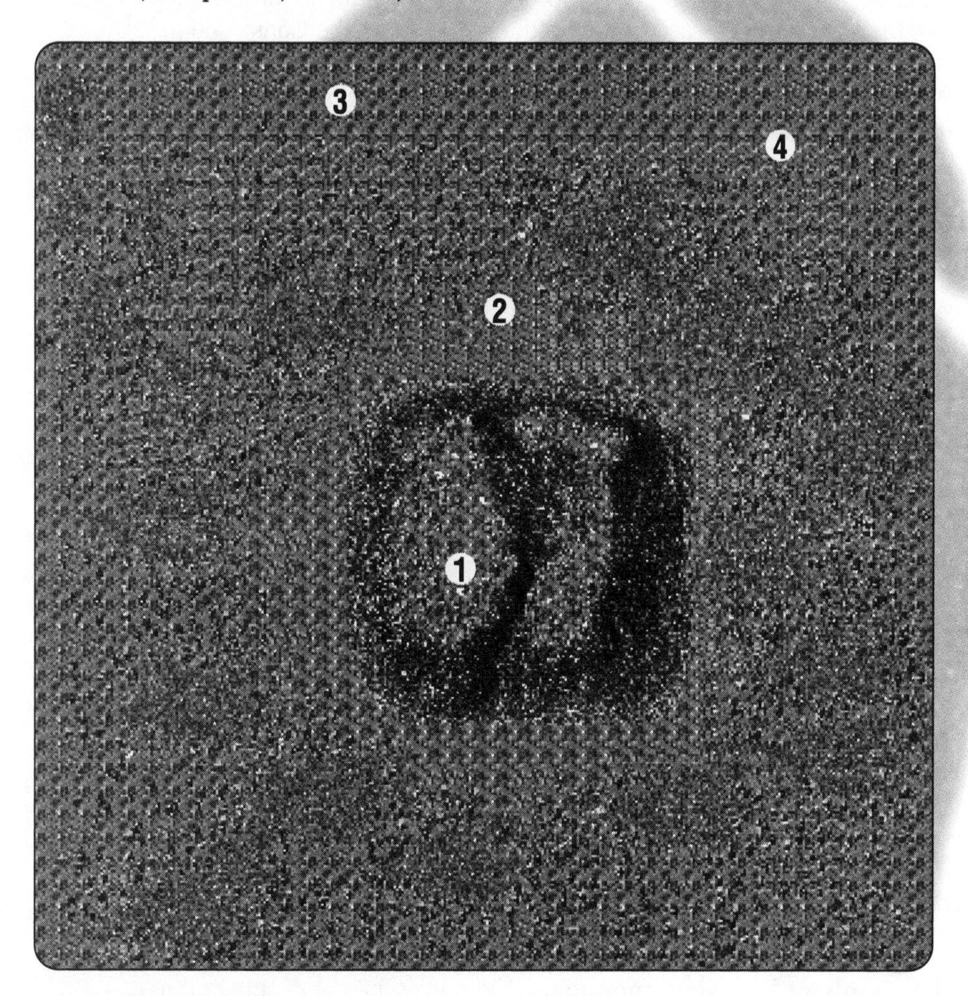

Mission Briefing

The title of this mission says it all. A large Arm force consisting of virtually every type of unit and weapon surrounds your small force, which is atop a mesa in the middle of the battlefield. Your troops are at half-strength. Repair all units, build an effective air and ground defense, and then slowly expand to remove all traces of Arm on the map.

How to Win

- **Build Radar Towers on the east and west sides of the two-level mesa.** Have the Commander build one of the towers and the Construction Kbot build the other. Immediately thereafter, order the Commander to repair all Core units. Set the Construction Kbot to building Metal Extractors on two or three of the five metal deposits on the mesa. Order the Commander to build several Solar Collectors and Wind Generators.

- **Prepare to defend yourself against Arm Spiders.** They will be the first to scale the walls, from the west. They're easily destroyed. After that, set the Construction Kbot to build a Kbot Lab and the Commander to build an Aircraft Plant. Build both of them near the south end of the mesa (1). Your Slasher and Crashers will provide the initial air defense. Your Diplomat will send off rockets against the enemy positions below. The Thuds and mobile artillery units will provide artillery support.

- **You must move quickly to build Kbots for defense.** Shortly after the Kbot Lab and Aircraft Plant are completed, five Fido assault Kbots will come over the north wall. Be ready for them by having your Commander near the north. His D-Gun can help remove them quickly, but also try to have your Pyro and Storms there as well. Put together a strike team of seven or eight PeeWees. They are going to attack a Merl circling from the west to the north. The Merl's rockets will cause major damage on the mesa unless you destroy it; it's accompanied by Zipper Kbots, so move your PeeWees down the north side of the mesa (2) to intercept it. Set your Aircraft Plant build Freedom Fighters as fast as possible to get a few on patrol above your position.

- **Build Jethros for air defense.** Shortly after the Fidos are taken care of, Arm Brawler gunships will begin to hover and rake the mesa with laser fire. Have Jethros ready to shoot back and focus what few Freedom Fighters you have on the Brawlers as well. The Slasher and Crashers will help. Set your Construction Kbot patrolling up and down the mesa, automatically repairing your units as they take damage.

- **Build a Construction Kbot and Construction Aircraft.** While you are defending the mesa with your Level-1 units, you must get your Level-2 units and structures under way. When the Construction Kbot is finished, have it build an Advanced Kbot Lab and then three Gaat Gun heavy lasers and three Pulverizer missile towers. Your Construction Aircraft should start on an Advanced Airfield. Have the Commander aid the building process once it's started. Also try to build at least two Spectre radar jammers, putting one at the north end and one at the south end of the mesa.

- **Next, build a couple of Punisher cannons.** Build one at the north side of the mesa and one at the west side. The Arm forces will continue to arrive in waves, and they can be beaten back if you keep your production going. Your goal is to get Level-2 Vamps, Hurricanes, and Rapiers in the air as soon as possible. One target should be several Merl rocket launchers near point 3. Send your air force on them as soon as possible. You don't want them anywhere near the mesa.

- **Don't move off the mesa until your air superiority is clear.** The mesa will be very crowded by now. Take six Cans and ten Pyros down the north slope and set up a perimeter. Keep sending additional Cans and Pyros to that area, defending against attacking Fidos and Zippers. On the mesa, have an Advanced Construction Kbot start building an Intimidator, assisted by the Commander to speed things up. Your air force should now be building up a growing Level-2 presence that is patrolling 360 degrees around the mesa. Protected by the Cans and Pyros, have the Commander build a Vehicle Plant just north of the mesa (2) as you expand to come off the mesa. Crank out as many Raiders and Slashers as possible—set the plant to build a dozen of each. The area surrounding the mesa is excellent for tank engagements, and this can be a fascinating armored engagement. The northeast corner of the map (4) has the smallest Arm presence, so expand in that direction to give yourself room.

- **Use your tanks in groups of six to eight units.** Support their efforts as they sweep either west or east by having your Rapiers, Hurricanes, and Vamps in separate squadrons that hit targets that are engaging the tanks. Take your time in cleaning the map and keep your production high.

A variation on this strategy is to move your troops off the mesa to the east, instead of the north. Build a Vehicle Plant earlier, and then try to move to an Advanced Vehicle Plant. This will turn the battle into more of a major tank battle, but it's riskier because of the Arm air and rocket units around the map.

Mission 25:

Empyrrean's Final Stand

Difficulty rating: Hard

Objective: This is the final mission, the point where you must defeat Arm and all of its forces once and for all. You must destroy a huge Arm presence in the northern section of the battlefield. As part of your mission, you must also kill the Arm Commander.

Starting forces: Commander, 2 Thuds, 2 Pyros, 1 Can

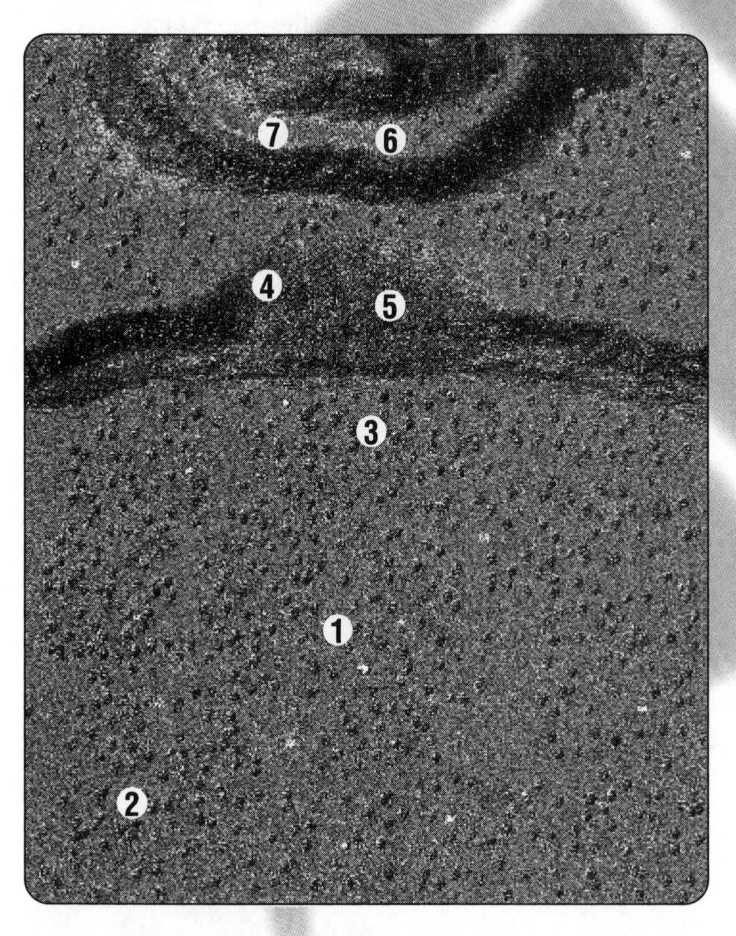

Mission Briefing

The remainder of Arm's forces are spread out around a large hill in the upper half of the battlefield. The Arm Commander is partially obscured under a tree (4) near the front lines. But there's no sense making a suicide run to destroy him early, because you also have to destroy every other Arm unit to win the mission. This calls for another extended period of base construction, army and air force building, and a step-by-step siege of the entrenched enemy.

How to Win

- **Pull back your forces from your starting position (1) toward the southwest corner (2),** and look for three metal deposits in that area. You must have time to build up the Core army and air force before you attract much attention from the massive Arm force to the north. The first line of Arm defenses (3) contains Samson missile launchers, Luger mobile artillery units, Bulldogs, Fidos, and several Brawlers. After finding three or four metal deposits and starting your production, build a Kbot Lab, a Vehicle Plant, and then an Aircraft Plant. As each is completed, begin a construction unit first, then begin producing Kbots, tanks, and Freedom Fighters, respectively.

- **Build four or five Crashers and Slashers for anti-air defenses first.** While your Level-1 factories are churning out a mix of Kbots, vehicles, and Freedom Fighters, get your advanced factories under way. This is where you will spend most of your time and resources developing Level-2 Cans, Pyros, Reapers, Pillagers, Diplomats, Vamps, Rapiers, and Hurricanes. The attacks won't start right away, but they will begin before you reach the ability to make Level-2 weapons. So, maintain a defense line composed of Level-1 Thuds, Storms, Instigators, and Raiders. As you spread your base east from the southwest corner, you will find six metal deposits to tap. Keep your troops near the south so that they don't stray towards the enemy.

- **Move your Reaper tanks, Diplomat rocket launchers, and Pillager artillery units behind a wall of Pyros and Cans (1).** Mix in Level-1 Crashers and Slashers for additional air cover. As you move forward from point 1 to point 3, you will start to attract waves of Jeffys, Stumpys, and Lugers. Next will come Fidos and Brawlers. Keep a couple of Deleter radar jammers with your group, ordering each of them to guard a Reaper tank. Also bring along at least two Informer mobile radar units and one or two construction units for repair purposes. Arm forces will begin their usual repeated attacks. When you get within range of the Defender missile towers and Sentinel heavy-laser towers at point 5, immediately begin targeting them with your Diplomats. Send a few Kbots forward to help visually identify where the Defenders and Sentinels are located.

- **When you reach the hills, begin to build Gaat Guns and Pulverizers.** By now, the Arm air force will be out in strength, and must be met by the Vamps and Rapiers you have been building in the south. Hold back eight to ten Phoenix bombers until your air force is starting to rule the skies. Then, launch repeated waves of Vamp and Phoenix attacks on the Arm units between points 5 and 6. Remember that the Arm Commander must be destroyed, and he can be a target for your air strikes near point 4. Support the air units with your Diplomat rockets. Use the Gaat Guns to defend the hills against Arm counter-attacks and target the Arm air units with Pulverizers. During this time, you must make sure that you have set your factories to produce eight to ten of each of your primary Kbots, vehicles, and aircraft. You will be too busy to go back and mess with factory output; you'll barely have the time to order new units into the front line.

- **Attack Arm's Big Bertha.** There is a Big Bertha at point 7 that will begin to cause you trouble as you approach the first line of hills. Strike that gun hard with your bombers. Arm also has captured Phoenix bombers, about ten of them. They will attack in waves, and begin raining bombs. There are also Merls and Guardians near point 6, so expect the artillery barrages to intensify as you advance north. There is nothing you can do but dig in at the hills near point 5, build long-range guns, and keep sending in air strikes. The advance will take quite a while between points 5 and 6, so keep your factories humming. This is a war of attrition at this point, and whoever produces the most in the shortest time will be the winner.

- **Bring up more tanks and Cans to charge the hills.** With the Bertha destroyed and a couple of Guardians gone, bring up more tanks and Cans to charge the hills at point 6. Keep construction units busy reclaiming metal during this long period leading up to the final attack. By now the Arm air forces should be largely gone, so keep up the continual Vamp and Phoenix attacks on the hills to the north. It will take a while longer to finish off the last of the Arm defenders.

Try a different strategy on this mission by holding back your units from attacking until you have a massive war machine in place, including at least two Intimidator long-range cannons. By using the Intimidators to systematically rid the hills of the Sentinel and Defender emplacements, you won't take as many casualties when you finally rush the hills at point 5 and, later, point 6.

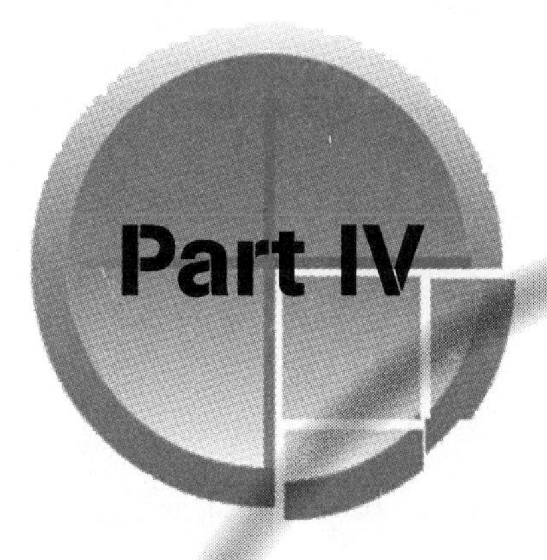

Multiplayer Total Annihilation

Both sides lay in ruins. Their civilizations had long since vanished, their once vast military complexes were smashed. Their armies were reduced to a few scattered remnants, which continued to battle on ravaged worlds. Their hatred fueled by millenia of conflict, they would fight to the death. For each, the only acceptable outcome was the complete and utter annihilation of the other.

Long ago the galaxy had known peace, and it would soon know peace again.

+CONTOUR#

(Will show the 3D contour mesh in the game; replace # with a value between 1 and 5, and then **CONTOUR** by itself to clear)

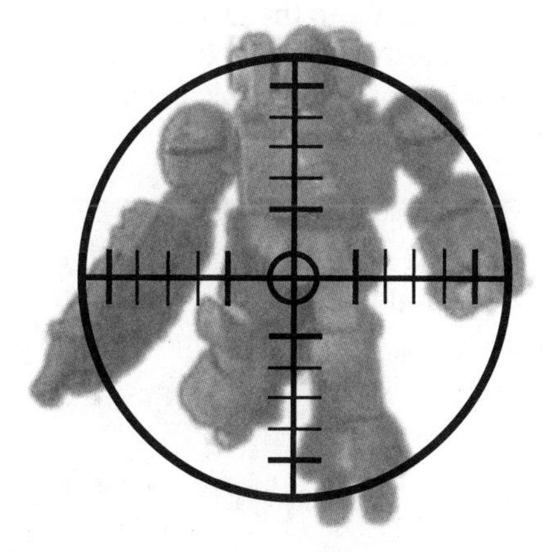

Multiplayer and Skirmish Modes

Total Annihilation is arguably the most player-customizable multiplayer strategy game ever to hit the online world. Virtually every component of game play can be included or excluded, depending on what players want to do. There are four different versions of multiplayer games, all of which feature some kind of human-to-human play. The Skirmish mode, which features single-player gaming against up to three computer-controlled AI players, has many of the same options as multiplayer. Differences between the two are noted.

Setting Up Your Multiplayer Game

Like so many things about *Total Annihilation*, your options in multiplayer games are a gamer's dream. You can configure your multiplayer games in different ways. Here are some tips on making the most of your options.

Spawning

The designers of *Total Annihilation* have built into the product a feature called *spawning*, which means that more than one person can play the game without actually having a TA CD-ROM in their computers. This encourages multiplayer participation and enables your friends to try out the game with you first before buying it.

A single TA CD-ROM permits up to three players on three different computers to participate in a game at the same time without two of the players having a disc in their computer. Two players with TA discs permit up to six players to engage in a multiplayer game. And three players with TA discs in their computers can spawn up to ten players simultaneously.

Find the latest information on spawning at the *Total Annihilation* web site:

http://www.totalannihilation.com

Understanding Your Multiplayer Options

Multiplayer TA games fall into four different connection categories. The two modes that allow more than two players to compete head-to-head are Internet play and Local Area Network (LAN) play. Internet play can be carried out through a variety of entertainment services, listed below. Modem and Serial connection play are two-player games with two computers connected either via a telephone line or a serial cable. When you click the Multiplayer option on the TA main screen, the screen changes to the Select Connection Screen so that you can make a decision about which multiplayer connection you would like.

Select Connection Screen

- **IPX for LAN play.** LANs are proliferating around the world as many companies and some individuals connect multiple computers into local-area networks in their businesses or homes. The drawback to LAN play is that it requires considerable resources to link up multiple computers this way, and most companies do not relish the idea of having their LANs used for gaming. If you do have access to a LAN for gaming, this option helps you configure the game for network play. Insert Icon TIP

Getting started: Select the Multiplayer option button from the main screen. Click the IPX selection. TA will detect if your computer is connected to a network, and present you with the Select Game screen. For more details see the Select Game Screen section in this chapter.

- **TCP/IP connection for DirectPlay.** By far the most popular form of multiplayer gaming now takes place over the Internet, hosted by any of a number of entertainment service providers that generally charge a fee or accept advertising as a part of their service. Some of the most popular services are hosting *Total Annihilation* games. Each of these services and web sites requires that you have online access through an Internet service provider (ISP).

- **http://www.totalannihilation.com** takes you to the official *Total Annihilation* web site hosted by Cavedog Entertainment.
- **Unit Download** enables you to download to your computer the latest new units and structures that Cavedog has placed on its web site for you to add to your TA game.
- **Service Providers** lists those entertainment service providers that will be hosting multiplayer *Total Annihilation* games. You find this option just below the Unit Download button. Click on any of them in order to get more information about their services and/or to be taken directly to their web sites.

Getting started: You will have to have Internet access through an Internet (or online) service provider. If you select the TCP/IP option, you will see a screen that asks for a TCP (transfer control protocol). This is the address number that your computer uses when connected to the Internet. If your system is on a local-area network (LAN), leave the number blank and the game will automatically find the number that the network uses. If you are not on a network, you will have to ask your ISP if your system has a permanent IP address or if it is generated new every time you log on to the Internet. See the "Readme" text file on your TA CD-ROM for more detailed information on setting up and hosting Internet games for two to four players.

- **Modem Connection for DirectPlay.** This option enables you and another player to connect via your modems and a telephone line to engage in two-player games. You must have a 28.8 kpbs or higher modem.

Getting started: Selecting the Modem play option takes you to a telephone number selection screen. If you are dialing the other player, enter that phone number and select Dial. If you will be answering a call from another player, press Answer. When a connection is made, both players will be presented with the Battle Room screen for further choices.

- **Serial Connection for DirectPlay.** This option enables you to physically connect two computers in the same room through a cable connected to the computers' serial ports. Once you have a cable connected between the two computers and the game is installed on both systems, TA will search to find the correct serial port and speed for you.

Getting started: When you select this method of play from the Multiplayer menu, you next see a screen in which you select the serial port through which your computer is connected to the other computer and the connection speed between the two.

Select Game Screen

For Internet and LAN games, this screen lists the available games you can join and preferences set by each game's host. To join a game, you click on the appropriate name on the list, then enter your name, and press Join. (On a LAN, you can press Watch.)

- **Name of Game**—this is an entry box that displays the name of the game you wish to join.
- **Map Name**—tells you which of the over 30 maps is being used in this game.

- **Cmdr**—determines whether the game ends with a Commander's death or continues the game after any or all of the Commanders are destroyed.
- **Ping**—this number shows, in milliseconds, the amount of time it is taking your computer to bounce a signal to the computer hosting the game and back again. The lower the number, the faster the transmission you will get for game play.
- **LOS**—there are three line-of-site options in *Total Annihilation:*
  - **True** gives all units and structures a true line of sight, which means that hills, forests, mountains, and other obstructions can block what they can see.
  - **Circular** gives all units and structures a line of sight that includes everything within a circle of where each might be at any given moment.
  - **Permanent** enables you to see whatever is happening at any point through which one of your units has passed. This mode is particularly useful when you capture an enemy unit or structure, because you then see whatever that unit or structure has seen.
- **Map**—displays whether the game started with an unmapped battlefield that must be explored to be seen or a mapped battlefield in which the entire map is displayed
- **Metal and Energy**—shows the starting amounts of metal and energy, usually set at 1,000 units of each at the start of a game
- **Plyrs**—indicates the number of players who engage in a particular game
- **Status**—shows whether the game is currently under way, being formed, or is closed to other players
- **Your Name**—an entry box for your name
- **Password**—an entry box for a game that is using a password to access
- **New**—enables you to move to the Create New Game screen to start your own TA multiplayer game
- **Update**—updates the information listed in the Select Game screen
- **Watch**—for LAN games, an option to watch a game in progress without being a part of the action
- **Join**—enables you to join the game of your choice after the above information has been entered

Create New Game Screen

This screen is where you will set the basic parameters for a new game that you wish to host. The Password option gives you a chance to set a password so that only those players who have the password can enter the game. When you have entered this information, then you are taken to the Battle Room screen.

- **Enter Game Name:** enter any game name of your choosing
- **Enter Your Name:** type in the name you are using
- **Password:** enter a password if you wish to have only those people who know the password able to join.
- **Next:** takes you to the Battle Room screen

Battle Room Screen

Here you sign in, select a side and color, and decide whether to attempt an alliance with another player or players. Most of the selections in the Battle Room screen are identical to choices noted above, with the exception of Resolution and Memory. Resolution shows the graphic resolution you wish to use in the game. For almost all computers, except the fastest systems (above 200 Mhz), Cavedog Entertainment recommends the 640 x 480 resolution for optimum graphics speed. Memory lists the available RAM (Random Access Memory) of your computer. Some of the multiplayer maps require 32MB RAM.

Additional Multiplayer Options

Two more options give you a tremendous range of flexibility in your TA gaming experience—Cheat Codes and Build Restriction.

- **Cheat Codes.** This indicates whether or not any Cheat Codes, are allowed or disallowed in the current game.
- **Build Restriction.** This selection bar takes you to the Build Restriction menu from which you can select or de-select virtually all units and structures to use in the game.

Opting for the Skirmish Mode

Almost all of the options described for Multiplayer gaming apply to the Skirmish games you will play against up to three computer-controlled opponents on the same maps you use in Multiplayer mode. The only significant difference in game selection is that in Skirmish mode you can select whether you wish the game to be Easy, Medium, or Hard. Medium is the default selection. The other two choices don't change the enemy AI, but merely affect the amount of metal and energy the sides have and with how many units and structures they begin.

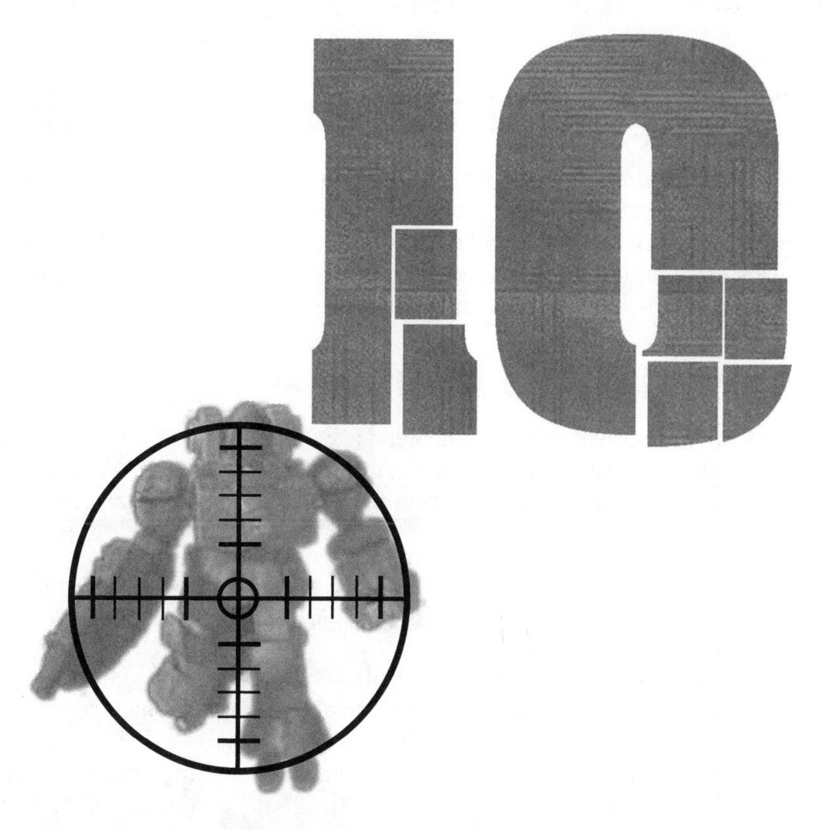

10 Multiplayer Strategies

The best way to enjoy *Total Annihilation* is to play against other people. Not that the single-player missions aren't challenging in their own right, but nothing beats playing against live opponents. However, before you venture on your multiplayer war path, you should first digest the tips in this chapter and you might stand a better chance against your bloodthirsty online opponents. Note: TA's skirmish mode uses the same maps that are in the multiplayer games and provides a terrific way to practice your strategies against AI opponents before you tackle other players.

Basic Multiplayer Strategies

Like any real-time strategy game, *Total Annihilation* favors those players who can move faster and accomplish more than other players. If you can handle four tasks in TA while your enemy completes only two, you're already ahead of him or her. Improving your speed and your success begins with the basics of multiplayer gaming: learning the maps by heart, knowing your opponents, and familiarizing yourself with the keyboard shortcuts.

Memorize the Maps

Study the multiplayer maps in Chapter 11. Each of them has been designed and play-balanced for a certain numbers of players. Know your map(s), and you will immediately have an edge over your enemy in terms of your construction and resource-building efforts—regardless of the number of your opponents.

- **Use choke points.** Many of the maps have natural choke points and barriers that channel movement around the map in certain ways. Finding the best choke points on a map is one way to gain a critical early advantage over those unfamiliar with the map.
- **Build mobile units that apply to the terrain.** Kbots such as PeeWees, Fidos, and Rockos are able to maneuver on rocky, mountainous terrain far better than tanks, which favor open ground for their best maneuverability and speed. On the other hand, on island campaigns and lava maps, getting air power flying over the natural barriers can be much more effective than sending Kbots out early—they will be blocked by water and lava.
- **Remember where the metal is located.** Once you play on a given map a few times, you will begin to remember where individual metal deposits are located. Make a note of them as you are playing and you will soon have a list of deposit locations that will save precious time on the same map in the future.
- **Use the relative sizes of the maps to your advantage.** One of TA's advances is the use of very large maps. When playing on these big maps, your style of play should change. On large maps, send out scout vehicles in arcs around your position to find metal deposits and natural terrain elements as fast as possible. Big maps give players a sense that they have time to build their bases before being attacked. This is true, but it can also work to your advantage if you surprise an opponent early in a game with a *blitzkrieg* attack. On small maps, however, you should attack earlier than on big maps.

On a very large map, build an Aircraft Plant as early as possible. Then build a scout aircraft that can quickly cover the entire map on long-range recon missions. You will very quickly see where your enemies are.

Know your opponents

Each player you encounter has certain styles and techniques of play that he or she will apply time and time again. For direct-connect modem and serial games and most LAN games, you will probably know the person, or people, you are playing against. As you play them over time, make mental notes of their tendencies. Ask yourself:

- **Is my opponent an offensive or defensive player?** Most players end up being either defense-oriented or offense-oriented. Although their strategies do change based on the map and the number of other players, after a couple of games against the same person, you should notice certain styles of play. Of course, they notice elements of *your* game play as well. Be a student of other players. Watch their regular patterns, then figure out ways to stop them.

- **Does my opponent favor ground initiatives or air initiatives?** Beginning players are usually overly fascinated by air power, and tend to build it too early as a fundamental strategic component instead of a supporting strategic component. On maps that favor the swift movement of ground units, develop your Kbot and vehicle plants before you invest in aircraft. When playing more than one other person, always develop anti-aircraft Jethros or Crashers and Samson or Slashers early in development—at least one of your opponents will build aircraft very early, and you need to be prepared.

- **Does my enemy form alliances?** Some players love to form alliances in multiplayer games (see the section Choosing an Ally in this chapter), especially when they can add an ally with a complementary strength that minimizes an individual weakness. Forming alliances with players you don't know is risky business, because an alliance can be broken at any time. Get to know a player, if possible, before you accept or propose an alliance.

- **Is my opponent a fast or slow builder?** No other element of game play in TA is as important as how quickly and effectively you can construct factories to build other units and structures. You must build as effectively as you do swiftly for this aspect to help you strategically. That means knowing *what* and *when* to build fast. A slow, methodical builder doesn't have much of a long-term chance in a multiplayer game. Enter each game with a good idea of what you want to build and move as quickly as possible.

When competing against one or more players who are strongly defensive, extend the outside edge of your base at least twice as far as you normally would. This way, if an enemy scout finds one of your units or structures closer than expected to that base, the player will tend to build an even tighter base because of the perceived threat.

Use Keyboard Shortcuts

In single-player games, you have the luxury of pausing a mission or a skirmish in order to double-check a keyboard shortcut. That's not the case in multiplayer TA. An element of being fast and effective in the game is understanding which key strokes can help you streamline your actions. All of the keyboard shortcuts are helpful; the following seven shortcuts, however, are crucial in multiplayer games.

- **Tab.** In multiplayer games, pressing Tab presents you with a pop-up menu at the bottom of the screen that enables you to share your resources, your units, and any information you may have. The submenus include:
  - **Allies**—which gives you the names of other players in the game and enables you to propose alliances with one or more of them.
  - **Share**—which enables you to transfer to any player any energy and metal resources, units, and the map information that you have.
  - **Control**—which enables the host player to reject a player from the game, permit someone to watch the game, or open and close the game to other players.
- **Shift key.** When using the Build menu, hold down the Shift key to queue up multiple commands. One of TA's strong points is that you don't have to spend as much time building individual units one by one. Set multiple orders using the Shift key, and then move on!
- **F3.** This key selects the unit that last reported in or chatted information to you. You should use some degree of Chat to receive at least minimum information from your troops. With so much going on around the battlefield, it's easy to lose track of units that are coming under attack, discovering enemy positions, or completing building tasks. When you receive a message on screen from one of your units, hit the F3 key to go immediately to that unit. Nothing is worse than having an idle construction unit because you forgot to check its progress on a building project.
- **Ctrl-Z.** One of the most helpful key commands, Ctrl-Z selects all units of the same type. Just click on one of them and then press Ctrl-Z to include all other units of that type. The best use for this is with aircraft. Unless you form a selected group of aircraft before they start flying (pressing Ctrl plus 1–9 keys), your aircraft can be literally all over the map. Click on one gunship or bomber, for example, then hit Ctrl-Z, and send them all the same command.
- **Ctrl-C.** You will use this key combination many times in a game. In the thick of battles, your Commander can get lost among the dozens of other units. Hit Ctrl-C to automatically select the Commander and center the screen on him.
- **D.** When the Commander is selected, this activates the all-powerful Disintegrator Gun, or D-Gun. It takes 400 energy units for each blast.
- **Tilde (~).** The tilde key toggles the damage bars and squad numbers on and off for all units on your side. Playing with these indicators on is very helpful in keeping track of which units need to be repaired during combat. Leave this turned on to better see the status of your troops.
- **Ctrl-A, Ctrl-B, Ctrl-F, Ctrl-S, and Ctrl-V.** Select all (A) your units, builders (B), factories (F), VToLs (V), or all visible units on screen (S) with these key combinations. These combinations are very effective for getting out of bad situations in a hurry, especially against more than one opponent when you want to pull your troops back from a multiplayer battle situation.

Select the aircraft and use the T key to track your scout aircraft early in the game. You will see all of your enemies that the scout sees during the tracking session.

Varying Your Moves

Every game has its own rhythm, but there are strategies common to almost all early-, middle-, and late-stage multiplayer games that will be of some help.

Early-Stage Strategies

The beginning of a game is the most crucial period. It sets the pace and the direction that you will have to live with for the rest of the game. There are several areas of strategy that you should keep in mind.

- **Resources.** In the early stage of a game, send out scouts that will destroy some or all of an enemy's resources; it can be a crippling blow. To prevent that from happening to you, assign guards to your resource generators right from the start. The more players in a game, the more important it is for you to guard your resources early.
- **Construction.** Build construction plants and then mobile construction units as quickly as you can to get ahead of as many of your opponents as possible. Also, place factories in the direction of your opponents if you know their positions. This keeps an armored structure between your base and your enemies, and it lets the units that are produced become immediately available on the front line.
- **Communication.** Offer an alliance early to see the response from one or more of your opponents. If you ally early in a game, share as much information as possible at that time and keep chatting back and forth when new information becomes available. Remember to set your communications so that only allies will see your messages.
- **Combat.** Your aggressive enemies will send out scouts right away. Have either scout vehicles, Kbots, or Light Laser Towers up early to prevent hit-and-run scouting attacks. Set at least one patrol at least a half-screen away from your base so that you have an early warning system. And generally avoid early combat unless your strategy is based on harassing the enemy from the start.

Mid-Game Strategies

By the middle of a game, resources should be flowing, several advanced plants and construction units should be available, and you should know where your enemies are located. The strategies change at this point in several ways.

- **Resources.** In a crowded multiplayer game, delay building energy and metal storage structures until you have factories on line and advanced units being produced. This means that early in the game you should be very efficient at using just enough energy and metal so that you don't run out and you don't have excess. Also, before choosing an ally at this stage in the game, you should find out who has the greatest resource inventory, and then share immediately.

- **Construction.** After the initial phase of a game, gear your efforts toward advanced construction plants. You must stay ahead in the arms race, especially when it comes to getting access to Level-2 weapons. On large maps with few players, expand the perimeter of your base as often as possible to take in more territory and metal deposits and to spread your base so that a nuclear attack won't destroy most of it.

- **Communication.** Battles become large engagements midway through the game, and it's important to keep track of your allies' situations by comparing notes. It's also a time when priorities change, and so do alliances. If you haven't formed an alliance by now, and you're starting to lose ground, seek out an ally for support.

- **Combat.** Major assault initiatives and campaigns are under way during this phase of the game. If you are playing an offensive, attacking game, expect to find more resistance at enemy bases. If you are playing a defensive, conservative game, expect large multistage attacks from your opponents. You must keep your production high during this period, so protect your factories at all costs.

Late-Stage Strategies

By now, trends have begun to develop that reveal who has the power and the momentum. This is another moment when reassessing alliances and strategic plans is necessary.

- **Resources.** By now, your base should have Moho Mines and Fusion Plants if you've been successful. If there were four or more players at the start of a game, at least one of them is now defeated, perhaps even two. If it was a three- or two-player contest at the start, then it should be apparent who is on the winning track. Your search for more metal resources should intensify, and you should try to capture metal and energy structures from opponents. Also, if you're losing, then propose an alliance with a player with the best resources.

- **Construction.** Your advanced construction units should now be producing Level-3 weapons, such as long-range cannons and nuclear missiles. If you have built several construction units and advanced construction units, your building projects can be speeded up a great deal by using all of them and the Commander to boost the build rate.

- **Communication.** If you find yourself on the losing end of things at this stage, try forging an alliance with another player who needs help. The tide of a game can be changed dramatically by an alliance of two players who individually are losing ground. Make sure that such an alliance includes as much detailed information back and forth as possible to effectively attack and defend one another.

- **Combat.** The big guns of Level-3 can make this the most enjoyable or the most frustrating part of the game, depending on whether or not you have the weapons doing the firing. For allies, trading such units as Bulldog and Goliath tanks or Merl rocket launchers can result in wild end games in which the tide of battle shifts back and forth as allies support one another with weapons trades.

It's just barely possible for one Commander to D-Gun another Commander and still live. But the shot must be as your Commander is about to move behind a large obstruction, such as a hill or large rock.

Choosing an Ally

Total Annihilation's Ally option is a step ahead of other alliance strategy games. You can exchange information privately via chat, share any of your units, and give away as much of your resources as you wish. The reciprocal nature of these trades brings strategy-game alliances to a new level of interaction.

Forming Alliances

- **Propose an alliance that complements the strengths and weaknesses of the two players.** Unlike some other strategy games in which alliances are two separate armies just agreeing not to fight one another, TA's alliance feature enables you to exchange units, resources, and information that can truly shore up your weak areas and add strength to those of your partner. If you're flush with metal resources but low on tanks, for example, an alliance with another player with the opposite situation changes the game tremendously.
- **Decide on responsibilities and opportunities.** A successful alliance usually divides up certain duties and responsibilities. If you like to set up defensive fortresses and your ally likes to command attacking troops, then agree beforehand to that arrangement. Always go into an alliance with a specific idea of what each of you brings to the other.
- **Choose an ally from the enemy camp.** When selecting an ally in a multiplayer game, choose someone who is playing the other side—Arm or Core—so that you get the best of both sides' unique units; for example, Arm's Zeus lightning-gun Kbot and fast-attack Zipper as well as Core's Goliath super-heavy tank.
- **Play to your strengths.** There is no strategic advantage to agree to an alliance when it plays to an area of your game that is weak. You know where your real strengths lie, and you must communicate that to your ally before you both agree to join forces.

Breaking Alliances

- **Dissolve your alliance.** Some TA players form alliances like the one between Hitler and Stalin in 1939—as a marriage of convenience that will soon be called off. These things can come back to haunt you, however, if you abuse the alliance relationship in TA. A player who has been on the losing end of an alliance with you will think twice before accepting another such arrangement.

- **Change partners, change goals.** Alliances are based on certain conditions and expectations that exist at a particular point in the game. Those conditions can change, and so should your alliances. If you decide to go out on your own, try to follow alliance etiquette by first announcing to your ally that you wish to withdraw from the arrangement and then offer some time period during which you and your former ally can prepare to be enemies.

Sharing Resources, Units, and Information

- **Share for balanced resources and power.** There is never a perfect trade, but among allies your sharing of resources should have some parity. Agree in advance of an alliance what will be shared and in what quantities. The alliance must work for both sides. Exchanging one PeeWee for a Moho Mine won't take the alliance very far.

- **"Lend" a resource generator to an ally.** One of the most innovative alliance strategies is to "lend" an ally one or more of your resource generators. You do this by sharing, say, a Moho Mine or a Fusion Reactor that is inside your base. Your ally gets to use its production, but you can take it back at anytime just by having your Commander recapture it.

Mercenary Alliances

- **Hire yourself out for a price.** In games where you find yourself outgunned but still powerful—knowing that it will be tough to match your opponents for the rest of the game—you can offer to be a spoiler for one of the other players in exchange for extra resources or units. This can be especially helpful if you have no construction units and can bargain for at least one of your ally's to help you in the long run.

- **Concentrate on having one strong suit that you can exploit.** In closely fought multiplayer games, having one area of development in which you clearly dominate can fetch a good exchange price from a potential ally, who otherwise might not be interested. Let's say that you have a powerful air force, clearly much stronger than a neighbor's. Propose that, for a fee, you will ally and share your aircraft with him for a time.

Forced Alliances

- **Threaten your weaker opponents.** You aren't in this game to win friends and influence people. So, with that in mind, consider blackmailing your weaker opponents into alliances of convenience—convenient for you, that is. Threaten to blow up an enemy base if your offer of an alliance is not accepted. A powerful player can gain an ally or two by simply threatening to destroy them immediately if they don't accept an alliance. With their alliance, you leave them alone, and they keep supplying you with resources, units, and information to use against stronger enemies.

- **Pull out of an alliance before you fulfill your part of the sharing agreement.** Sure, you'll be a pariah after that; no one will trust you, and for good reason. But, hey, you now have a material advantage that you can exploit to defeat everyone else. Just plan to leave town after the game.

Building Restrictions into Your Strategies

Total Annihilation allows you to configure both the types of units and the number of units that are in any multiplayer game. This enables you to customize games that play to your particular strengths or that will help you improve an area of play that is weak.

Restricting Types of Units

- **Set up all-ground, all-air, or all-sea games.** By restricting the types of units in a multiplayer game, you can put together games that minimize some aspects of play and maximize others. This is one way of handicapping TA games among players of different strengths. For example, an experienced player who is a whiz at using air power can be brought back to earth in a game that uses only ground units.

- **De-select all fast-attack units.** To take away the advantage for a player who is known as a fast-attack, slashing-offense opponent, restrict the unit types to exclude Zippers, Jeffys, and other quick-moving units. Play the game only with slower moving units.

Restricting Numbers of Units

- **Reduce the number of units to simplify the game.** Let's face it. Some players are more adept at handling dozens and dozens of units than others. To simplify a game, try reducing the number of available units for everyone to four or five each. This works against players who love to amass huge numbers of forces and then fight a war of attrition.

- **Reduce the number of units in categories of strength for your opponent.** If you can play a great ground campaign, but air power is your weak point. Set up a game that enables you to maximize the number of ground units, but severely restricts the number of air units.

Strategic Variations

There are many variations on multiplayer strategies, and being creative is part of the fun in multiplayer gaming. Here are a couple of examples to get you started.

- **Threaten mutually assured destruction.** For opponents who like to send in their Commander to start blowing up your base, thus crippling your efforts from the start, broadcast a message that anyone doing so will be fired on by your Commander. The threat is that when your Commander blows up another Commander, both sides are eliminated from the game (provided the Commander Dies option is selected).
- **Try the "undefended base" strategy.** For two- or three-player multiplayer games, one aggressive offensive strategy is to leave your own base undefended while you pour every unit of energy and metal into mobile units that can take the fight to the nearest enemy base. By raiding that base, and perhaps others, you capture energy and metal storage structures and generators while—you hope—crippling the capacity of the opponent. The more players in a game, however, the riskier such a strategy is. Your base is sure to be overrun by someone else while you're out raiding your neighbors.

TA is a multiplayer's dream, and you will certainly discover your own strategies as you play the game. Now it's time for you to get acquainted with the maps on which you will be spending so much of your TA time. Get to know them well!

Hot Keys

Giving Orders	
A	Attack order
G	Guard order
M	Move order
P	Patrol order
S	Stop order
D	Disintegrator Gun
C	Capture order
R	Repair order
E	Reclaim order
H	Shares resources with another player
Shift	Press to queue up multiple commands
Enter	Activates the message bar
Esc	Cancels the current command
In Control	
Ctrl-A	Selects all of your units
Ctrl-B	Selects all Builders
Ctrl-C	Centers screen on/selects Commander
Ctrl-D	Self-destructs selected units (toggles on/off)
Ctrl-F	Selects all factories
Ctrl-S	Selects all units currently on the screen
Ctrl-V	Selects all VToLs
Ctrl-1–Ctrl-9	Assigns selected units to a squad
Alt-1–Alt-9	Activates previously assigned squad
F2	Pauses game/brings up the Options menu
- / +	Reduces/increases the game speed
Managing Unit Info	
B	Build menu for that unit
O	Order menu for the current unit
1 - 9	Menu for the current unit
, (comma)	Previous menu for that unit
. (period)	Next menu for that unit
~ (tilde)	Toggles damage bars on the units
F1	Displays info on selected unit
F3	Takes you to the unit that last chatted
F12	Clears all chat messages
N	Scrolls to the next unit off screen
T	Tracks the selected unit

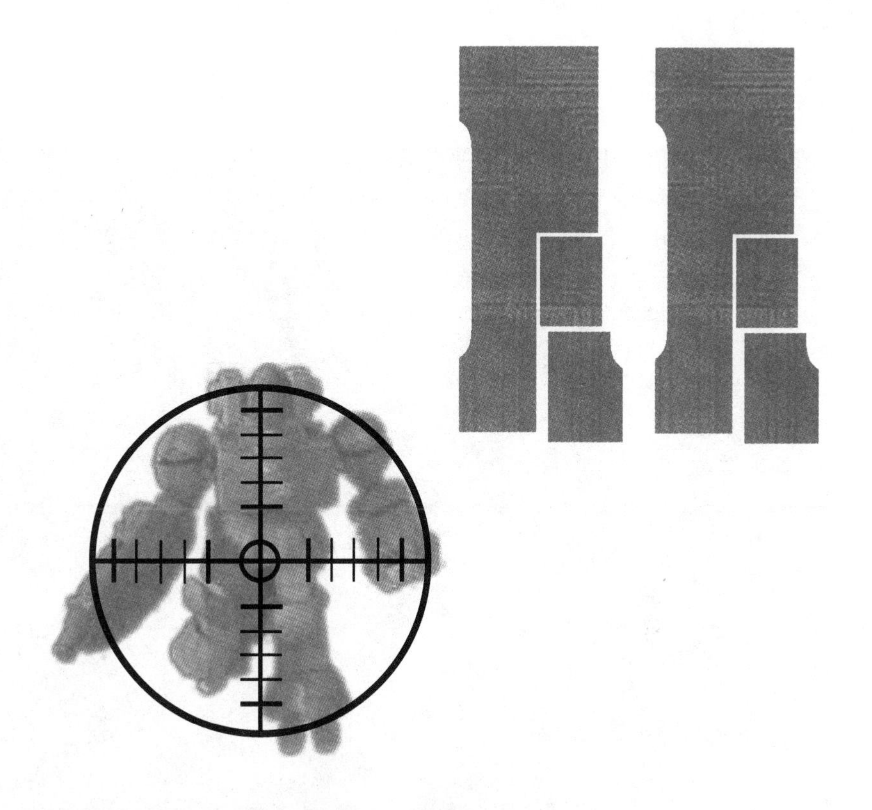

Multiplayer Maps

This chapter presents more than 30 multiplayer- and skirmish-mode maps, broken down by name, size, number of players, and a brief tip. *Size* tells you how many screens the map is wide and high (a "screen" is that portion of the map you see at any one time in the main game screen); *number of players* tells you for how many players the map has been play-balanced. The maps range in size from relatively small 8 x 8 maps to massive 40 x 40 maps that require 32MB of RAM. The starting positions are designed so that players begin with relatively equal chances to succeed. You may be able to play some of the 32MB maps on a computer that has 16 to 24MB RAM; in that case, you should limit the number of total units that each player can use in that game from 200 each to 75 or 100 each. (Slowing the game down with the minus (-) key to "-5" may also help.)

Anteer Strait

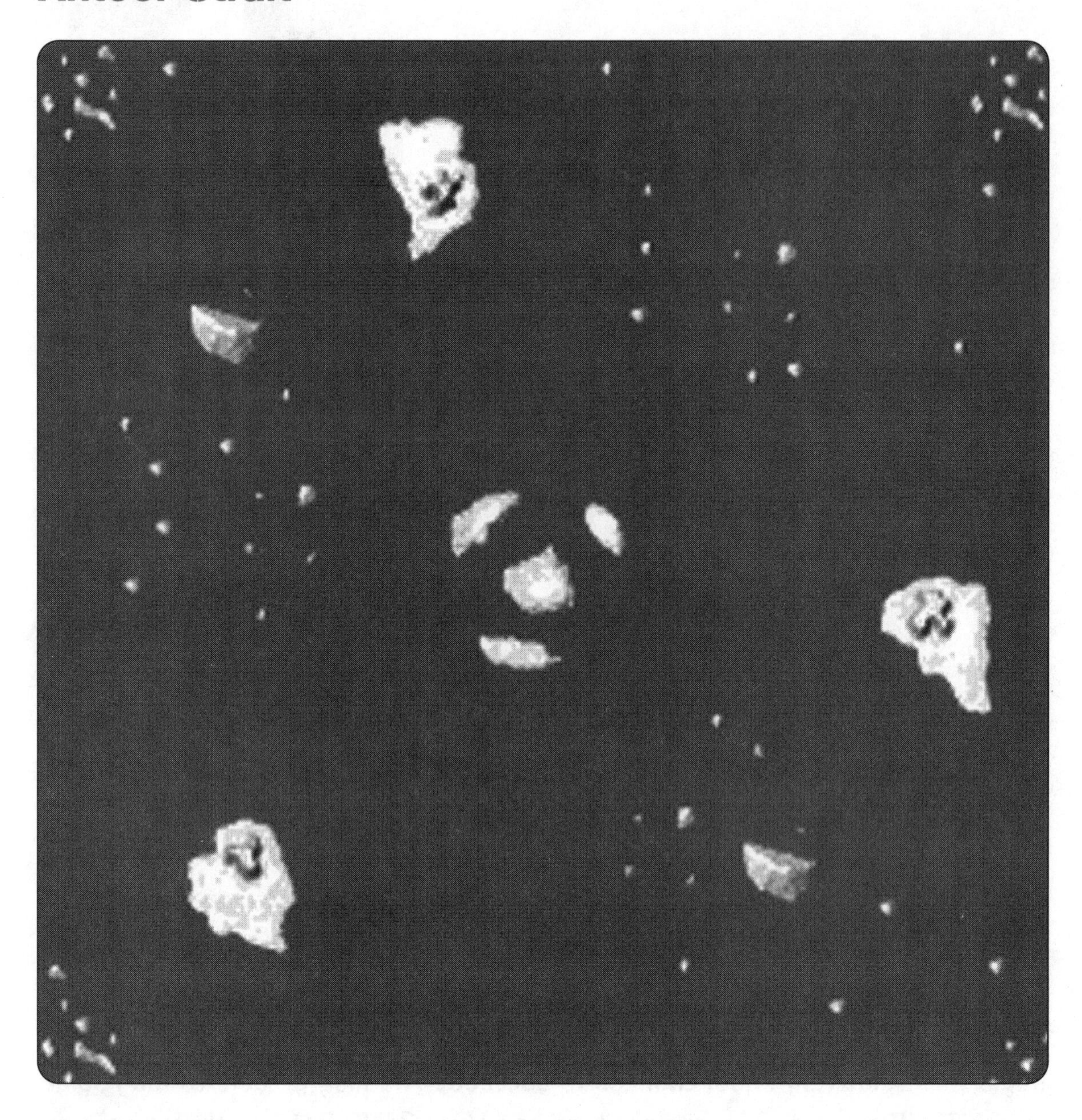

Size: 18 x 18

Number of Players: 3

Description: This is a very large water map on an ice world covered by icebergs and islands.

The icebergs can be used to block naval guns. There is a lot of metal on the four islands in the center of the map. Prevent your enemies from building there unopposed.

Ashap Plateau

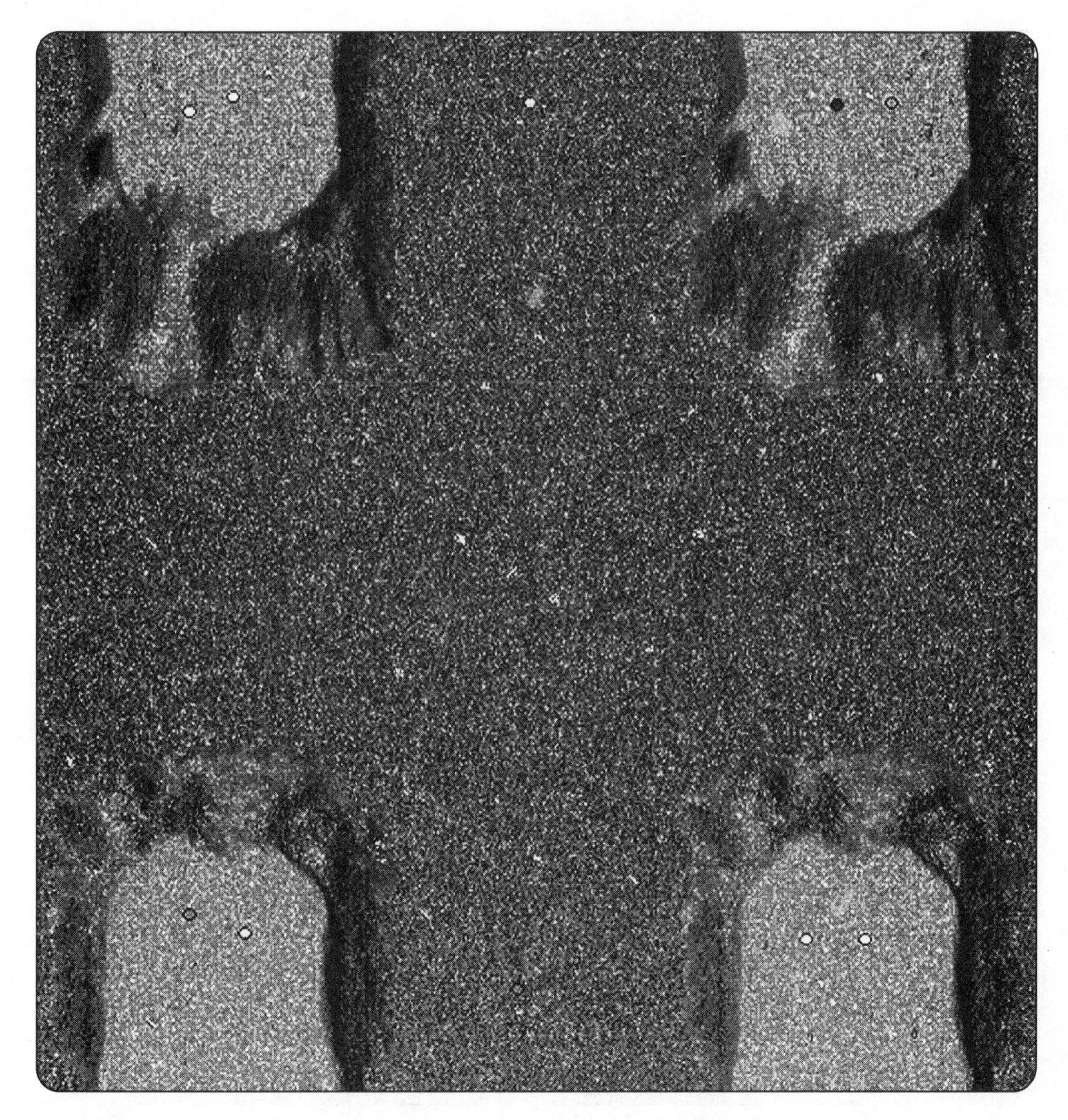

Size: 8 x 8

Number of players: 2 or 4

Description: There are two north-facing and two south-facing mesas, each having ramps. Most of the ground below the mesas is too rough to build large factories. But there is sufficient space for Radar Towers and Laser Towers.

There is very little metal on top of the mesas, forcing players to descend and fight it out for the metal resources. This is not a map for defensive-oriented players; you must be aggressive to get enough metal.

Caldera's Rim

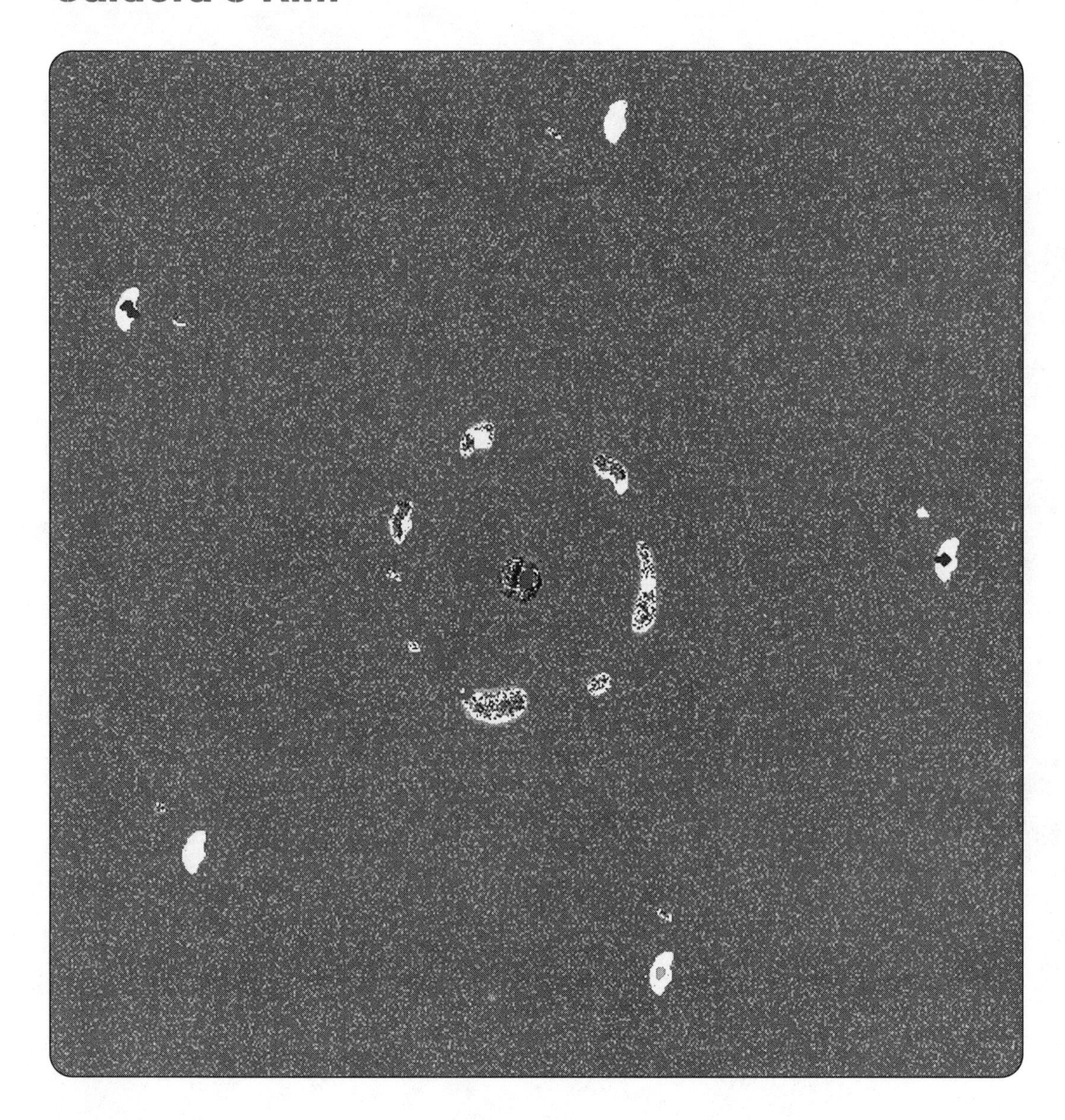

Size: 29 x 29

Number of players: 2 or 5

Description: This is an island map, with an outer ring of five islands and an inner ring of islands surrounding a sunken volcano.

Maintain a presence in the center islands. There are rich metal sources near the sunken volcano. Even if you cannot possess it, keep your enemy under fire so that he cannot develop with it.

Coast to Coast

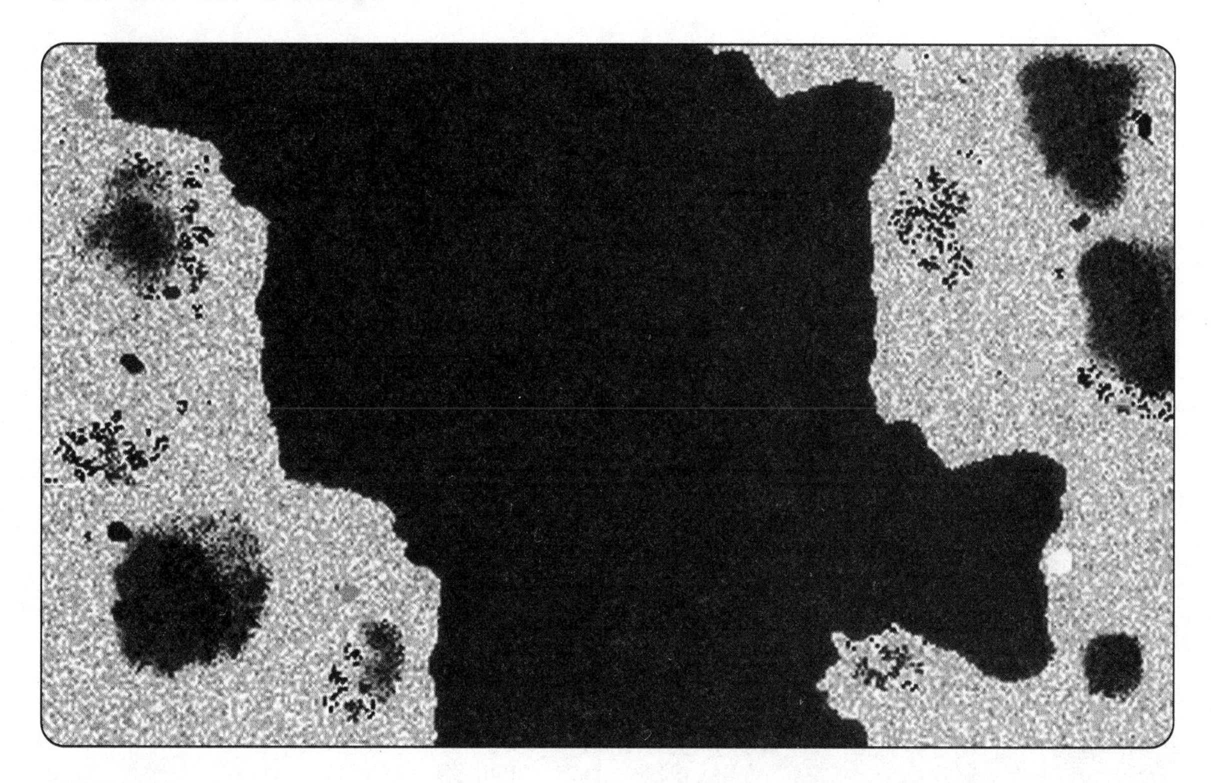

Size: 7 x 4

Number of players: 2

Description: There are two large land masses, one on the east and the other on the west. A fairly large body of water is in between.

This map lends itself to air battles. Get your Aircraft Plant started early. There is not enough ocean for big naval battles, so don't push your construction in that direction.

Dark Side

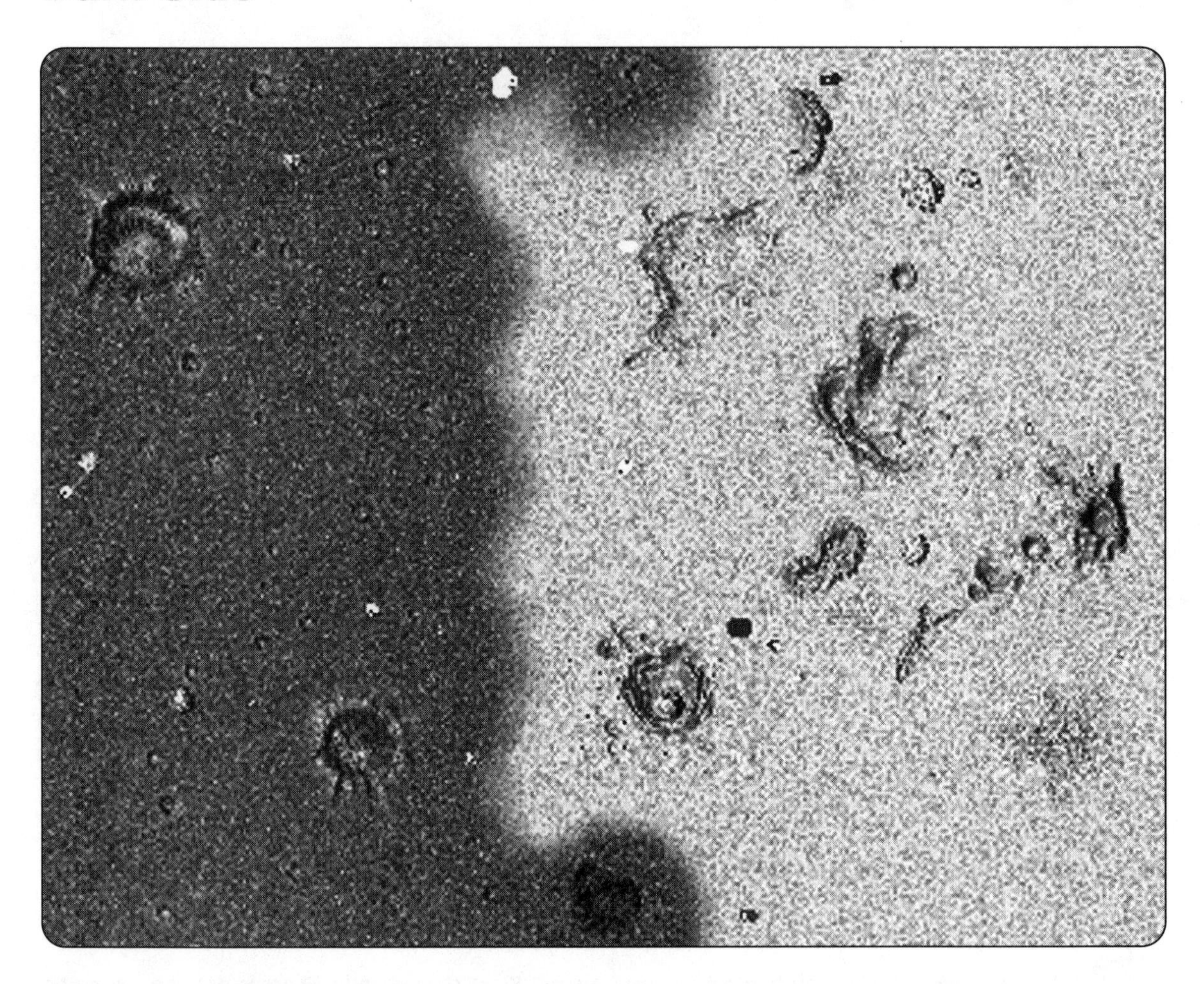

Size: 8 x 6

Number of players: 2 or 3

Description: This is a lunar map with basaltic seas on the left and white lunar highlands on the right.

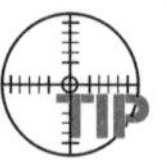

Each of the three large craters has metal at the bottom. It is a small map, which means you have to get down into the craters quickly and grab the metal.

The Desert Triad

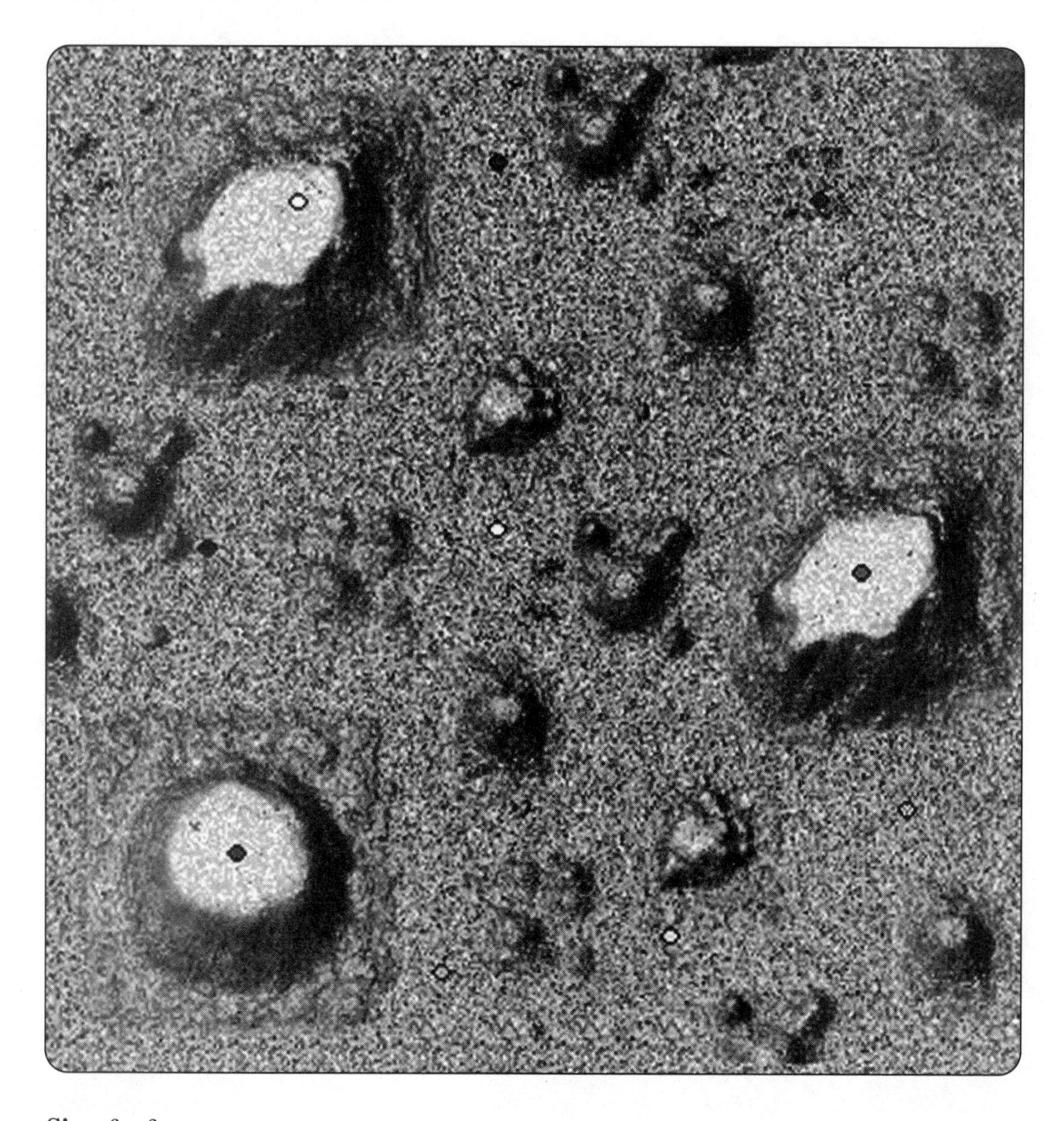

Size: 6 x 6

Number of players: 2, 3 or 6

Description: You begin on one of three very tall mesas whose walls are so steep that almost no unit can climb them. This is a secure place to build a base.

This map plays best in 3-player contests. It is largely an air war among the mesas. On the map floor, however, there is a good amount of metal and geothermal vents. Try sending your Commander to the map floor for more resources.

Etorrep Glacier

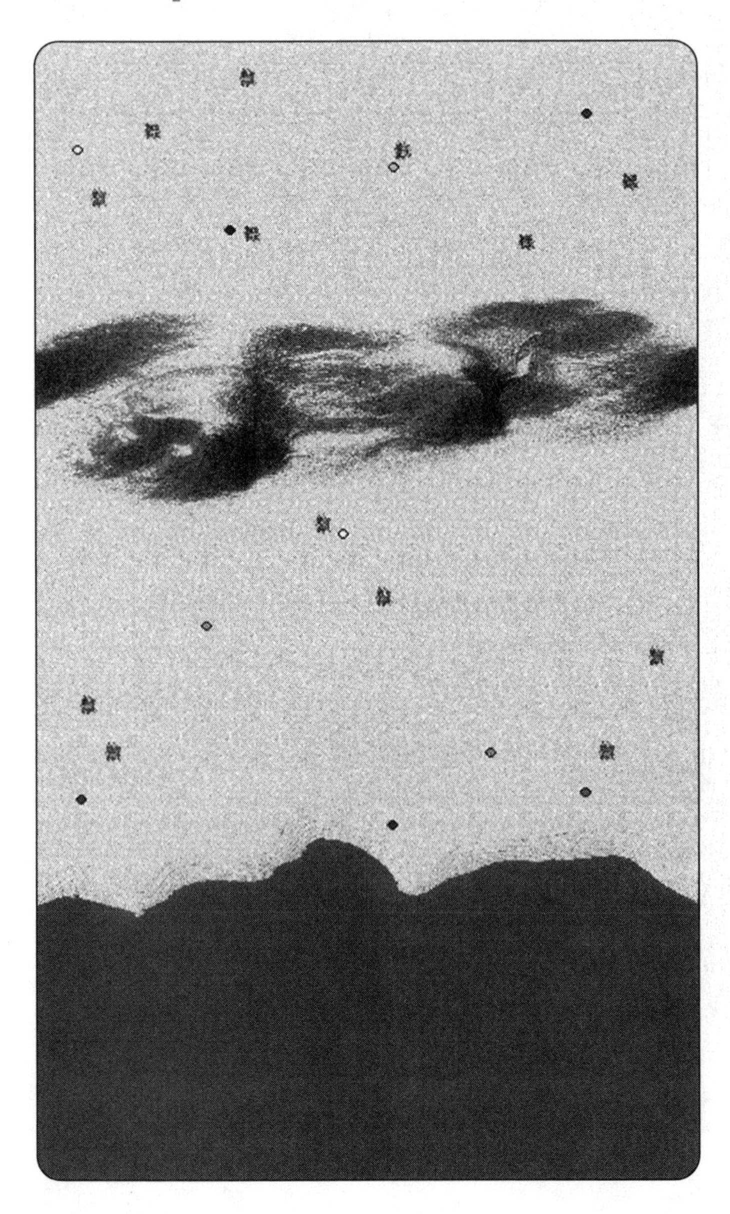

Size: 5 x 9

Number of players: 2 or 3

Description: This is an ice world. At the north end of the map, there is a huge wall of ice and at the south end some water.

Tips: Scramble to get to the top of that ice wall, a good position from which to build your base.

Evad River Confluence

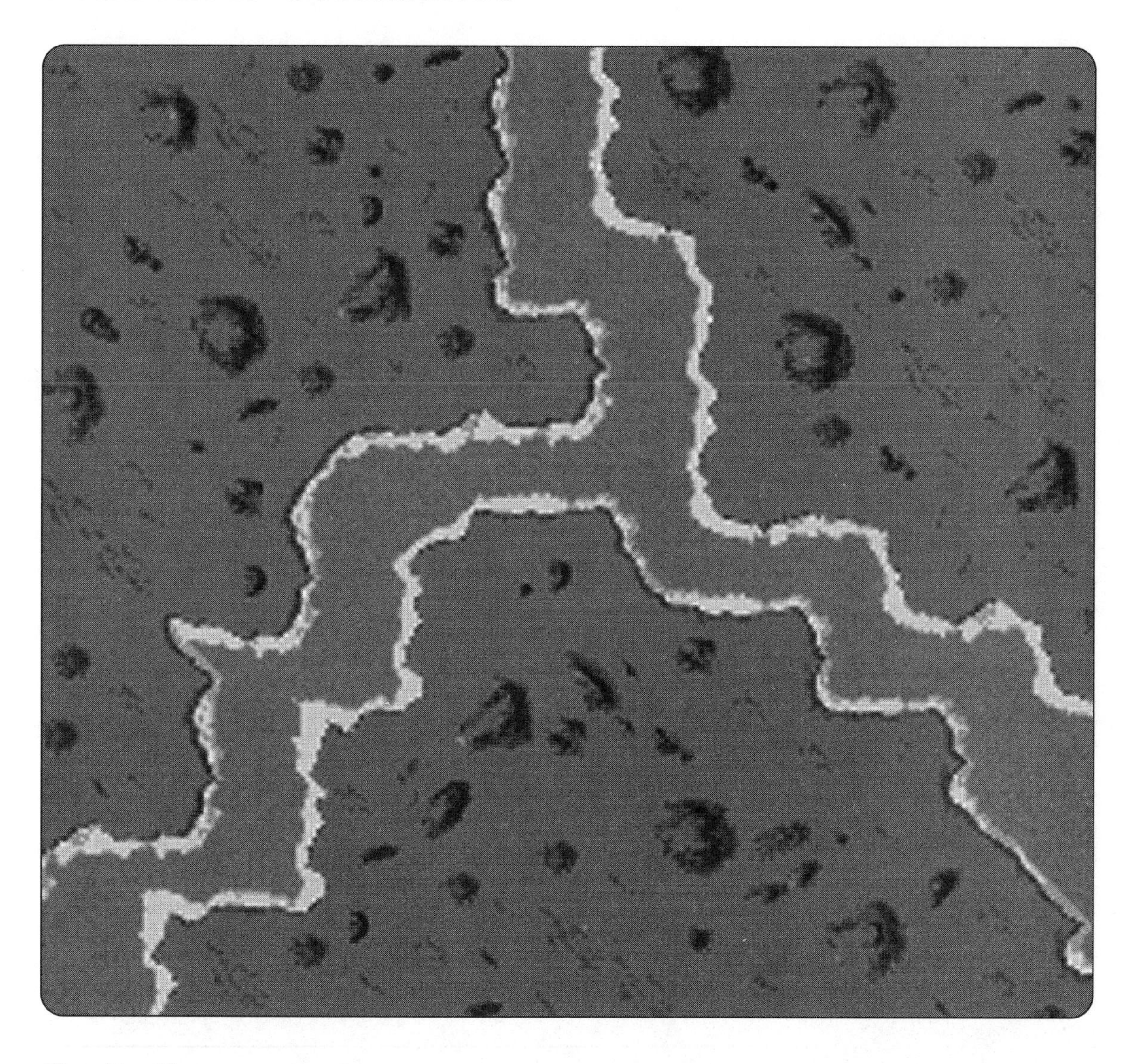

Size: 11 x 10

Number of Players: Up to 10

Description: Two rivers join in the middle of the map, dividing the map into three equal areas.

Don't worry about immediate tank rushes because of the water separating the players. In the land area where the three rivers come together, there is a fair amount of metal. Try to control that area.

Fox Holes

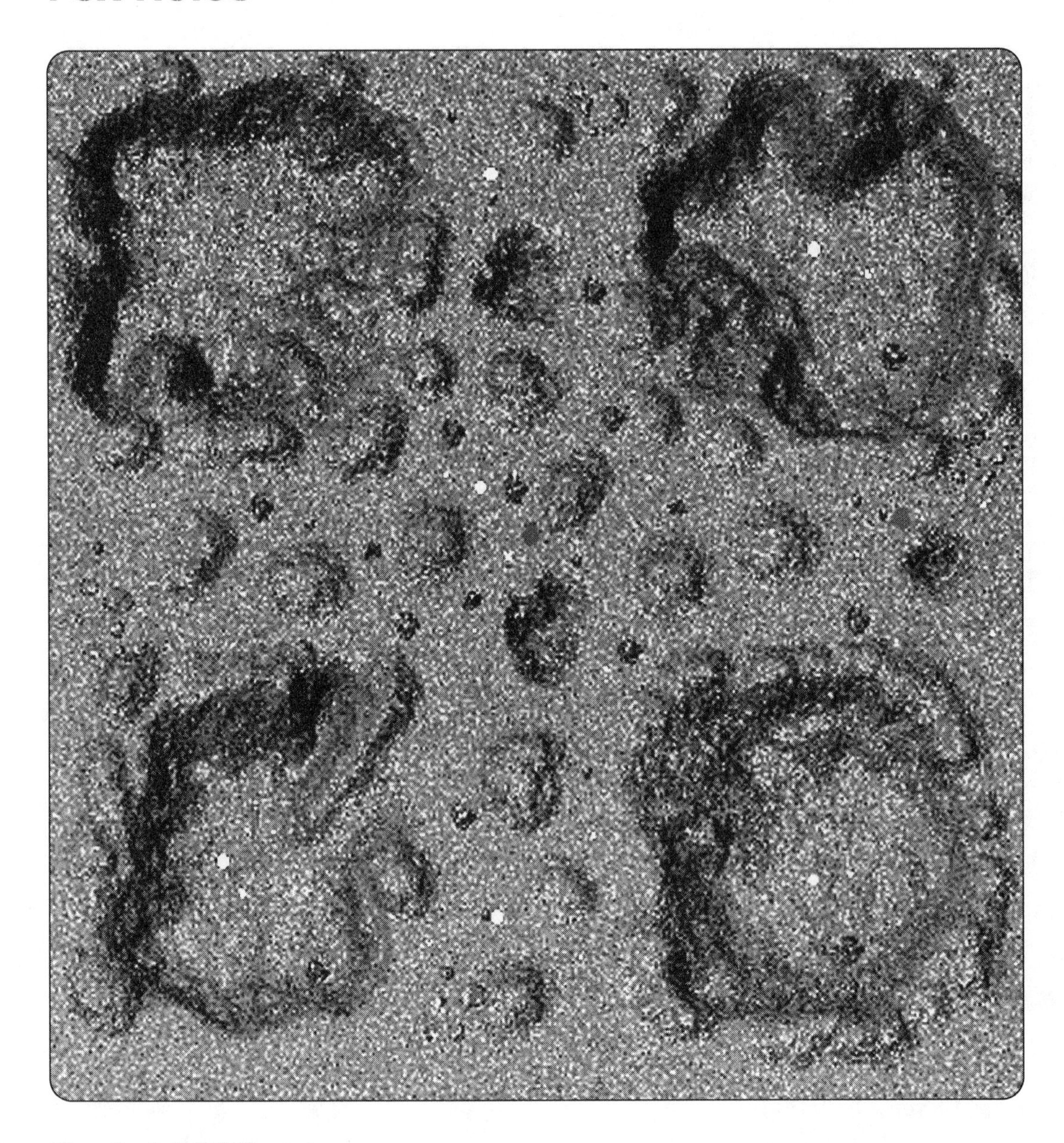

Size: 9 x 9 (a 32MB map)

Number of players: 2, 3, or 4

Description: There are four large craters on this lava world, with a ramp in the middle.

This map lends itself to short, violent battles. Head for the high ground, where the metal is more plentiful.

Full Moon

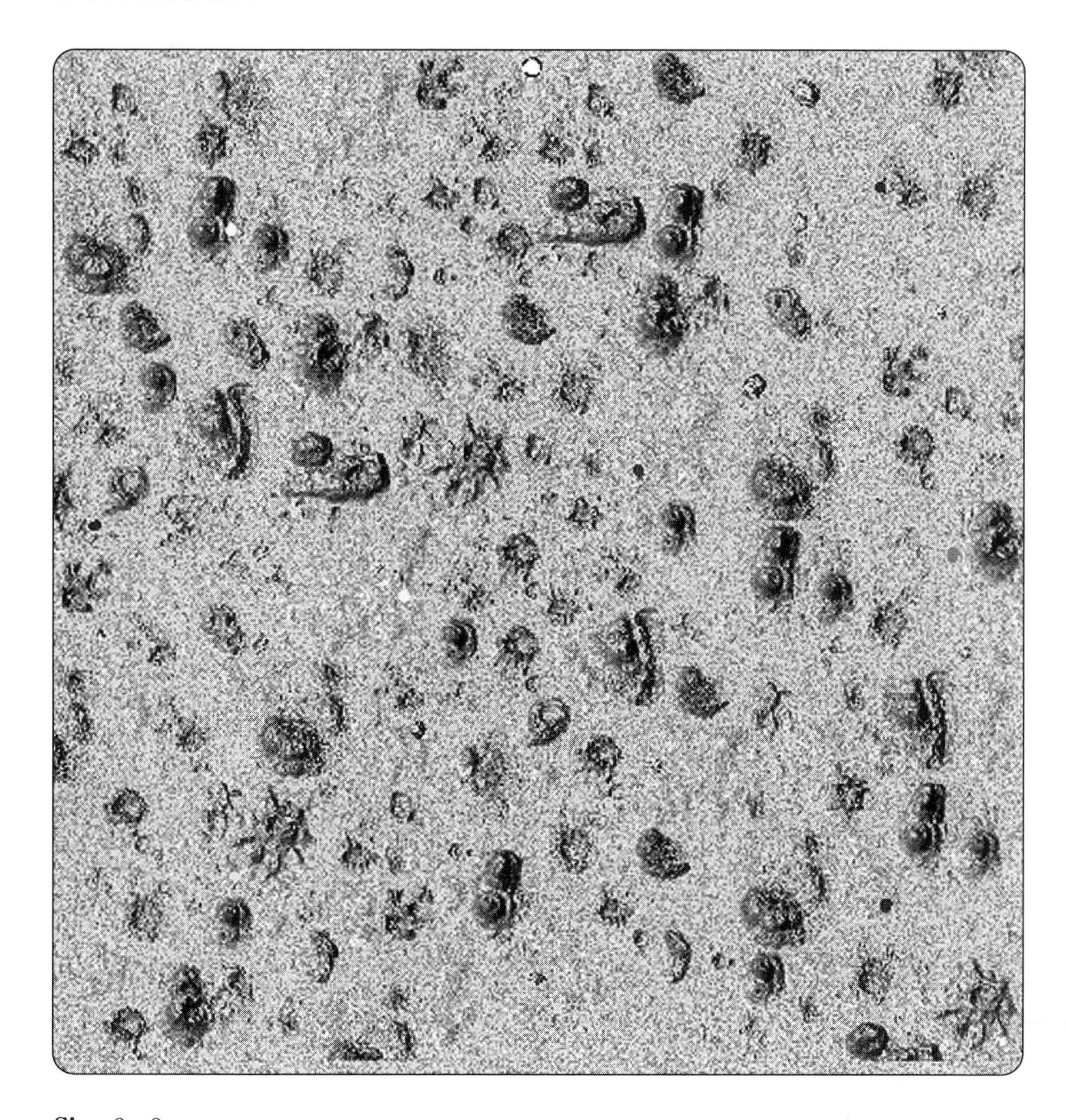

Size: 8 x 8

Number of players: 2, 4, or 8

Description: This lunar landscape is covered with many small hills.

Players should use the hills to block enemy fire, then jump out and fire back. One recommendation is to play this map without aircraft. It was built with that in mind.

Gods of War

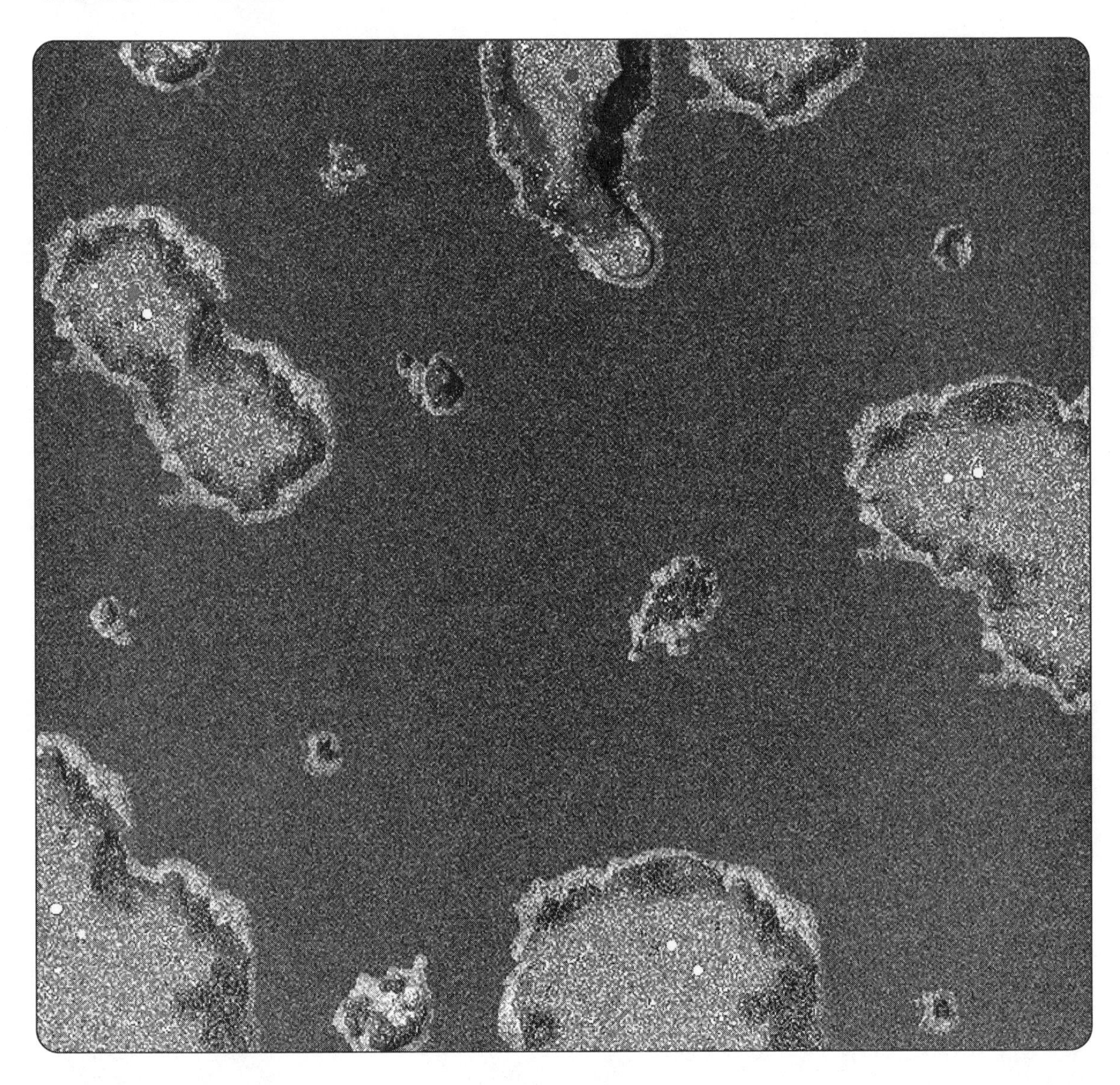

Size: 9 x 8

Number of players: 5

Description: This is an asymmetrical water map dotted with islands.

Build aircraft right away in addition to a Shipyard.

Great Divide

Size: 5 x 8

Number of players: 2

Description: A mountain range runs east to west, broken midway by a mountain pass.

One player starts in the north and one in the south. The mountain is tall enough to block even big guns from firing over it. The mountain is a bit closer to the south than the north. The northern approach has a gentler slope on which you can build. The southern approach is steeper, but affords places to hide from artillery.

Greenhaven

Size: 16 x 16

Number of players: 2, 4, or 8

Description: There are many small hills, with no dominating terrain features.

The hill located in the northwest corner of the map offers protection on two sides and is more easily defended than the other hills.

Hundred Isles

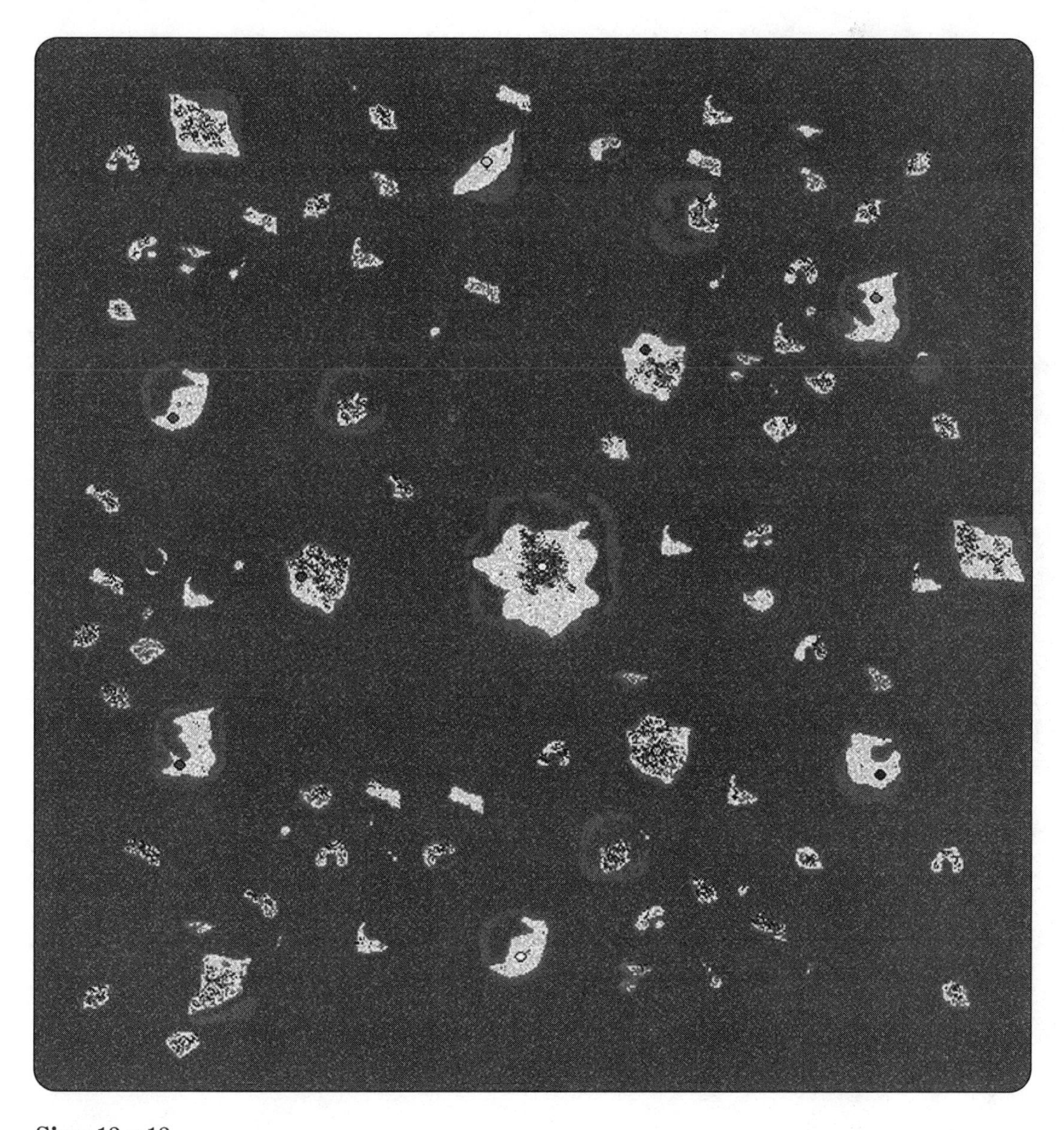

Size: 12 x 12

Number of players: 2, 3, or 6

Description: There are 106 islands, some of them very small.

A number of the islands have reefs with approaches so steep that amphibious tanks can't climb them. This can help establish lines of defense. Big ships are powerful on this map. The large island near the center has metal deposits.

Kill the Middle

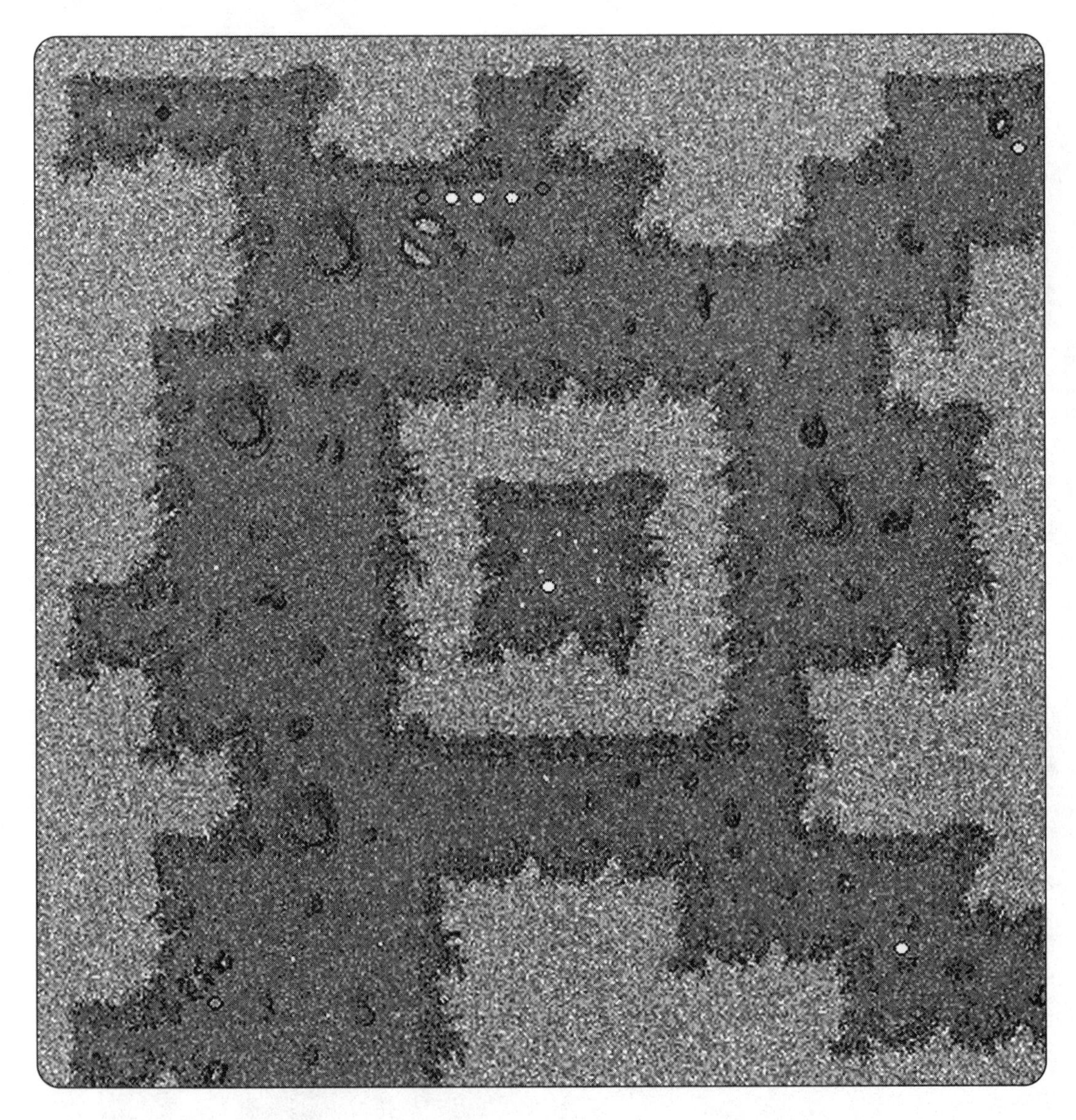

Size: 13 x 13

Number of players: 2 or 3

Description: This lava world features a center metal-rich island surrounded by other land masses that are connected to one another.

The three-player game is designed so that the two people who start at either corner of the map must gang up on the player who starts on the metal-rich center island. Because of the lava surrounding the island, the two outer players must build aircraft or long-range guns to reach the island.

King of the Hill

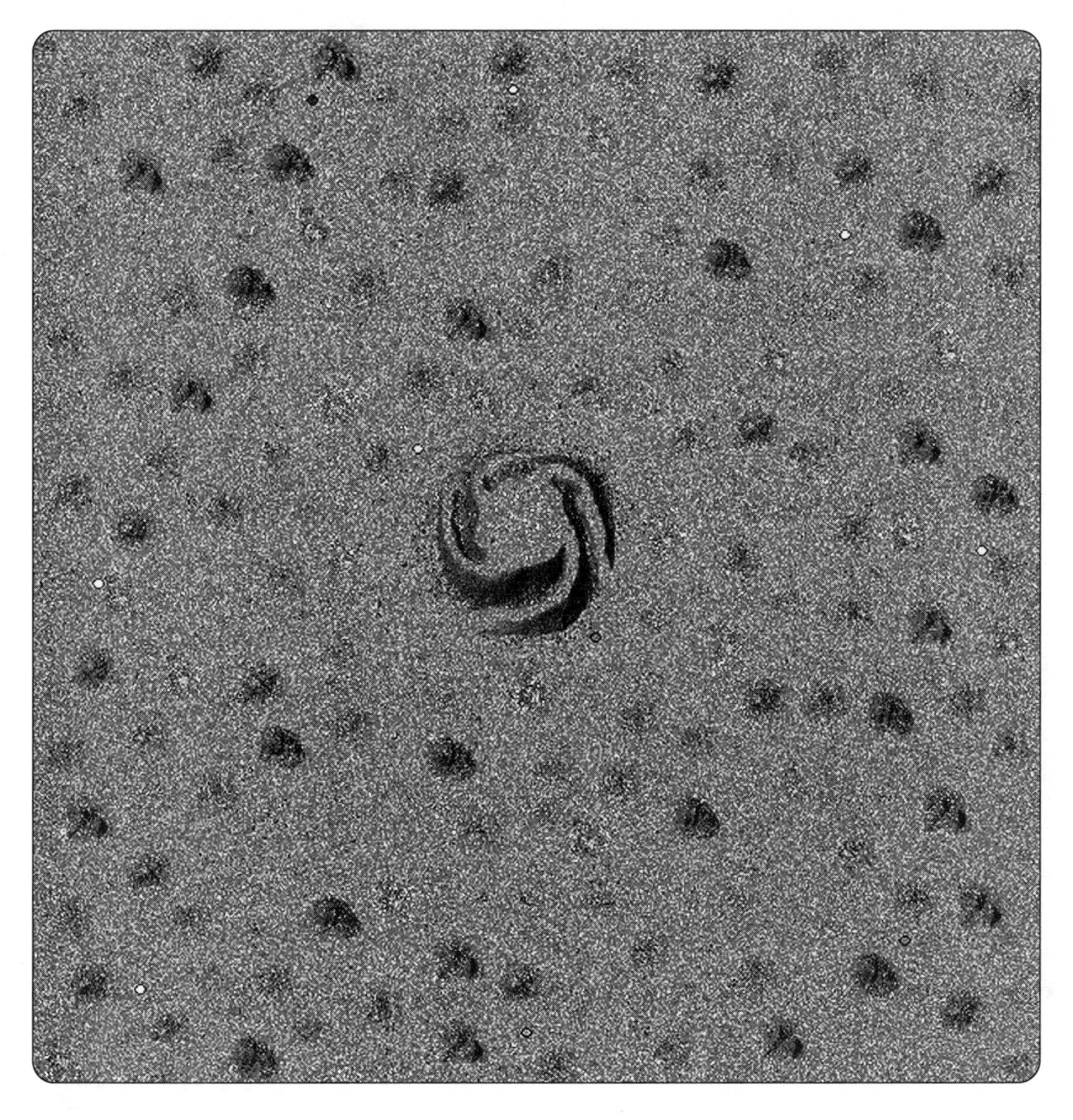

Size: 16 x 16

Number of players: 2, 3, or 4

Description: The map is dominated by a large hill with four spiral ramps. The closer to the center of the map you go, the more metal you will find.

TIP **The name says it all. This is a fight to see who can be king of the hill.**

Lava High Ground

Size: 8 x 8 (32MB map)

Number of players: 2, 3, or 4

Description: There are four flat areas in the corners and a central area that contains lots of metal. The map works best with 3 or 4 players.

Head for the high ground. You should climb to the central region to get ahead of your enemy. If possible, get there early and sow Dragon's Teeth to block your opponent's access.

Lava Run

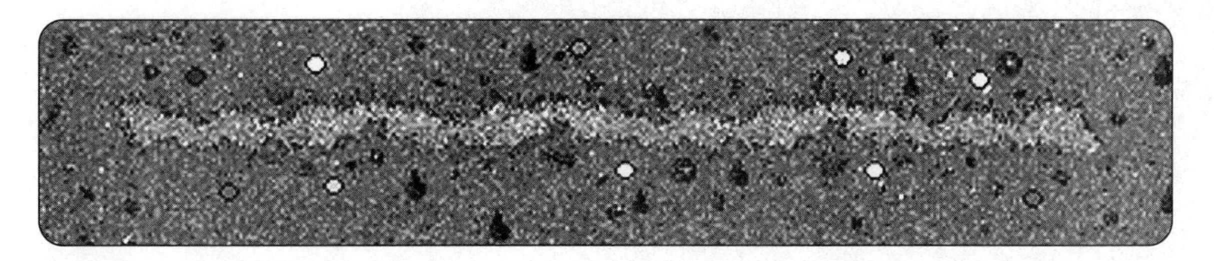

Size: 24 x 4

Number of players: 3, 4, 5, 6, 7, 10

Description: A narrow strip of lava runs almost the complete width of the map. Players are placed on either side. You cannot cross the lava, but you can fire across it.

You are smart if you ally with the person directly across the lava from your position, to avoid being weakened by constant battles while building.

Lava 2 Hills

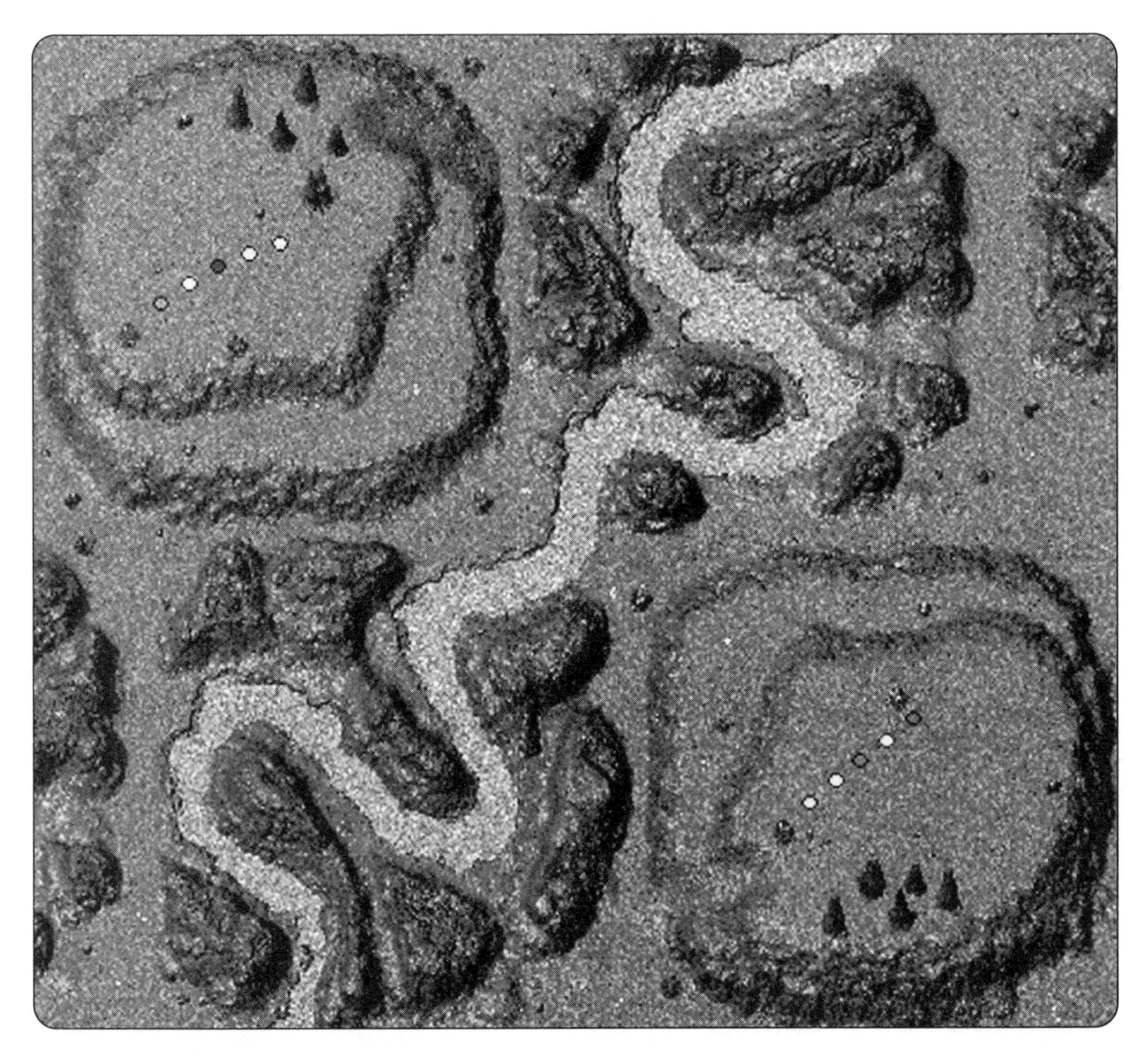

Size: 9 x 8 (32MB map)

Number of players: 2 (possible to have team play with even number of players)

Description: Two very large mesas dominate this map, with one in the northwest and one in the southeast. A meandering stream of lava cuts across the map from the northeast to the southwest.

Air power will be necessary to get across the lava. The mesas also offer good locations from which to position long-range artillery.

Lava Mania

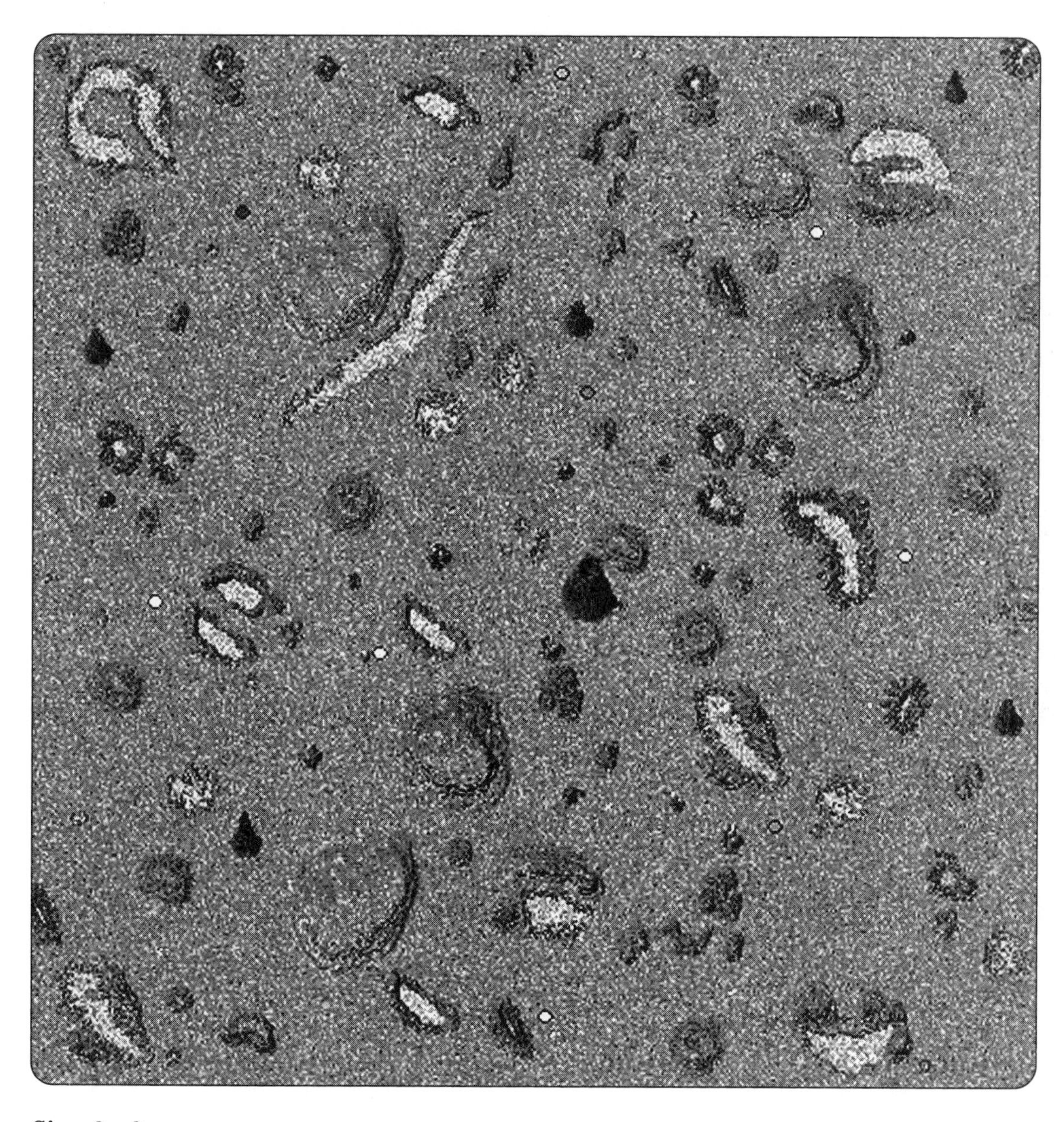

Size: 8 x 8

Number of players: 2, 4, or 8

Description: There are small puddles of lava all over the map. Players fight across the map, working their way around the lava pools.

There is an area in the northwest corner where a player can build a base behind a thin strip of lava and Dragon's Teeth to avoid a ground rush.

Metal Heck

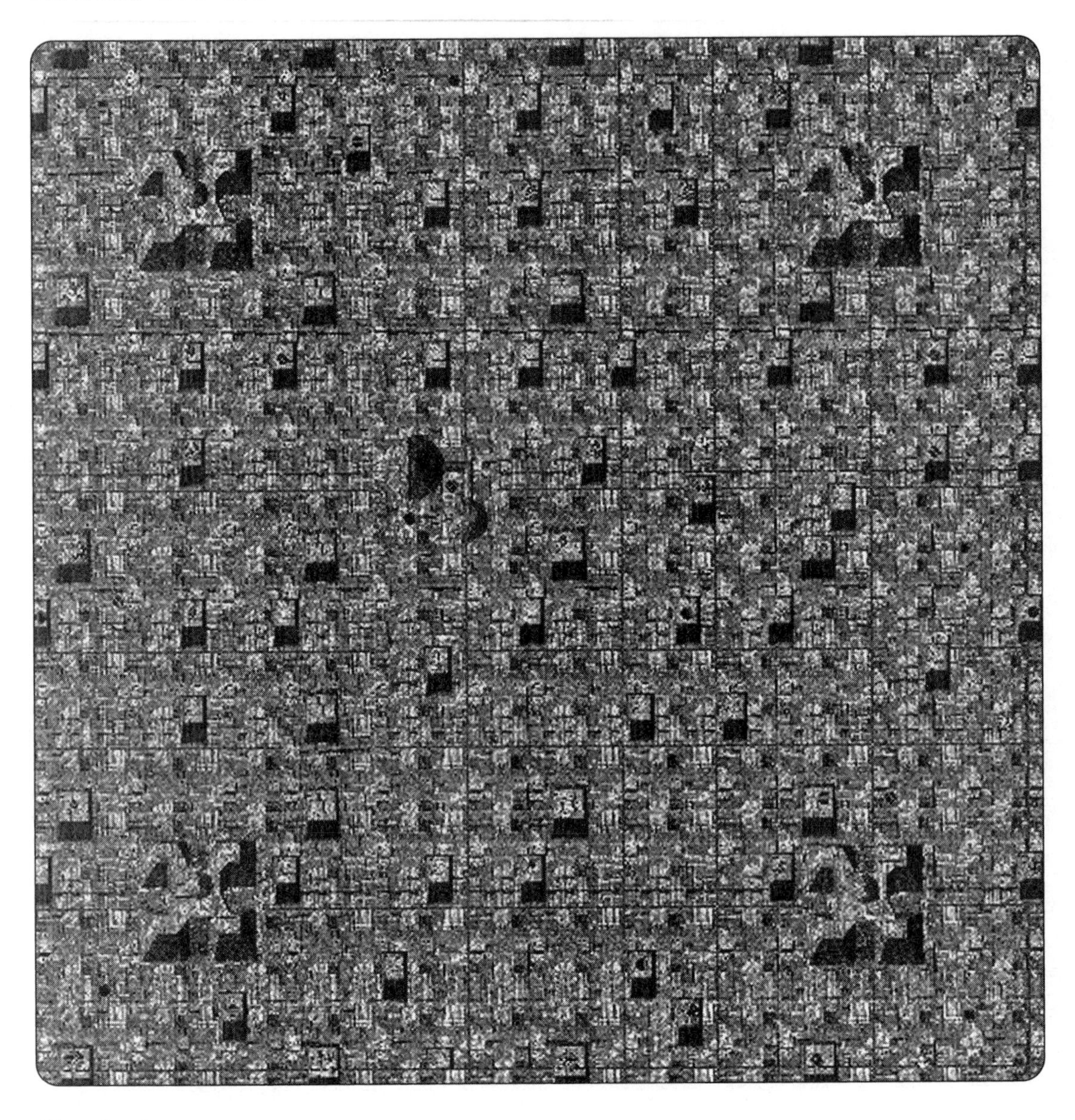

Size: 8 x 8

Number of players: 2, 3, 4, 5, 7, or 8 (with 3, 5, or 7 players there are different starting positions for better play balance.)

Description: This is a metal world. There's plenty of metal and a lot of steam vents.

Although the map is a relatively open one, there are enough raised levels to hide behind and partially protect bases from artillery.

Over Crude Water

Size: 18 x 18

Number of players: 2 or 4

Description: The map is on an oil-slick metal world, with many bridges and small islands, almost a maze.

Solidify your position by blocking off bridges around you .

Pincushion

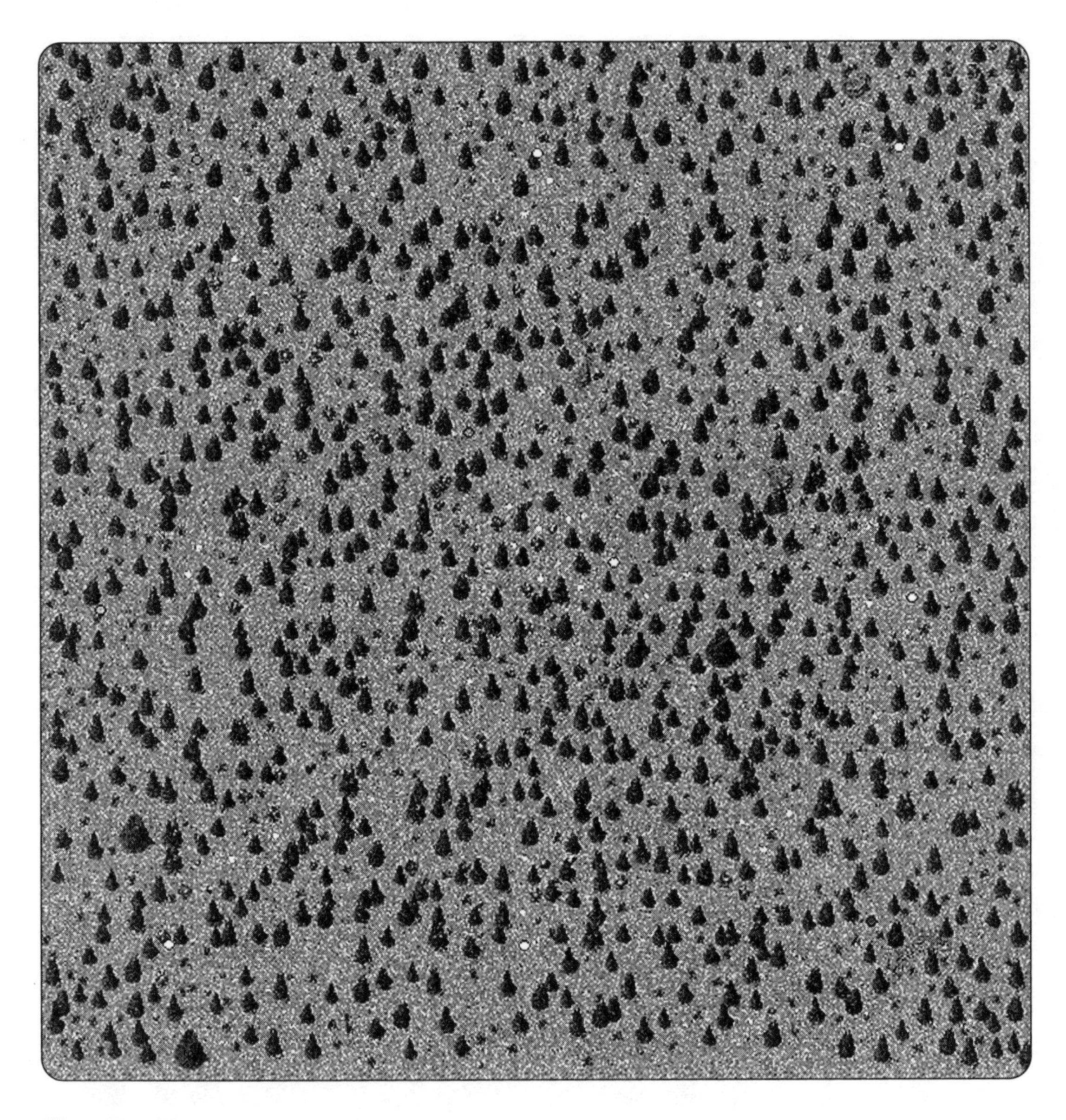

Size: 13 x 13

Number of players: 2, 4, or 8

Description: Tall spires that cause problems for long-range guns dominate this map. Their shells clip the spires, causing them to be less effective.

Short-range, heavy-damage weapons are best on this map. You can reclaim energy from the nodes. Build larger passageways for larger units by reclaiming the nodes in a systematic way across an area.

Red Hot Lava

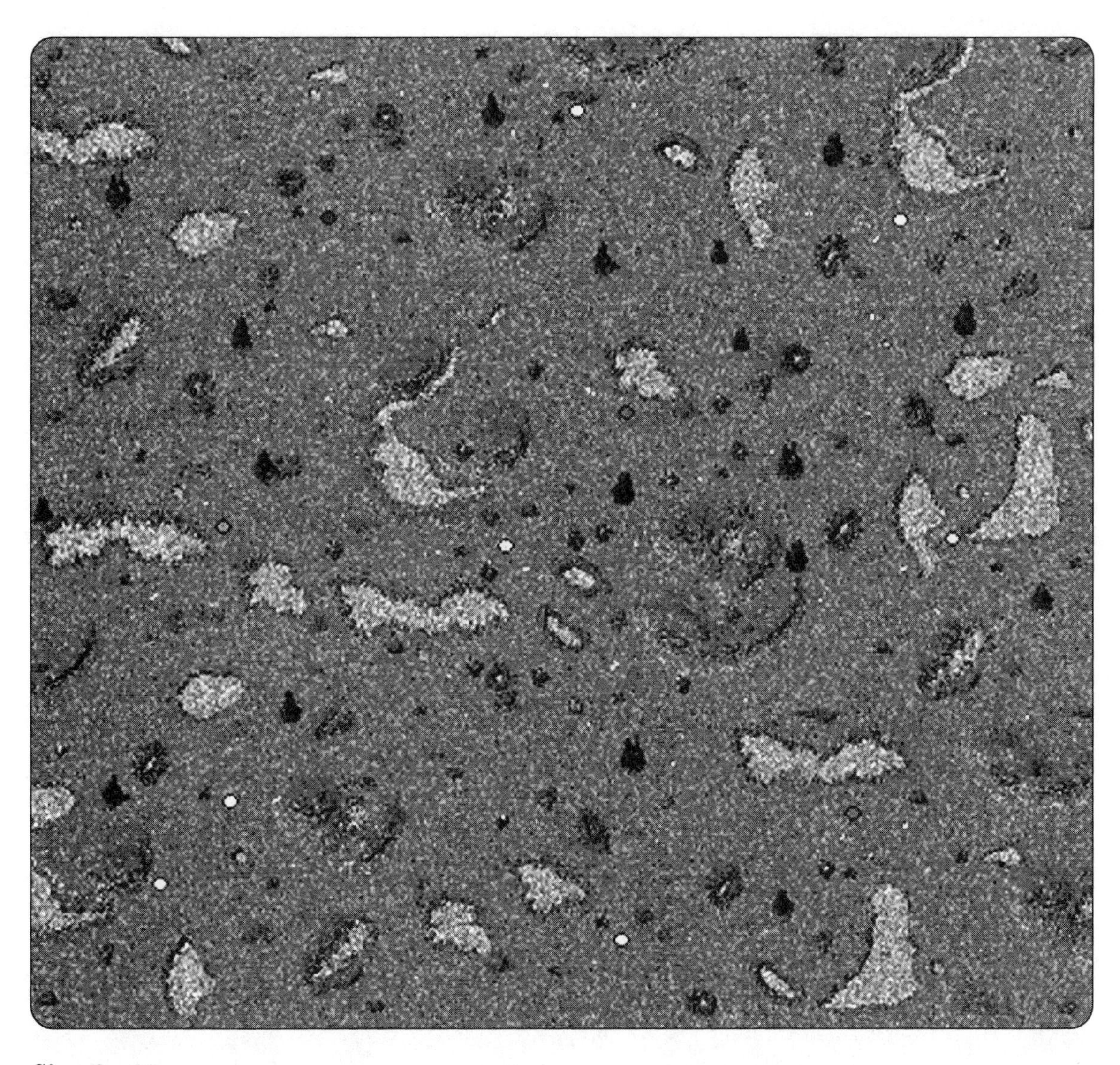

Size: 8 x 11

Number of players: 2, 4, or 8

Description: The map is covered with small puddles of lava and plenty of small hills.

From the west edge of the map, there is a stream of lava that runs toward the center. This makes it difficult for players in the northwest and southwest to get at one another.

Red Planet

Size: 9 x 9

Number of players: 2 or 4

Description: Small and medium hills dot the map. This tends to be a free-for-all.

Use some of the taller hills as partial barricades against enemy fire. But, there's not much cover.

Red Triangle

Size: 16 x 16

Number of players: 2, 3, or 6

Description: A large triangle of land occupies the center of the map. Three smaller islands are on the outside. Most of the map is water. The action starts in the middle, so there's intense fighting right away.

If you are getting stomped in the middle of the map, try moving out to one of the three islands and building your base there.

Ring Atoll

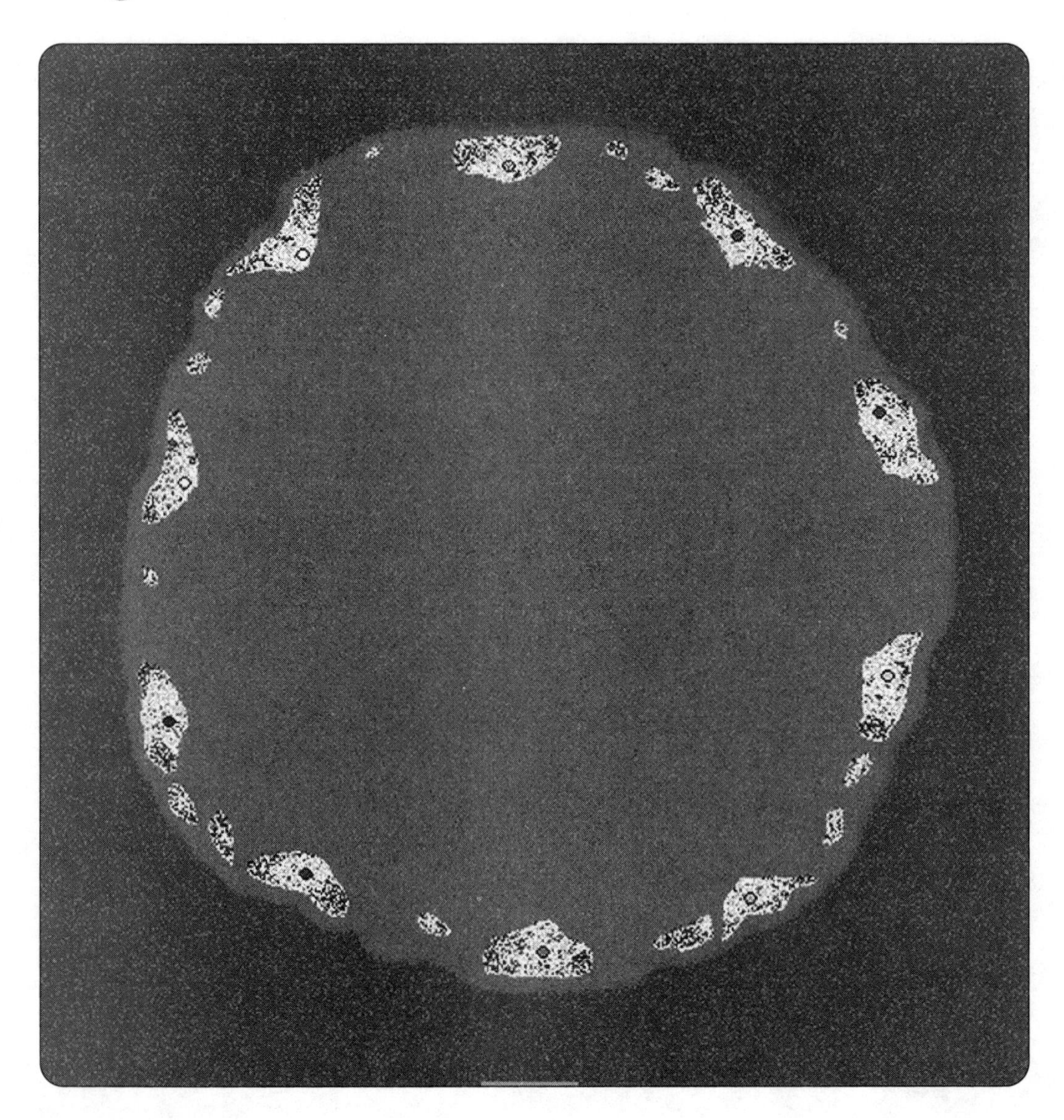

Size: 20 x 20

Number of players: 2, 5, or 10

Description: The map is composed of a large central sea of very shallow water that all ground units can move through. Most ships cannot be used in the water, except for small scout ships and destroyers in certain areas. Islands surround the water.

TIP **Because of the ring of islands, you build and fight others on nearby islands either in a clockwise or counterclockwise direction.**

Rock Alley

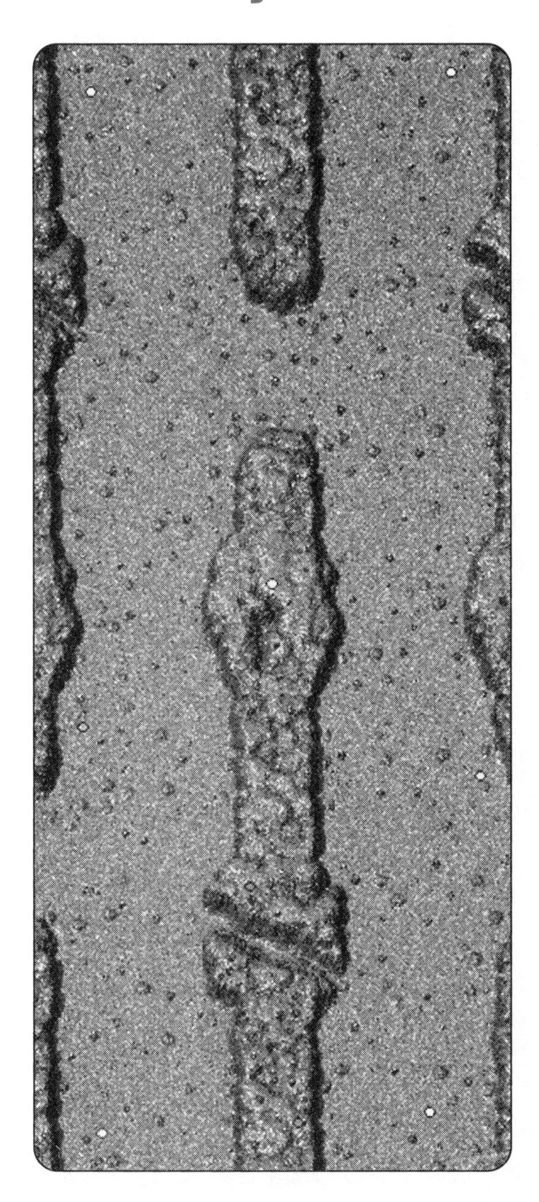

Size: 9 x 21

Number of players: 2

Description: Two valleys run north-south, with a huge mountain in between.

There is not much metal in the valleys. You will need to climb the mountain to find more at the top. This is a good map to play without aircraft so that the game becomes much more of a valley-floor ground war. (Agree to turn off the Aircraft Plant as an option.)

Seven Islands

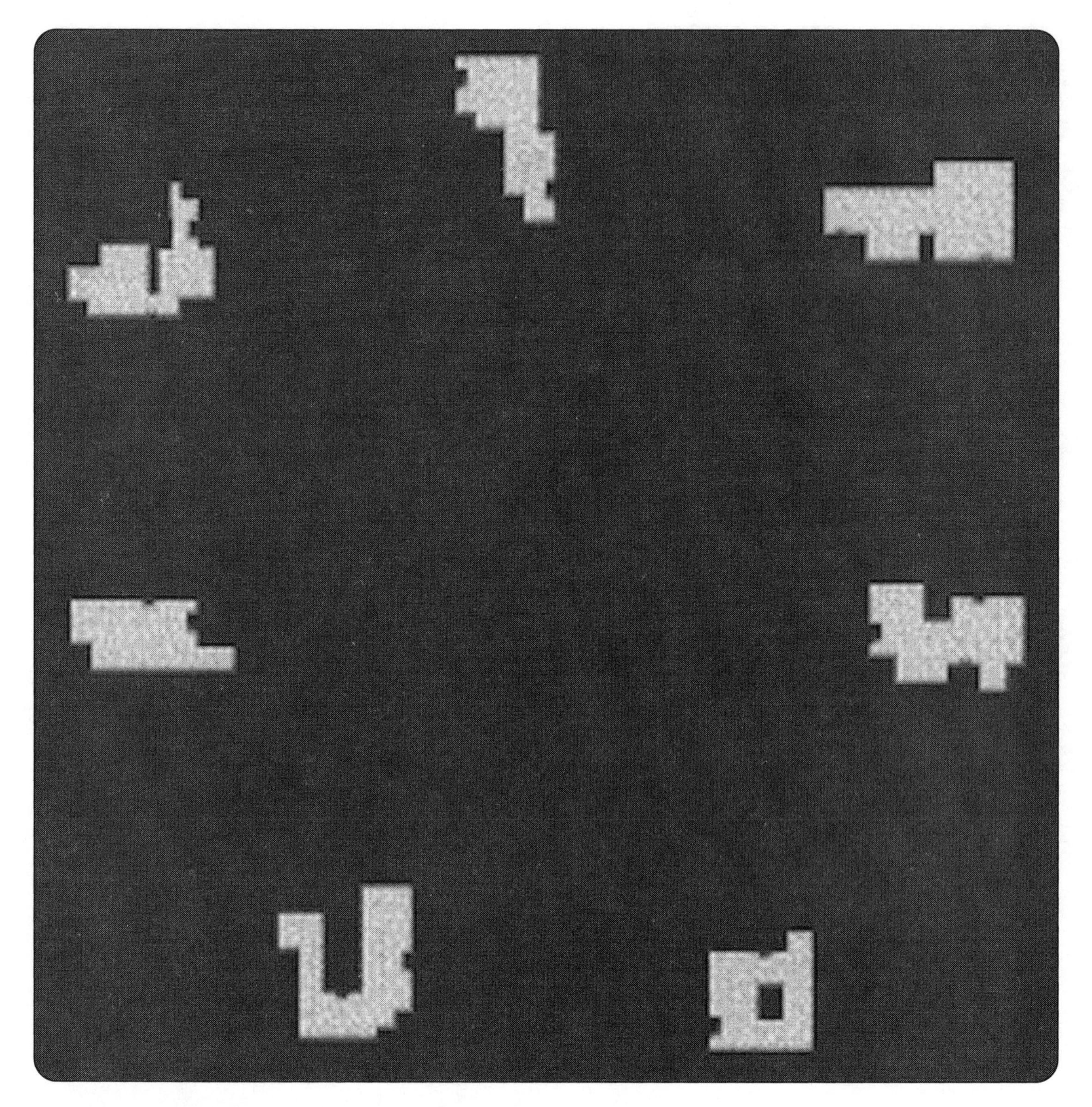

Size: 40 x 40 (a 32MB map)

Number of players: 2 or 7 (can also play with 3)

Description: Seven irregularly shaped islands are on this map, set on a metal world with large stretches of black ocean between them.

TIP **This is the ultimate naval battle map. It is easy to get metal and geothermal power. You are able to afford to build big ships and have huge naval battles.**

Sherrwood

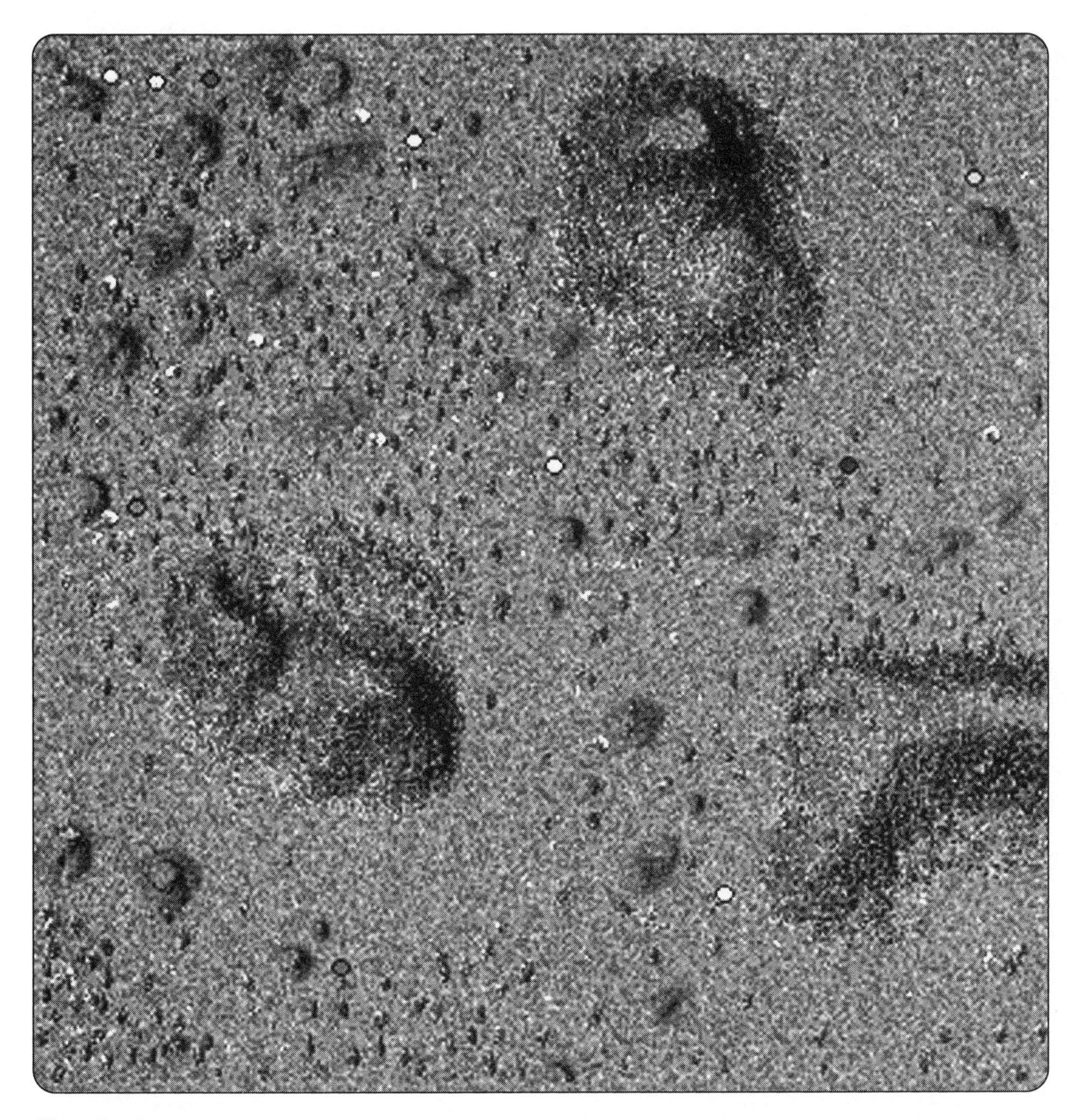

Size: 6 x 6

Number of players: 2 or 3

Description: This is a small map with three large hills that dominate your strategy.

Because of the hills, you are relatively immune from being shelled. A good tactic is to protect your most important units and structures behind the hill. You cannot get everything behind it, so choose those factories and units that are the most expensive.

Shore to Shore

Size: 29 x 5 (a 32MB map)

Number of players: 2 (can also have good team play)

Description: This map features two opposing coastlines separated by a large ocean.

This map is so big that even Big Bertha and Annihilator guns cannot reach one another. However, try building a Bertha or an Annihilator on one of the islands closer to your enemy to shell the opposite coastline.

Two Continents

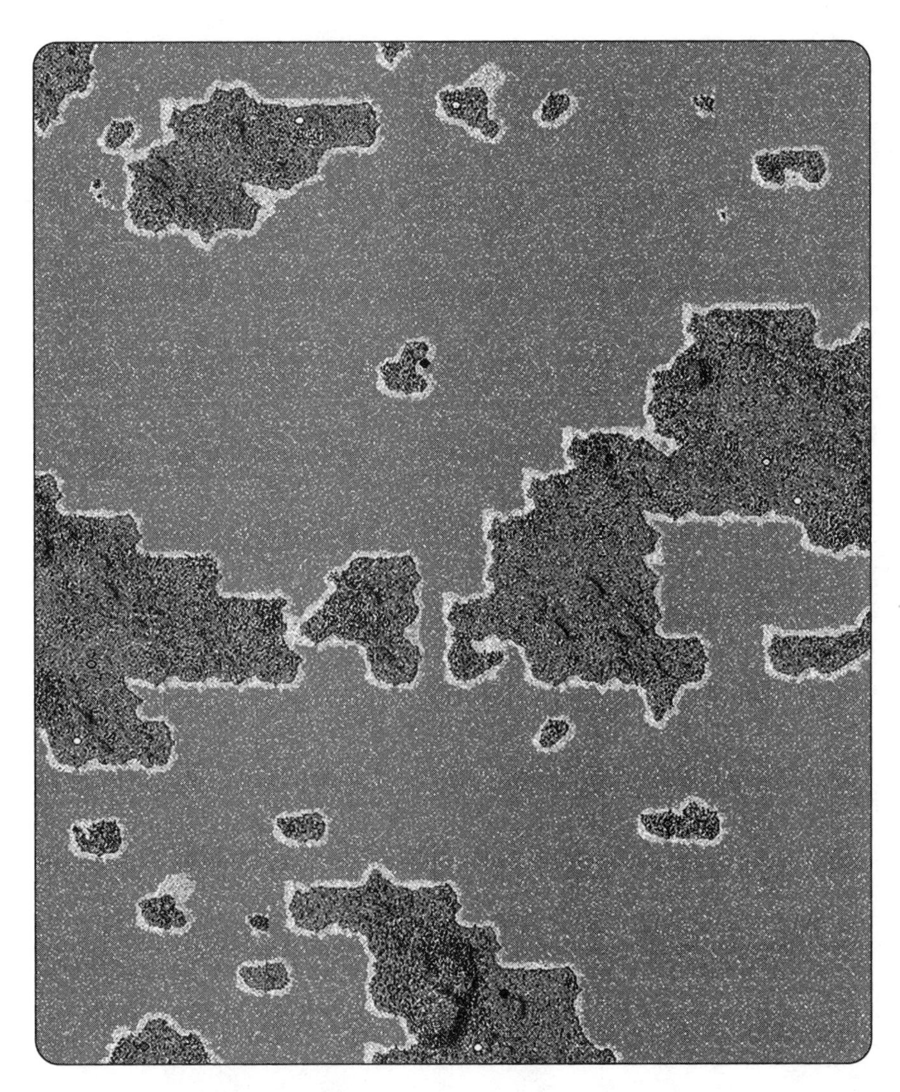

Size: 22 x 25 (a 32MB map)

Number of players: 2 or 4

Description: There are two continents, east and west, and two smaller islands, north and south. A narrow strait in the center of the map allows ships in the North and South oceans to reach each other. Players who are on the two north and south islands have more metal deposits near them because they can't get to the metal in the middle.

The players on the East and West continents must move to the center of the map to find meal. The player on the northern island should place Torpedo Launchers in the water to keep enemy subs from reaching the waters North of the island. The southern island features a mountain that can act as a barrier to enemy shells.

Yerrot Mountains

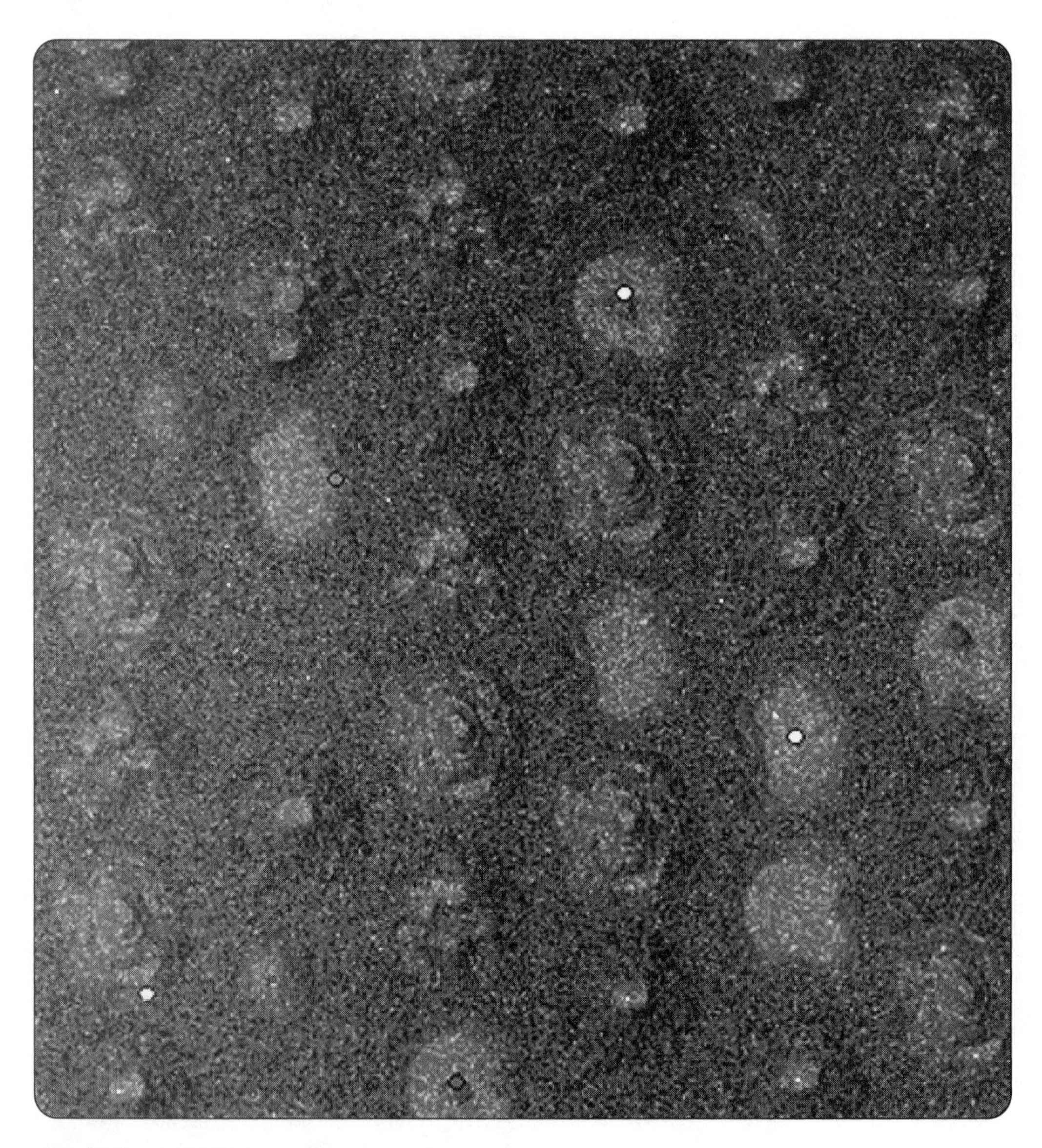

Size: 27 x 23 (32MB map)

Number of players: 2, 3, 4, or 6

Description: This map has the most mountainous terrain of any *Total Annihilation* map. There are flat valley floors for bases, and that's where you begin. The map is so large that even Guardian long-range cannons can't reach from one valley to the next.

TIP There's a good amount of metal on the valley floor. Much of the rough, flat ground around you is unsuitable for large buildings.

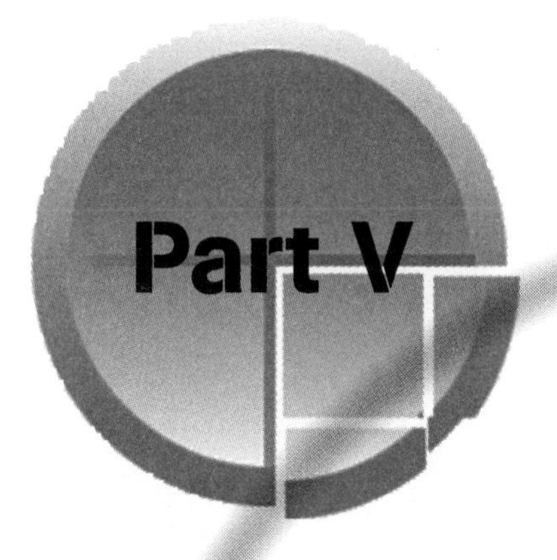

Inside Total Annihilation

One of the things we've done is to say, "We don't like a resource-management system in which you have to constantly micromanage all these little units that get in the way of war strategy." The player can now assume that materials are going where they need to go, that metal and energy get to the factory. Let's focus on where we want to put our tanks, where we want our artillery. Otherwise, it gets to be like a SimCity-type game, not a war-strategy game.

—Chris Taylor

+DITHER

(Changes the gray line-of-sight stuff to a dither)

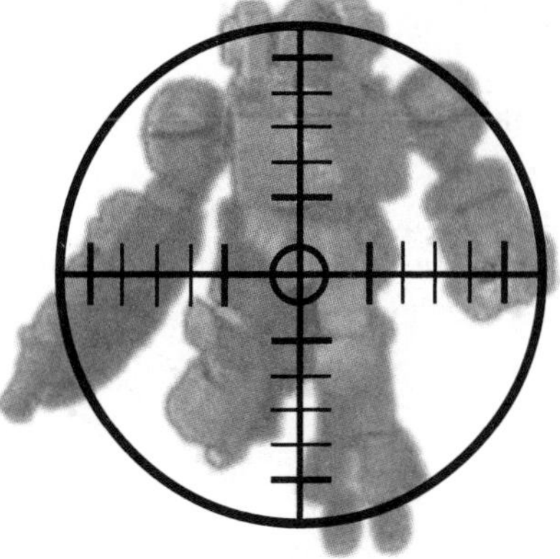

Cavedog's Best Ten Strategies

Who better to ask for hints and tips about *Total Annihilation* than the game designers, programmers, and artists who have been living and breathing it for the past two years? For your use, here are some favorite hints, tips, and preferences from ten of the most experienced *Total Annihilation* players in the world—at least for now.

Brian W. Brown

Programmer

Offensive or defensive player: Balanced, but leans toward strong defenses.

Favorite strategy: "The first vehicle I build is a Jeffy, a couple of them. I send them out in wider and wider patrol scans. As soon as they've discovered some things, such as metal deposits, I walk the Commander or a Construction Vehicle over and start building. For attack strategy, I tend to take out stationary emplacements first—Laser Towers and Guardians—because they do the most damage."

Best advice for TA newcomers: "Build lots of information-gathering units and structures, such as Radar Towers; Advanced Radar Towers, especially. I build them redundantly, all over the place, so I know when the enemy is coming. Go crazy with Radar Towers; they're cheap."

Favorite unit: "Stumpys. They're good all-purpose units."

Clay Corbisier

Art Designer for Arm Units

Offensive or defensive player: "Defensive. Although it doesn't always get me real far!"

Favorite strategy: "First, I'll get a Vehicle Plant going and then a Construction Vehicle built. I'll send my Construction Vehicle way up to the other end of the map and have it build another base up there. Eventually, I'll send an attacking force in toward the enemy from two sides."

Best advice for TA newcomers: "I like to get a couple of Construction Vehicles out there building Laser Towers around my base. Then I have a couple of other Construction Vehicles building Dragon's Teeth blockades between them and the enemy. Not only can't the enemy get through, they're getting nailed while they're trying to do it."

Favorite unit: "Advanced Laser Towers. They're really powerful, and you can set them up on hills and in valleys, then get a crossfire going and just mow the enemy down when they try to get to you."

Nathan Doster

Lead Mission Designer

Offensive or defensive player: Balanced, but leans toward defensive.

Favorite strategy: "I like to be creative with units. There's a lot that can be done with Arm's Zipper, for example. [These units] move very quickly. They can move into somebody's base, take out a critical unit, and be out of there before the guy can react. Keep them moving—don't let them stop!"

Best advice for TA newcomers: "On missions, players should realize that we have an incredible number of variables, all acting and interacting. At any given time, what is happening and what the player does will affect what the AI does and the response of the units that I've placed. This is not as simple a game as many people are used to playing."

Favorite unit: "The Brawler is one of my favorites. It's a gunship that hovers and can be just deadly. And it's neat to watch. Also, the Spider tank is underrated. It can go up virtually anything. The only thing it can do is paralyze. But let's say you have a very powerful enemy unit that's doing a great deal of damage. If you can get a spider tank within range of him, he's paralyzed. And now you have time to do something about it. Even to the extent that your Commander go in and capture it."

Clayton Kauzlaric

Lead Artist

Offensive or defensive player: "Defensive. I like to build up a really hefty base."

Favorite strategy: "I like to climb up the technology tree as fast as possible, getting a Fusion Reactor, getting a Moho Mine, getting a huge income and tons of storage."

Best advice for TA newcomers: "Take care of your income. It's really tempting to start clicking buttons and building stuff. Before you know it, there's a zero for energy or metal. Once you're out of metal or energy, you're seriously hurting."

Favorite unit: "Tanks and planes. Scouting is my first big thing!"

Bartosz Kijanka

Artificial Intelligence Support Programmer

Offensive or defensive player: "I tend to be defensive, but I really don't know exactly what I'm going to do until I perceive my opponent's personality. Is he going to take an offensive or defensive approach?"

Favorite strategy: "If I'm left alone for a significant amount of time, I'll tend to focus on my economy and build up my resources more than I'll worry about a military buildup. That's to build up quicker, and then later on have more resources to throw at my opponent."

Best advice for TA newcomers: "Always make sure you have multiple Construction units, because if you lose those early on, then the game's as good as over. Put one or two away from the front lines so you have a backup economy if you get heavily assaulted."

Favorite unit: Aircraft Construction units. "When you get the Aircraft Construction unit you can send it halfway across the map. Then you can issue a bunch of commands to it."

Jake McMahon

Assistant Producer

Offensive or defensive player: Offensive. "I love harassing people!"

Favorite strategy: "My strategy is to keep people uncomfortable at all times, and to keep the battle at the enemy's base, not mine. That way, they're always reacting to me. My own base is undefended. For instance, I like to put a crawling bomb on an air transport, then send it on its way. Track it with the T key, and when it gets close to the target, hit Ctrl-D, and then count down 5-4-3-2-1—it takes out a huge area, about three-quarters of a screen."

Best advice for TA newcomers: "You really need to be aggressive. Try to capture as much of the map as possible. It's just open territory, so if you can hold it with one unit, then you've got that territory, and that's a huge benefit."

Favorite unit: "One of my favorites is the Can. Anything near a Can dies. If an enemy patrol comes across a group of Cans, all of their units die. They're slow and they waddle, but they put anything down that comes near."

Jeff Petkau

Artificial Intelligence Designer

Offensive or defensive player: "I'm pretty aggressive. If somebody walks his Commander near me, I'll take him out no matter what the personal cost to me!"

Favorite strategy: "Build everywhere. Spread your base over the whole world!"

Best advice for TA newcomers: "For the missions, they're not very difficult if you're cautious all the way through. But they really encourage you *not* to be. Invaders will come in, and your Commander is sitting there and he'll wipe them out in two seconds. He'll take a few steps more and wipe out another army by himself. And the missions encourage you to walk him another two steps farther out. All of a sudden, he's dead! Be cautious."

Favorite unit: "I'd have to say Construction Aircraft."

Kevin Pun

3D Animator

Offensive or defensive player: "A little bit of both. I like to send stuff out to the enemy, to try to attack as soon as possible. But I do keep my defenses up."

Favorite strategy: "At the beginning of a game, I start building PeeWees right away, and send them off so that the other guys won't have a chance to defend themselves. I send them out to find the enemy and bug the enemy. It's a guerilla war-type tactic."

Best advice for TA newcomers: "Build a Fusion Reactor as soon as possible. Develop resources quickly. Also, go after Moho Mines for a steady stream of metal."

Favorite unit: "Since I built the Kbots, I've been using them a lot. I use tanks, but I think the Kbots are fresh and cheap. You can build a hundred of them fairly quickly."

Richard Smith

Assistant Game Designer

Offensive or defensive player: Balanced, but leans toward offensive.

Favorite strategy: "Depends on the map. If I'm on a very small map, I forget everything else and build up my army quickly because I know I'm going to need them. But on larger maps I like to force an artillery duel with the enemy."

Best advice for TA newcomers: "At the center of your base, have a Construction Kbot patrol back and forth in an area. Send any of your damaged units back to the Construction bot, and any wounded unit that comes near it will be healed."

Favorite unit: "I love radar jammers. I build twenty of them and will cluster them about so that if I lose one or two I'm still hidden. If you destroy an enemy's radar jammer, then all of a sudden a big blank area of the map turns bright red on the radar display—and you know where you can start launching things."

Chris Taylor

Game Designer

Offensive or defensive player: "I would say defensive, but it depends on who I'm playing. It's fun to build a massive base and say, 'Come and get me, if you want! I'm ready for ya!'"

Favorite strategy: "I like to build nukes. If an enemy doesn't invade my base early, I can nuke them off the map. For example, I had a canyon situation in which I wanted to take a convoy through, but there were trees and metal from destroyed bots. So, I nuked the area to flatten everything. The last thing I saw before I sent the nuke in were metal, trees, and an enemy Spider Kbot moving through. When I looked again after the nuke, it was like a Sears parking lot."

Best advice for TA newcomers: "When you put Light Carriers out, aircraft can use them as automatic repair facilities. The aircraft will automatically return to the Carrier when they've taken enough damage."

Favorite unit: "Depending on who I'm playing, my favorite changes. But, if forced to pick one, it would have to be the Zeus. It has a lot of personality and has huge firepower."

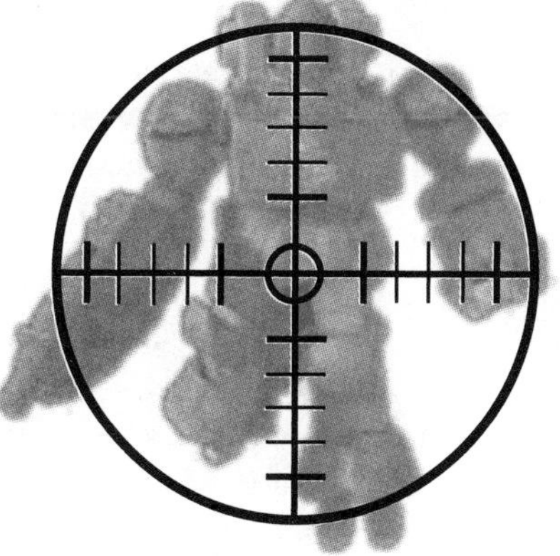

Behind the Scenes with Ron Gilbert and Chris Taylor

Ever wondered what goes through the minds of game developers as they scheme to bring you the next big thing in computer entertainment? Here's your chance to find out more about what TA producer Ron Gilbert and TA designer Chris Taylor think about their game, the creative process of game design, the computer game industry, and the future of computer gaming.

It was just about two years ago, in the fall of 1995, when Ron Gilbert and Chris Taylor first began discussing the ideas that would become *Total Annihilation*. At that time, Taylor had been a successful developer of sports games for Electronic Arts; Gilbert, who had developed such computer game classics as *The Secret of Monkey Island*, had been building Humongous Entertainment, a very successful publisher of children's entertainment software, with partner Shelley Day. In their modest Woodinville, Washington, headquarters not far from Seattle, Gilbert and Taylor built the Cavedog team that completed *Total Annihilation* in August 1997—on schedule! This interview took place during the frantic hours shortly before the game's release.

Bateman: *Now that you've put two years of work into* Total Annihilation, *what's your feeling about it and what do you like best?*

Taylor: I'm really happy with it. It's exceeded my expectations and I'm thrilled with the results. I do believe we've achieved a dream goal. There are so many little details and interrelationships that I love. For example, just today we added a new feature: A construction vehicle can guard any other construction vehicle, and when you order the first construction vehicle to build something, the other one automatically helps.

Gilbert: What I like best is that *Total Annihilation* really plays very differently than the other strategy games. We didn't just take a *Warcraft* or a *Command & Conquer* and come up with a bunch of new units, which seems to be what a lot of other people are doing. We added a lot of very fundamental game play dynamics that are different from what other people are doing. You know, you get into a big multiplayer game of TA and it plays a lot differently than *Command & Conquer* does, and I really like that.

Bateman: *Let's talk about the multiplayer option. I know that you want multiplayer* Total Annihilation *to offer something different from other multiplayer games.*

Taylor: Yes, we have state-of-the-art Internet technology and some of the smartest guys in the business working on our stuff. For example, when we were looking at allied play, we said "Why should we only let players give units to their allies? Why should we restrict a person like that?" Instead, we made it so that allies can give anything they want to anybody they want. We just give the player that choice. You hit the Tab key, and there's a Share button to let you give mapping information, energy and metal, or units—three areas.

Gilbert: Most of that kind of choice came from Chris and me sitting down and saying, "What about this feature?" And then we'd argue about it for an hour, and then realize, "Why are we arguing about this? Let's put them both in." So, anything we came up with we would just stick in there and let people turn it on and turn it off. Why should we decide if you can give resources or not. We'll just allow it. Why should we decide if you want a right-click interface or a left-click interface? Let's just give players both. So, what we tried to do is anything we thought was a good idea, rather than picking the way it should be, we just left it up to the player.

Bateman: *Some of the multiplayer maps require 32 MB of memory to play, and I know you want even bigger maps.*

Taylor: Yeah, I'd love to see people get into some worlds that are so huge they have gigantic weekend-long tournaments, attracting lots of press while these guys are slugging it out. There's a Watch Mode that allows a fourth "person" to observe three-player games. For example, through a mechanism we have for the Internet, a producer could produce a show of the game, moving a camera around; and somebody would be broadcasting that over the Internet, with people watching. One person, the producer, would be deciding where the camera would point to. I'll see if we can push it to five—four people playing and one watching. The Internet is exciting like that because it can give a much bigger audience to tournament-style play.

Gilbert: That's one of the reasons I'm excited about our multiplayer stuff and being able to ally with others. I'm definitely a defensive TA player. I tend to spend a lot of time building up my base, and building up my defenses, which is probably why I lose a whole lot. I tend to become very, very entrenched. It takes a while for people to get rid of me. But I'm not the kind that just goes and conquers land. It's really neat to be able to set up two people where one guy sits there and builds the base and will be the defense and the other guy can go out and conquer territory—and to be able to very quickly toss resources and units back and forth between the two people and act like a single army. In other games, like *Red Alert*, when you're allied with somebody it's really like you're two separate armies but you're just not fighting. And the way we thought about allies in TA is it should really be one army with two different players.

Bateman: *As people play TA, they're finding new, creative ways of using some of the units that help the game play evolve. How is that happening?*

Taylor: Crawling bombs are a good example. They're units you can build that go across the world, over the highest mountains and over the bottom of the ocean floor. They crawl at a really slow rate, and they crawl right into your base and blow up. Well, if you've got five cents worth of defense, you can blow it up. The bomb will take out an area, but it'll blow up outside the range of, say, the laser tower, which we designed so you can build a fundamental defense to protect against this very devastating unit.

What people were doing was sending these bombs in to other players' bases until they learned to build defenses for them. In response, players took air transports and began picking up the crawling bombs and flying them in as suicide bombs. Air transports are expensive. But that technique is a very effective weapon. However, if you build an air defense perimeter that is outside of your base at least a half-screen, that thing won't get anywhere near your base before it's taken out. People are going to move through these same changes as they play. Every time you get a new group of players, they go through this kind of evolution. For example, you can pick up a tank and set it on an aircraft carrier. Maybe your transport ship went down and you want to stack a couple of these tanks and have them offshore to move in. People will *discover* that. "Can I set that down on the deck of a ship?" Yeah, you can!

Bateman: *Ron, when you started Cavedog, what was your goal for the company?*

Gilbert: I wanted a company or a division in which we could do the non-children's games. My vision for the whole thing was that I wanted to create the type of environment that really good designers and programmers and artists could come to and build the vision that they had for games without a lot of bureaucratic stuff going on. I've worked at other companies, as has Chris, where you get a lot of—for lack of a better word—*suits* running around. You know, they've done a marketing survey and decided that green aliens are hot this month, so you've got to do green alien games. I wanted to create an environment that was run by people who love games. Shelley and I do; we're big gamers.

Bateman: *How did the Cavedog name come about?*

Gilbert: Chris and I were trying to come up with a name, and nothing was really sticking. One day, it was either Chris or Clayton who came in and said, "How about Frozen Yak Entertainment?" And we said, "Wow! We really like that! Let's live with that for awhile." So we lived with that for a couple of weeks, and we all liked it. And then Chris came in and said "How about Cavedog Entertainment?" And we really liked that, too. But half the people liked Cavedog and half the people liked Frozen Yak, and we went around and around and around. Finally we had to make a decision. So, I pulled a penny out of my pocket and said, "I'm going to flip this coin. Heads it's Frozen Yak Entertainment; tails it's Cavedog Entertainment. Let's all agree that we're going to live with whatever the penny says." So, I flipped the coin and it came up Cavedog. Not one scrap of marketing research. I'm proud of that."

Bateman: *So, Chris, where did you come up with "Cavedog?"*

Taylor: I was working away on TA. It was the only title we were working on then. Ron said we needed to come up with a name. I worried about it the most, and came up with *so* many names, dozens and dozens of names. I'd be driving down streets looking at signs, and I was on this kick with Frozen Yak. An animal kick. Well, I woke up one morning, and Cavedog popped into my head. I thought no one would like it. So I held onto it for awhile and then told Ron and others, and they liked it.

Bateman: *When Chris approached you, did you already have in mind the type of game you wanted to do first?*

Gilbert: No, not at all. I didn't want Cavedog—and I still don't want Cavedog—to be pegged down to a particular genre of games. I want to be able to do lots of different things. So, when Chris came to me with the game, I hadn't been thinking of something like this to begin with.

Bateman: *Is there a certain number of games that you'd like Cavedog to publish each year?*

Gilbert: I don't think it's really so much a number of games. Just making sure that we're always producing really good stuff that we believe in. I don't want to get into a situation where we're just trying to get bigger and bigger and bigger, and we're putting out junk to have market share. If we come out with a bunch of games one year and not very many the next year, just because of how many good ideas there were, that would be OK with me.

Bateman: *Chris, one of your goals was to minimize the kind of micro-management in TA that in some previous games becomes tedious and frustrating.*

Taylor: The analogy is that of a general in a real war, and we're trying to put you in that position. Think of Patton. Patton never had to go back and make sure there was enough steel or to see if lunch was coming. If you're a general and you're doing your job out in the field, you just worry about how to use the tanks. We set it up for the economy to be continual—a continual income of energy and metal.

Bateman: *How did the soundtrack to TA come about?*

Taylor: When I think of war, I can't get *Apocalypse Now* out of my head. You know, Wagner's *Ride of the Valkyries*. It pushed a button; that charge, that feel, that rush. I told Jeremy Soule, TA's composer,

that I wanted that feel in the game. For him it was some of the most difficult music he had ever composed. But, I kept pushing, and got the best out of him. He did a great job. We had the Northwest Sinfonia record the soundtrack. As the action in the game changes, the music shifts. There's battle music and then there's more, you know, base-building music. It doesn't switch immediately; the tempo and music transition as game play changes.

Bateman: *Now that the game is out, will there be add-on packs for TA in the future?*

Gilbert: We're building a secondary team that will do all the add-on packs; they'll be dedicated to doing nothing but supporting *Total Annihilation* throughout the next year. Chris is going to go on and build *Total Annihilation 2.*

We'll come out with four different expansion packs over the next year, plus what we release from our web site. The expansion packs will not include just more tanks and more aircraft. One of our expansion packs will include insectoid units, which are like the Spider Kbots—mechanical, but spiders. And they will reproduce; spiders that build themselves. So that new pack will be a completely different experience. We'll also have a pack that we call psionics—mind control, where you now have a whole new set of weapons. When they are employed you get to control any unit in their vicinity, a whole different game play. We want our expansion packs to be very different, not just more of the same. We'll use Cavedog's web site for more of the same—better radar, better tanks, etc.

With the add-on packs, I really want to be able to respond to what people like and don't like about the game. So, other than the first one that will come out in January or February, I want to get a feel for the landscape before we start going into those. People may pick up on certain units or certain types of game play, and I want to be able to give them what they want with those packs.

Bateman: *I understand you've got some wacky units coming?*

Gilbert: We're definitely going to do that, although we don't have any concrete ideas. Chris and I have talked about doing some really bizarre things—like, clown Kbots—a hundred of them get out of a Volkswagen and they all run around. Just doing some really fun stuff like that. People like to take their games seriously, but they also like it when you poke a little fun. The way we'll have all the add-on units structured, if you don't like the clown Kbots, just turn them off. Don't play with them.

Bateman: *Where do you see the future of gaming? Is technology or creativity leading right now?*

Gilbert: The only thing that I'm not pleased about is that I wish there were more people playing games. I really would like it—and not just for financial reasons. As a designer, I like to have as many people as possible play what I do. You can sell three or four hundred thousand copies of something, which is a big hit today, but I'd like a lot more people to be playing what I do than just that many.

In terms of technology versus creativity, it's a balance. Occasionally you get a game that comes out that's a technology marvel and no game play, and it sells a ton. Sometimes you get other games that come out that have a lot of game play and no technology. If you look at *Command & Conquer*, that sold over a million copies. There's nothing technically fascinating about that game. We could have built that game on the Commodore 64 back in 1986. I wish I'd thought of it. That's an example where the game play in that product was really what made it go, not the technology.

Bateman: *Chris, what gives you the biggest hope about computer gaming in the near future?*

Taylor: The Internet. It's improving and we're getting better bandwidth and lower latency. And we're getting more RAM with our computers. When you get a multiplayer war game going in a gigantic world, it's just a whole different experience. In the future, we'll be able to play massive wars with people all over the world. [Laughs] It doesn't get any better than that!

The TA team: *(back, from left to right)* Jon Mavor, Clay Corbisier, Kevin Smith, Jake McMahon, Rick Lambright; *(middle, from left to right)* Rebecca Coffman, Jeremy Soule, Lawton Watkins, Chris Taylor, Mike Fisher, Brian Brown, Bart Kijanka, Scott Robinson, Clayton Kauzlaric, Jeff Petkau, Mark West; *(front, from left to right)* Kurt Pfeiffer, John Baron, Kevin Pun

Appendix

+NOWISEE

(Exposes the map and turns off line of sight so you can see everyone)

Arm and Core Structure and Unit Statistics

This appendix features detailed unit and structure variables for both Arm and Core that you can dig through for comparisons—for those of you who can't get enough of *Total Annihilation*. The information provided is broken down by these categories:

Name—lists the name of each unit or structure.

Level—indicates the Technology Level of each unit and structure.

Description—provides a short definition of each unit and structure.

Range—indicates the shooting range for all armed units and structures. The range is given as Short, Medium, Long, or Very Long. Short indicates line-of-site short-range weapons such as the PeeWee, Flash tank, or Commander. Medium indicates a longer-range line-of-sight weapon, such as the Freedom Fighter jet, Light Laser Tower, or Samson missile truck. Long flags a weapon that shoots beyond its own line of sight, such as a Ranger missile ship or a Guardian cannon. Very Long indicates the longest-range weapons in the game, such as the Big Bertha cannon or the Retaliator nuclear missile launcher. Note that artillery units and structures that fire shells or missiles can increase their range by being on top of hills, ridges, and mountains.

Build Cost Energy and **Build Cost Metal**—is measured in energy or metal units. The costs are subtracted directly from the energy and metal reserves that you have accumulated. This is separate from the Build Time for each unit and structure.

Armor—variables are measured in the number of hit points each unit or structure can withstand before being destroyed. Those points change dramatically depending on the distance and the number of units firing at the same target. For comparative purposes, Armor is expressed as Light, Medium, and Heavy. Use the Armor variables here as a comparative chart of relative armor strength under all types of fire.

Speed—represents how rapidly a unit moves on the battlefield and is measured in abstract units for comparative purposes.

Build Units—lists the number of seconds it takes to build a unit or structure. Build Units depend on the build speed of the construction plant or unit doing the building. There are seven work speeds, ranging from the Commander (300 units per second) to a Construction Aircraft (50 units per second). Construction units working together add up their work speeds to increase their speed. For example, the Commander and a Construction Aircraft together build at 350 units per second. Calculate the number of seconds it takes to build a unit or structure by dividing the Build Speed into the total number under Build Units. Build Speeds break down as follows: *Commander:* **300**; *Advanced Kbot Lab, Advanced Vehicle Plant, Advanced Aircraft Plant, Advanced Shipyard, and Advanced Constrution Vehicle:* **200**; *Advanced Construction Kbot:* **160**; *Construction Ship:* **125**; *Kbot Lab, Vehicle Plant, Aircraft Plant, Shipyard, Construction Vehicle,* and *Advanced Construction Aircraft:* **100**; *Construction Kbot:* **80**; *Construction Aircraft:* **50**. For those Arm and Core structures that can be built by more than one construction unit, the different Build Speeds and build times are indicated in the corresponding A, B, and C columns.

Prerequisites: There are 16 units and structures that can build other units and structures. The Commander builds four basic construction plants which, in turn, each builds a Level-2 mobile construction unit. These mobile units can each build an advanced construction plant. And three of those advanced plants each builds an advanced mobile unit. (See Chapter 3 for the Arm and Core unit build hierarchies.)

Arm Structure and Unit Statistics

Name	Level	Description	Range	Build Cost		Armor	Speed	Build Units	Build Speed			Seconds to Build			Prerequisites	Weapons
				Energy	Metal				A	B	C	A	B	C		
Adv. Aircraft Plant	2	Construction plant	—	4,521	2,210	Medium	—	17,376	50			348			C-AP-CA	—
Adv. Construction Aircraft	2	Construction plant	—	12,096	220	Light	7.6	24,763	200			124			C-AP-CA-AAP	—
Adv. Construction Kbot	2	Construction Kbot	—	5,784	300	Medium	0.6	13,432	200			67			C-KL-CK-AKL	—
Adv. Construction Vehicle	2	Construction aircraft	—	4,263	481	Medium	1.6	10,397	200			52			C-VP-CV-AVP	—
Adv. Kbot Lab	2	Construction plant	—	3,277	2,007	Heavy	—	13,520	80			169			C-KL-CK	—
Adv. Shipyard	2	Construction plant	—	2,402	2,524	Medium	—	13,310	125			106			C-S-CS	—
Adv. Vehicle Plant	2	Construction plant	—	3,200	1,984	Medium	—	14,950	100			150			C-VP-CV	—
Advanced Radar Tower	3	Radar tower	—	1,830	125	Light	—	4,800	100	160	200	48	30	24	Any ACU	—
Air Repair Pad	3	Aircraft repair platform	—	8,510	425	Light	—	21,953	100	160	200	220	137	110	Any ACU	—
Aircraft Plant	1	Construction plant	—	1,370	850	Medium	—	7,240	300			24			C	—
Annihilator	3	High-energy cannon	Long	25,025	3,985	Medium	—	75,071	100	160	200	751	469	375	Any ACU	Cannon
Atlas	1	Air transport	—	2,479	107	Light	7	5,500	100			55			C-AP	—
Big Bertha	3	Long-range cannon	Very long	64,680	4,184	Medium		85,185	100	160	200	852	532	426	Any ACU	Cannon
Brawler	2	Gunship	Medium	6,249	314	Light	6.6	14,385	200			72			C-AP-CA-AAP	Laser
Bulldog	2	Heavy assault tank	Medium	2,994	467	Heavy	1.1	5,675	200			28			C-VP-CV-AVP	Cannon
Colossus	2	Light carrier		11,257	1,372	Heavy	2.3	25,394	200			127			C-S-CS-AS	—
Commander	10	Leader	Short	34,125	29,854	Heavy	1.2	95,897							Chris Taylor	Laser, D-Gun
Conqueror	2	Cruiser	Long	8,608	1,719	Heavy	2.5	17,789	200			89			C-S-CS-AS	Long-range cannon
Construction Aircraft	1	Construction aircraft	—	4,320	105	Light	6.9	8,844	100			88			C-AP	—
Construction Kbot	1	Construction Kbot	—	2,410	120	Light	0.8	5,597	100			56			C-KL	—
Construction Ship	1	Mobile construction unit	—	2,130	255	Medium	2.1	5,121	100			51			C-S	—
Construction Vehicle	1	Mobile construction unit	—	2,030	185	Light	1.4	4,951	100			50			C-VP	—
Crusader	1	Destroyer	Medium	4,537	898	Medium	2.9	9,391	100			94			C-S	Cannon; dpth chrgs
Defender	2	Missile tower	Medium	843	79	Light	—	1,843	50	80	100	37	23	18	Any CU; not S	Missiles
Dragon's Teeth	2	Perimeter defense	—	250	10	Heavy	—	520	50	80	100	10	7	5	Any CU; not S	—
Energy Storage	1	Storage structure	—	2,430	240	Medium	—	12,710	300			42			C	—
Eraser	2	Radar jammer	—	1,326	73	Light	1	4,937	200			25			C-KL-CK-AKL	—
Fido	2	Assault Kbot	Medium	3,556	398	Medium	1.75	10,827	200			54			C-KL-CK-AKL	Gauss cannon
Flash	1	Light tank	Short	870	106	Light	2	1,676	100			17			C-VP	Cannon
Freedom Fighter	1	Fighter aircraft	Medium	3,234	99	Light	10	9,182	100			92			C-AP	Laser
Fusion Reactor	3	Power generator	—	36,058	5,130	Heavy	—	93,768	100	160	200	938	586	469	Any ACU	—
Galactic Gate	10	Space teleporter	—	1,865,294	213,965	Heavy	—	3,742,578							—	—
Geothermal Powerplant	2	Power generator	—	9,568	520	Light	—	13,078	50	80	100	262	163	131	Any CU; not S	—
Guardian	2	Plasma cannon	Long	7,687	1,946	Medium	—	10,377	50	80	100	208	130	104	Any CU; not S	Plasma cannon
Hammer	1	Artillery Kbot	Medium	1,187	151	Light	1.1	2,340	100			23			C-KL	Plasma cannon
Hawk	2	Stealth fighter	Long	6,893	254	Light	12	15,285	200			76			C-AP-CA-AAP	Missiles
Hulk	1	Transport ship	—	4,639	919	Medium	1.9	14,538	100			145			C-S	—
Invader	2	Crawling bomb	—	5,473	61	Light	0.42	7,901	200			40			C-KL-CK-AKL	Crawling bomb
Jammer	2	Mobile radar jammer	—	1,621	97	Light	1	5,933	200			30			C-VP-CV-AVP	—
Jeffy	1	Scout vehicle	Short	564	37	Light	3	1,465	100			15			C-VP	Light Laser
Jethro	1	Anti-air missile Kbot	Medium	1,219	128	Light	1.4	2,631	100			26			C-KL	Missiles

Arm Structure and Unit Statistics

Name	Level	Description	Range	Build Cost		Armor	Speed	Build Units	Build Speed			Seconds to Build			Prerequisites	Weapons
				Energy	Metal				A	B	C	A	B	C		
Kbot Lab	1	Construction plant	—	1,130	705	Medium	—	6,760	300			23			C	—
Light Laser Tower	1	Laser Tower	Medium	2,546	262	Light	—	4,662	300			16			C	Light laser
Lancet	2	Torpedo bomber	Medium	6,438	378	Light	9.7	14,096	200			70			C-AP-CA-AAP	Torpedo bombs
Luger	2	Mobile artillery	Medium	2,140	264	Light	1	2,830	200			14			C-VP-CV-AVP	Anti-sliver cannon
Lurker	1	Submarine	Medium	3,724	1,151	Light	2.1	8,194	100			82			C-S	Torpedoes
Merl	2	Mobile rocket launcher	Long	2,746	462	Light	1.2	4,592	200			23			C-VP-CV-AVP	Rockets
Metal Extractor	1	Resource provider	—	521	50	Light	—	1,800	300			6			C	—
Metal Maker	1	Resource converter	—	687	0	Light	—	2,605	300			9			C	—
Metal Storage	1	Storage structure	—	535	305	Medium	—	2,925	300			10			C	—
Millenium	2	Battleship	Long	20,731	4,404	Heavy	2	42,730	200			214			C-S-CS-AS	Cannons
Moho Mine	3	Metal extractor	—	8,700	1,508	Medium	—	35,750	100	160	200	358	223	179	Any ACU	—
Peeper	1	Air scout	—	1,475	40	Light	12	2,585	100			26			C-AP	—
Peewee	1	Kbot	Short	697	53	Light	1.8	1,452	100			15			C-KL	Machine guns
Phoenix	2	Strategic bomber	Medium	7,624	209	Light	9.5	16,064	200			80			C-AP-CA-AAP	Bombs
Piranha	2	Submarine killer	Medium	5,481	1,448	Light	2.4	13,767	200			69			C-S-CS-AS	Torpedoes
Protector	3	Nuclear missile defense	Long	88,000	1,437	Light	—	95,678	100	160	200	957	598	478	Any ACU	Anti-nukes
Radar Tower	1	Radar tower	—	750	49	Light	—	1,137	300			4			C	—
Ranger	2	Missile ship	Long	7,804	2,348	Medium	1	15,317	200			77			C-S-CS-AS	Missiles
Retaliator	3	Nuclear missile launcher	Unlimited	52,134	1,010	Medium	—	178,453	100	160	200	1,785	1,115	892	Any ACU	Nuclear missile
Rocko	1	Rocket Kbot	Medium	964	117	Light	1.2	1,946	100			19			C-KL	Rockets
Samson	1	Mobile missilelauncher	Medium	1,027	119	Light	1.5	1,941	100			19			C-VP	SAM missiles
Seer	2	Mobile radar	—	941	85	Light	1.1	3,186	200			16			C-VP-CV-AVP	—
Sentinel	2	Heavy laser tower	Long	5,398	584	Medium	—	9,575	50	80	100	192	120	96	Any CU; not S	Heavy laser tower
Shipyard	1	Produces Ships	—	775	615	Medium	—	6,050	300			20			C	—
Skeeter	1	Scout ship	Medium	985	100	Light	3.8	2,062	100			21			C-S	Missiles
Solar Collector	1	Power generator	—	760	145	Light	—	2,495	300			8			C	—
Sonar Station	2	Sonar structure	—	403	20	Light	—	912	125			7			C-S-CS	—
Spider	2	Spider assault vehicle	Medium	2,200	230	Light	1.5	6,075	200			30			C-VP-CV-AVP	Paralyzer
Stumpy	1	Medium assault tank	Medium	1,246	165	Light	1.7	2,404	100			24			C-VP	Plasma cannon
Thunder	1	Bomber	Short	5,496	130	Light	9	10,155	100			102			C-AP	Bombs
Tidal Generator	2	Power generator	—	768	82	Light	—	2,188	125			18			C-S-CS	—
Torpedo Launcher	2	Torpedo launcher	Medium	2,658	904	Medium	—	4,120	125			33			C-S-CS	Torpedoes
Triton	2	Amphibious tank	Medium	2,300	298	Medium	1.3	4,112	200			21			C-VP-CV-AVP	Cannon
Vehicle Plant	1	Construction plant	—	1,000	620	Medium	—	6,500	300			22			C	—
Wind Generator	1	Power generator	—	509	52	Light	—	1,603	300			5			C	—
Zeus	2	Lightning-gun Kbot	Short	2,228	267	Light	1	5,478	200			27			C-KL-CK-AKL	Lightning gun
Zipper	2	Fast-attack Kbot	Short	2,221	151	Light	2.53	6,768	200			34			C-KL-CK-AKL	Medium Laser

C = Commander; KL = Kbot Lab; VP = Vehicle Plant; AP = Aircraft Plant; S = Shipyard; CK = Construction Kbot; CV = Construction Vehicle; CA = Construction Aircraft; CS = Construction Ship; AKL = Adv. Kbot Lab; AVP = Adv. Vehicle Plant; AAP = Adv. Aircraft Plant; AS = Adv. Shipyard; ACK = Adv. Construction Kbot; ACV = Adv. Construction Vehicle; ACA = Adv. Construction Aircraft; CU = Construction Unit (for those structures that can be built by any of the mobile construction units); ACU = Adv. Construction Unit (for those structures that can be built by any of the adv. mobile construction units)

Core Structure and Unit Statistics

Name	Level	Description	Range	Build Cost Energy	Build Cost Metal	Armor	Speed	Build Units	Build Speed A	Build Speed B	Build Speed C	Seconds to Build A	Seconds to Build B	Seconds to Build C	Prerequisites	Weapons
A.K.	1	Kbot	Short	696	56	Light	1.72	1,523	100			15			C-KL	Machine gun
Adv. Aircraft Plant	2	Mobile construction unit	—	4,422	2,191	Medium	—	17,232	50			345			C-AP-CA	—
Adv. Construction Aircraft	2	Mobile construction unit	—	12,824	231	Light	7.5	26,001	200			130			C-AP-CA-AAP	—
Adv. Construction Kbot	2	Mobile construction unit	—	6,096	325	Medium	0.6	13,963	200			70			C-KL-CK-AKL	—
Adv. Construction Vehicle	2	Mobile construction unit	—	4,504	455	Medium	1.5	10,806	200			54			C-VP-CV-AVP	—
Adv. Kbot Lab	2	Construction plant	—	3,625	1,972	Heavy	—	14,000	80			175			C-KL-CK	—
Adv. Shipyard	2	Construction plant	—	2,325	2,460	Medium	—	13,080	125			105			C-S-CS	—
Adv. Vehicle Plant	2	Construction plant	—	3,520	1,947	Medium	—	15,410	100			154			C-VP-CV	—
Advanced Radar Tower	3	Long-range radar	—	1,920	122	Light	—	4,960	100	160	200	50	31	25	Any ACU	—
Air Repair Pad	3	Repair pad	—	8,540	430	Light	—	21,587	100	160	200	216	135	108	Any ACU	—
Aircraft Plant	1	Construction plant	—	1,340	830	Medium	—	7,180	300			24			C	—
Avenger	1	Fighter	Medium	3,181	101	Light	11	9,196	100			92			C-AP	Air-to-Air missiles
Commander	10	Leader	Short	35,838	23,512	Heavy	1.07	97,852							Chris Taylor	—
Construction Aircraft	1	Mobile construction unit	—	4,580	110	Light	6.7	9,286	100			93			C-AP	—
Construction Kbot	1	Mobile construction unit	—	2,540	130	Light	0.9	5,818	100			58			C-KL	—
Construction Ship	1	Mobile construction unit	—	2,375	260	Medium	2.1	5,537	100			55			C-S	—
Construction Vehicle	1	Mobile construction unit	—	2,145	175	Light	1.3	5,146	100			51			C-VP	—
Crasher	1	Missile Kbot	Medium	1,224	129	Light	1.25	2,636	100			26			C-KL	Missiles
Crock	2	Amphibious tank	Medium	2,310	295	Medium	1.2	4,119	200			21			C-VP-CV-AVP	Cannon
Deleter	2	Mobile radar jammer	—	1,757	100	Light	1.05	6,404	200			32			C-VP-CV-AVP	—
Diplomat	2	Mobile rocket launcher	Long	2,470	427	Light	1.1	4,002	200			20			C-VP-CV-AVP	Rockets
Doomsday Machine	3	High-energy cannon	Medium	14,245	2,140	Heavy	—	39,276	100	160	200	393	245	196	Any ACU	Energy cannon
Dragon's Teeth	2	Perimeter defense	—	300	11	Heavy	—	565	50	80	100	11	7	6	Any CU; not S	—
Energy Storage	1	Storage structure	—	2,490	250	Medium	—	12,750	300			43			C	—
Enforcer	1	Destroyer	Long	4,505	887	Heavy	2.93	9,368	100			94			C-S	Cannon, dpth chrgs
Envoy	1	Transport ship	—	4,786	887	Medium	1.8	13,663	100			137			C-S	—
Executioner	2	Cruiser	Long	8,551	1,724	Heavy	2.4	17,050	200			85			C-S-CS-AS	Cannon, depth charges
Fink	1	Air scout	—	1,369	36	Light	11	2,156	100			22			C-AP	—
Fortitude Missile Defense	3	Nuclear missile defense	Long	92,321	1,508	Light	—	96,450	100	160	200	965	603	482	Any ACU	Anti-nukes
Fusion Power Plant	3	Power generator	—	37,865	5,004	Heavy	—	94,281	100	160	200	943	589	471	Any ACU	—
Gaat Gun	2	Heavy laser tower	Long	5,443	589	Medium	—	9,622	50	80	100	192	120	96	Any CU; not S	Laser tower
Galactic Gate	10	Space teleporter	—	1,982,431	197,485	Medium	—	3,421,694							—	—
Geothermal Powerplant	2	Energy generator	—	9,375	505	Light	—	12,875	50	80	100	258	161	129	Any CU; not S	—
Goliath	2	Very heavy assault tank	Medium	3,906	697	Heavy	0.8	7,058	200			35			C-VP-CV-AVP	Cannon
Hive	2	Light carrier	—	11,715	1,379	Heavy	2.2	25,271	200			126			C-S-CS-AS	—
Hurricane	2	Strategic bomber	Medium	8,050	220	Light	9.1	16,269	200			81			C-AP-CA-AAP	Bombs
Informer	2	Mobile radar	—	1,209	86	Light	1.4	4,223	200			21			C-VP-CV-AVP	—
Instigator	1	Assault tank	Short	887	110	Light	1.9	1,737	100			17			C-VP	Cannon
Intimidator	3	Long-range cannon	Long	62,520	4,328	Medium	—	93,237	100	160	200	932	583	466	Any ACU	Plasma cannon
Kbot Lab	1	Construction plant	—	1,250	680	Medium	—	7,000	300			23			C	—

Core Structure and Unit Statistics

Name	Level	Description	Range	Build Cost		Armor	Speed	Build Units	Build Speed			Seconds to Build			Prerequisites	Weapons
				Energy	Metal				A	B	C	A	B	C		
Light Laser Tower	1	Laser tower	Medium	2,608	268	Light	—	4,724	300			16			C	Laser
Metal Extractor	1	Resource provider	—	514	51	Light	—	1,874	300			6			C	—
Metal Maker	1	Resource converter	—	700	0	Light	—	2,682	300			9			C	—
Metal Storage	1	Storage structure	—	550	320	Medium	—	2,925	300			10			C	—
Missile Frigate	2	Missile ship	Long	7,628	2,283	Medium	0.9	15,126	200			76			C-S-CS-AS	Missiles
Mobile Artillery	2	Mobile artillery	Medium	1,535	251	Light	0.9	2,723	200			14			C-VP-CV-AVP	Anti-sliver cannon
Moho Mine	3	Advanced metal extractor	—	9,121	1,450	Medium	—	32,500	100	160	200	325	203	163	Any ACU	—
Pulverizer	2	Missile tower	Medium	805	76	Light	—	1,749	50	80	100	35	22	17	Any CU; not S	Missiles
Punisher	2	Plasma cannon	Long	7,585	1,887	Medium	—	10,268	50	80	100	205	128	103	Any CU; not S	Plasma cannon
Pyro	2	Flamethrower Kbot	Short	2,200	260	Light	1.5	3,750	200			19			C-KL-CK-AKL	Flamethrower
Radar Tower	1	Radar tower	—	800	50	Light	—	1,137	300			4			C	—
Raider	1	Medium assault tank	Medium	1,241	169	Medium	1.6	2,376	100			24			C-VP	Cannon
Rapier	2	Gunship	Medium	5,778	294	Light	7.6	13,294	200			66			C-AP-CA-AAP	Lasers
Reaper	2	Heavy assault tank	Medium	3,048	473	Medium	1.2	5,730	200			29			C-VP-CV-AVP	Cannon
Roach	2	Crawling bomb	—	5,471	65	Light	0.4	7,899	200			39			C-KL-CK-AKL	Crawling bomb
Searcher	1	Scout ship	Medium	917	95	Light	3.6.	1,877	100			19			C-S	Missiles
Shadow	1	Bomber	Short	5,691	131	Light	8	10,750	100			108			C-AP	Bombs
Shark	2	Submarine killer	Medium	5,245	1,356	Light	2.5	12,529	200			63			C-S-CS-AS	Torpedoes
Shipyard	1	Construction plant	—	750	600	Medium	—	6,000	300			20			C	—
Silencer	3	Nuclear missile launcher	Unlimited	48,768	975	Medium	—	181,243	100	160	200	1,812	1,133	906	Any ACU	Nuke missile lnchr
Slasher	1	Missile launcher	Medium	947	116	Light	1.45	1,820	100	160	200	18	11	9	C-VP	Missiles
Snake	1	Submarine	Medium	3,902	1,199	Light	2.05	8,729	100	160	200	87	55	44	C-S	Torpedoes
Solar Collector	1	Power generator	—	790	141	Light	—	2,416	300			8			C	—
Sonar Station	2	Sonar structure	—	399	20	Light	—	900	125			7			C-S-CS	—
Spectre	2	Radar jammer	—	1,453	70	Light	1	5,439	200			27			C-KL-CK-AKL	—
Storm	1	Rocket Kbot	Medium	985	118	Light	1.25	1,969	100			20			C-KL	Rockets
The Can	2	Armored assault Kbot	Short	3,500	420	Medium	0.5	7,500	200			38			C-KL-CK-AKL	Hvy plasma cannon
Thud	1	Artillery Kbot	Medium	1,161	147	Light	1.13	2,171	100			22			C-KL	Plasma Cannon
Tidal Generator	2	Power generator	—	752	81	Light	—	2,094	125			17			C-S-CS	—
Titan	2	Torpedo bomber	Medium	6,588	364	Light	9.5	13,722	200			69			C-AP-CA-AAP	Torpedo bombs
Torpedo Launcher	2	Torpedo launcher	Medium	3,058	931	Medium	—	4,233	125			34			C-S-CS	Torpedoes
Valkyrie	1	Air transport	—	2,695	115	Light	7	5,889	100			59			C-AP	—
Vamp	2	Stealth fighter	Long	6,973	257	Light	12	15,924	200			80			C-AP-CA-AAP	Missiles
Vehicle Plant	1	Construction plant	—	1,100	600	Medium	—	6,700	300			22			C	—
Warlord	2	Battleship	Long	19,741	4,181	Heavy	2.15	40,640	200			203			C-S-CS-AS	Heavy cannon
Weasel	1	Scout vehicle	Short	575	38	Light	2.8	1,515	100			15			C-VP	Laser
Wind Generator	1	Power generator	—	523	55	Light	—	1,687	300			6			C	—

C = Commander; KL = Kbot Lab; VP = Vehicle Plant; AP = Aircraft Plant; S = Shipyard; CK = Construction Kbot; CV = Construction Vehicle; CA = Construction Aircraft; CS = Construction Ship; AKL = Adv. Kbot Lab; AVP = Adv. Vehicle Plant; AAP = Adv. Aircraft Plant; AS = Adv. Shipyard; ACK = Adv. Construction Kbot; ACV = Adv. Construction Vehicle; ACA = Adv. Construction Aircraft; CU = Construction Unit (for those structures that can be built by any of the mobile construction units); ACU = Adv. Construction Unit (for those structures that can be built by any of the adv. mobile construction units)

Core

Name	Range	Armor	Prerequisites	Weapon
A.K.	Short	Light	C-KL	Machine gun
Adv. Aircraft Plant	—	Medium	C-AP-CA	—
Adv. Construction Aircraft	—	Light	C-AP-CA-AAP	—
Adv. Construction Kbot	—	Medium	C-KL-CK-AKL	—
Adv. Construction Vehicle	—	Medium	C-VP-CV-AVP	—
Adv. Kbot Lab	—	Heavy	C-KL-CK	—
Adv. Shipyard	—	Medium	C-S-CS	—
Adv. Vehicle Plant	—	Medium	C-VP-CV	—
Adv. Radar Tower	—	Light	Any ACU	—
Air Repair Pad	—	Light	Any ACU	—
Avenger	Medium	Light	C-AP	Air-to-Air missiles
Commander	Short	Heavy	Chris Taylor	—
Construction Aircraft	—	Light	C-AP	—
Construction Kbot	—	Light	C-KL	—
Construction Ship	—	Medium	C-S	—
Construction Vehicle	—	Light	C-VP	—
Crasher	Medium	Light	C-KL	Missiles
Crock	Medium	Medium	C-VP-CV-AVP	Cannon
Deleter	—	Light	C-VP-CV-AVP	—
Diplomat	Long	Light	C-VP-CV-AVP	Rockets
Doomsday Machine	Medium	Heavy	Any ACU	Energy cannon
Dragon's Teeth	—	Heavy	Any CU; not S	—
Enforcer	Long	Heavy	C-S	Cannon; dpth chgs
Envoy	—	Medium	C-S	—
Executioner	Long	Heavy	C-S-CS-AS	Cannon; dpth chgs
Fink	—	Light	C-AP	—
Fortitude Missile Defense	Long	Light	Any ACU	Anti-nukes
Fusion Power Plant	—	Heavy	Any ACU	—
Gaat Gun	Long	Medium	Any CU; not S	Laser tower
Galactic Gate	—	Medium	—	—
Geothermal Powerplant	—	Light	Any CU; not S	—
Goliath	Medium	Heavy	C-VP-CV-AVP	Cannon
Hive	—	Heavy	C-S-CS-AS	—
Hurricane	Medium	Light	C-AP-CA-AAP	Bombs
Informer	—	Light	C-VP-CV-AVP	—
Instigator	Short	Light	C-VP	Cannon
Intimidator	Long	Medium	Any ACU	Plasma cannon
Light Laser Tower	Medium	Light	C	Laser
Missile Frigate	Long	Medium	C-S-CS-AS	Missiles
Mobile Artillery	Medium	Light	C-VP-CV-AVP	Anti-sliver cannon
Moho Mine	—	Medium	Any ACU	—
Pulverizer	Medium	Light	Any CU; not S	Missiles
Punisher	Long	Medium	Any CU; not S	Plasma cannon
Pyro	Short	Light	C-KL-CK-AKL	Flamethrower
Raider	Medium	Medium	C-VP	Cannon
Rapier	Medium	Light	C-AP-CA-AAP	Lasers
Reaper	Medium	Medium	C-VP-CV-AVP	Cannon
Roach	—	Light	C-KL-CK-AKL	Crawling bomb
Searcher	Medium	Light	C-S	Missiles
Shadow	Short	Light	C-AP	Bombs
Shark	Medium	Light	C-S-CS-AS	Torpedoes
Silencer	Unlimited	Medium	Any ACU	Nuke missile lnchr
Slasher	Medium	Light	C-VP	Missiles
Snake	Medium	Light	C-S	Torpedoes
Sonar Station	—	Light	C-S-CS	—
Spectre	—	Light	C-KL-CK-AKL	—
Storm	Medium	Light	C-KL	Rockets
The Can	Short	Medium	C-KL-CK-AKL	Plasma cannon
Thud	Medium	Light	C-KL	Plasma cannon
Tidal Generator	—	Light	C-S-CS	—
Titan	Medium	Light	C-AP-CA-AAP	Torpedo bombs
Torpedo Launcher	Medium	Medium	C-S-CS	Torpedoes
Valkyrie	—	Light	C-AP	—
Vamp	Long	Light	C-AP-CA-AAP	Missiles
Warlord	Long	Heavy	C-S-CS-AS	Heavy cannon
Weasel	Short	Light	C-VP	Laser

C = Commander; KL = Kbot Lab; VP = Vehicle Plant; AP = Aircraft Plant; S = Shipyard; CK = Construction Kbot; CV = Construction Vehicle; CA = Construction Aircraft; CS = Construction Ship; AKL = Adv. Kbot Lab; AVP = Adv. Vehicle Plant; AAP = Adv. Aircraft Plant; AS = Adv. Shipyard; ACK = Adv. Construction Kbot; ACV = Adv. Construction Vehicle; ACA = Adv. Construction Aircraft; CU = Construction Unit (for those structures that can be built by any of the mobile construction units); ACU = Adv. Construction Unit (for those structures that can be built by any of the adv. mobile construction units)

Arm

Name	Range	Armor	Prerequisites	Weapon
Adv. Aircraft Plant	—	Medium	C-AP-CA	—
Adv. Construction Aircraft	—	Light	C-AP-CA-AAP	—
Adv. Construction Kbot	—	Medium	C-KL-CK-AKL	—
Adv. Construction Vehicle	—	Medium	C-VP-CV-AVP	—
Adv. Kbot Lab	—	Heavy	C-KL-CK	—
Adv. Shipyard	—	Medium	C-S-CS	—
Adv. Vehicle Plant	—	Medium	C-VP-CV	—
Adv. Radar Tower	—	Light	Any ACU	—
Air Repair Pad	—	Light	Any ACU	—
Annihilator	Long	Medium	Any ACU	Cannon
Atlas	—	Light	C-AP	—
Big Bertha	Very long	Medium	Any ACU	Cannon
Brawler	Medium	Light	C-AP-CA-AAP	Laser
Bulldog	Medium	Heavy	C-VP-CV-AVP	Cannon
Colossus	—	Heavy	C-S-CS-AS	—
Commander	Short	Heavy	Chris Taylor	Laser, D-Gun
Conqueror	Long	Heavy	C-S-CS-AS	Cannon
Construction Aircraft	—	Light	C-AP	—
Construction Kbot	—	Light	C-KL	—
Construction Ship	—	Medium	C-S	—
Construction Vehicle	—	Light	C-VP	—
Crusader	Medium	Medium	C-S	Cannon; dpth chgs
Defender	Medium	Light	Any CU; not S	Missiles
Dragon's Teeth	—	Heavy	Any CU; not S	—
Eraser	—	Light	C-KL-CK-AKL	—
Fido	Medium	Medium	C-KL-CK-AKL	Gauss cannon
Flash	Short	Light	C-VP	Cannon
Freedom Fighter	Medium	Light	C-AP	Laser
Fusion Reactor	—	Heavy	Any ACU	—
Geothermal Powerplant	—	Light	Any CU; not S	—
Guardian	Long	Medium	Any CU; not S	Plasma cannon
Hammer	Medium	Light	C-KL	Plasma cannon
Hawk	Long	Light	C-AP-CA-AAP	Missiles
Hulk	—	Medium	C-S	—
Invader	—	Light	C-KL-CK-AKL	Crawling bomb
Jammer	—	Light	C-VP-CV-AVP	—
Jeffy	Short	Light	C-VP	Light Laser
Jethro	Medium	Light	C-KL	Missiles
Lancet	Medium	Light	C-AP-CA-AAP	Torpedo bombs
Light Laser Tower	Medium	Light	C	Light laser
Luger	Medium	Light	C-VP-CV-AVP	Anti-sliver cannon
Lurker	Medium	Light	C-S	Torpedoes
Merl	Long	Light	C-VP-CV-AVP	Rockets
Millenium	Long	Heavy	C-S-CS-AS	Cannons
Moho Mine	—	Medium	Any ACU	—
Peeper	—	Light	C-AP	—
Peewee	Short	Light	C-KL	Machine guns
Phoenix	Medium	Light	C-AP-CA-AAP	Bombs
Piranha	Medium	Light	C-S-CS-AS	Torpedoes
Protector	Long	Light	Any ACU	Anti-nukes
Ranger	Long	Medium	C-S-CS-AS	Missiles
Retaliator	Unlimited	Medium	Any ACU	Nuclear missile
Rocko	Medium	Light	C-KL	Rockets
Samson	Medium	Light	C-VP	SAM missiles
Seer	—	Light	C-VP-CV-AVP	—
Sentinel	Long	Medium	Any CU; not S	Heavy laser tower
Skeeter	Medium	Light	C-S	Missiles
Sonar Station	—	Light	C-S-CS	—
Spider	Medium	Light	C-VP-CV-AVP	Paralyzer
Stumpy	Medium	Light	C-VP	Plasma cannon
Thunder	Short	Light	C-AP	Bombs
Tidal Generator	—	Light	C-S-CS	—
Torpedo Launcher	Medium	Medium	C-S-CS	Torpedoes
Triton	Medium	Medium	C-VP-CV-AVP	Cannon
Zeus	Short	Light	C-KL-CK-AKL	Lightning gun
Zipper	Short	Light	C-KL-CK-AKL	Medium Laser

C = Commander; KL = Kbot Lab; VP = Vehicle Plant; AP = Aircraft Plant; S = Shipyard; CK = Construction Kbot; CV = Construction Vehicle; CA = Construction Aircraft; CS = Construction Ship; AKL = Adv. Kbot Lab; AVP = Adv. Vehicle Plant; AAP = Adv. Aircraft Plant; AS = Adv. Shipyard; ACK = Adv. Construction Kbot; ACV = Adv. Construction Vehicle; ACA = Adv. Construction Aircraft; CU = Construction Unit (for those structures that can be built by any of the mobile construction units); ACU = Adv. Construction Unit (for those structures that can be built by any of the adv. mobile construction units)